RĀGS AROUND THE CLOCK

Rāgs Around the Clock

A Handbook for North Indian Classical Music, with Online Recordings in the Khayāl Style

David Clarke
Music by Vijay Rajput
with
Murad Ali, Imre Bangha, Mahmood Dholpuri,
Fida Hussain, Shahbaz Hussain, Jonathan Katz
and Athar Hussain Khan

Dr Vijay Rajput (Hindustani vocal) accompanied by Prof. David Clarke (tānpurā), Recital Room, Newcastle University, 25 April 2024. Image: John Donoghue (www.jdphotographer.co.uk). Licence held by Newcastle University.

OpenBook Publishers

https://www.openbookpublishers.com

ISBN Paperback: 978-1-80064-807-4

ISBN Digital (PDF): 978-1-80064-809-8

ISBN Digital ebook (EPUB): 978-1-80064-810-4

ISBN HTML: 978-1-80064-813-5

DOI: 10.11647/OBP.0313

Cover image: Companion Persuading Radha as Krishna Flutes, folio from the "Lambagraon" Gita Govinda (Song of the Cowherd). India, Himachal Pradesh, Kangra, ca. 1825. Opaque watercolour and gold on paper. Gift of the Michael J. Connell Foundation (M.71.59.7), Los Angeles County Museum of Art. Wikimedia, public domain, https://commons.wikimedia.org/wiki/File:Companion_Persuading_Radha_as_Krishna_Flutes,_Folio_from_the_%27Lambagraon%27_Gita_Govinda_(Song_of_the_Cowherd)_LACMA_M.71.49.7.jpg

Cover design by Katy Saunders.

Contents

Online Albums: Track List vii

Rāg Samay Cakra vii

Twilight Rāgs from North India viii

Preface and Acknowledgements xi

Biographical Notes xiii

Transliteration and Other Textual Conventions xv

Prologue: First Encounters xvii

Introduction: Origins, Overview, Contexts xxi

1. CONCEPTS, CONVENTIONS, HISTORY AND CULTURE 1

1.1 Elements of Indian Classical Music 2

1.2 *Sargam* Notation 3

1.3 *Rāg* 5

1.4 *Tāl* 8

1.5 Tānpurā Drone, *Svar* 11

1.6 *Rāg* and Time: *Samay Cakra* 13

1.7 Khayāl: Stylistic and Performance Conventions 17

1.8 Khayāl: Ornamentation 19

1.9 Khayāl: Origins 27

1.10 V. N. Bhatkhande 30

1.11 The *Guru-Śiṣyā Paramparā* 32

1.12 *Riyāz* 41

2. A CYCLE OF *RĀGS*: *RĀG SAMAY CAKRA* 43

2.1 The Album and Its Supporting Materials 44

2.2 The Song Texts 46

2.3 Notating the *Bandiś*es (and Performing Them) 49

2.4 Terminology Used in the *Rāg* Specifications 53

2.5 The *Rāg*s 54

3. EXPLORATIONS AND ANALYSES (I): *RĀG SAMAY CAKRA* 97

3.1 Introduction 98

3.2 How Do You Sing an *Ālāp*? 99

3.3 How Do You Sing a *Choṭā Khayāl*? 126

4. EXPLORATIONS AND ANALYSES (II): *TWILIGHT RĀGS FROM NORTH INDIA* **163**
4.1 Introduction 164
4.2 Rāg Bhairav: Texts, Notations and Commentaries 165
4.3 How Do You Sing a *Baṛā Khayāl*? Performance Conventions, Aesthetics, Temporality 187
Epilogue: *Laya/Pralaya* 204

Glossary of Terms Used in Hindustani Classical Music 207
References 213
List of Audio Examples 219
List of Figures 223
Index 227

Online Albums: Track List

Rāg Samay Cakra

Music

1	Rāg Bhairav (5:06)
2	Rāg Toḍī (5:47)
3	Rāg Śuddh Sāraṅg (5:12)
4	Rāg Brindābanī Sāraṅg (3:53)
5	Rāg Bhīmpalāsī (5:15)
6	Rāg Multānī (4:45)
7	Rāg Pūriyā Dhanāśrī (7:39)
8	Rāg Bhūpālī (7:03)
9	Rāg Yaman (7:22)
10	Rāg Kedār (3:48)
11	Rāg Bihāg (5:30)
12	Rāg Mālkauns (6:57)
13	Rāg Megh (4:32)
14	Rāg Basant (4:47)

Bandiś Texts, Spoken

15	'Dhana dhana murata' (Rāg Bhairav) (0:33)
16	'Laṅgara kā̃karīyā' (Rāg Todī) (0:23)
17	'Aba morī bāta' (Rāg Śuddh Sāraṅg) (0:33)
18	'Raṅga le manavā' (Rāg Brindābanī Sāraṅg) (0:41)
19	'Hamarī kahī mitavā' (Rāg Bhīmpalāsī) (0:28)
20	'Runaka jhunaka' (Rāg Multānī) (0:22)
21	'Pā̃yalīyā jhanakāra' (Rāg Pūriyā Dhanāśrī) (0:22)
22	'Gāīye Gaṇapatī' (Rāg Bhūpālī) (0:23)

23 ‘Śyām bajāi’ (Rāg Yaman) (0:27)

24 ‘Bola bola mose’ (Rāg Kedār) (0:27)

25 ‘Abahū̃ lālana’ (Rāg Bihāg) (0:32)

26 ‘Koyalīyā bole ambuvā’ (Rāg Mālkauns) (0:28)

27 ‘Ghanana ghanana’ (Rāg Megh) (0:24)

28 ‘Phulavā binata’ (Rāg Basant) (0:30)

Twilight Rāgs from North India

Rāg Bhairav

1 *Ālāp* (2:55)

2 *Baṛā khayāl* in *vilambit ektāl*: ‘Bālamavā more saīyā̃’ (18:22)

3 *Choṭā khayāl* in *drut ektāl*: ‘Suno to sakhī batiyā’ (11:58)

Rāg Yaman

4 *Ālāp* (3:14)

5 *Baṛā khayāl* in *vilambit ektāl*: ‘Kahe sakhī kaise ke karīe’ (19:39)

6 *Choṭā khayāl* in *drut tīntāl*: ‘Śyām bajāi’ (10:30)

To students and teachers of Indian classical music everywhere

Preface and Acknowledgements

Rāgs Around the Clock is a compendium for the study and exploration of Hindustani (North Indian) classical music. It comprises the present volume, by David Clarke (henceforth DC), and two albums by khayāl singer Vijay Rajput (henceforth VR), around which the contents of the book are organised. The albums, along with audio examples extracted from them and analysed below, are available to stream and download at https://doi.org/10.11647/OBP.0313#resources, or from the book's companion website at https://research.ncl.ac.uk/ragas/.

Our title invokes the notion—still very much alive within the Hindustani tradition—that a *rāg* should be performed at its proper time (*samay*). This principle is reflected in the recorded performances. Our first album, *Rāg samay cakra*, is a cycle (*cakra*) of *rāg*s, turning through successive phases of the day and night; while the second album, *Twilight Rāgs from North India*, presents *rāg*s from particularly evocative times of the diurnal cycle. As well as providing an introduction to Hindustani *rāg* music in theory and practice, this work offers perspectives on the khayāl vocal style and its musical processes, in pursuit of the question: what is it that khayāl singers do when they perform? We hope the contents will appeal to anyone drawn to such music—whether inside or outside the academy: whether newcomer, aficionado (*rasika*), student, teacher, researcher or lay listener.

In addition to embracing the *samay* concept, *Rāgs Around the Clock*, through its commentaries and analyses, distinctively showcases the vocal idiom—the *gāyakī*—of a single artist, VR. In so doing, it offers a window onto the Kirānā *gharānā*, a stylistic lineage of Indian musicians that goes back several generations. Vijay ji was a disciple (*śiṣyā*) of the late Pandit Bhimsen Joshi (1922–2011), one of the *gharānā*'s most revered latter-day exponents and a bearer of India's highest civilian award, the *Bhārat Ratna*. Among Bhimsen Joshi's gurus was the equally renowned Sawai Gandharva (1886–1952), who in turn was taught by the founder of this branch of the Kirānā *gharānā*, Abdul Karim Khan (1872–1937). This lineage (*paramparā*) continues into the present day through the teaching of artists like VR, with DC numbering among his students.

Which brings us to a further distinctive feature of this project: the musical relationship of its principal collaborators, namely that of guru and *śiṣyā*. Although our subject is not that relationship *per se* (the topic perhaps of future, autoethnographic work), it nonetheless subtly conditions much of the content. At one point or another, VR has passed down all of the featured *rāg*s to me, DC; and much of what I understand generally about *rāg* and the performance of khayāl comes from the experience of taking instruction (*tālīm*) from my guruji.

In its very grounding as oral/aural culture, that experience encompasses knowledge of a kind that eludes complete capture by concepts or theory. This ineffable dimension is perhaps an aspect of Indian music's acknowledged spiritual content. Western philosophy might couch this as a dialectic between theory and practice, between mind and body, between the subjective experience of the performer and the objective properties of the musical material. Either way, the question of the limits of theory and the subjective experience of what lies beyond it becomes a running theme in the later stages of *Rāgs Around the Clock*.

Another aspect of subjectivity acknowledged here is the heart connection between teacher and disciple and between fellow students—manifested also in their collective devotion to musical tradition. These are important, anthropological facts about the music, and although this book is not principally a work of ethnomusicology, such themes are reflected within its narratives—most explicitly in the (auto)ethnographic vignettes of its Prologue and Epilogue, which seek to draw wider cultural understanding from the stories of people and their relationships.

In the same vein, we should note that, despite its focus on the individual artist, Indian classical music is a fundamentally collaborative enterprise, sustained by interlocking—and these days international—networks of gurus, disciples, friends, fellow artists and contacts. So too, *Rāgs Around the Clock* would not have been possible without our numerous collaborators and supporters, to whom we are deeply indebted. Not least among these are the consummate accompanists on our albums—Murad Ali (sāraṅgī), Athar Hussain Khan (tabla) and Mahmood Dholpuri (harmonium) on *Rāg samay cakra*; Shahbaz Hussain (tabla) and Fida Hussain (harmonium) on *Twilight Rāgs from North India*. No less important have been our language advisers, Jonathan Katz and Imre Bangha, who provided scholarly translations of the song texts and offered invaluable guidance regarding the finer points of language. Sudipta Roy (who appears in the Epilogue) also helped with translation and read earlier versions of the text. David de la Haye recorded and mastered the spoken song texts of *Rāg samay cakra*, and John Ayers was the sound engineer for *Twilight Rāgs*. Behind the scenes, Richard Widdess generously commented on earlier drafts of the book, and has been a much-valued supporter and critical friend. We are grateful too to the second, anonymous peer reviewer of our original proposal, whose suggestion that the book be expanded led to additional chapters that have, we hope, given the book greater heft. I (DC) of course take responsibility for the final contents and for any unconscious remnants of my culture's colonial past.

Thanks are also due to Newcastle University, whose Institute for Creative Arts Practice (NICAP) provided financial support for the initial development of the book, and whose School of Arts and Cultures provided a grant towards the costs of publishing it in open access form. Financial support for the recordings was provided by the Centre for Excellence in Teaching and Learning (CETL) for Music and Inclusivity, funded by the Higher Education Funding Council for England between 2005 and 2010, and led by the International Centre for Music Studies (ICMuS) at Newcastle University.

Last but not least, an enormous thank you to Alessandra Tosi and her team at Open Book Publishers—for themselves being open to the idea of this book; for their commitment and their editorial and technical professionalism; and, especially, for their patience.

Biographical Notes

Born in New Delhi, Vijay Rajput started learning music at the age of eight. He acquired his initial training in the khayāl vocal style from Pandits M. G. Deshpande, Vinay Chander Mudgal and Madhup Mudgal. Subsequently, he studied for several years under *Bhārat Ratna* Pandit Bhimsen Joshi, one of India's most eminent vocalists. Vijay gained his PhD from the University of Delhi in 2003 with a thesis on the life and works of Sawai Gandharva. He is in demand as a performer in India, the UK and on the wider international stage. He has sung at many festivals, including the Sawai Gandharva Bhimsen Mahotsav in Pune. He has been based in Newcastle upon Tyne since 2004, and since 2006 has taught students from many musical backgrounds at Newcastle University.

David Clarke is Emeritus Professor of Music at Newcastle University. His wide-ranging musical and academic interests include music theory and analysis, music and philosophy, and Hindustani classical music. His musicological publications include articles, books and book chapters on twentieth-century western music, music and consciousness, and Hindustani classical music. He has studied the khayāl vocal style with Dr Vijay Rajput since 2004, and has undertaken study and participated in workshops with Pandits Rajan and Sajan Misra, Ramakant and Umakant Gundecha, Smt Veena Sahasrabuddhe and Pandit Uday Bhawalkar.

Athar Hussain Khan is a highly regarded tabla player who began learning with his uncle, Ustād Shane Ahmed Khan, at the age of seven. He subsequently studied with Ustād Manu Khan of the Ajrara *gharānā*, which ranks among India's principal tabla lineages. He has performed at major festivals throughout India as well as internationally.

Murad Ali is one of the best-known contemporary exponents of the sāraṅgī, and has played an important role in the resurgence of the instrument. He inherits a family tradition of sāraṅgī playing that goes back six generations, having studied intensively with his grandfather, Ustād Siddique Ahmad Khan, and his father, Ustād Ghulam Sabir Khan. He has accompanied many of the world's greatest exponents of Indian classical music, and is esteemed as a solo performer, composer and fusion artist.

The late Mahmood Dholpuri began his musical training under his grandfather, the sāraṅgī player Buddha Khan, going on to learn harmonium from various gurus, including Nasir Ahmad Khan of the Delhi *gharānā*. Mahmood Dholpuri became a highly respected and well-loved accompanist to many of the tradition's greatest vocalists, including Pandit Bhimsen Joshi, Pandit Jasraj and Begum Parveen Sultana. He was awarded the civilian honour *Padma Śrī* in 2006.

Shahbaz Hussain is a UK-born tabla virtuoso. He started learning from his late father Ustād Mumtaz Hussain, a prominent vocalist, at the age of five. He is a disciple of Ustād Faiyaz Khan of the Delhi *gharānā*. He studied further and gave major performances with Ustād Shaukat Hussain Khan and Ustād Allah Rakha Khan. Shahbaz Hussain performs internationally, giving solo performances and accompanying many of the most acclaimed masters of Hindustani classical music.

Fida Hussain is a cherished harmonium accompanist to many world-class soloists, including Lakshmi Shankar, Ustād Fateh Ali Khan and Sharda Sahai. He is also a vocalist and former theatre performer.

Dr Jonathan Katz is Lecturer in Classics at Brasenose College, Oxford, Emeritus Fellow at St Anne's College, Oxford, and Quondam Fellow at All Souls College, Oxford. He is a scholar of ancient Greek, Latin and Sanskrit, and researches South Asian music through Indian-language sources. He is a practitioner of Hindustani classical music and an accomplished western-classical pianist.

Prof. Imre Bangha is Associate Professor of Hindi in the Faculty of Asian and Middle Eastern Studies, University of Oxford. He specialises in early Hindi literature and has expertise in a range of languages including Braj Bhāṣā, Urdu, Bengali and Hungarian.

Transliteration and Other Textual Conventions

Western readers may be aware that the languages of the Indian subcontinent deploy writing systems other than the Latin/Roman alphabet—for example, Hindi and Sanskrit are written in Devanāgarī (देवनागरी) script. In transliterating text from these and other languages (such as Braj Bhāṣā) into Roman/Latin font, I have followed the conventions of the International Alphabet of Sanskrit Transliteration (IAST), closely related to ISO 15919. This involves the use of diacritics—for example, a line (macron) to indicate lengthened vowels, a tilde (~) to indicate nasalised vowels, and underdots or overdots to indicate retroflex consonants or nasalisation of a preceding vowel. Such a formalised system may be unfamiliar even to South Asian speakers, who, in everyday writing, would be more likely to transliterate 'Rāg Toḍī' as 'Raag Todi'. But IAST is favoured in scholarly practice because it makes for more precise and rigorous representation of spoken—and indeed sung—sounds (explained further in Section 2.2).

The front matter of most academic books on Indian music customarily details preferences regarding a host of further issues surrounding transliteration, orthography and other conventions. Here, briefly, are mine:

- Italics are generally used for non-English technical terms (for example, *bandiś*), but not for proper names (for example, of instruments, musical genres and *rāgs*).
- Quotations from non-English texts are generally presented un-italicised in quotation marks.
- Indic words that have entered common western usage have been left in their westernised versions—hence 'sitar', not 'sitār'; 'tabla' not 'tablā'.
- Similarly, I have retained commonly anglicised versions of place names and languages, etc.—for example, 'Delhi' not 'Dillī', 'Hindi' not Hindī'.
- I have omitted diacritics from names of people—thus, 'Bhatkhande', not 'Bhātkhaṇḍe'; and the honoric *jī* is rendered as 'ji'—for example, 'Vijay ji', 'guruji'.
- In general, I have used the Hindavi (i.e. Hindi/Urdu) terms *rāg*, *tāl* and *ras*, rather than their Sanskrit counterparts *rāga*, *tāla* and *rasa*.
- The suppression of the implicit vowel 'a' (aka *schwa*), which occurs under certain circumstances in spoken Hindavi, is normally reflected in transliteration—hence, '*tān*' not '*tāna*'. However, this is a difficult principle to apply entirely

> systematically (see Choudhury et al. 2004; Dhore et al. 2012), and occasionally I have adopted alternative, commonly recognised transliterations, such as 'Devanāgarī' rather than 'Devnāgarī'. Moreover, in the transliteration of *song* texts, I have, on the advice of our translators, followed the complementary norm: showing the 'a' that would be suppressed in speech—for instance, 'jhanakāra' not 'jhankār'. This is because that vowel *is* pronounced when sung and is essential to musical and poetic metre. I expand further on this matter in Section 2.2, where readers will also find a guide to essentials of pronunciation.

Finally, a note on geographic terminology is warranted. While our chief concern is with North Indian—Hindustani—classical music, some of the principles under discussion are not totally distinct from those of South Indian—Karnatak—classical music; hence I use the more general term 'Indian classical music' when wanting to reflect shared aspects of this heritage. More generally still, I tend to use the term 'Indian Music' to refer to aspects of culture and practice that extend beyond the classical sphere; and 'South Asian music' when the context pertains more specifically to the period following the Partition of 1947.

Prologue: First Encounters

The date of Vijay ji's arrival in the United Kingdom is etched indelibly in his memory: '2004, September tenth', he will tell you without a moment's hesitation. I (David) have heard his story several times (this version comes from a dialogue we had in November 2022): a chance conversation with a friend in New Delhi who alerted him to a newspaper advertisement for a teacher of Indian classical music in—of all places—Newcastle upon Tyne in the North East of England; the decision to quit a comfortable administrative post in the armed forces entertainment wing of India's Ministry of Information and Broadcasting; the experiment of going West, like so many South Asian musicians before him. Vijay's musical career was already on the rise: he was gaining repute in his own country as a Hindustani vocalist; he had been a disciple of one of India's most famed khayāl vocalists, Pandit Bhimsen Joshi (1922–2011); and before that had studied with several esteemed teachers at the Gandharva Mahavidyalaya in New Delhi. Now here was an opportunity to 'just see' what might be possible in a different climate and in a professional role explicitly to do with making music.

Ethnomusicologist Philip Bohlman writes of the significance of first encounters in the experience of world music (2002: 1–5). My own first encounter with Vijay came not long after his arrival in Newcastle from New Delhi. I remember introducing myself to him at the home of Dr A, a local general medical practitioner (GP), of Indian heritage, who, with his then wife, also a GP, was seeking to re-launch a working musical *gurukul* within their own house, complete with a new resident guru (Vijay). From Vijay's side, this was his first encounter with any country outside of India, and as we said Hello that Saturday morning in 2004, he looked a little overwhelmed by the momentousness of the step he had taken; it was a hard decision, his wife, Noopur, still in India, a baby on the way (they would join him a few months later). I also remember he looked young, in his early thirties; if this meant he didn't conform to the traditional image of a guru as an older paternalistic figure, it did mean that he had the optimism and energy of someone in the first half of life to seize an opportunity and make something of it—'destiny', he told me, many years later.

When Vijay notes that his journey west followed in the footsteps (or, more accurately, the flightpath) of many South Asian artists before him, he points to a bigger historical context of outward migration from the Indian subcontinent, and the emergence of Indian music within an increasingly internationalised world during the twentieth century, and especially since the 1960s. The big names who have criss-crossed the globe—including Ravi Shankar (1920–2012), Alla Rakha (1919–2000), Zakir Hussain, Hariprasad Chaurasia—are only part of the story. To this we can also add a much larger population of working musicians who have settled abroad or who practice as artists of second- or third-generation South Asian heritage. In the UK, these individuals have helped Indian music take root not only in London, but also in regional cities such as Leeds, Birmingham, Leicester, Manchester, Liverpool and, of course, Newcastle upon Tyne. Since arriving in Newcastle, Vijay has not only been responsible for growing Indian music in his adopted home, but has also established networks as a teacher and performer across those other regional and metropolitan centres, as well as continuing to build his artistic reputation in India.

That wider global movement since the late twentieth century has in turn been decisive for Westerners' first encounters with Indian music. My own happened many years before meeting Vijay: an all-night concert at Dartington Hall in the mid-1980s, which featured world-class Indian artists resident at Dartington, or domiciled elsewhere in the UK, or on tour from the subcontinent. 'First encounters with world music are never isolated, passing events', Bohlman reminds us; they engender a new awareness that 'seldom leaves us untouched, rather it transforms us, often deeply' (2002: 2, 1). True: that night opened me up to Indian music in a way that I never expected and that would never leave me. I was then a doctoral student researching the music of English composer Michael Tippett (1905–98), and it would be another fifteen years before I would take up Hindustani classical music as a practice; and then only tentatively while I developed my career as a lecturer in western music theory and analysis at Newcastle University. My first teacher was a guru from the earlier incarnation of Dr and Dr A's *Gurukul* project in Newcastle—a highly versatile Bengali musician (both vocalist and tabla player) called Arun Debnath. But not long after I got off the starting blocks, the venture folded, and our emergent community was without a teacher for a couple of years, until the doctors put out feelers to India and Vijay was hired.

Soon after our introduction, I took my first lesson with him. 'You know Rāg Yaman?', he asked. 'Yes', I replied. And so we began—'Piyā kī najariyā ...'. I realised from the start that Vijay's teaching was going to involve a step change from what I had previously encountered—even closer to the face-to-face *guru-śiṣyā paramparā* in which knowledge is transmitted orally. My notebook, into which my previous teacher had neatly written compositions, exercises, sequences of *tān*s and so on, was now my responsibility should I want to continue using it. It quickly became strewn with my own chaotic jottings as I struggled to make on-the-fly notations of what Vijay was singing to me. But I have welcomed this as part of a different dialogue, which we have evolved over some twenty years on and off. As from my previous guruji, I have learned from Vijay a range of *rāg*s and compositions; but also, because we have had more years together, an ever-stronger sense of *gāyakī*—vocal style—and of the deeper learning culture of Indian classical music.

Our relationship has been a complex one: not quite the straightforward *guru-śiṣyā* model, partly because I am about a decade older than Vijay, partly because of our different personalities and cultural standpoints, and partly because of my own professional position as a university professor of music. At the same time, when I take *tālīm* from him, I sit at his feet like any other student, and submit to his guidance, encouragement, and sometimes chastening judgements. My periodic experiences of learning with other gurus, during workshops or field trips to India, have only deepened our connection, because those activities have deepened my relationship with the culture of Hindustani music, and ultimately this is of a piece with the bond between guru and *śiṣyā*.

We have become friends and collaborators, Vijay and I. Among other things, we have worked together to introduce Hindustani classical music to students at Newcastle University. *Rāgs Around the Clock*, which comes out of this experience, is perhaps our most significant joint venture to date, as well as being a document of our *guru-śiṣyā* relationship. Although there is in one sense a clear division of labour within this project—with Vijay the lead artist on both of the accompanying albums, and myself the author of this book—much of what I write here channels his knowledge and insights, and I trust his presence will be sensed throughout much of the following text. For my own part, this venture has been an important milestone in a re-versioning of myself—an internalised cultural dialogue that contains something of ethnomusicologist Mantle Hood's notion of bimusicality (Hood 1960). For, I now realise, I have had to become a musician and a musicologist twice over: once in the western classical sphere, and once again in the domain of Hindustani classical music. If that journey has been elicited by something bigger than both Vijay and me, I nonetheless offer *praṇām* to my guruji for everything he has so generously given his at times wayward *śiṣyā*.

Introduction: Origins, Overview, Contexts

This book has been a long time coming. Its roots go back to a teaching initiative implemented by myself (David Clarke, henceforth DC), Vijay Rajput (henceforth VR), and tabla maestro Shahbaz Hussain, at Newcastle University in the late 2000s. Since that time, we have together offered short courses—modules, in UK higher-education parlance—to Music students, under the banner *Indian Music in Practice*. Our aim is simple: we offer students the opportunity to 'learn about Indian music by *doing* it'. To elaborate, and to pinpoint the spirit of the present compendium: we seek to cultivate two-way traffic between practice and theory: between practice informed by technical, historical, cultural and aesthetic knowledge, and knowledge experienced through embodied musical engagement. The practice in question is the *guru-śiṣyā paramparā* (master-disciple lineage), in which students learn face-to-face from teachers steeped in their musical heritage. Our own students do this not to become professional performers (which would take vastly more than a module or two), but rather to learn through a lived encounter with the music and its cultural and historical situation.

Rāgs Around the Clock develops resources produced during this venture, putting them into the public domain where they may be used and adapted under their Creative Commons licence by students, teachers and practicing musicians—indeed by anyone who enjoys and would like to know more about Hindustani classical music in general and the k͟hayāl vocal style in particular. Further, these materials are supplemented with analytical writings offered as a contribution to research in the field. The compendium is designed both as a set of resources from which readers can select as they wish, and as a monograph which can be read in a sequence essentially progressing from simpler treatments to more complex ones.

As the first word in our title suggests, a key concept is *rāg*—arguably *the* fundamental notion in Indian classical music. *Rāg* elusively denotes a number of things: the way melody in general is organised and shaped; a kind of modal system; a corresponding world of feeling and imagination. Musicians also talk of performing particular *rāgs*—from a corpus of hundreds (some claim thousands), each with its own name. And an essential part of a vocalist's or melody-instrumentalist's training is to acquire a repertoire of *rāg*s and associated songs or compositions. In the Hindustani tradition, musicians need to know *rāg*s suitable for various times of the day or night—for each *rāg* has its appropriate time, or *samay*. Hence, *Rāgs Around the Clock*. Hence also the title of the book's first companion album: *Rāg samay cakra*. Here, VR sings a cycle (*cakra*) of *rāg*s according to their performing times, from dawn to the small hours; he also includes two seasonal *rāgs*—Megh, for the rainy season, and Basant, for the springtime—illustrating a further connection between *rāg* and cyclic time.

 https://doi.org/10.11647/OBP.0313.00

While *rāg* performances often last the best part of an hour, and sometimes longer, an accomplished musician can capture the essence of a *rāg* in just a few minutes. On *Rāg samay cakra*, VR presents fourteen *rāg*s in capsule performances lasting around five minutes each. The inspiration here was *The Raga Guide*, a scholarly introduction to Hindustani *rāg* in book form by Joep Bor (1999) and fellow scholars, with attached CDs comprising concise performances by internationally renowned artists. The musicians follow the example of the earliest recorded performers of Indian music, who, working within the limitations of 78 rpm (revolutions per minute) gramophone technology, showed themselves 'capable of bringing out the essence of the ragas in just a few minutes' (Bor et al. 1999: 5). Our initial motive was to curate an album for VR's students, comprising *rāg*s he commonly teaches and particularly cherishes. While our own collection is less epic (featuring fourteen *rāgs* rather than seventy-four), it is more explicitly focused on the particular *gāyakī* (vocal idiom) of a single artist and on the khayāl style. Despite their brevity and didactic purpose, the performances are fully idiomatic—intended to be musically satisfying in their own right.

To complement these compressed renditions, we also include a second album, *Twilight Rāgs from North India*, which presents two concert-length performances lasting around thirty-five minutes each. Here, we showcase two *rāgs* fundamental to Hindustani classical music, and redolent of the passage from night to day and vice versa: Rāg Bhairav, sung at sunrise, and Rāg Yaman, sung after sunset. The long-form presentation gives VR time to explore the musical depths of each *rāg* through the many facets of the khayāl style.

These two albums, then, form the unifying focus around which the four parts of *Rāgs Around the Clock* are organised. Part 1 comprises a series of essays that introduce readers to relevant theoretical concepts and contexts, and that illustrate how musical practice is permeated by convention, culture and history. These accounts are mostly short, mirroring the compression of the performances on *Rāg samay cakra*. Like those recordings, the essays may be imbibed in any order, though they are similarly organised in a meaningful sequence. They present selected concepts that are part of the common working knowledge of musicians. Traditionally, this knowledge has been transmitted within a learning culture shaped by myth as much as scholarship, and no less entwined in ideology than any other musical practice, from whichever corner of the globe. This is not to say that the myths and ideologies of Indian classical music have not been productive or enabling; indeed, they are inseparable from its history and discourses. But it is to point to the need for commentary and analysis also informed by critically aware research—a principle we have sought to uphold by drawing most of our information from peer-reviewed scholarship, and by distinguishing this from the tropes and narratives of the tradition.

Part 2 presents supporting materials for *Rāg samay cakra*: a commentary on each *rāg*; a notation of the song (*bandiś*) chosen for its performance; and a transliteration and translation of the text, produced in collaboration with Jonathan Katz and Imre Bangha. On the one hand, these materials serve as a resource for students wanting to learn (or learn about) these *rāg*s and their *bandiś*es. On the other hand, this collection adds to numerous other published examples of *rāg* curation in online and offline formats. The most eminent of these include not only *The Raga Guide*, but also Suvarnalata Rao and Wim van der Meer's website, *Music in Motion* (https://autrimncpa.wordpress.com/), which presents annotated transcriptions playable in real time of commissioned *rāg* recordings by world-class artists. To these we may add Patrick Moutal's *A Comparative Study of Selected Hindustānī Rāga-s* (1997/1991) and its related website (http://www.moutal.eu/); and Nicolas Magriel and Lalita du Perron's magisterial *The Songs of Khayāl* (2013), whose second volume presents painstaking transcriptions and sound clips of numerous *bandiśes* from historic recorded performances. Valuable examples of non-academic online collections include *Ocean of Ragas* by Sudhir V. Gadre (http://www.oceanofragas.com/) and *Tanarang* by Prakash Vishwanath Ringe and Vishwajeet Vishwanath Ringe (http://www.tanarang.com/).

In Parts 3 and 4 of *Rāgs Around the Clock*, I (DC) offer detailed commentaries on the book's two companion albums in a series of article-length essays that explore the different stages of a *rāg* performance. Part 3 revisits *Rāg samay cakra*: in separate sections, I explore the questions 'How do you sing an *ālāp*?' and 'How do you sing a *choṭā khayāl*?' These are questions of obvious practical relevance to performers; and this way of couching things similarly invites listeners to understand the music from the singer's perspective. It also seeks to abstract some of the deeper principles of khayāl through close analysis of VR's performances. In what is one of the book's main research strands, I attempt to codify these principles as a set of theoretical rubrics in order to formalise what gurus convey orally and demonstrate musically to their students. At the same time, this inquiry builds in its own critique of the status of such rubrics. On the one hand, they tantalisingly point to a possible performance grammar that Hindustani musicians might unconsciously imbibe during their long training. On the other hand, when tested against practice, such rubrics sometimes become fuzzy or provisional; their status tends toward the heuristic—a term I use a lot in this book, appropriately enough, given that pedagogy is among its subjects.

These and other ideas are pursued further in Part 4, which considers the second album, *Twilight Rāgs from North India*. In Section 4.2, I extend the analysis of *choṭā khayāl* principles from Part 3, this time looking at VR's extended *drut khayāl* from his Bhairav performance. Among other things, I explore the phenomenology of the khayāl performer as they respond to the perpetual question: what do I do next? In an adaptation of ideas from Daniel Dennett's multiple drafts theory of consciousness (1991), I conjecture whether every rubric or principle of performance might not vie for selection at any given moment within a pandemonium of possibilities operating below the threshold of consciousness.

To dramatise a little: what begins to emerge here is the thought that to perform khayāl involves a negotiation between the forces of order, regulated by convention, and the energy of the inchoate, simmering in the unconscious of the individual performer. I speculate about this phenomenology further in a dialogue with my fellow *śiṣyā* Sudipta Roy in the Epilogue of this book; but before this, in Section 4.3, I thematise similar tensions in an analysis of VR's *baṛā khayāl* from his Yaman performance on *Twilight Rāgs*. I seek to do justice to this, the weightiest stage of a khayāl performance, by showing how its essence lies in a deep-rooted tension between metrical and anti-metrical orderings of time—as captured in the terms *nibaddh* and *anibaddh*.

It is in the nature of Indian classical music that no artist is an iconoclast; rather each adds their personal voice to the panoply of their forebears and contemporaries. So too with Indian-music scholarship—including the present collaboration between VR and myself: what is new is not a paradigm-shifting reset of known parameters, but rather a re-synthesis of received understanding shaped by our individual backgrounds and by our longstanding *guru-śiṣyā* relationship. Viewed within the wider musicological landscape, *Rāgs Around the Clock* joins a growing tradition of collaboration between Indian and western musical and musicological investigators. Our predecessors (and their works) include Neil Sorrell and sāraṅgī player Ram Narayan (1980); Martin Clayton and k͟hayāl singer Veena Sahasrabuddhe (1998); sarod player Ali Akbar Khan and George Ruckert (2021/1998); and dhrupad singer Ritwik Sanyal and Richard Widdess (2004). Such cross-cultural collaborations matter. They matter in the wider global dissemination of one of the world's significant classical traditions, and they matter in signifying a maturation of the western reception of Indian music; each work enriches that tradition by creating new knowledge and perspectives. We hope that the musical and intellectual contribution of *Rāgs Around the Clock* will in its own way play a part in this continuing inter-cultural dialogue.

1. CONCEPTS, CONVENTIONS, HISTORY AND CULTURE

https://doi.org/10.11647/OBP.0313.01

1.1 Elements of Indian Classical Music

Survey the scene when a Hindustani classical music performance is in full flow, and you will see and hear a number of things going on simultaneously. Centre stage is the main artist (or artists). He or she may be an instrumentalist or vocalist; and if a vocalist they may be supported by one or more accompanists on melody instruments, such as harmonium or sāraṅgī (a bowed instrument with many sympathetic resonating strings). Then there will be one or more percussionists, usually playing tabla (a pair of hand drums) or possibly pakhāvaj (a barrel drum used in the dhrupad style). And in the background to all this is the constant buzzing drone of one or more tānpurās, long-necked lute-like instruments—these days increasingly supplemented, sometimes even supplanted, by their digital counterparts.

Much of the joy and intensity of Indian classical music comes from the fact that it is substantially improvised; unlike its western counterpart it is not performed from notation, but is extemporised in the moment. Even so, the performers do not produce their ideas from a void. Rather, they generate them from well-recognised conventions and structures that help them mobilise a stock of musical materials and formulas acquired over many years of practice into ever new variants. (For more detailed discussions, see Sanyal and Widdess 2004: 130, 143; Slawek 1998; Zadeh 2012.)

The rich inventiveness of a live Indian classical music performance draws ultimately on a small number of fundamental musical elements and their organising concepts. These are: (i) melody, organised by the modal principles of *rāg*; (ii) rhythm, organised by the cyclic principles of *tāl*; and (iii) drone, which fixes the tonic note of the *rāg* as a continuous sounding presence—in Indian classical music there is no concept of key change, and no functional harmony as such. The resonance and manifold overtones of the drone-sustaining tānpurā embody a further fundamental concept in Indian music that also permeates melody: *svar*. This term could be superficially translated as 'note', but it signifies something richer and more aesthetically resonant.

These concepts are explored in the following sections. Prefacing these discussions, we also consider *sargam* notation—part of the common tongue of musicians, and, as a solmisation system, essential to the discussion of scales, in turn an important component—though arguably not the substance—of *rāgs*. In the later sections of Part 1, I provide perspectives on the k͟hayāl vocal style and also explore aspects of history and culture that inform the lifeworld of Hindustani musicians.

1.2 *Sargam* Notation

Although Indian classical music is principally an oral tradition, notation is no stranger to it and is in practice embedded in the oral transmission of musical ideas. The identification of tabla strokes with *bols* (words) is one example of such oral notation (see Section 1.4). So too is the naming of notes (*svar*) under the system known as *sargam*—a term derived from the first four scale steps, Sā, Re, Ga, Ma. *Sargam* notation is a solmisation system: like western sol-fa, it indicates scale degrees, not absolute pitches. The system tonic, Sā, can be placed at whatever pitch suits the performer or the circumstances; all the other scale degrees are placed relative to it.

The terms for the full heptatonic gamut are: Sā, Re, Ga, Ma, Pa, Dha, Ni. For convenience, these are often abbreviated to their first letter, but they are in fact the short forms of longer Sanskrit names—*ṣaḍj, ṛiṣabh, gāndhār, madhyam, pañcam, dhaivat* and *niṣād*. While musicians usually use the shortened note names ('sing Pa') they not infrequently use the longer ones too ('sustain *pañcam*'). These details are summarised in Figure 1.2.1 (of course, in their original Sanskrit form, these syllables and words would be represented in Devanāgarī characters, not the Roman ones used here and in western transliteration generally).

Scale degree	Abbreviation	Note name (short)	Note name (full)
1	S	Sā	*ṣaḍj*
2	R	Re	*ṛiṣabh*
3	G	Ga	*gāndhār*
4	M	Ma	*madhyam*
5	P	Pa	*pañcam*
6	D	Dha	*dhaivat*
7	N	Ni	*niṣād*

Fig. 1.2.1 Scale degrees/note names in *sargam* notation. Created by author (2024), CC BY-NC-SA.

Indian classical music normally operates within a three-octave compass, and the register in which a note is to be sung or played can also be included in the notation. This is the case in the notation system of Vishnu Narayan Bhatkhande (1860–1936), which is used by many Hindustani musicians, and which we have adapted in notating the song compositions in *Rāgs Around the Clock*. Under these conventions, notes in the lower octave are notated with a dot below the note name; notes in the upper octave with a dot above; and notes in the middle octave with the note name only. For example: Ṣ = lower tonic (*mandrā* Sā); S = middle tonic (*madhya* Sā); and Ṡ = upper tonic (*tār* Sā).

Pitches can be inflected upwards or downwards. Letters without modifications indicate the natural (*śuddh*) form of a note. A line below a letter indicates its flat (*komal*) form—applicable to Re, Ga, Dha and Ni; hence R̲ = *komal* Re, flattened 2nd. In Hindustani classical music only the fourth scale degree can be sharpened; this is known as *tivra* Ma, and is indicated with a wedge above the note name, thus: Ḿ. These five inflections added to the seven natural notes theoretically make available a full twelve-note chromatic gamut, though not all notes are available in any given *rāg*, and these are not arranged in equal temperament. Rather, *svar*s may be subject to microtonal inflection (*śruti*) according to the *rāg*.

Already this hints at a much more extensive and complex theoretical background. The discussion of microtones, of different possible divisions of the octave (for example into twenty-two *śruti*s), is just one aspect of a large body of theoretical treatises (*śāstra*s) on Indian music and related arts. Many of these have been lost, but the oldest known is the *Nāṭyaśāstra* of Bharata Muni (in fact a treatment of theatre from the early first millennium CE); while the earliest known example of *sargam* notation is found on the Kuḍumiyāmalai Inscription dating from seventh- or eighth-century Tamil Nadu (see Widdess 1979; 1995: 104–24; 1996). The principal language of these works is Sanskrit, but scholars such as Françoise 'Nalini' Delvoye and Katherine Butler Schofield (née Brown) shed light on a further corpus of Indo-Persian texts written between the thirteenth and late-nineteenth centuries that highlight the significance of Muslim scholars and artists in the Hindustani tradition (see Nijenhuis and Delvoye 2010; Brown 2003, 2010). Further, the bigger context for Hindustani music also includes the contribution of Sikh musicians, gurus and scholars (see, for example, recent work by Gurminder Kaur Bhogal (2017, 2022), Harjinder Singh Lallie (2016), and Kirit Singh (2023)).

It is useful for musicians to be aware of the theoretical and historical hinterland behind their practice; for, in truth, Indian classical music has constantly evolved out of a complex and elliptical relationship between oral discipular traditions (*sampradāya*) and canonical works of theory (*śāstra*). The quotidian use of *sargam* notation by practitioners—as a way of talking about music, of communicating knowledge and ideas about it, of making things happen with it (in the context, say, of a class or a rehearsal)—is one example of the mediation of practice by theory. But the implications of this confluence extend beyond pragmatics. The way notation transmutes sounds into concepts (like Sā, Re, Ga ...), the way it structures them into a systemic relationship, the way it brings a pattern and an order to our musical thinking—all these features condition our experience of the music, and pre-empt any naïve dislocation between orality and literacy, and between improvisation and composition.

Critical twists and turns in this argument are possible. For example, Dard Neuman (2012) interrogates notation and classificatory knowledge as ideological aspects of the modernisation of Indian music ushered in by the likes of Bhatkhande in the earlier twentieth century. Neuman cites accounts of how hereditary musicians (of the kind Bhatkhande tended to disparage) would traditionally withhold information about a *rāg* and inhibit the use of *sargam* notation until the student had memorised and absorbed the material in an embodied way—though, even then, information was withheld only temporarily, not suppressed permanently.

At subsequent points in this book—notably in Section 4.3—we will again have occasion to consider the creative tensions between notation and practice. For now, it is sufficient to underline notation's mediating significance in our contemporary musical world, and to note its historical presence in arguments (traced in Powers 1992) for what makes Indian classical music classical—*śāstrīya saṅgīta*.

1.3 *Rāg*

Rāg is the source from which all melodic invention in Indian classical music flows. If its concept cannot be finally captured in language this is because *rāg* has an aesthetic as well as a technical dimension; it is a world of feelings *and* a mode of tonal organisation.

Because Indian classical music organises tones under melodic rather than harmonic principles, *rāg* can in certain respects be thought of as a *modal* system. It is indeed considered as such in *Grove Music*'s capacious article on Mode (Powers et al. 2001), which notably locates *rāg* in a pan-Asian and wider global context. One of the modal features of *rāg* is that it is built on scale forms. A *rāg* must deploy no fewer than five and may have up to seven scale degrees, with varying inflections. In other words, its scales may take pentatonic, hexatonic or heptatonic form (known as *auḍav*, *ṣāḍav* and *sampūrṇ*, respectively). However, ascending and descending scale forms (*āroh* and *avroh*) may differ. For example, the ascending form of Rāg Bihāg (heard on Track 11 of *Rāg samay cakra*) is based on a pentatonic scale with a natural fourth degree, while its descending counterpart deploys a heptatonic scale with a sometimes sharpened fourth. Sometimes but not always: when and how to execute the sharpened scale degree, so as to enhance rather than disturb the feel of the *rāg*, is just one of the subtleties a student must learn from their teacher—and just one instance of how the technical and aesthetic blur into one another.

From this we begin to see how a *rāg* amounts to something much more than its raw scale form. In one *rāg*, certain notes may be particularly prominent (these may be termed *vādī* and *saṃvādī*) while others are only fleetingly touched upon or used to pass between adjacent pitches. In a different *rāg* using the same scale, degrees of relative prominence may differ, as may the way one note moves to another. Compare, for example Rāg Toḍī and Rāg Multānī (Tracks 2 and 6 respectively of *Rāg samay cakra*), both of which have flattened second, flattened third, sharpened fourth and flattened sixth degrees, but each of which deploys these notes with different emphases, grammars and expressive palates. Perhaps their most explicit difference lies in their respective *vādī* and *saṃvādī* pitches: in Todī, <u>Dha</u> and <u>Gha</u>; in Multānī, Pa and Sā. Furthermore, every *rāg* has its distinctive melodic turns of phrase—a characteristic that bears out Harold Powers' claim that 'a rāga is not a tune, nor is it a "modal" scale, but rather a continuum with scale and tune as its extremes' (Qureshi et al. 2020: §III.2.i.a). And certain notes in a *rāg* may receive particular ornamentation or microtonal inflections (*śruti*), or both—listen, for example, to the distinctive oscillation (*āndolan*) around the flattened second and sixth degrees of Rāg Bhairav (Track 1 of *Rāg samay cakra*; Tracks 1–3 of *Twilight Rāgs*).

These, then, are some of the ways in which *rāg* combines and colours tones to generate subtleties of mood and emotion—or *ras*. While there is no history of formal correlation between the terms, musicians sometimes invoke *ras* as a way of indicating the appropriate affect of a *rāg*—as we sometimes do in our commentaries in Section 2.5 of this book. The Sanskrit word *rasa* literally means 'juice' or 'essence' or 'flavour', and came to denote a theory of emotion in Hindu aesthetics that goes back to Bharata Muni's *Nāṭyaśāstra* (2006/1989: 70–85), compiled in the early centuries of the first millennium CE. Bharata outlined eight *rasa*s, of which the most relevant to <u>kh</u>ayāl are probably *śṛṅgāra* (romance), *karuṇa* (compassion or pathos), and *vīra* (heroism); so too is a ninth *rasa*, *śānta* (peace), which was adopted by later theorists.

Another way in which a *rāg* acquires its identity is through its *differences* from similar *rāg*s. Hence, part of the work of learning a *rāg* is also to acquire familiarity with its relatives. In our commentaries we have taken care to indicate, where relevant, some of the salient similarities and differences between a *rāg* and its neighbours. This points to the fact that *rāg*s are organised into families—although exactly how one construes the interrelationships of the several hundred *rāg*s in an ever-evolving repertory has historically been a moot point. *Rāg*s both invite and resist totalising classification systems, and over the centuries *rāg*s themselves and their systems of organisation and taxonomy have mutated or been supplanted by new ones. For example, the *rāga–rāginī* system, in which a series of principal (male) *rāg*s were construed as governing their own family of 'wives', held currency in various versions between the fourteenth and early-nineteenth centuries, but eventually became obsolete when it no longer seemed to conform to actual usage. Joep Bor et al. (1999: 2–4) provide a historical sketch of this and other classification systems; see also Harold Powers and Richard Widdess's more extended account (in Qureshi et al. 2020: §III.1.ii).

A key reformer in modern *rāg* taxonomy was V. N. Bhatkhande (a figure discussed at greater length in Section 1.10). Bhatkhande organised *rāg*s into ten groups, each identified by a parent scale, which he termed *ṭhāṭ*—as shown in Figure 1.3.1.

Ṭhāṭ	Scale
Kalyāṇ	S R G Ḿ P D N Ṡ
Bilāval	S R G M P D N Ṡ
Khamāj	S R G M P D N̲ Ṡ
Bhairav	S R̲ G M P D̲ N Ṡ
Pūrvī	S R̲ G Ḿ P D̲ N Ṡ
Mārvā	S R̲ G Ḿ P D̲ N Ṡ
Kāfī	S R G̲ M P D N̲ Ṡ
Āsāvarī	S R G̲ M P D̲ N̲ Ṡ
Bhairavī	S R̲ G̲ M P D̲ N̲ Ṡ
Toḍī	S R̲ G̲ Ḿ P D̲ N̲ Ṡ

Fig. 1.3.1 Bhatkhande's *ṭhāṭ*s and their scale types (after Powers 1992: 13). Created by author (2024), CC BY-NC-SA.

It needs to be stressed that the ten *ṭhāṭ*s and their associated scale types remain abstract, theoretical constructs. One would never imagine 'performing' the Kalyāṇ *ṭhāṭ* as such, but one might be aware when performing certain *rāg*s, such as Yaman, Bhūpālī, Kedār and Kalyāṇ itself, that they are related through being members of this *ṭhāṭ*—at least according to Bhatkande's construction. But then, like so much else in Bhatkhande's life and work, this system remains contentious—among other reasons because it contains many inconsistencies and anomalies (a number of *rāg*s do not fit readily into it), and because scales are not the only, nor even necessarily the main, principle through which *rāg*s can be defined and related. These were arguments made by, among others, Omkarnath Thakur (1897–1967), 'the most articulate and persuasive of Bhatkhande's detractors' (Powers 1992: 18). Yet, for all this, Bhatkhande remains a continuing, if qualified, point of reference, both for performers and theorists (see, for example, Nazir Jairazbhoy's (1971) extended application of Bhatkhande's *ṭhāṭ* system).

While we cannot adequately recreate the sound worlds of the now obsolete *grāma-jāti*, *grāmarāga* and *deśī-rāgā* systems, which range from the early first to the early second millennia, scholars such as Widdess have nonetheless adduced 'evidence for continuity and change in musical concepts, structures and performance' across these antecedents of our present-day *rāg* system (1995: 371). So, if the evolutionary timescale of this process and the discontinuities within it warn us not to construe *rāg* as something unchanging or timeless, this evidence nonetheless points to its sheer historical depth.

1.4 *Tāl*

Tāl is the term used for the cyclic organisation of rhythm in Indian classical music. In the Hindustani tradition, the job of projecting and sustaining the *tāl* falls chiefly to the tabla player—or pakhāvaj player in a dhrupad performance. Common *tāl*s include *tīntāl* (based on a sixteen-beat cycle), *ektāl* (based on twelve beats), *jhaptāl* (ten beats), *rūpak tāl* (seven beats), *keharvā tāl* (eight beats; used for light classical music, including devotional bhajans) and *dādrā tāl* (six beats; also used for light classical music, including ṭhumrī).

A *tāl*'s feeling of endless recurrence seems of a piece with the unchanging background drone on Sā; but what gives a *tāl* its cyclic quality? This is a more complex matter than might at first appear (a point explored in Clayton 2000: chapters 4–5). Some obvious features include the unchanging length of each *tāl* cycle (*āvartan*), measured as a fixed number of beats (*mātrās*); and the unbroken succession of one cycle by the next. Moreover, each *tāl* organises its cycle in a characteristic way that gives it a unique shape and flow. This is related to the fact that *tāl* is not only cyclic but also *metrical*: the *mātrās* of a *tāl* cycle are organised into subdivisions known as *vibhāg*s (broadly similar to western music's grouping of beats into bars). This gives a *tāl* its distinctive pattern. Consider Figure 1.4.1, which shows the metrical profile of *tīntāl*, one of the most common *tāl*s in Hindustani classical music. Looking along the top row of this figure, you can see how one *āvartan* (cycle) comprises sixteen *mātrās* (beats) organised into four *vibhāg*s (subdivisions) of four *mātrās* each:

mātrā	1	2	3	4	5	6	7	8	9	10	11	12	13	14	15	16	1 ...
ṭhekā	dhā	dhin	dhin	dhā	dhā	dhin	dhin	dhā	dhā	tin	tin	tā	tā	dhin	dhin	dhā	dhā ...
clap pattern	clap				clap				wave				clap				clap
notation	x				2				o				3				x
	sam				*tālī*				*khālī*				*tālī*				*sam*

Fig. 1.4.1 *Tīntāl*: metrical structure and clap pattern. Created by author (2024), CC BY-NC-SA.

One way in which this metrical structure can be communicated is through its *clap pattern*. This is partly a didactic device, but it is not absent from performance either. In a live concert, audience members can often be seen discreetly tapping out the *tāl*'s clap pattern with their fingers or on their knee; and in the Karnatak tradition, vocalists themselves may overtly execute the clap pattern as they sing. The details of the clap pattern for *tīntāl* along with its accompanying notation are shown in the bottom three rows of Figure 1.4.1, and can be explained as follows:

- The beginning of each *vibhāg* is signalled with a clap or a wave depending on its place in the cycle (see third row up).
- Beat 1 of the entire cycle is known as *sam* (see bottom row). In *tīntāl* and almost all other *tāl*s, this is indicated with a clap, which is notated 'x' (a notable exception is *rūpak tāl*, which begins with a wave). Because *tāl*s are cyclic, *sam* simultaneously marks both the beginning of each *āvartan* and the end of the

preceding one. It is structurally the most significant feature of a *tāl*, and, after an accumulation of several *āvartans*, *sam* can mark a climactic point of release.

- By contrast, the complementary point of a *tāl* (and its associated *vibhāg*) is termed *khālī*, meaning 'empty'; this point is signalled with a wave, and is notated 'o'. In *tīntāl, khālī* falls on beat 9, at the opposite pole to *sam*, giving this *tāl* a distinctive symmetrical aspect. Some *tāl*s have more than one *khālī*—for example, *ektāl*, discussed below.
- Stressed beats other than *sam* are termed *tālī*, and, like *sam*, are clapped. In *tīntāl* these are found on beats 5 and 13, and are notated with the numbers 2 and 3, denoting the second and third claps of the cycle (see second row up in Figure 1.4.1).

This technical description perhaps risks making the structure seem more complex than it actually is. The best way to grasp these points in the first instance is simply to count the beats out loud and clap or wave in the correct place, repeating this until the pattern is ingrained in the body. A further important point is made by Neil Sorrell, who reminds us that *sam* (or *tālī*) and *khālī* do not simplistically correspond to stressed and unstressed beats as they might in western metre (Sorrell and Narayan 1980: 117). *Sam* might be a point of focus, a locus of organisation, but it is not necessarily articulated with a major accent (*rūpak tāl* is a case in point). Similarly, *khālī* may be associated with lighter strokes, but in symmetrical *tāl*s such as *tīntāl* it is nonetheless a complementary point of focus that is in its own way structural—as *saṃvādī* is to *vādī* in a *rāg*, we might conjecture.

Just as a *rāg* is more than a scale, so a *tāl* is defined by more than the number of its beats or its combination of claps and waves. In the Hindustani tradition, another way in which a *tāl* is expressed is through its *ṭhekā*—a pattern of drum strokes unique to the *tāl* and complementing the clap pattern. Drum strokes in Indian classical music are taught and identified by their *bols* (meaning 'words'), such as 'nā', 'tin', 'ghe', 'ke'; and the *ṭhekā* for any given *tāl* combines such strokes into a unique sequence. For example, the *ṭhekā* for *tīntāl* is as shown in the second row of Figure 1.4.1, beginning with the *bols* 'dhā, dhin, dhin, dhā'. These particular *bols* onomatopoeically convey the simultaneous combination of a percussive stroke on the smaller, tuned tabla drum (*dāyā̃*) and a resonant stroke on the larger one (*bāyā̃*). Conversely, the strokes that follow *khālī*, on beats 10–13 (... tin tin tā | tā...), do not involve the larger drum, and hence the feel is lighter at this point. All musicians should know the *ṭhekā* of any *tāl* they are using. So, students should practice speaking it out loud until it becomes second nature, and then combine it with the relevant clap pattern. Again, this is a way to know the shape and flow of a *tāl* experientially.

The tabla player may decorate the *ṭhekā*, but usually ensures it remains discernible. This helps the vocal or instrumental soloist remain oriented within the *tāl*, so that after improvisatory passages they are able to resume the composition at the right point. Hence, all the performers have a stake in *tāl* and need constantly to hold it in their awareness. The same goes for the audience: because the *tāl* forms the organising metrical framework against which the musicians improvise, listeners who are able to follow it are likely to gain greater insight into the performers' invention—hence the subtle participation of audience members in keeping time, a gesture of identification with the musicians.

While almost all the compositions on the *Rāg samay cakra* album are in *tīntāl*, the *bandiś* for Rāg Basant deploys *ektāl*, as do several compositions on *Twilight Rāgs from North India*. Details of this twelve-beat *tāl* are given in Figure 1.4.2. Note here how *ektāl* has two *khālī vibhāg*s, yet in the first of these, on beat 3, *khālī* is simultaneously associated with a wave within the clap pattern and a heavy tabla *bol* within the *ṭhekā*. The converse is also true on *mātrā* 5, where a *tālī* in the clap pattern corresponds with a *khālī bol* ('tū') in the *ṭhekā*. These seeming contradictions between *ṭhekā* and clap pattern—discussed at greater length by Martin Clayton (2000: 65–6)—reinforce Sorrell's point that *sam* and *khālī* do not necessarily correspond to phenomenal stress or accentuation.

mātrā	1	2	3	4	5	6	7	8	9	10	11	12	1 ...
ṭhekā	dhin	dhin	dhāge	tirakiṭa	tū	nā	kat	tā	dhāge	tirakiṭa	dhin	nā	dhin ...
clap pattern	clap		wave		clap		wave		clap		clap		clap
notation	x		o		2		o		3		4		x
	sam		*khālī*		*tālī*		*khālī*		*tālī*		*tālī*		sam

Fig. 1.4.2 *Ektāl*: metrical structure and clap pattern. Created by author (2024), CC BY-NC-SA.

Tāls can be performed across an entire gamut of speeds, but Hindustani classical music nominally uses three categories of *lay* (tempo): *vilambit* (slow); *madhya lay* (medium tempo); and *drut* (fast). While these represent quite broad tempo bandwidths as measured by the metronome, each has its own personality. *Madhya lay*, for example, does not just occupy a mid-point between *vilambit* and *drut lays*, but has an unhurried, relaxed character of its own. It is also possible to perform in *ati vilambit* (very slow) and *ati drut* (very fast) *lays*—the former usually the hallmark of a *baṛā* (large, grand) *khayāl* (as discussed in Section 4.3); the latter often coming into play at the culmination of many an extended instrumental or vocal performance (I make a detailed analysis of just such a *drut khayāl* in *ektāl* by Vijay Rajput (henceforth VR) in Section 4.2).

1.5 Tānpurā Drone, *Svar*

The tānpurā, a long-necked fretless lute, is responsible for providing the most elemental feature of Indian classical music: its drone. This instrument is ostensibly easy to play, requiring only that the player pluck the open strings at an unchanging tempo—different from that of the other artists—remaining outside the accumulation of speed and intensity characteristic of Indian classical music performances (see Clayton 2007 for an empirical investigation of these conditions). Arguably, tānpurā players do not overtly perform, but occupy a liminal place both inside and outside the performance.

Nowadays the tānpurā drone is often generated digitally, either by electronic śruti boxes or—increasingly commonly—by smartphone apps. Although ostensibly for practise purposes, such devices are commonly plugged into the sound system of concert performances, boosting the sound of the live tānpurās. Occasionally, in an instrumental performance, the live tānpurā might be entirely obviated by its electronic counterpart softly unfurling its drone in the background.

The tānpurā player's relatively low status in the performer hierarchy is mitigated by the fact that he or she may be a senior student of the principal artist; hence this accompanying role can carry a degree of kudos. If the soloist is a singer, the tānpurā-playing student may be solicited to provide short periods of vocal support during a performance. And for all its modest technical demands, the tānpurā itself is held in high esteem—philosophically because it embodies *svar* (see below), and practically because it provides the essential reference point for the other performers' tuning.

Most tānpurās have four strings that are plucked in a steady repeating sequence. The middle two strings are tuned to the tonic in the middle register (*madhya* Sā); the lowest to the lower-octave tonic (*mandrā* Sā); and the second lowest usually to the lower fifth degree (Pa) or, if that note is not present in the *rāg* being performed, to some other appropriate scale degree—most usually the fourth (Ma) or seventh (Ni).

What gives the instrument its characteristic buzz is the sandwiching of a cotton thread between each string and the flat bridge at a key nodal point. This generates a cascade of harmonics—an effect known as *javārī*, meaning 'life-giving' (see Datta et al. 2019). It is to this acoustic panoply that the soloist attunes, listening to the vibrations and seeking to match and intensify them. Musicians sometimes say that all the notes of a *rāg* are already there in the sound of the tānpurā; the performer's job is merely to tap into them and release them.

This is the experience of *svar*—not merely 'note' in the prosaic sense of a specific pitch with a specific amplitude and duration, but also a phenomenal convergence of sound and self, of tone and feeling. *Svar* can be coloured and enhanced by the *śruti* (microtones) that lie within it; and as one *svar* melts into the next, so this concept blends into that of *rāg*. Some musicians also invoke a relationship between *svar* and *nād*—a term for musicalised sound that has metaphysical resonances going back to the Vedic era (ca. 1500–500 BCE) (see Beck 1995; Rowell 1998). Related to this are philosophical ideas such as *nāda yoga*—the oneness of mind and body achieved through sound—and *nāda brahma*—the convergence of sound and consciousness.

As evocative as these ideas are, we have to be careful about regarding them as essential or universal (see Clayton 2000: 6–7, 10–13). For one thing, the omnipresence of a tonic drone in Indian classical music is probably a relatively recent development. Research by Chaitanya Deva (1980b: 47–75), Lewis Rowell (1998: 293), Bonnie Wade (1998: 195–8) and Widdess (1995: 7)—based variously on the historical evidence of iconography, instrument construction and primary textual sources—suggests that this performing practice may go back to no earlier than the fifteenth century. In the present day, notions such as *nāda yoga* and *nāda brahma* hold greater currency for some genres, *gharānās* and individual musicians than others. They feature, for example, in the discourse of certain lineages of the dhrupad style, such as the Ḍāgar *bānī* (notably the Gundecha brothers), and among some exponents of the Kirānā *gharānā*, including VR.

1.6 *Rāg* and Time: *Samay Cakra*

The title of our book, *Rāgs Around the Clock,* references a convention fundamental to Hindustani classical music: that a *rāg* should be performed at its proper time. The Sanskrit term for this principle is *samay cakra*—where *samay* means 'time', or, more specifically, 'at the appointed time or right moment' (Monier-Williams 1899), and *cakra* denotes 'wheel' or 'circle'.

There is no single agreed representation of this time cycle (see Wade 2004/1999: 77–8). One example, from a now superseded incarnation of the ITC Sangeet Research Academy website, divides the diurnal cycle into twelve segments—as shown in Figure 1.6.1. Under another convention—the one we adopt in *Rāgs Around the Clock*—day and night are each divided into four quarters, or *prahar*s. The Sanskrit *prahara* literally means 'watch' as in the watch of a guardsman; a similar word, *prahāra,* means a striking or hitting, as in the sounding of the hours on a gong. This eightfold schema is represented, in conjunction with the *rāg*s of our albums, in Figure 1.6.2.

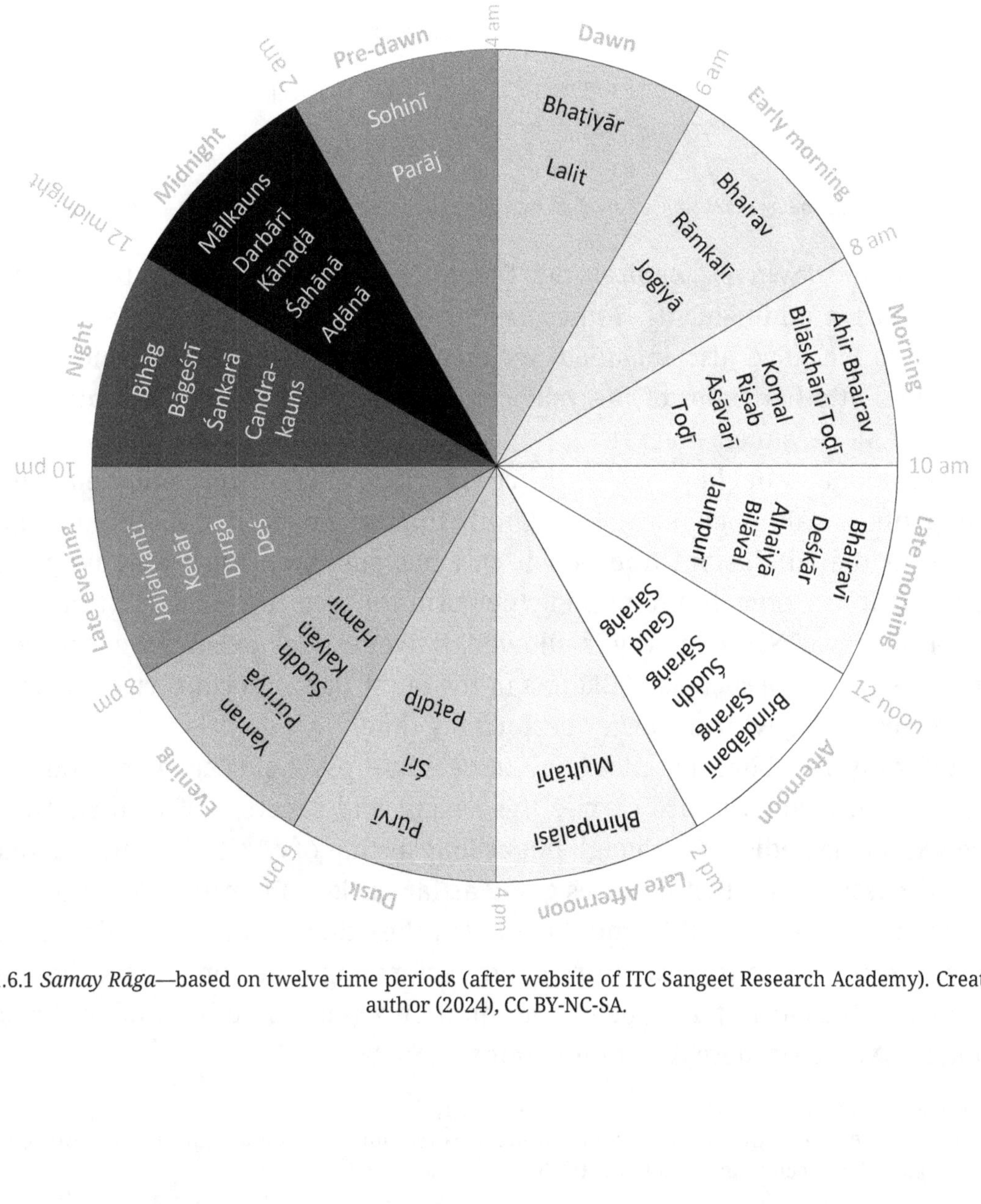

Fig. 1.6.1 *Samay Rāga*—based on twelve time periods (after website of ITC Sangeet Research Academy). Created by author (2024), CC BY-NC-SA.

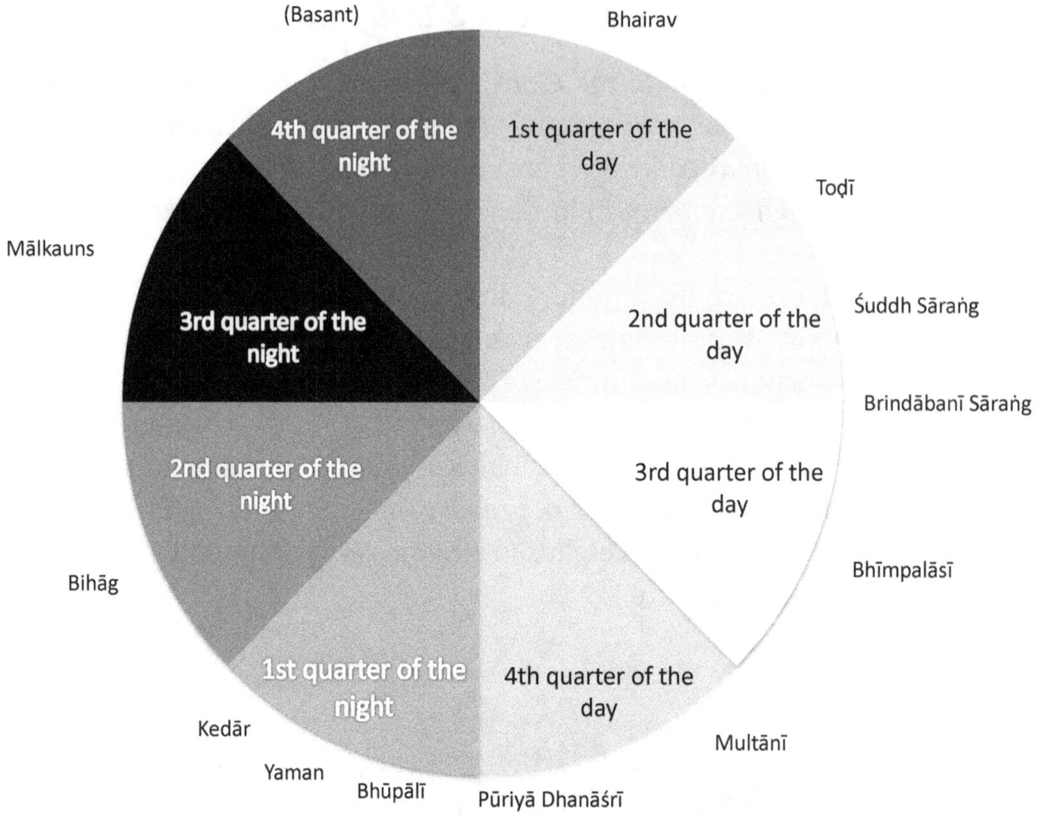

Fig. 1.6.2 *Rāg samay cakra*—based on eight time periods. Created by author (2024), CC BY-NC-SA.

Beginning with the dawn *rāg*, Bhairav, our first album, *Rāg samay cakra* takes us through to Rāg Mālkauns, a midnight *rāg*. Some *rāg*s have associations with the annual cycle of the seasons, so we have also included performances of Rāg Basant, which celebrates springtime and at other times of the year can be performed in the final quarter of the night, and Rāg Megh, a monsoon *rāg*.

Just how essential—and how old—is the connection between *rāg*s and their sanctioned performing times? Although Karnatak (South Indian) music has largely dropped the association, in the Hindustani tradition it still has currency. Musicians may privately practise a *rāg* at any time, but to publicly perform a *rāg* at the incorrect time would be to invite disapproval. Some leeway is allowed, however—for example, in the licence to perform a late-night *rāg* such as Mālkauns in the latter part of a concert, provided that it does not precede a *rāg* with an earlier performing time.

This culturally regulated practice may have some psychological basis. But, as with so many cultural factors, it also carries the weight and sanction of history. The *samay* principle has a long pedigree, although not as long as that of *rāg* itself. Antecedents of the latter are discussed in written treatises going as far back as Bharata's *Nāṭyaśāstra*, dated between approximately 500 BCE and 500 CE. On the other hand, the earliest sources in which we find connections between *rāg* and performing time come from the medieval period. Possibly the earliest documented account of *rāg* and time is found in the *Saṅgīta-makaranda* of Nārada, where the author states:

> One who sings knowing the proper time remains happy. By singing *raga*-s at the wrong time one ill-treats them. Listening to them, one becomes impoverished and sees the length of one's life reduced. (Part 1, *sloka*s 23–4; as cited in Daniélou 2003: 95.)

Typically of such treatises, Nārada's work is difficult to date with precision. In his introduction to the 1920 edition of the text, Mangesh Rāmakrishana Telang locates it between the seventh and eleventh centuries CE (Nārada 1920: viii–x), a view consistent with M. Vijay Lakshmi's overview of the extant scholarship (1996: 40–1, 65). On these views, the treatise would predate Śārṅgadeva's early thirteenth-century *Saṅgīta-ratnākara* (1978, 2023/1993), one of the most important medieval treatises on Indian music, and another early source that links *rāg* and performing time (Śārṅgadeva 2023/1993: chapter II). However, Widdess (personal communication) queries whether the *Saṅgīta-makaranda* is the earlier text, since it anticipates the later *rāga-rāgiṇi* system; Widdess nonetheless acknowledges that it may be the earliest *rationalisation* of *rāg*–time association (as opposed to the mere assertion of the principle in treatises such as the *Saṅgīta-ratnākara* and the *Bharata-bhāṣya* of Nānyadeva). By contrast, Shripada Bandyopadhyaya implicitly endorses the view of Nārada's treatise predating Śārṅgadeva's; in his chronological exposition, Bandyopadhyaya places the *Saṅgīta-makarand* between the *Bṛhad-deśī* of Mataṅga (ca. sixth to eighth century) and the *Saṅgīta-ratnākara* (thirteenth century), and also comments that 'Saranga Deva … followed in the footsteps of his predecessors, denying only the principles of masculine and feminine Rāgas expounded by Nārada Muni in his work "Sangeet Makaranda"' (1977:17).

Another account of time theories in the early sources is given by Mukund Lath (1987), who remains sceptical about any 'psycho-physiological' basis (see also Wade 2004/1999: 78–9). Lath reminds us that another important figure in the promotion of time theory was the twentieth-century musicologist Bhatkhande (discussed in Section 1.10, below). Bhatkhande integrated time theory with his *ṭhāṭ* system, which groups *rāg*s into families based on their scale form (as recounted in Section 1.3). He attempted to show how *rāg*s associated with the same performing time often also have commonalties in their scale form. For example, *rāg*s using flattened second and natural third and seventh degrees are commonly associated with dawn or dusk (*sandhi prakāś rāg*s). Bhatkhande also argued that *rāg*s sung in the hours of darkness tend to prioritise the lower tetrachord of the scale (*pūrvaṅg*), while those sung in the daylight hours favour the upper tetrachord (*uttaraṅg*). These correlations and others are also raised by Chaitanya Deva (1980a: 19–20) in an account not dissimilar to Powers' paraphrase of Bhatkhande (cf. Powers 1992: 15–16); subsequent engagements with Bhatkhande's theories can be found in work by N. A. Jairazbhoy (1971: 61–4). Powers tells us that Bhatkhande looked to treatises written between the fifteenth and eighteenth centuries—rather than to earlier texts such as the *Saṅgīta-ratnākara*—for theoretical evidence of the living practice he knew, and on which to develop his own time theory and *ṭhāṭ* system (1992: 11). But Powers also relates how practitioners such as Thakur disparaged Bhatkhande's system and looked back to the earlier treatises for his own theories of *rāg* organised on principles other than scalic ones.

Where does this leave us? On the one hand, critiques such as Thakur's point to the often self-confessed inconsistencies in Bhatkhande's system, and to the lack of any conclusive empirical evidence for the association between *rāg* and *samay*. On the other hand, in the absence of any subsequent alternative systematic theory, Bhatkhande's word continues to hold considerable authority—a point conceded by Bor et al. (1999: 4). There may be no objective resolution to the issue. The connection between *rāg* and time is arguably not an essential one, but is made 'natural' or 'real' as part of a historically mediated cultural practice that also has regard for the ambience of each phase of the diurnal cycle. Rāg Yaman, for example, can be felt to tap into the stillness of the early evening, the sun just set, the day's work completed; complementing this, the *rāg*'s tone colours—Ni and Ga in reposeful prominence, Re their congenial mediator, Ma gently yearning, all resonating peaceably against the prevailing tonic—feed back into those sensibilities and reinforce them. Deva (1980a: 20) makes a similar point about *sandhi prakāś* (twilight) *rāg*s:

> *Sandhi* means a junction: the passing of night into day and day into night. There seems to be a psychological significance in this. For, it is the time of mental twilight between the conscious and the non-conscious: a time when one sits for prayer and meditation. The dissonances engendered by [*komal*] *ri*, [komal] *dha* and [suddh] *Ni* go well with the 'dreamy' state of mind during these hours.

Deva's subsequent ruminations (ibid.) include the observation that some twilight *rāg*s have both *tivra* and *suddh* Ma, presumably resonating with their liminal place in the time cycle.

The global diaspora of South Asian musicians and their music adds a further twist to these experiences. For example, the subtropical daylight hours and climate of northern India do not map comprehensively onto more remote northern or southern latitudes. At VR and David Clarke's (henceforth DC) own geographic location at 55 degrees North, where the length of daylight varies significantly between Summer and Winter solstices, there may be no right time or ambience for certain *rāg*s at certain points of the year. Consider Rāg Yaman once again, which in India would be sung after sunset in the first quarter of the night, between around 6 and 8 pm. At midsummer in the North of England, however, the sky may not be fully dark even at midnight, the time of Rāg Mālkauns. As nature and culture slip out of sync in these different geographic contexts, it requires a work of the imagination (the meaning of *k͟hayāl*), to reunite India and the foreign land (an idea so often invoked in k͟hayāl songs) in our minds.

1.7 Khayāl: Stylistic and Performance Conventions

All the *rāg*s in *Rāgs Around the Clock* are performed in the khayāl style—a vocal idiom that rose to pre-eminence in the eighteenth century and has remained centre stage among Hindustani classical vocal genres ever since. Aesthetically, khayāl occupies a middle ground between the older, more sober dhrupad style and the romantic, light-classical genre of ṭhumrī. In Section 1.9 we will look at some recent perspectives on the historical origins of khayāl, but first it will be useful to examine some of its present-day conventions. What is it that performers expect to do, and that listeners expect to hear, in a khayāl performance?

Khayāl is an Indo-Persian/Arabic term meaning 'imagination', a quality reflected in the music's largely improvised nature. The vocalist must extemporise within the constraints of *rāg* and *tāl*, also drawing inspiration from one or more short song compositions (*bandiś*es) based on just a few lines of poetry. The texts are usually devotional or romantic, or maybe both, since divine and human love are not opposed in this imaginative world (a topic discussed further in Section 2.2).

A khayāl performance may be expansive, or concise, or somewhere in between. A fully-fledged presentation—which normally begins a recital and in present-day practice might last 30–60 minutes—will comprise all of the components listed in the outline below: *ālāp*, *baṛā khayāl* and *choṭā khayāl*. For shorter performances, it is possible to perform just an *ālāp* and a single *choṭā* (small) *khayāl*. It is this latter, simpler framework that students first aspire to master, and that forms the basis for all fourteen tracks of our first album, *Rāg samay cakra*. By contrast, the second album, *Twilight Rāgs from North India*, presents two extended *rāg* renditions, both of which include a *baṛā* (large) *khayāl*; this provides a model for more advanced students. The three stages of the schema below are cross-referenced to further, in-depth explorations undertaken in Parts 3 and 4 of this book, which are also illustrated by examples from VR's performances.

1. *Ālāp*: an unmetred, meditative exploration of the chosen *rāg*, improvised by the soloist without tabla accompaniment (cf. Section 3.2). If followed by a *baṛā khayāl*, this may be very short, as *ālāp* principles are in any case impregnated within the first phase of that section.

2. *Baṛā* (large) *khayāl*: the most substantial section of an extended khayāl performance (cf. Section 4.3). The inception of a *baṛā khayāl* is marked by the entry of the tabla, which joins the voice and establishes a slow, or very slow, *tāl*—hence, this stage is sometimes known as a *vilambit* (slow) *khayāl*. A *baṛā khayāl* is based around a rhythmically fluid composition, and comprises two principal phases:

    a. The soloist sings the first part (*sthāī*) of the composition (*bandiś*) and then embarks upon an extended series of improvisations that retain an *ālāp*-like feel, despite the presence of the *tāl*, and create a sense of staged development (*baṛhat*). Each improvisation ends with the opening motif (*mukhṛā*) of the composition, which articulates *sam* (the beginning/end point of each cycle of the slow *tāl*). The music gradually intensifies, rising in register until the soloist achieves and sustains the upper tonic (*tār* Sā). This triggers the second part (*antarā*) of the composition, which is followed by the second phase of the *baṛā khayāl*.

b. The soloist returns to the *mukhṛā* of the first part of the composition, and the feel now becomes more dynamic (the tempo may also move up a gear) as the soloist improvises using a variety of devices, such as:
   - *Laykārī*—syncopated rhythmic play.
   - *Bol bāṇṭ*—rhythmic play with the words of the song text.
   - *Tāns*—melodic runs and patterns, which come in several varieties:
     - *Ākār tāns*—sung to the vowel ā.
     - *Bol tāns*—using the words of the composition.
     - *Sargam tāns*—using *sargam* syllables.
     - *Gamak tāns*—performed with a heavy shake around the note.

The intensity continues to build, leading to the next stage of the performance.

3. *Choṭā* (small) *khayāl*: a faster or up-tempo *khayāl*—hence also known as *drut* (fast) *khayāl*—based around a further *bandiś* in the chosen *rāg*, with improvised elaborations (cf. Section 3.3). Again, the *bandiś* is in two parts: *sthāī* and *antarā*. The soloist is at liberty either to sing both parts at the outset or (quite commonly) to delay the introduction of the second part until completing a significant period of improvisation around the first. The first line of each part (especially that of the *sthāī*) usually receives the most emphasis, and is often treated as a refrain (*mukhṛā*). Between statements, the soloist improvises using a similar repertory of devices to that listed above for the *baṛā khayāl*.

The performance may continue with one or more further compositions, often with a corresponding increase in *lay*. It sometimes concludes with a *tarānā*, deploying a composition based on non-semantic syllables such as *ta, na, de, re, nūm*. This could be considered as an optional, fourth section of the performance.

1.8 Khayāl: Ornamentation

Ornamentation is a vital aspect of *rāg* music in its many guises. Indeed, there is probably no type of Indian music in which ornamentation does not in some way play a part. Degrees and styles of ornamentation vary according to genre, *gharānā* (stylistic school), performer, mood and circumstance: relatively sparingly in dhrupad, fulsomely in ṭhumrī, abundantly in some light music and film music idioms. Midway along this continuum is khayāl, which has its own repertory of ornaments, some distinctive to itself, others held in common with related genres. Pick a few seconds of any track on the albums accompanying this book, and you will hear that many of the notes VR sings are either ornament*ed by* or ornament*ing* some other note—sometimes subliminally, discreetly, delicately; at other times overtly, effusively, exuberantly.

Terminology with respect to ornamentation is beset by ambiguity. The word *alaṅkār*, often used in Hindustani music to mean adornment or decoration, may also (or instead) be used by musicians to mean sequential practise exercises. Meanwhile, in Karnatak music, the general term for ornament is *gamak*, which, confusingly, signifies a particular kind of ornament in Hindustani music. Moreover, different musicians or different stylistic schools may mean slightly or appreciably different things by individual names of ornaments.

My aim here is not to definitively resolve such ambiguities, but rather to offer my own window onto their complexities. To my knowledge, the most perspicacious account in English of ornamentation in khayāl is by Nicolas Magriel (Magriel and du Perron 2013, I: Chapter 6), who does not shy away from ambiguities of terminology. Here I offer a more concise treatment, which is based on VR's *gāyakī*, and adds further to this not entirely reconcilable mix of viewpoints. In what follows, I will consider the main classes of ornament in khayāl, providing short audio illustrations from *Rāg samay cakra*, with accompanying notations.

Kaṇ

A *kaṇ* is a single, delicate note that lightly touches the longer note it precedes—like a grace note in western music (meanings of *kaṇ* include 'particle', 'speck' or 'grain'). This embellishment is a common khayāl fingerprint, but is also found in other performing styles (sometimes under other names). In the *ālāp* of Rāg Bhūpālī on *Rāg samay cakra* (*RSC*), VR presents several strings of consecutive *kaṇ svar*s, whose elegance and simplicity capture the spirit of this guileless pentatonic *rāg*. A short illustration is given in Audio Example 1.8.1, with notation in Figure 1.8.1 (*kaṇ*s shown in superscript); at this point we hear VR approaching and quitting *tār* Sā.

Audio Example 1.8.1 *Kaṇ*: Rāg Bhūpālī (*RSC*, Track 9, 00:56–01:17)
https://hdl.handle.net/20.500.12434/41671299

^{P}GP$^{\dot{S}}$D, Ṡ———— $^{\dot{S}}$D Ṡ$^{\dot{S}}$D^{D}P^{P}G—, G–^{G}RP–^{P}G—,

Fig. 1.8.1 *Kaṇ*: notation of Audio Example 1.8.1. Created by author (2024), CC BY-NC-SA.

A related type of ornament can sometimes be found *following* a sustained note. The terminal position and near-subliminal quality of such decorations perhaps explains why they are seldom mentioned in accounts of ornamentation in khayāl, and why they seem to have no agreed name. They are an aspect of the style, nonetheless; at the end of many a sustained note in VR's performances (especially in *ālāp*s) one can hear him make a little oscillation: slightly wider than a vibrato, barely audible as a tiny flicker or two below (or occasionally above) the main note. Audio Example 1.8.2 captures two such instances, following sustained Pa in Rāg Kedār; the notations in Figure 1.8.2 indicate the terminal ornament with a tiny 'v' symbol, one per oscillation.

Audio Example 1.8.2 *Kampit*/'after-*kaṇ*':
(a) Rāg Kedār (*RSC*, Track 10, 00:52–00:58)
(b) Rāg Kedār (ibid., 01:01–01:07)
https://hdl.handle.net/20.500.12434/8f23eb8c

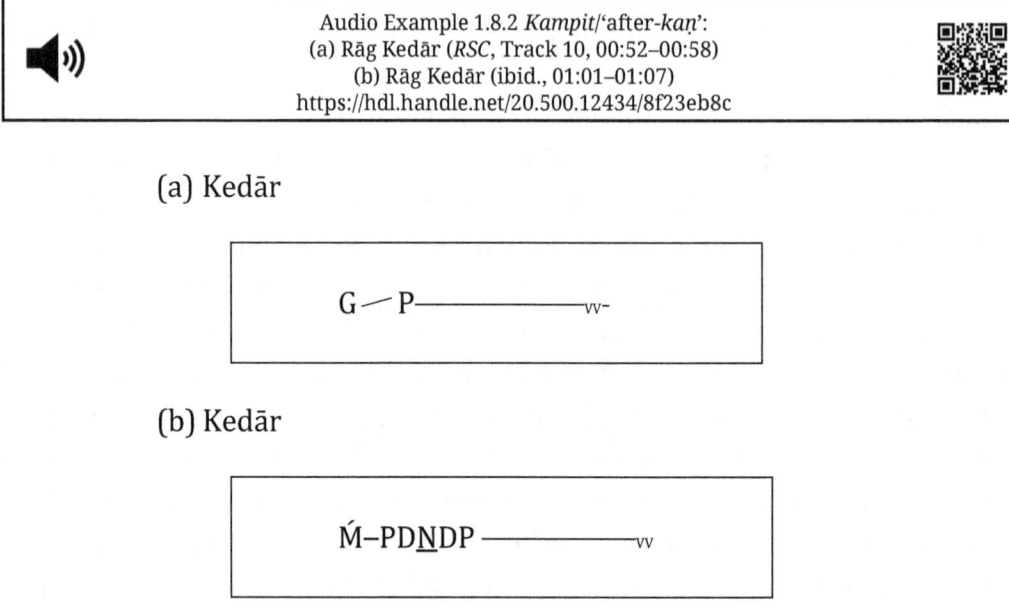

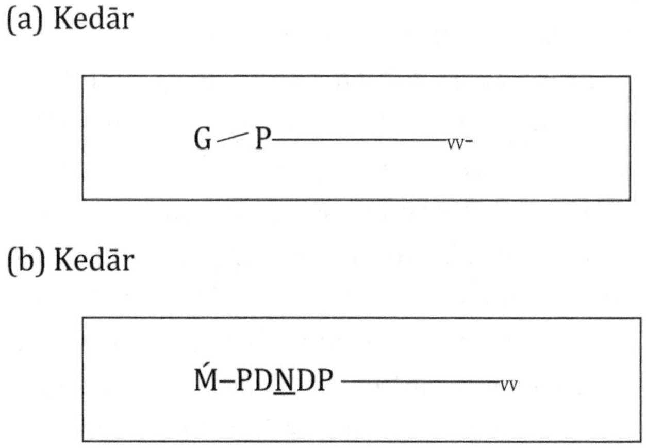

Fig. 1.8.2 *Kampit*/'after-*kaṇ*': notation of Audio Example 1.8.2. Created by author (2024), CC BY-NC-SA.

Magriel coins the term 'after-*kaṇ*' for such tiny gestures, and aptly describes them as 'barely-sounded afterthoughts at the end of sustained tones ... ways of "rounding-off" the "sharp" ends of a steadily-intoned note' (Magriel and du Perron 2013, I: 300). These figures have at least some of the qualities associated with the ornament known as *kampit* or *kampan*, which means 'tremble' or 'shake'—a kind of vibrato, which does not decisively voice any note outside of the sustained one (cf. Sanyal and Widdess 2004: 163–4).

Mīṇḍ

Mīṇḍ denotes a gliding motion between two notes. Although this resembles a *glissando* in western music, it has a different aesthetic significance here. Fluidity between pitches is something of a norm in Indian music: the passage from note to note often feels seamless (more like swimming than stepping, as I heard one musician put it). So we might say that *mīṇḍ* projects this kind of motion from the background of consciousness, where it operates subliminally, into the foreground, where it becomes expressively salient. Its qualities vary according to how quickly or slowly it is executed and over what distance; it may also fleetingly touch other notes along the way.

Mīṇḍ may be among the defining attributes of a *rāg*. In Mālkauns, for example, slow and ponderous *mīṇḍ* enhances its gravity as a *gambhīr* (serious) *rāg*. Parts (a) and (b) of Audio Example 1.8.3 capture two such characteristic moments: the first between *mandra* Ni and Dha, the second between Ga and Sā. Part (c) of the example is taken from Rāg Megh, also a *gambhīr rāg*. Here, the repeated *mīṇḍ* between Ma and Re at the beginning of the extract and the slow glide from Ni to Pa at the end feel like tender expressions of entreaty appropriate to the romance of the rainy season. In the notation of these extracts in Figure 1.8.3 (and throughout this volume), *mīṇḍ* is indicated with either an upward or downward oblique line, according to the direction of the glide.

Audio Example 1.8.3 *Mīṇḍ*:
(a) Rāg Mālkauns (*RSC*, Track 12, 00:47–00:53)
(b) Rāg Mālkauns (ibid., 01:52–02:04)
(c) Rāg Megh (*RSC*, Track 13, 00:40–01:02)
https://hdl.handle.net/20.500.12434/64451d35

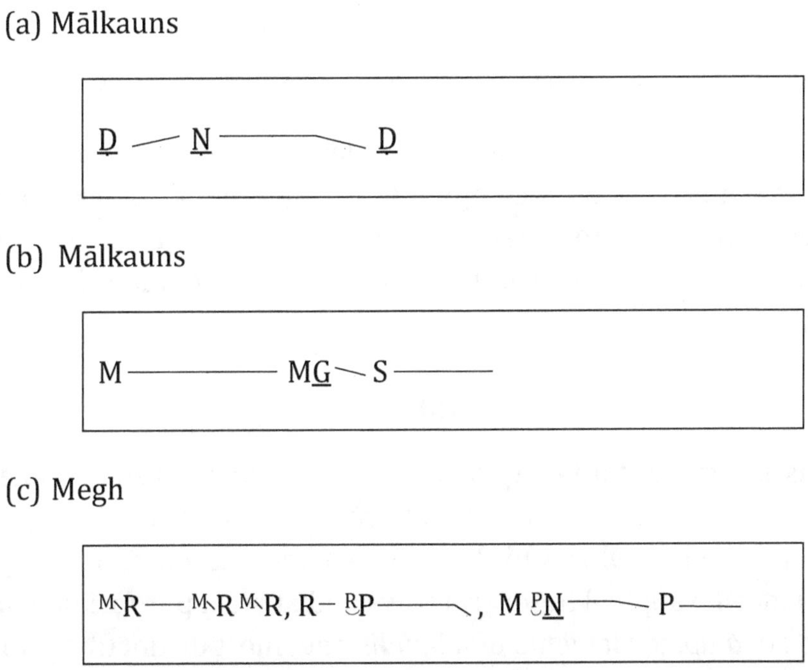

Fig. 1.8.3 *Mīṇḍ*: notation of Audio Example 1.8.3. Created by author (2024), CC BY-NC-SA.

Āndolan

While *mīṇḍ* signifies a glide between two notes, *āndolan* (also *āndolit*) denotes a gentle oscillation within a single *svar*. This has the effect of colouring its sound quality and amplifying its inner life. In Rāg Bhairav, this effect is conventionally applied to the *vādī* and *saṃvādī* tones, Re and Dha—as we hear in parts (a) and (b) of Audio Example 1.8.4. Here, VR also fleetingly catches the notes above, Ga and Ni, as if mixing these notes into Re and Dha respectively in order to capture the blended colours of the dawn twilight. *Āndolan* may also be judiciously used in other contexts. In part (c) of the audio example, we hear it applied plaintively to Dha of Mālkauns. In the corresponding notations (Figure 1.8.4), *āndolan* is indicated with tilde symbols (~~~).

Audio Example 1.8.4 *Āndolan*:
(a) Rāg Bhairav (*RSC*, Track 1, 00:13–00:26)
(b) Rāg Bhairav (ibid., 01:33–01:40)
(c) Rāg Mālkauns (*RSC*, Track 12, 02:56–03:02)
https://hdl.handle.net/20.500.12434/9b88bcac

(a) Bhairav

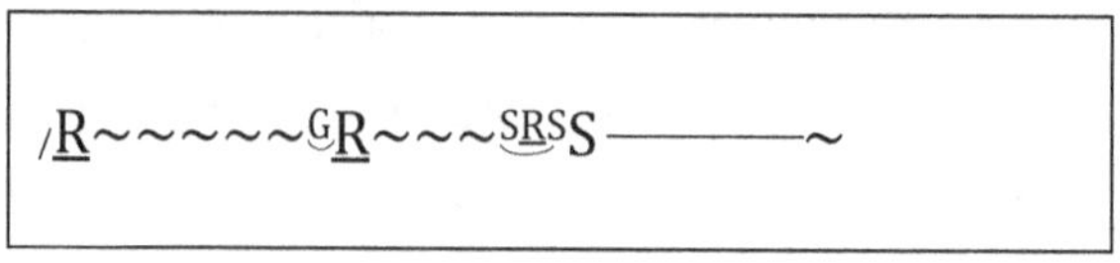

(b) Bhairav

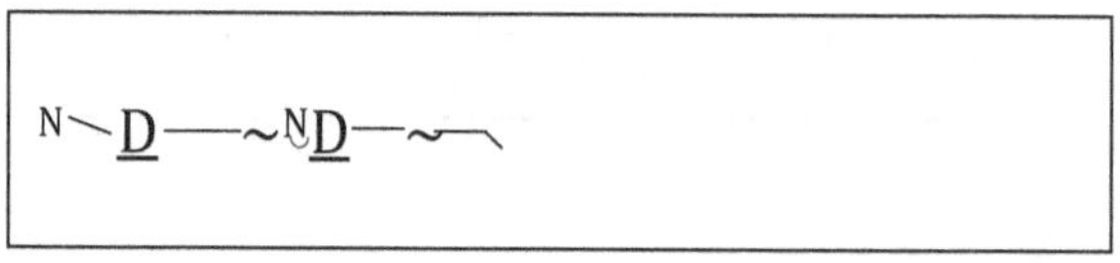

Fig. 1.8.4 *Āndolan*: notation of Audio Example 1.8.4. Created by author (2024), CC BY-NC-SA.

Not for the first time in these illustrations (nor the last), we can observe how the particular ornament under the microscope is complemented by others (for example, *mīṇḍ*). The several types of ornament work together towards the same end of conveying the particular *ras* (emotional 'juice') of the *rāg*; learning how to combine them in this way is part of the khayāl singer's art.

Gamak

In Hindustani classical music, the term *gamak* is used to indicate a wide shake or oscillation around a series of notes. Its presence in khayāl is a legacy of the genre's historical connection with dhrupad, in which this form of ornament is a definitive stylistic feature. In khayāl, *gamak* may be applied in several ways and at any appropriate point. It can add colour to *ālāp*, to *bol ālāp*, to elements of a *bandiś* and, most distinctively, to *tāns*. VR tells of how Bhimsen Joshi (1922–2011) was influential in introducing *gamak tāns* into khayāl, and was regarded as an archetypal exponent: 'When guruji sang *gamak*, you could feel the stage shake'.

VR certainly continues his teacher's legacy within the Kirānā *gharānā*; some instances of his *gamak* are captured in Audio Example 1.8.5 and indicated in Figure 1.8.5 with wavy lines. In (a), VR applies *gamak* to a decorative flourish (*murkī*) that precedes sustained Dha near the opening of Rāg Bhairav—thus combining types of ornament. In (b), he employs *gamak* in the *bandiś* of Rāg Pūriyā Dhanāśrī, during the second half of its second line. Again, this applies one decoration to another: the melodic contour here is already a *tān*-like decoration of the original version of the melody, which the notation shows in paler font. In (c), VR sings an extended *gamak tān* in the latter stages of a *choṭā khayāl* in Rāg Yaman. Given that *tāns* themselves may be regarded as decorating a *rāg* (Mittal 2000: 121–2), then, again, we here find decoration applied to decoration.

Audio Example 1.8.5 *Gamak*:
(a) Rāg Bhairav (*RSC*, Track 1, 00:26–00:30)
(b) Rāg Pūriyā Dhanāśrī (*RSC*, Track 7, 02:46–02:53)
(c) Rāg Yaman (*RSC*, Track 9, 05:24–05:32)
https://hdl.handle.net/20.500.12434/9f944a0b

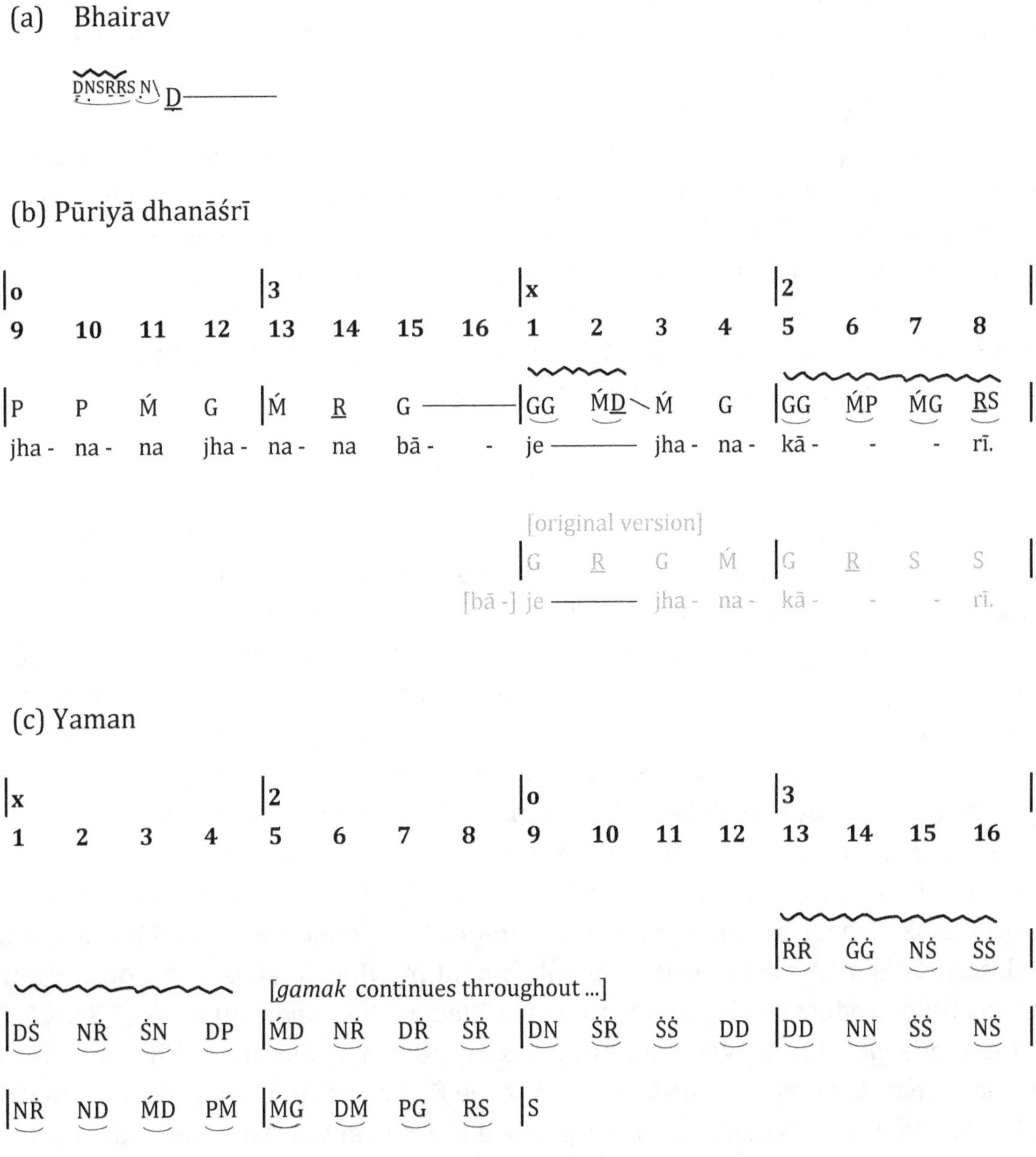

Fig. 1.8.5 *Gamak*: notation of Audio Example 1.8.5. Created by author (2024), CC BY-NC-SA.

Ordinary human beings are helped in transcribing such breathtakingly rapid *gamak tāns* by software such as Transcribe! which makes it possible radically to slow down the recording. This has the effect of rendering the depth of *gamak* even more vividly, but can also exacerbate the ambiguity of what one hears (cf. Magriel and du Perron 2013, I: 329). In general, the magnitude of the shake in *gamak* is sometimes so great that it can be near-impossible to discern the target pitches beneath—though a singer should always have these clear in their own mind, and a listener may also be able to divine them from the context (see Sanyal and Widdess 2004: 165–6). There is also no obvious consensus as to whether the shake should begin above or below the decorated note. Ali Akbar Khan (1922–2009) and George Ruckert do not consistently prescribe any single approach in their various exercises for sarod (2021/1998: 207, 211); Widdess provides a spectrographic analysis of dhrupad *gamak* sung by Ritwik Sanyal, which shows a clear V-shaped motion from above the notes, to below them, and back again (Sanyal and Widdess 2004: 165); Magriel's transcriptions of *gamak* in khayāl do not suggest any generalisable inferences about direction of execution, but do underscore how the ornament is rarely heard in isolation from others (Magriel and du Perron 2013, I: 328–33).

Gamak is perhaps the most distinctively Indian of ornaments, and may initially sound alien to the ears of other cultures. But in its extremity, it points to two wider aspects of ornamentation in Hindustani classical music. First, we might hear it as amplifying the inner life of *svar*—in this case maximally so, like a volatile version of *āndolan*. Second, this most literally visceral of decorations reminds us of the bodily nature of ornament: the delicate ones too need a certain physicality to execute; and ornaments, in the guise of jewellery, are a traditional form of body adornment in Indian culture.

Kaṭhkā and *Murkī*

No two commentators, it seems, will agree on what kinds of ornament are signified by *kaṭhkā* and *murkī*. The two related terms have a range of inconsistent definitions, from a kind of mordent to an elaborate string of decorative notes. Some musicians treat the two words as actually or virtually synonymous (VR is in the latter camp). Magriel, who surveys many performers' use of these and other terms, in the end takes the pragmatic decision to use *kaṭhkā* to signify all their possible meanings (Magriel and du Perron 2013, I: 305–7). Bor et al. define *murkī* as 'a fast and delicate ornament involving two or more tones, similar to a mordent' (1999: 181), but provide no corresponding gloss for *kaṭhkā*.

If delicacy is one possible connotation of *murkī*, a degree of force, percussiveness, or the action of cutting is sometimes associated with *kaṭhkā* (Magriel and du Perron 2013, I: 306). Ashok Ranade invokes the Hindi *khaṭaknā*, 'to create a sharp clashing sound', and describes *kaṭhkā* as 'a melodic embellishment in which a cluster of notes is quickly and forcefully produced prior to the note projected as the important note' (2006: 222); he also mentions *murkī* as a synonym, but gives no further elaboration. Khan and Ruckert describe *kaṭhkā* as 'a type of *murkī*, involving the fast repetition of a note (lit., knocking)' (2021/1998: 346). So it would not be wise to see these characteristics as clear markers of one type of ornament or the other.

Audio Example 1.8.6 *Kaṭhkā/murkī*:
(a) Rāg Kedār (*RSC*, Track 10, 00:17–00:26)
(b) Rāg Kedār (ibid., 01:07–01:14)
(c) Rāg Bhīmpalāsī (*RSC*, Track 5, 01:29–01:37)
https://hdl.handle.net/20.500.12434/61687ef7

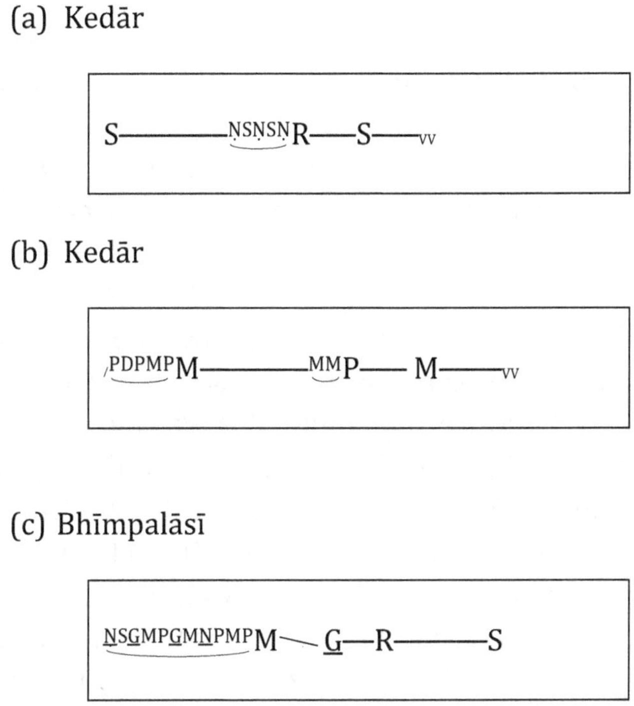

Fig. 1.8.6 *Kaṭhkā/murkī*: notation of Audio Example 1.8.6. Created by author (2024), CC BY-NC-SA.

Audio Example 1.8.6 and its accompanying notation in Figure 1.8.6 give three salient extracts from *Rāg samay cakra*; I also played these to VR for his opinion regarding their nomenclature. In the first extract (a), from the *ālāp* of Kedār, we hear a motion from sustained Sā to sustained Re via a very rapid double oscillation between Ṇi and Sā (which could also be heard as a blurred reiteration of Sā); VR seemed happy to label this figure as *kaṭhkā*—which might be consistent with a conception, that includes, but is not limited to, the emphatic repetition of a note. Conversely, he thought that the final extract, (c), in which Ma of Bhīmpalāsī is approached by a delicate and wide-ranging run, was a clear case of *murkī*. As for the second extract, in which Ma of Kedār is prefaced via a turn-like figure around Pa, VR exclaimed 'I don't know; it could be *kaṭhkā* or *murkī*—or both!' In the same conversation, he described another attribute of *kaṭhkā* as decorating a note from either side; and also suggested that *murkī* might be a more free-formed kind of run; since both notions seem to apply here, this might partly explain his equivocation. Importantly, VR also indicated that he does not think of these ornaments by name when he performs: 'I just sing, I don't really know what they're all called!' His experience chimes with Magriel's observation that 'musicians rarely use any of these terms in verbal discourse although their music is replete with the nuances they signify' (Magriel and du Perron 2013, I: 305).

Cultural and Aesthetic Significance

The loose fit—and sometimes blatant gap—between the theory and practice of ornament need not be seen as a deficit. The many ambiguities and divergences between word and music instead tell us that ornamentation is performed in a constant state of invention and evolution. The creative process involves not a pick-and-mix of prefabricated, rigidly defined objects that must be rigorously named and categorised, but rather a continuous arising of adornments that constantly blend and vary their form in the moment and movement of imagination. The way ornamentation in Hindustani classical music teases our ability to name, and perpetually eludes it, perhaps points to its very essence.

Whereas modern western conceptions may associate ornament with artifice and superficiality, the Sanskrit *alaṃkāra* meant 'things which make *alam* [sufficient], which give strength required for something ... which bestow a consecrated condition upon a person' (Gonda 1975: 271; see also Ali 2004: 163). This notion has resonances in the history of Indian court culture, not only in the Mughal era (1526–1857), in which Hindustani classical music flourished, but also going back to the early medieval courts of the Gupta era and beyond (fourth to seventh centuries)—as described in Daud Ali's major work on that topic (2004: 19, 162–70). Ali recounts how this was a culture in which aesthetic adornment operated as a sign of courtly fitness and moral accomplishment—a culture consistent with representations in Bharata's *Nāṭyaśāstra* (Ali 2004: 148). In Bharata's work, we find canonical lines regarding decoration in music (Bharata 2006/1989: 407 [Chapter 29, Slokas 72–6]): 'A song devoid of Alaṁkāra resembles the night bereft of the Moon, [a] river deprived of water[,] [a] creeper that has not blossomed, and a woman unadorned'. Here, then, from the early centuries of the common era, in lines that remain pertinent to the present day, we have evidence of the essential place of ornament in Indian music.

1.9 Khayāl: Origins

For all that many of its songs invoke Hindu deities and legends, khayāl developed and flourished in and around the Muslim courts of the Mughal era. One problem is that we do not know exactly what the music would have sounded like in the earlier centuries of its evolution. Like the music itself, accounts of khayāl's history have tended to be transmitted orally, accruing a variety of myths in the process. For a factually grounded account of the genre's origins it is important to look to reliable scholarship based on consultation of the available manuscript sources.

Significant among such historical treatments is Katherine Butler Schofield's (née Brown) revisionist essay 'The Origins and Early Development of Khayal' (2010). Brown painstakingly pieces together an account whose authority is based on the evidence of Indo-Persian sources. Interestingly, and perhaps provocatively, it differs in key respects from received wisdom. Taking the earliest known uses of the term *khayāl* in the manuscript sources as a starting point, Brown surmises that a form of the genre may have first appeared at the Mughal court between 1593 and 1637—significantly later than the life of Amir Khusrau (1253–1325) to whom the invention of khayāl is commonly attributed.

Alternative protagonists in Brown's account include the Qavvāls of Delhi—Sufi musicians who were regarded as the primary exponents of khayāl throughout the seventeenth century (Brown 2010: 168ff.). They cultivated the *raviś* (style) of Amir Khusrau, which included the genres of qaul, tarānā and—in some accounts—khayāl. However, Brown argues that khayāl was not a direct inheritance from Amir Khusrau, but was rather part of a legacy in which the Qavvāls synthesised his *raviś* with other influences. Important among these was a genre known as cutkulā, which was a legacy of Sultan Husain Shah Sharqi of Jaunpur (r. 1458–83).

Significant in the nexus between Delhi and Jaunpur was the figure of Shaikh Bahauddin Barnawi (d. 1628/9), associated with the village of Barnawa, East of Delhi (ibid.: 174–8). A renowned musician, he is known to have composed khayāl. His great-grandfather, Shaikh Pir Buddhan (d. 1498) was the *pīr* (spiritual master) and fellow connoisseur of Husain Shah Sharqi of Jaunpur (ibid.: 177), and hence may have been a conduit for the transmission of cutkulā—and its subsequent evolution as khayāl—into the lineage of the Barnawa shaikhs. Indeed, Brown conjectures that the circumstances were exactly right for Shaikh Bahauddin Barnawi himself to have been a creator of khayāl (ibid.: 178). And among the Shaikhs' retinue were qavvāls—a possible line of transmission to the Qavvāls of Delhi.

Crucial to these many interconnections are the religion and culture of Sufism, especially its Chishti Order. This is the common denominator that links many of the protagonists and places in Brown's account: Amir Khusrau, Husain Shah Sharqi, the Qavvāls, the Barnawa Shaikhs, other khayāl exponents such as Shaikh Sher Muhammed (seventeenth century), and the centres of Delhi and Jaunpur. A possible channel of transmission could have been Sufi *samā'* gatherings—ecstatic devotional assemblies in which khayāl, or generic variants of it, may have been sung (ibid.: 180–2). Importantly, such gatherings were sympathetic to Hindu devotional imagery—a fact which remained salient for the evolution of khayāl in later centuries. There seemed to be no contradiction in Muslims singing songs informed by the Hindu *bhakti* tradition, in which the pain of separation between lovers (most emblematically Rādhā and Kṛṣṇa) might be implicitly equated with longing for union with the divine (ibid. 186–7).

Brown's already complex narrative forms part of an even more complex wider picture. Although any extended exploration of the subsequent history of khayāl is beyond the scope of this account, several points are worth briefly highlighting.

First, khayāl, alongside various other forms of Hindustani music, eventually established a place in the secular court *mehfil* of the Mughal empire in the seventeenth century. While dhrupad was the pre-eminent classical genre (with Tānsen (ca. 1500–89) its most prominent exponent) in the court of Akbar the Great (r. 1556–1605), we know from Faqīrullāh's *Rāg Darpan* (*Mirror of Music*, compiled mid-seventeenth century), that two khayāl singers were listed in the retinue of the Emperor Shah Jahan (r. 1627–58) (Wade 1997: 1–2), albeit that dhrupad was still in the ascendant at this point. It was by the beginning of the reign of Aurangzeb (r. 1658–1701), that khayāl probably began to rival dhrupad, in popularity if not prestige (Brown 2010: 182–4).

Secondly, while khayāl had acquired the characteristics of a classical form by this time, it had arisen and would continue to develop through cross-fertilisation with other styles and genres, and through a confluence of classical (*mārga*) and regional (*deśī*) features. Madhu Trivedi tells of a flourishing of the musical arts in the first half of the eighteenth century under Emperor Muhammad Shah (r. 1719–48), which also included a diversification of patronage. *Mehfils* were 'arranged by nobles, affluent people and eminent musicians [and] attracted large audiences. As a result the number of professional artists increased greatly' (Trivedi 2010: 83). Paradoxically, the crisis of the Mughal empire at this time (which marked the beginning of its disintegration) further fostered this diversification. After the invasion and sacking of Delhi by the Safavid Persian Emperor Nādir Shah (1688–1747) in 1739, court artists were forced to find employment from a wider sphere of patrons, and this was complemented by a cross-pollination of classical and folk (*dhun*)-based forms (ibid.: 84).

Thirdly, under this changing political and social background—increasingly marked by the British presence in India—khayāl flourished during the eighteenth, nineteenth and early twentieth centuries across various Northern Indian centres of patronage, including Delhi, Gwalior, Lucknow, Benares, Baroda, Rampur, Calcutta and Bombay (Bor and Miner 2010; Wade 1997: 5–10).

Fourthly, there is the question of Ni'mat Khan, also known by his pen name Sadāraṅg (1670–1748). Ni'mat Khan was active in the early eighteenth century, and is canonical in histories and orally transmitted stories of khayāl. He was a celebrated player of the bīn (a form of lute), a famed exponent of dhrupad and khayāl, and a renowned teacher. Sulochana Brahaspati (2010: 271–5) describes how he was not only favoured by the Emperor Muhammad Shah, but also established an important musical lineage associated with Rampur, which included his nephew Firoz Khan, known under the pen name Adāraṅg. Trivedi credits Ni'mat Khan with the 'renovation' of khayāl through features still recognisable in today's versions of the genre (2010: 84). On the other hand, Brown refutes claims that he uniquely popularised or classicised khayāl—though she concedes him a place within the broader landscape of the genre (2010: 189–91). She argues that Ni'mat Khan's espousal of khayāl under the patronage of Muhammad Shah may have been related to his need to distance himself from his association with dhrupad, which he practiced under the earlier patronage of the eventually discredited Emperor Jahandar Shah (r. 1712–13) and his concubine Lal Kunwar. If this was the case, the strategy worked: to this day, songs referencing Sadāraṅg (by no means all of which are authenticable) continue to circulate in the k͟hayāl repertory.

1.10 V. N. Bhatkhande

Any student or enthusiast of Hindustani classical music will sooner or later encounter the figure of Vishnu Narayan Bhatkhande, whose name has indeed already surfaced several times in this book. A seminal scholar-musician, Bhatkhande was instrumental in ushering Indian music into the modern era. He organised four All-India Music Conferences held between 1916 and 1925 (see Trasoff 2010). His lifelong efforts to modernise the way Indian music was taught, understood and practiced was of a piece with the momentous social, cultural and historical changes of India's struggle for independence from the British. He published a substantial body of historical and theoretical writings on Indian music, some in Sanskrit, some in his mother tongue, Marathi (some of which were translated into Hindi). To this day, his legacy remains pertinent, if contentious, to practitioners and scholars of South Asian music.

Three traces of Bhatkhande's influence can be discerned in *Rāgs Around the Clock*. First, his time theory of *rāg* is of obvious relevance (cf. Section 1.6). Secondly, in our descriptions and specifications of individual *rāg*s (in Section 2.5, below), we have drawn on his *Kramik pustak mālikā* (1937)—a six-volume compendium of *rāg* commentaries and *bandiś* transcriptions compiled from hereditary musicians of his day (a copy sits on VR's bookshelf, and is a not-infrequent reference point in our lessons). Thirdly, in our transcription of *bandiś*es we have adapted Bhatkhande's notation method, since this is almost universally recognised by present-day Hindustani musicians.

Typically of many modernisers, Bhatkhande achieved historical significance and influence through a process of othering—strategically differentiating himself from rival individuals, peoples, ideas and tendencies. He asserted a future Indian music against a colonial western present—a future underpinned by an institutionalised learning culture distinct from the hereditary musical lineages of India's own past. To this end, he and Rai Umanath Bali established an academy for the study of Hindustani music in Lucknow in 1926, originally known as Marris College (see Katz 2017: 109–16). Bhatkhande's vision of Indian music as a culturally unifying force in a new, independent nation was an ostensibly secular one. In this he differentiated himself from his rival reformer Vishnu Digambar Paluskar (1872–1931), whose own urban music academies—which bear the name Gandharva Mahavidyalaya and remain operative today—were intimately connected to Hindu nationalism and the notion of a return to the imagined Vedic roots of a pre-Muslim era.

Janaki Bakhle discusses Bhatkhande and Paluskar against the wider political background of their projects in her 2005 monograph *Two Men and Music*. Bakhle's account of Bhatkhande is especially polemical, highlighting his antagonism toward the very hereditary Muslim musicians whose musical knowledge he solicited. She underlines how he characterised them as illiterate; how he held them responsible for a perceived decline of Indian music into degeneracy; and how he regarded them as imperilling their musical legacy by relying solely on oral transmission within their own *khāndān*s (family lineages). Bakhle's evidence includes Bhatkhande's own journal, which documents his frustration at what he perceived as the shortcomings of musicians such as the sarod player Karamutallah Khan (Bakhle 2005: 109–13). Max Katz, on the other hand, evidences an altogether more cordial and constructive relationship between Bhatkhande and the sarod player Sakhawat Hussain Khan (1877–1955), who was an important figure in the establishment of Marris College (Katz 2017: 116–22). Yet Katz also argues that this relationship was played out against the wider backdrop of a Hindu–Muslim communalist struggle in which the former group was to achieve ascendancy—both within the College and within India as a whole (2017: 100–28).

Bhatkhande's ultimate goal was to systematise and unify Indian music—to present it as a classical tradition of equal stature to that of the West. His invention of a musical notation system was part of this; and so was his search for a theoretical and historical basis for Indian music that would demonstrate systemic linkages between its various forms (one goal, eventually abandoned, was to unify the Hindustani and Karnatak traditions). Yet, he was unable to find conclusive evidence for such a unified picture. For all his scholasticism, his research eventually led him to believe that Indian music as actually practiced in his own day had only a relatively short history of some two to three hundred years, and that ancient canonical treatises such as the *Nāṭyaśāstra* of Bharata or the thirteenth-century *Saṅgīta-ratnākara* of Śārṅgadeva were of limited relevance (Bakhle 2005: 105–6, 114–16). In his attempt to write a systematic theory of his own, his *Hindustānī-saṅgīta-paddhati*, he placed more value on treatises written between the fifteenth and eighteenth centuries (see Powers 1992: 11), which he believed had a more discernible relationship to modern-day musical practice.

Bhatkhande remains an ambiguous figure—canonised and criticised in equal measure. Authors such as Sobhana Nayar (1989) and Shripada Bandyopadhyaya (1977) are unstinting in their praise of him and unequivocal about his significance. Others, as we have seen, can be searing in their critique. Yet even Bakhle is careful to consider the nuances, ambivalences and contradictions in Bhatkhande's thinking. His musical theories have been criticised by scholars and musicians on theoretical and practical grounds, yet he remains a key point of reference for many (for example, Jairazbhoy 1971). In a sympathetic appreciation, Sulochana Brahaspati (2010: 278–9) reminds us that in his youth Bhatkhande learned the vīṇā as 'a disciple of the [Muslim] maestros of Rampur', and that the historical texts he found valuable included sources in Urdu and Persian. As the musical and geopolitical debates into which he pitched continue to play out in the present day, we can only continue to hold his formidable achievement and the contradictions in his outlook in tense juxtaposition.

1.11 The *Guru-Śiṣyā Paramparā*

Introduction

The content of Indian classical music is organically connected to the way it is taught. The subtleties of *rāg*, *svar* and *śruti*; the spontaneity of improvised performance; the oftentimes elliptical relationship between melody and *tāl*; the emotional flavour (*ras*) that can be savoured in every phrase and ornament: these elements of the music's lifeblood flow from its distinctive oral pedagogy founded on the immediacy of face-to-face communication and the bond between student and teacher. This historically longstanding tradition, which has the figure of the guru at its heart, is known as the *guru-śiṣyā paramparā*.

Let us consider these words in turn. 'Guru' means more than simply 'teacher': it carries connotations of 'master' or 'preceptor', and has a history going back to the Vedas, the foundational texts of Hinduism. As Joel Mlecko explains (1982: 34): '*Gu* means "ignorance" and *ru*, "dispeller." The guru is a dispeller of ignorance, all kinds of ignorance'. Similarly, *śiṣyā* means more than merely 'student': it implies discipleship and devotion. Finally, *paramparā*, means 'lineage' or 'succession': it points to a would-be unbroken transmission of knowledge as *śiṣyās* themselves eventually become gurus and pass on their skills and wisdom to the next generation.

These Sanskrit terms have their Urdu equivalents in Muslim traditions of learning—a significant point given the prominence of Muslim hereditary lineages in Hindustani classical music. The Muslim counterparts of guru and *śiṣyā* are *ustād* and *śāgird*; and the equivalent of *paramparā* is *silsilā*. As James Kippen puts it (2008: 127): 'what both [sets of terms] have in common, in an ideal sense, is a system where the master becomes the complete role model for the disciple not only in terms of the transmission of musical understanding and the technical means to perform it but also in terms of moral and ethical integrity, self-realization, vision, and personal depth'. What both versions of the tradition also have in common is the place of the student as a member of the master's household, with its intimate and immersive learning environment. This last feature continues to be regarded as the ideal milieu for the passing-on of musical knowledge and its attendant values, even though, since the twentieth century, it has been challenged by other learning systems that have emerged from it or have sought to displace it.

Which brings us to a further crucial aspect of the *guru-śiṣyā paramparā*: the impact of modernisation. The tradition's passage into modernity goes hand in hand with the rise of a Hindu middle class that began to cohere in the nineteenth century (Van der Meer 1980: 122–6), came to prominence contemporaneously with the Indian independence movement (Neuman 1990: 18–21), and achieved dominance in India after independence and Partition in 1947 (ibid.: 142). Voices in recent anglophone musicology (for example, Bakhle 2005, Katz 2017) have critically examined how this also involved an emerging Hindu hegemony over hereditary Muslim musicians. However, complementing this, Justin Scarimbolo (2014) argues for softening 'polarized understandings', based on his research into the agency of Brahman musicians 'beyond nationalism' during the colonial era.

What remains clear is that, in the earlier twentieth century, the Hindu middle-class sphere became fertile ground for the learning of Indian classical music (and largely remains its habitus in India today). Since that time, musical pedagogy has taken institutional form within specialist music academies or music departments of universities (the earliest modern Indian universities were founded on the colonial model of London University in 1857). Alongside such establishments, gurus and *ustāds* continue to teach privately, but often along lines closer to western musical tuition—what Regula Burkhardt Qureshi terms the 'Indian bourgeois version of music lessons' (2009: 168).

To summarise and elaborate a little: we have so far identified three particularly important moments in the long duration of the *guru-śiṣyā paramparā*. First, its historical antecedents in the figure of the guru in the Vedic era (dating back to probably the second millennium BCE); second, the significance of hereditary musicians as tradition bearers, who were already a presence in the court culture of the Delhi Sultanate (which arose in the thirteenth century) and further flourished under the Mughal dynasty (from the sixteenth to the nineteenth centuries); third the impact of modernity, with its attendant shift in the nineteenth and twentieth centuries to a middle-class culture of musical pedagogy and consumption. To these three moments we might add a fourth: a problematic side to the *paramparā*, arguably rooted in its patriarchal underpinnings, that has begun to loom especially large in the twenty-first century.

It is important to stress that these moments do not resolve into a unified, seamless historical chronology or narrative. As Bakhle reminds us (2005: 257–8), 'no single historical trajectory is adequate to the task of telling the robust history of music'. Nonetheless, these themes, with their overlaps and interpenetrations, will form important elements in the following discussion of the *paramparā*. My starting point, however, will be what is probably the tradition's most crucial aspect (also mentioned above): the fact that the student has historically acquired their musical training through living in (or near) their teacher's household, in an environment where learning becomes inseparable from daily living. If this account takes more extended form than the other essays so far in this book, this is largely because of the sheer significance of the *paramparā* to Indian classical music, and because its social, historical and cultural features throw considerable light on the practice as a whole.

The Tropes of the Tradition

What are the sources of our knowledge of the *guru-śiṣyā paramparā*? Like so much else in Indian culture, much of what we know *about* the tradition has been orally transmitted *within* it, through stories and anecdotes. These have assumed a status close to myth or lore. Such narrative themes are often termed *tropes*; and if they project a highly idealised picture of the relationship between master and disciple that is not always realised in practice, this seems essential to sustaining and reproducing the ethos and ethic of the learning culture (for does not every musician speak devotedly of their *ustād* or guruji?).

Another source of our knowledge comes from scholarly accounts by ethnomusicologists who themselves have experienced musical discipleship as part of their fieldwork. These accounts include writings by Daniel Neuman (1990: 43–58) who learnt sāraṅgī with Ustād Sabri Khan (1927–2015); Qureshi (2009) who, some years later, learnt with the same *ustād*; Kippen (1988; 2008), who studied tabla with Ustād Afaq Hussain (1930–90); Magriel (2001), also a disciple of Ustād Sabri Khan; and Wim van der Meer (1980: 138–50), who studied voice with Pandit Dilip Chandra Vedi (1901–92). Our knowledge of the *guru-śiṣyā paramparā* is also informed by historians' investigations of the *guru* concept in ancient Vedic sources. Further insight is afforded by musicological genealogies of hereditary musicians, and by related accounts of the *gharānā*s (stylistic schools) of the later nineteenth and earlier twentieth centuries (see for example, Das Sharma [Dasasarma] 1993; Neuman 1990; Wade 1997).

Salient within these sources is the idea that the traditional locus of musical instruction is the guru's own home. This point is underlined by, among others, Qureshi (2009), who describes first-hand how pedagogical transmission is predominantly oral, and how the distinctive feature of discipleship under a hereditary musician is that the *śagīrd* or *śiṣyā* live with or near their *ustād* or guru as an actual or honorary family member. Qureshi recounts how the Urdu phrase 'sīna ba sīna', which loosely means 'from heart to heart', was interpreted by her *ustād*, Sabri Khan, as meaning in effect 'from father to son'—thus stressing the intimate, familial nature of this culture (2009: 167–71). Familial might also mean quasi-familial—in that non-family members can also be admitted to the teacher's circle and treated as a family member (as in Qureshi's own case)—or extended familial—in that teaching may also be from grandparent to grandchild, uncle to nephew etc. This domain extends out into a wider kinship network or community, known as *birādarī* or 'brotherhood' (ibid.: 170).

In this familial setting—often known as a *gurukul* (meaning, roughly, domain or clan of the guru)—teaching, learning, practice (*riyāz*), talk about music, and the goings-on of everyday life blend seamlessly (Neuman 1990: 54–5). This is a particularly congenial environment for younger family members to learn in. Magriel (2001: 104–40) observed how the young sons and nephews of several hereditary *ustād*s were inducted into learning music almost by osmosis, since music making was going on around them all the time as extended family and community flowed in and out of the house. Learning for these youngsters was in the first instance informal, even playful, and gradually became more formalised and focused as they got older and acquired competence. The *ustād*s' aspiration was for this younger generation to become professional artists themselves, and so pass on the tradition and continue the family lineage (assuming the potential was there and the opportunities for a career looked favourable). Such hereditary musicians are known as *khāndānī* (Neuman 1990: 58).

The admission of non-family members into discipleship is one way that Hindu musicians have learnt from Muslim teachers and vice-versa; it has also enabled the diversification of traditions, and, in the more recent past, made it possible for western musicians to study with South Asian masters. Nonetheless, entry by non-family members into a guru's or *ustād*'s domain has historically been difficult to negotiate. Another trope among musicians' stories is of having to demonstrate the seriousness of their intent to a potential guru or *ustād*, who might in the first instance appear indifferent or even discouraging. Van der Meer provides examples of such stories, some of them legendary (1980: 144–8); Kippen's account of his own experience of gaining admission as a disciple of Ustād Afaq Hussain is also paradigmatic (2008: 125–6, 128–9); and VR himself recounts how, after initially approaching Pandit Bhimsen Joshi in person to take him on as his *śiṣyā*, it took another two years before the master finally confirmed he would teach him, during which time VR would repeatedly turn up to Joshi's concerts in Delhi, sometimes playing tānpurā for him, understanding that the whole process was a test of his patience and commitment (Rajput 2012).

Once admitted into the guru's household, a student's devotion might continue to be tested before they are formally accepted and begin *tālīm* (tuition). A further trope among musicians' stories is of being expected to perform menial chores for their guru, such as doing his shopping, running errands, and generally making his life more comfortable—all of which could be seen as a demonstration of their submission (Kippen 2008: 129; Neuman 1990: §55). During this probationary phase, the student typically sits in on other students' lessons, learning by immersion, rather than being directly taught.

Eventually, if convinced by the student's commitment and general good character, the master may formally take them on as a *śiṣyā* or *śāgird*. This rite of passage is traditionally marked by a ceremony known as *gaṇḍā bandhan*, at which a thread is tied around the wrists of master and disciple, symbolising the bond between them. Kippen describes this ceremony as a mixture of Muslim and Hindu ritual (2008: 130); Qureshi (2009: 171–4) references the ceremony by its Muslim name—*śāgirdī*—in an account of sāraṅgī player Nasir Khan's admission into discipleship under his uncle, Ustād Sabri Khan. Such ceremonies are undergone by hereditary and non-hereditary musicians alike; indeed, the distinction between the categories would seem to be erased from this point. The *śiṣyā* commits to a life devoted to musical learning and its attendant values, and the guru commits to the *śiṣyā* as if their own offspring, and to passing the tradition on to them. If not already a family member, the *śiṣyā* is henceforward treated as such, and refers to fellow students as their *guru-bhāī* or *guru-bahan* ('guru brother' or 'guru sister'). There is a strongly affective dimension in all these relationships: another trope has it that the guru should love his student like (or more than) he loves his own son, and the *śiṣyā* love his guru like (or more than) he loves his own father (Neuman 1990: 45–50).

At the *gaṇḍā bandhan* ceremony, the *śiṣyā* customarily makes a financial offering known as a *guru dakśinā*; and although further offerings may also be subsequently made (even expected), notionally these would not be regarded as direct payment for *tālīm* which in principle is given freely (Neuman 1990: 51–2). 'Guruji never asked for payment', confirms VR; in other accounts of the *guru dakśinā*, the *śiṣyā* simply pays what they can afford. What the guru has to offer is regarded as being beyond price (as it were, outside of any commodity exchange); in return the *śiṣyā* is expected to adapt his own behaviour, showing respect and obedience. Even after initiation, a *śiṣyā* continues to undertake tasks and favours (such as carrying the guru's instrument, bringing his food to the table) as acts of respect and gratitude (Neuman 1990: 46, 51). Reverence is also conventionally shown in the ritual greeting (*praṇām*) of touching a guru's feet.

Perspectives from History

The historical depth of the *paramparā*—and of lineages within it—matters. There is status for a musician in hailing from a long and distinguished pedigree. Lines of descent from father to son (patrilinear) or from blood relative to blood relative (consanguineal) are known as *khāndān*, and its members as *khāndānī*; wider family groups connected by actual or potential marriage ties are known as *birādarī* (Neuman 1990: 95–9; Qureshi 2009: 170–1). Scholars seeking to compile genealogies must contend with sometimes misremembered or conflicting accounts (where brothers may have been confused with father and son or vice-versa (Neuman 1990: 166)) and sometimes tenuous claims by musicians to have belonged to the *khāndān* or *birādarī* of a particularly eminent *ustād* in order to enhance their own prestige. Even if some might be stretching a point to claim themselves *khāndanī* of the legendary sixteenth-century dhrupad singer Tānsen, present-day continuities with the four singing styles (*bānīs*) dating back to Akbar's court, and with instrumental lineages putatively originated by the sons and daughters of Tānsen, mean that this is at least imaginable (ibid.: 147–8, 164–5). Neuman asserts that the likely limit point of any hereditary musician's plausible ancestry would be the Sufi musician Amir Khusrau who was a famed singer in the era of the Delhi Sultanate. Before and alongside this, one would need to look to pedagogical lineages of Hindu temple musicians, which were not necessarily hereditary (ibid.: 85, 104, 105). For that matter, not all lineages associated with courts were Muslim—for example, Tānsen and his teacher, the equally legendary Swami Haridas (1480–1573), were both Brahmans (though the former is said to have become a Muslim when he entered Akbar's court).

A further aspect of lineage is the institution of the *gharānā*, which was 'conceived in the mid-nineteenth century and born in the twentieth', as Neuman puts it (1990: 146). In seeking to distinguish a *gharānā* from a *khāndān* (beyond the fact that the former concept has a more recent historical provenance), we might say that *gharānā* more strongly implies the idea of a stylistic school. *Gharānās* are often named after their place of origin (for example, Gwalior, Agra, Delhi, Kirānā) or their founder or most eminent pioneer (for example, sitarist Imdad Khan). *Gharānās* may be predominantly vocal or instrumental, or reputed for both. Each *gharānā* is distinguished from the others by particular forms of performance style which have evolved across successive generations (Deshpande 1987; Wade 1997). For example, while the vocal strand of the Kirānā *gharānā*, with which VR is affiliated, is known for its purity of *svar* and for giving less priority to *lay* (as can be heard from historic recordings of its founder, Abdul Karim Khan), the reverse is true for the Agra *gharānā* (Deshpande 1987: 41–5).

Although lines of transmission between generations of a *gharānā* may be hereditary, this is not universally the case. For example, tracing back a line of pedagogy back from VR within the Kirānā *gharānā*, we have Pandit Bhimsen Joshi, Pandit Sawai Gandharva (1886–1952) and Ustād Abdul Karim Khan (1872–1937), none of whom are consanguineal. For a *gharānā* to be recognised as such, it must customarily have at least three generations; it is not enough for a teacher and his students to declare themselves a *gharānā*. Despite their often geographic titles, *gharānās* do not necessarily designate physical or geographic communities. Membership is generally consolidated through identification with a performance style, and some artists may identify with more than one *gharānā* (for example, Bhimsen Joshi's singing style also drew influence from musicians of other *gharānās* (Wade 1997: 194)). Conversely, although the *gharānā* concept did not arise until the nineteenth century, once established, *gharānās* tended retrospectively to reconstruct their roots back to earlier generations. At stake here was what Neuman terms 'the politics of pedigree'—the need for agency and influence, which became particularly acute at a time when the princely courts that supported professional hereditary musicians were in decline (Neuman 1990: 146–7; 145–67).

As might be surmised, paternalism and patriarchy are notable features of the *guru-śiṣyā paramparā*; in recounting its social structure, it is difficult not to reproduce the implicit tendency to represent the actors as male. So it is important to stress that women have also had a longstanding place in Indian classical music (Post 2000), albeit not outside the relations of patriarchy. As Neuman explains and documents (1990: 97–9; 248–53), wives and mothers had a role in preserving and expanding the hermetic lineages of *khāndans*. Women also historically constituted their own class of hereditary musicians (ibid.: 100–2), as temple dancers and court musicians (*devadāsīs*, *tawaīfs*)—professional functions that overlapped with that of courtesan. In the temple and courtly milieux of their day, such women were highly regarded for their cultural knowledge and artistic prowess. However, they became vilified under colonial Victorian moralising attitudes in the nineteenth century, and under related social reforms in the early twentieth that included the banning of temple dancers (Post 2000). Women subsequently regained respectability within Indian classical music largely through middle-class (and predominantly Hindu) teaching academies such as Paluskar's Gandharva Mahavidyalaya (Bakhle 2005), which, significantly, allowed non-hereditary aspiring musicians access to tuition. Hereditary female performers nonetheless maintained a place as professional musicians, though needed to take steps to sanitise their former courtesan associations. Learning with respected gurus and *ustāds* was one way to do this, which gave them affiliation with *gharānās* (Neuman 1990: 100–1; 207–8). The suffix *bai*—which can be intended honorifically—is not uncommonly added to the first names of professional female performers (ibid.: 100).

Qureshi (2002) sees the endogenous culture of hereditary musicians as reproducing the feudal relationships in which they were employed. When their princely or landowner patrons could dismiss them on a whim, it was understandable that musicians would keep the only commodity they had—their artistic skills and knowledge—within the family. Such a feudal mentality partly explains the patriarchal authority one can still find operating in the *ustād-śāgird/guru-śiṣyā* culture of today—where the guru or *ustād* tends to be regarded as a figure of absolute authority.

An even longer historical view reveals the guru as a venerated, near-deified religious figure within the deep past of Hinduism. According to Mlecko (1982: 34), '[i]n his earliest role the guru was a teacher of the Vedas and the various skills needed for their study, such as grammar, metrics, etymology and mnemonics'. Mlecko stresses the importance of orality in the transmission of this knowledge in which 'proper accent and pronunciation' were paramount (ibid.); and it was the milieu of the *gurukul* that afforded the close personal contact necessary to this learning process. In other words, the institutions of both guru and *gurukul*, as we have continued to see them in the pedagogy of Indian classical music, were already operative at a very early historical stage—in what Mlecko loosely terms 'ancient India', probably meaning the first millennium BCE or earlier. Indeed Mlecko evidences the importance attributed to the guru within the scriptures themselves—for example in the *Ṛg Veda*, *Yajur Veda* and several of the *Upaniṣads*, dating variously from the second millennium BCE to the early centuries BCE. The writers of these texts often impute divinity to the guru, some depicting him as a figure from whom even the gods learn. Jan Gonda's account (1965: 229–83) similarly evidences the exalted status of the guru as well as the antiquity of the guru concept, which he argues as being co-extensive with Hinduism. Mlecko likewise illustrates the continuity of these ideas through the Hindu epics and tantrism. He goes on to demonstrate their later historical evolution in the medieval *bhakti* tradition and beyond (1982: 47–52), in which the guru becomes emancipated from his priestly or Brahminical origins and becomes a figure within popular devotional movements (see also Sooklal 2010).

The Impact of Modernity

The *guru-śiṣyā paramparā* has continued to evolve under late modernity. Since the twentieth century, the *paramparā* has had to find a way to survive without the patronage of princely courts and wealthy *zamīndārs* (hereditary landowners)—with the concert hall largely taking the place of the *mehfil* (courtly gathering), the academy functioning as an alternative site of pedagogy to the *gurukul*, and liberal-democratic social relationships beginning to impinge on the feudally-sanctioned authoritarianism of the guru.

In modern times many gurus or *ustāds* still teach from their own home, but students are more likely to be visitors than live-in family members, taking their lesson perhaps weekly rather than daily, and commonly availing themselves of smartphone technology to record their class as a way of maintaining their teacher's virtual presence between lessons. Alternatively, or additionally, a guru might be employed by one or more educational institutions. Taking the residency of bansurī maestro Pandit Hariprasad Chaurasia at the Rotterdam Conservatory as a case study, Huib Schippers (2007) analyses how such artists manage traditional *guru-śiṣyā* teaching styles against the regulative processes of qualification-awarding institutions, as well as balancing their students' needs against the itinerant lifestyle of a performer on the international stage. The profile of many jobbing modern gurus takes the form of a freelance portfolio career in which they operate as self-employed individuals juggling performing and private and institutional teaching commitments across various locations.

The physical *gurukul* has also taken new forms. Some teachers rent alternative premises—in effect an annexe to their home—from which to teach students locally. Others have developed purpose-built *gurukuls* complete with residential accommodation for national and international students. One example would be the Gundecha brothers' Gurukul Dhrupad Sansthan in Bhopal, where, even though the scale is large, the core pedagogical principles remain daily face-to-face contact with the gurus and the sustaining of a community of *śiṣyās* who predominantly live together (Sankaran 2020). The Kolkata-based ITC Sangeet Research Academy is another example, with its more formal institutional infrastructure, research library and associated scholars; notwithstanding all this, the Academy's key objective remains to cultivate performers in the *guru-śiṣyā paramparā* (Kashalkar 2013).

Such modern *gurukuls*, which resist the idea of a formal curriculum or syllabus, remain distinct from Indian university music departments and music schools which offer tuition for a formal award such as a degree. As Andrew Alter summarises it (paraphrasing

Banerjee 1986), tuition in these latter institutions is likely to be syllabus-based, involve a variety of teachers rather than a single guru, be delivered to groups of students rather than individuals, and emphasise musical literacy and academic training alongside practical tuition (Alter 2000: 447–8). Yet, even in the face of more institutionalised and externally regulated models, such as the western-influenced, curriculum-based, academy, the *guru-śiṣyā paramparā* continues to be acclaimed by performers as the essential pathway to learning Indian classical music, with the guru or *ustād* as its lynchpin.

Problematics of the *Paramparā*

The image of the guru conveyed in most narratives about the *paramparā* is an idealised one. Sanyukta Kashalkar (2013: 83) puts it thus (in a statement mirrored on a now-superseded version of the ITC Sangeet Research Academy website): 'To the Shishya, the Guru symbolises the art itself, while for the Guru, the Shishya signifies the continuity of the art. The Guru shares the sacred knowledge of the art only with kindred souls, sincere in their quest'. Given human nature, however, any individual guru or *ustād* may map more or less perfectly onto the quasi-divine ideal they inherit; and a properly critical assessment of the *guru-śiṣyā paramparā* needs also to address its shadow side.

Problems, perhaps as longstanding as the tradition itself, have not gone unacknowledged. Mlecko's historical long view includes the statement that '[g]urus can be completely selfless, desiring nothing for themselves or they can be avaricious, seeking only an easy livelihood off the naive or guilt-ridden—they use the *śiṣyās*' (1982: 55). Kippen too gives an account of 'the problems of exploitation and manipulation' by musical *ustāds* (2008: 134–7), including a commonly referenced complaint: the guru who teaches 'with a closed fist'—who, in other words, is parsimonious with the knowledge he passes on to his students (see also Slawek 2000: 462–3). The field also has its stories of gurus no less prone than other human beings to addiction and desire; stories of sexual misconduct, harassment and abuse have also come to light.

One aspect of the tradition's grating up against modernity is the way these behaviours are, in the earlier twenty-first century, being publicly called out, especially via social media; the *guru-śiṣyā paramparā* is now also experiencing its #MeToo moment. At the time of writing, this tendency has reached the point where some gurus are themselves calling for reform. Karnatak vocalist and writer T. M. Krishna has been at the spearhead: 'Let me say it as it is', he writes, '[t]he parampara is ... structurally flawed' (Krishna 2020: n.p.). He continues:

> we need to reimagine our structures of learning. The system must begin with respect for students, and recognition of their independence and rights as individuals. This is vital because the power structure is naturally tilted in favour of the guru. But for this to happen, we need to first 'humanise' gurus. The parampara that demands obedience and unquestioning deference, only because someone is a guru, needs to be demolished. Simply put, gurus must be respected for being domain experts—nothing more.

Krishna holds fire—at least in this article—on what this reimagining might be, while insisting he is not arguing for the institutionalisation of teaching. The issue is perhaps whether what is distinctive and valuable about the *guru-śiṣyā paramparā* can be transmuted into something compatible with liberal-democratic values. For the personal, affective and relational aspects of the *guru-śiṣyā paramparā* at its best still represent something valuable and humanising. Indeed, against the increasing regulation and corporatisation of learning institutions in countries such as the UK (and their growing culture of transactionalism between students and teachers) the values of the *paramparā* might, paradoxically, suggest a more salutary critical alternative.

Krishna is surely right to argue for re-constructing gurus as nothing more (or less) than human beings, and for unburdening them of the status of gods—a status which risks the corresponding infantilisation of the *śiṣyā*. Yet in order not to lose what is heart-centred in the tradition, perhaps we might still aspire for gurus and *ustād*s ethically to function as something beyond domain experts. Kashalkar chooses her words well in the above quotation when she says the guru *symbolises* the art itself and that its continuity is *signified* by the *śiṣyā*. For this potentially defends both parties from the mistake of attributing these qualities to them *a priori*—from conflating the individuals with the art they hold in trust. In reality both (human) parties might fall short of the ideal, but arguably they are less likely to do so if they recognise that neither is bigger than the tradition they uphold.

1.12 *Riyāz*

Like musical practitioners everywhere, Indian classical musicians practise for a purpose—indeed several purposes. They practise to improve: to increase their technical mastery of their voice or instrument. They practise to acquire knowledge: to internalise a repertoire of *rāg*s, *tāls*, compositions and more. They practise to learn how to perform: how to create and extemporise musical materials, and how to form them according to culturally recognised conventions of style and syntax. Above all, they practise in order ultimately to transcend these technical and material things: to reach for, and occasionally touch, moments of the intangible. This last purpose also relates to a *non*-purposive aspect of practise which is captured in the Urdu/Persian word by which Hindustani musicians know it: *riyāz*.

Riyāz construes practising as a devotional or spiritual act. It is often associated with another, Sanskrit term (familiar to yoga practitioners): *sādhana*. This refers to any daily practice aimed at attaining freedom from the ego. Despite this intent, the paradox is that *sādhana* 'should be undertaken without any specific goal in mind. [It] should be practiced for the sake of maintaining the practice, and as a means of cultivating discipline' (Yogapedia 2023). In the same vein, a musician's *riyāz* is also often undertaken as an end in itself rather than a means to an end—such as becoming a professional musician. *Riyāz* forms the very heart of musicians' musical lives and identities. They might routinely enquire of one another not when their last performance was, but how their *riyāz* is going.

In this sense, *riyāz* occupies the same idealised value-sphere as the relationship between guru and *śiṣyā*. Just as the guru ideally acts as spiritual preceptor, which makes him more than an everyday teacher; and just as the *śiṣyā* ideally approaches their learning with an attitude of discipleship, which makes them more than an everyday student; so *riyāz* is ideally undertaken—by both guru and *śiṣyā*—with mindful devotion, which makes it more than everyday practising.

And just as musicians' received wisdom about the *guru-śiṣyā paramparā* is transmitted through various narrative tropes, so too their understanding of *riyāz* is passed on through tales that have assumed the status of myth or lore. These principally concern (i) prodigious feats of *riyāz* (often told in respect of renowned *pandit*s or *ustād*s); (ii) the demonstration of bodily signs of *riyāz*; and (iii) the importance of formidable levels of repetition in doing one's *riyaz*. The following tale by eminent k͟hayāl singer Ajoy Chakrabarty (2002: 32) is entirely typical:

> My first *guru*, my father Sri Ajit Kumar Chakrabarty, used to have me practice one song or a single *taan* for up to eight hours at a stretch for several days. ... [He] would never let me stop until my practice was complete. If mother intervened at this time, he used to become angry and say, 'It is better to be childless than to have a worthless son'.

Daniel Neuman (1990: 31–43) recounts similar tales of musicians practising between eight and sixteen hours a day during the formative years of their training. He also tells of fellow sāraṅgī players inspecting the callouses on his cuticles as physical evidence of his *riyāz*: 'The practiced eye could gauge very accurately how much practice had been accomplished and from it ... the degree of dedication' (2002: 32). Comparable stories in respect of the sitar and sarod are told by Gerry Farrell (1986: 271).

While not every musician is in a position (or has the disposition) to practise the whole day or night long, the most significant principle of *riyāz*, regardless of the actual hours applied, is repetition. Commonly, Indian classical musicians spend a significant portion of their *riyāz* practising scales, *alaṅkār*s (ascending and descending sequential patterns), *palṭās* (similar, more developed patterns), *merukhaṇḍ* (permutation of a set of notes), *pakaḍ*s (catch phrases that capture the gist of a *rāg*) and *tān*s (running figurations). Sorrell provides a more detailed account of such practise techniques and how these eventually translate into performance (Sorrell and Narayan 1980: 67–91). Farrell notes that such routine exercises are practised at all stages of learning, by beginner and maestro alike, the only real difference being the speed of execution and level of sophistication (1986: 269).

A vital point is that in any *riyāz* session, one should not practise many items a few times, but one of them very many times. Again, this principle is enshrined in musicians' anecdotes. Chakrabarty writes: 'As I grew up, I became habituated to practising the same *taan*s 500–600 times throughout the night, understanding my father's and my gurus' demands and expectations' (2002: 32). Farrell discusses a *palṭā* 'which one of my teachers told me to play one thousand times (and he wasn't speaking figuratively!)' (1986: 268). As well as being the principal means of absorbing musical material, repetition (done mindfully) is regarded as an essential route to ironing out one's defects—if necessary to the point of exhaustion: 'you can take a small break if you start dying', vocalist Veena Sahasrabuddhe (1948–2016) is reported to have said (Phansalkar 2017: 48). Some gurus commend the use of a *mālā* (prayer beads) to count off repetitions (an aid more practicable for vocalists, who have their hands free, than for instrumentalists): a *mālā* usually has 109 beads, and is conventionally used when chanting *mantras*—significantly, a spiritual activity based on repetition.

Insistence on apparently pathological levels of repetition may seem like a means for a guru or *ustād* to assert their authority over a student, but essentially it is a way to enculturate a foundational pedagogical principle: a discipline; an almost meditative approach to internalising material at a beyond-conscious level. This is important because in improvised performance a musician needs automatically to reproduce and re-permutate musical ideas into new transformations without having to think (for there is no time for conscious thought when one is on the spot). Dard Neuman coins the term 'automaticity' for this process (2012: 438, 447 n. 3, 448 n. 16). He recounts how hereditary *ustād*s would seek to impede their students from thinking in their practising by withholding any technical or theoretical information about a *rāg*, *pakaḍ*, *palṭā* etc., even declining to use *sargam* note names, until the student had mastered the material in question (ibid.: 432–6). The aim was to achieve an essentially embodied practice—a 'body-instrument' in which the throat (in the case of vocalists) or hands (in the case of instrumentalists) 'think' for themselves (ibid.: 438–42, 445–6).

While not all Indian classical musicians aspire to become professionals, and while many undertake their practice and practising alongside other jobs or activities as part of busy, complex lives, a commitment to *riyāz*—and to repetition as its key technique—remains essential. The hard-won truth of the matter is that any musician is only as good as the quality and rigour of their *riyāz*. Only by this route do they ultimately attain the creative freedom in performance that can touch an audience's heart.

2. A CYCLE OF *RĀGS*: *RĀG SAMAY CAKRA*

Performers:

Dr Vijay Rajput (k͟hayāl vocalist)

with

Ustād Athar Hussain Khan (tabla)

Ustād Murad Ali (sāraṅgī)

Ustād Mahmood Dholpuri (harmonium)

 https://doi.org/10.11647/OBP.0313.02

2.1 The Album and Its Supporting Materials

Our first album, *Rāg samay cakra*, presents fourteen Hindustani *rāg*s in the k͟hayāl vocal style, performed by Dr Vijay Rajput (henceforth VR), a vocalist of the Kirānā *gharānā* (stylistic lineage). With his accompanists, VR takes the listener through a cycle (*cakra*) of *rāg*s ordered according to their designated performing times (*samay*): from the dawn *rāg* Bhairav to the midnight *rāg* Mālkauns (for a visual representation see Figure 1.6.2). As well as being identified with times of the day and night, *rāg*s are also associated with times of the year; and so the sequence ends with two seasonal *rāg*s: Megh, a *rāg* for the monsoon season, and Basant, a springtime *rāg* which may also be sung in the final quarter of the night. These performances are followed by supplementary tracks in which VR provides spoken renditions of the texts of the songs sung in each *rāg*. This is intended to help students who are not Hindu/Urdu speakers achieve correct pronunciation. The music was recorded in New Delhi in 2008; the spoken texts at Newcastle University in 2017, where the producer was David de la Haye.

All the performances on *Rāg samay cakra* take the form of an *ālāp* and *choṭā k͟hayāl*—literally 'small *k͟hayāl*'. We gave a thumbnail account of these performance stages in Section 1.7, but what follows is a further concise gloss.

In an *ālāp*, the soloist's job is to establish the *rāg*—its mood, its colours, its characteristic melodic behaviour. Listening to an *ālāp* is almost like overhearing an inner contemplation; the tabla is silent, so the vocalist has licence to extemporise, without being tied to any metre—an approach to rhythm known as *anibaddh* (similar to *senza misura* in western music). By contrast, the ensuing *choṭā k͟hayāl* is based around a short song composition (*bandiś*), and is sung in a rhythmic cycle (*tāl*) supported by the tabla—which means the rhythmic organisation is metrical (a condition termed *nibaddh*); the dynamic is interactive and accumulative. Hence, the overall trajectory—from the meditative beginnings of the *ālāp* to the climactic closure of the *choṭā k͟hayāl*—is a journey from ruminative inwardness to extravert exuberance.

As its name suggests, a *choṭā k͟hayāl* is a vehicle for shorter performances in this style. Even so, there is plenty of space for elaboration: not uncommonly a *choṭā k͟hayāl* will extend to around ten minutes—as on our second album, *Twilight Rāgs from North India* (Tracks 3 and 6). But it is also possible to give a satisfying and idiomatic *rāg* performance, including an *ālāp*, in around five minutes, as VR does throughout *Rāg samay cakra*. Because it is ostensibly simpler to master than the majestic, slow-tempo *baṛā k͟hayāl*, a *choṭā k͟hayāl* is usually what k͟hayāl singers first learn to perform. Hence, we intend that these compressed performances will be of value to students in the earlier stages of learning. But we hope that they will inspire more advanced students too. For a *choṭā k͟hayāl* presents its own challenges: it is usually sung up-tempo, at a speed ranging from medium fast to very fast—hence is also known as a *drut k͟hayāl* (fast *k͟hayāl*). This means the singer has to keep their wits about them through many extemporised twists and turns in which they interact with their accompanying artists; and physical as well as mental agility is required for the rapid delivery of virtuosic features such as *tān*s.

In Section 2.5 we provide supporting materials for each *rāg* of the album—namely:

1. A description of the *rāg*, including a technical specification and an outline of its musical and aesthetic characteristics.
2. A transliteration and translation of the *bandiś* text, as well as its original Devanāgarī version.
3. A *sargam* notation of the *bandiś* (composition).

In the intervening sections, we provide writings that help elucidate these materials. In Section 2.2 (relating to (2), above), we consider the poetic characteristics of the song texts, as well as the problematics of trying to produce any kind of definitive version of them; we also discuss conventions relating to their transliteration and pronunciation. In Section 2.3 (relating to (3), above) we explore issues to do with the musical notation of the *bandiś*es, given that historically they have been transmitted orally; we also provide information about the musical notation conventions applied in this book, and about how the *bandiś*es as notated relate to their delivery in actual performance. Finally, in Section 2.4 (relating to (1) above), we give a brief explanation of the technical terms used in the *rāg* specifications.

2.2 The Song Texts

Language and Poetics

Khayāl songs have a style and language all of their own—a point that Lalita du Perron drives home in her richly detailed account in *The Songs of Khayāl* (Magriel and du Perron 2013, I: 201–50). Even though, in the heat of performance, the words of khayāl compositions may get submerged under waves of invention and virtuosity, the texts remain important. They offer keys to the mood of a *bandiś*, and can spark the singer's imagination (the meaning of the word *khayāl*, let us recall). Hence, in our commentaries on the individual *rāgs* of *Rāg samay cakra* below (Section 2.5), we have extracted the *bandiś* texts, along with their translations, so that they can be perused in their own right, and so that students can familiarise themselves with them prior to, or in tandem with, learning the song melody.

A definitive version of a khayāl text is no more possible than a final version of its melody. Both are subject to mutation under oral transmission; both are susceptible to the vagaries of memory and imagination. Any individual artist may carry several variants of both tune and text in their head. Another challenge comes from the language itself. Khayāl songs are found in a range of North Indian regional languages and dialects, which may be related to Hindi but which do not take its modern standard form. Prominent among these is Braj Bhāṣā, which achieved status as a vernacular literary language between the late medieval era and the nineteenth century (Snell 1991), and continues to have currency in present-day musical genres such as khayāl, ṭhumrī and dhrupad. Mutabilities of phonology, grammar and spelling all add to the challenge of stabilising form and meaning. Further, there are the often allusive and ambiguous meanings of khayāl poems, which seldom exceed four lines and display numerous other stylistic idiosyncrasies (again, see du Perron's account).

Many of the common devotional and romantic tropes of khayāl poetry are illustrated in the texts of *Rāg samay cakra*. These include the veneration of deities; the pain of romantic separation; the entreaties of a lover; night-time assignations (and fear of being heard by the mother- or sister-in-law); images of nature (including birds, bees and mango trees); and celebrations of the seasons (notably springtime and the monsoon). Kr̥ṣṇa, typically depicted playing his flute, is often centre stage or rarely far from the scene. He is regarded as a figure who brings the divine and romantic into union. When not being adored by all, he is frequently seen being scalded by his consort, the *gopī* (cowherd) Rādhā, for his teasing, for his frequent absences, and for his assignations with a rival (*sautan*). Many of the song texts are sung from a female standpoint, and while Rādhā is rarely named as such, she is implicitly the archetype behind many of these songs of love and longing for the divine.

Transliteration and Pronunciation

Our edition of the texts has been a collaborative venture (where, inevitably, the roles have blurred a little). Initially, a Devanāgarī (देवनागरी) version of the *bandiś* texts was supplied by VR from his performer's perspective. This was then transliterated into Roman script by David Clarke (henceforth DC) and passed on to the translators; unless otherwise indicated, the English translations were composed by Jonathan Katz and Imre Bangha. Versions were then passed back and forth between collaborators, resulting in further modifications and refinements.

The oral transmission of k͟hayāl songs militates against any would-be final version of their texts. Performers might not sing every detail of the text as they would write it, nor write down the text (if they do so at all) exactly as they sing it. Sometimes the sounds of the words may take them in one direction while their possible meaning may lead a translator or editor in another. In our edition, alternatives to the actually sung version are shown in square brackets; conversely, round brackets are used for words that are sung, but which depart from the textual version.

In aiming for a scholarly transliteration from Devanāgarī into Roman script we have followed the conventions of IAST, the International Alphabet of Sanskrit Transliteration, a subset of ISO 15919 (see also the discussion above in Transliteration and Other Textual Conventions). Through its use of diacritics—dots, lines and other inflections above or below individual letters—this system provides a unique Roman counterpart for every Devanāgarī character. This may look a little more complicated or fussy than informal approaches to romanising Hindi or Urdu used in everyday vernacular practice, but it is simply more fastidious and does not take long to master; moreover it is helpful to singers in achieving correct pronunciation.

This is because IAST makes it possible to discriminate between closely related but distinct Hindavi (Hindi/Urdu) sounds in a way that is not possible with only the normal twenty-six characters of the Latin alphabet. For example, unlike English, Hindavi has two distinct 't' sounds: *dental*, with the tongue pressed against the front teeth; and *retroflex*, with the tongue against the roof of the mouth. In Devanāgarī script (used for Hindi and Sanskrit, among other languages), these are written as त and ट, and are transliterated as **t** and **ṭ** respectively. The same goes for the 'd' sounds द and ड, transliterated as **d** and **ḍ**. (For an admirably pragmatic online guide to Devanāgarī transliteration, see Snell 2016.)

We do not indicate every aspect of pronunciation here, but the following are particularly pertinent:

- A macron (line) over a vowel indicates the sound is lengthened—hence **ā** = 'aa', as in 'bar' in Standard English; **ī** = 'ee', as in 'teen'; **ū** = 'oo', as in 'loom'.
- A tilde (wavy line) over a vowel—for example, **ã**, **ĩ**, **ũ**—indicates nasalisation.
- A dot over an n—as in 'Sadāraṅg'—also indicates nasalisation.
- **C** is pronounced 'ch', as in 'cello' or 'church'.
- **Ś** and **ṣ** are both pronounced 'sh'—as in the English 'shoot'.
- **J** is pronounced as in 'January' or 'jungle'.
- **H** after a consonant—for example, **bh**, **dh**, **kh**—indicates that it is aspirated, i.e. pronounced with an additional puff of air.
- The underlined character **k͟h**—as in *k͟hayāl*—is pronounced further back in the throat than its non-underlined counterpart; these sounds are peculiar to Urdu words of Persian or Arabic origin.

- The short vowel **a** (known as *schwa* by phoneticists) is pronounced further forward in the mouth than the longer **ā**—especially when sung (see Sanyal and Widdess 2004: 173, n. 17). Hence 'p**a**ndit' is pronounced slightly like 'pundit', 't**a**blā' slightly like 'tublā'.

For more comprehensive guidance on pronunciation, readers should consult a primer such as Rupert Snell's excellent *Beginner's Hindi* (2003: viii–xviii) or the Hindi section of the website Omniglot, an online encyclopaedia of writing systems. Additionally, the transliterated song texts can be studied in conjunction with the recorded spoken renditions by VR found alongside the *rāg* recordings.

One further technicality should be noted. Spoken Hindavi, unlike Sanskrit, often suppresses an implicit '**a**' vowel after a consonant (a process termed *schwa deletion*). This is especially common at the end of a word—hence the Sanskrit '*rāga*' is pronounced '*rāg*' in Hindavi. However, in *sung* Hindavi, and in dialects such as Braj Bhāṣā, such suppressed vowels are *not* silenced; indeed their enunciation is often essential to the metrical structure of Braj poetry and song (see Snell 2016: 3–4). Hence, on the advice of our translators, we have included the normally suppressed **a** in our transliteration of the song texts—for example, 'dhan dhan murat' is sung (and hence transliterated) as 'dhan**a** dhan**a** murat**a**'; similarly, 'hamrī kahī mitvā' as 'ham**a**rī kahī mit**a**vā'.

2.3 Notating the *Bandiś*es (and Performing Them)

Prescriptive or Descriptive Music Writing?

Given that Hindustani classical music is primarily an oral tradition, its notation—while useful for teaching and musical analysis—raises a number of issues. In this regard, it will be useful to invoke the ethnomusicologist Charles Seeger's (1886–1979) well-known distinction between 'prescriptive and descriptive music writing' (Seeger 1958). The former type, typified by western staff notation, supplies *instructions* to the performer that are essential in rendering a piece. The latter, typically used in ethnomusicological transcription seeks to detail a *record* of musical sounds and events as actually rendered—which may be useful in documenting and scrutinising performances from non-notating cultures.

An exemplary use of *descriptive* notation can be found in Volume II of Nicolas Magriel and Lalita du Perron's *The Songs of Kh̲ayāl* (2013). Using an inflected *sargam* notation, Magriel seeks to capture every nuance of ornamentation and note placement in classic kh̲ayāl recordings. His aim is to illustrate—and in effect analyse—the mastery of the genre's greatest historical exponents, as found in their recorded legacy. By contrast, our approach in *Rāgs Around the Clock* is more *prescriptive* and heuristic. Our aim is generally to notate a simplified outline of a song (*bandiś*) to assist students in learning it (though on some occasions it will be useful to present more fully detailed descriptive notations of what VR actually sings).

For an authentic version of a *bandiś*, students will need to listen to their guru or *ustād* demonstrate it multiple times—either live or, as with *Rāgs Around the Clock*, in recorded form. Our (prescriptive) notation of the songs sung on *Rāg samay cakra* acts as nothing more (or less) than a pedagogical *aide memoire*, and largely corresponds to the on-the-spot sketch a student might make during their lesson. What is omitted is as significant as what is included. What is notated are the essentials. What is *not* notated are the stylistic nuances heard in the actual musical renditions—which is where VR's *gāyakī*—his distinctive style—is audible. Paradoxically, the abstraction of the notation helps make salient the nuances of the songs *as actually sung*, by their very absence.

Even in the short performances captured on *Rāg samay cakra*, one can often hear multiple variants of a *bandiś*, richly exceeding the simplified notation. Sometimes the sung version may only begin to conform to the notated one later in the performance; sometimes the notation may represent a composite distilled from different moments; sometimes what is notated may never be directly rendered as such but could be considered as a model of the song operating at the back of the performer's mind as they deliver it; or it may conform to a version transmitted and notated on a different occasion, which may be no less—or no more—'definitive'. So, rather than representing an idealised version of a *bandiś*, our notations form a practical or heuristic reference point that itself may transmute over time.

Notation Conventions

To notate the songs from our collection, we have developed a version of Vishnu Narayan Bhatkhande's (1860–1936) music writing system, as found, for example, in his multi-volume

Kramik pustak mālikā (1937), and informally applied by many Hindustani musicians. Although it would have been relatively straightforward to have made transcriptions using western staff notation, we have resisted that temptation, since it is not part of the currency of Indian music, and would bring with it a welter of distorting connotations (a point which resonates with Magriel's comments in Magriel and du Perron 2013, I: 91–2). The Bhatkhande-derived notation used here is, in any case, easy enough to decipher. Let us consider the example in Figure 2.3.1, which quotes the *antarā* (second part) of the famous Toḍī *bandiś*, 'Laṅgara kā̃karīyā jīna māro'—as sung by VR on Track 2 of *Rāg samay cakra* (from 04:14).

tīntāl

x				2				o				3			
1	**2**	**3**	**4**	**5**	**6**	**7**	**8**	**9**	**10**	**11**	**12**	**13**	**14**	**15**	**16**
: Ḿ	Ḿ	ᴰ\ G̲	-	Ḿ	-	D̲	D̲	Ṡ	-	Ṡ	Ṡ	N	Ṙ̲	Ṡ	- :
Su -	na	pa -	-	ve———		mo -	ri	sā -	-	sa	na -	nan -	dī -	yā.———	
D̲	Ġ̲	Ṙ̲	Ṡ	-	Ṡ	N	Ṡ	N	D̲	N	D̲	P			
Do -	-	rī	do -	-	rī	gha -	ra	ā	-	-	ve.———				

Fig. 2.3.1 *Bandiś* in Rāg Toḍī: notation of *antarā*. Created by author (2024), CC BY-NC-SA.

Each row of the notation represents one *āvartan* (cycle) of the *tāl*—in this case the 16-beat *tīntāl*. Individual beats (*mātrās*) are numbered in bold at the head of the notation on a horizontal axis. Vertical lines (broadly similar to barlines in western notation) mark off the subdivisions (*vibhāgs*) of the *tāl*; in the case of *tīntāl*, there are four *vibhāgs*, each lasting four *mātrās*. The clap pattern for the *tāl* is also shown according to convention: *sam* (the first beat) is indicated with 'x', *khālī* with 'o', and other clapped beats (*tālī*) with consecutive numbers.

The notes of the melody are given above the text, using the abbreviated syllables of *sargam* notation. A dot above a note name indicates that it is performed in the upper octave; a dot below, in the lower octave. Flat (*komal*) scale degrees are shown by underlining the note name (for example, R̲ = *komal* Re); the sharpened fourth degree, *tivra* Ma, is indicated with a wedge above the note name (i.e. Ḿ). Dashes signify that a note is sustained through the following beat(s). Oblique lines (/ or \) indicate a glide (*miṇḍ*) upwards or downwards between notes.

Superscripted note names are used for ornaments (discussed further at the end of this section). Since k̲h̲ayāl performances are often replete with subtle ornamentation and pitch bends, these are shown sparingly, in order not to clutter the notation; as stated above, our aim is not to capture every tiny detail of the performance but to convey the basic outline of the song for practical learning purposes.

The first line of both parts of a *bandiś* (*sthāī* and *antarā*) is conventionally repeated. To signal this, we apply repeat mark signs (: :) from western staff notation. While subsequent lines may also be repeated, and while the first line itself may be repeated several times over (often with variations), this is not usually indicated, since the matter is largely dependent on the context of any given performance and on the performer's mood.

Typically of the k͟hayāl style, all the *tīntāl bandiś*es in our collection begin not on *sam*, the first beat, but with a lead-in of several beats. (Although the *antarā* cited in Figure 2.3.1 does begin on *sam*, this is quite rare, and, in any case, the *sthāī* which opens the same *bandiś* begins on beat 14.) Not uncommonly, songs start on beat 9 (*khālī*), but they may begin earlier or later. Hence, the poetic lines of a song often straddle the rhythmic notational framework. This can be seen in Figure 2.3.2, which quotes the *sthāī* of the composition 'Koyalīyā bole ambuvā' in Rāg Mālkauns (Track 12 of *Rāg samay cakra* (from 03:28)). Here, the two lines of the stanza each extend from *khālī* to *khālī*.

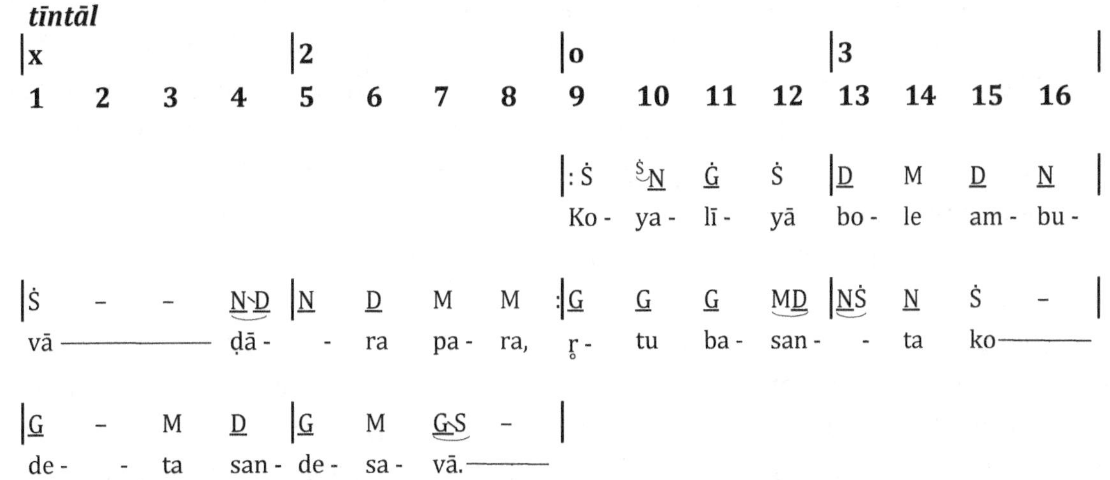

Fig. 2.3.2 *Bandiś* in Rāg Mālkauns: notation of *sthāī*. Created by author (2024), CC BY-NC-SA.

This figure also illustrates the use of bowed lines (like slurs in western notation) beneath note names to show notes grouped *within* a beat. For example, on beats 12 and 13 of the second line there are two notes per beat; and since notes grouped this way are normally sung more or less evenly, we can surmise that each note lasts half a beat. (In western terms, if a beat were represented by a quarter-note or crotchet, these would be equivalent to eighth-notes or quavers.) Furthermore, throughout the notations, bowed lines are also used to connect decorative notes (shown superscripted) to the note they are decorating. In Figure 2.3.2 this can be seen on beat 10 of the first line, where a *kaṇ* (grace note) on Ṡā is grouped in with the main note, N̲i.

From Notation to Performance

Finally, there is the question of how a *bandiś* as notated is deployed in performance—what, actually, do you do with this material; which portions of it do you sing when? Although the notations in this volume are, generally speaking, *prescriptive*, they do not unambiguously specify the order of things. Learning how to integrate the different components of a *bandiś* into a full *k͟hayāl* performance takes time to learn, but here are some initial rules of thumb:

1. Begin your *choṭā k͟hayāl* with the *sthāī* of the *bandiś*. It is customary to repeat the first line—usually once, but possibly several times, depending on context.

2. After the first line, sing the rest of the *sthāī*. The second line can also in principle be repeated, depending on the character of the composition, though this is less common than repeating the first line. Any further lines are usually sung only once.
3. Once you have sung the complete *sthāī*, reprise the first line.
4. The *antarā* follows similar, though not identical, conventions to the *sthāī*. The first line is usually repeated, other lines are less likely to be so. After the final line, you should return directly to the first line of the *sthāī*.
5. You may sing the *antarā* immediately after the *sthāī* or save it for later, while you improvise other material.

The improvisation of material can in fact apply to just about any stage of a performance. This is necessary because, while a *bandiś* usually takes little more than a minute to sing, a *choṭā khayāl* (even a compressed one) should last significantly longer: it is expanded through a variety of devices, such as *bol ālāp*, *tān*s and various forms of *laykārī*. But, throughout, the *bandiś* acts as the glue of the performance—the Hindi term carries the connotation of binding together (Ranade 2006: 71–4). For example, the first line of the *sthāī* usually acts as a refrain between developmental episodes; and the *antarā* may be revisited at a later stage.

The question of how to develop a *khayāl* is one of its key challenges. Ultimately this must be learnt from the guidance of one's teacher and the example of professional performances. While further discussion of this matter is beyond the scope of the present section, I will revisit it later in *Rāgs Around the Clock*, in Section 3.3, entitled 'How Do You Sing a *Choṭā Khayāl*?'. There, through a detailed analysis of VR's performances on *Rāg samay cakra*, I arrive at an expanded set of rubrics for performance, developing the ones sketched out above, and ultimately conjecturing whether all this might point to an implicit performance grammar for khayāl. But that more complex discussion is for later: for now, the above rules of thumb provide a starting point for how to apply the notations of Section 2.5 in practice.

2.4 Terminology Used in the *Rāg* Specifications

The description of each *rāg* in Section 2.5 begins with a technical specification of its key features. Unless otherwise indicated, we derive these thumbnails from Bhatkhande's *Kramik pustak mālikā* (1937), making his version of the information available probably for the first time outside the Marathi and Hindi editions of his opus. Page references to the relevant passages are given for each entry. Below, we provide a gloss on the terminology used:

Āroh–avroh—the ascending and descending form of the scale on which the *rāg* is based. Often this amounts to more than proceeding directly up and down: the representation may also capture the twists and turns of the scale along its path, according to the *rāg*. Bhatkhande uses commas to segment the scale formations, and sometimes plays with typographical spacing—presumably in order to reflect the *rāg*'s grammar. These conventions are reproduced in our own specifications, although exactly what Bhatkhande means by their layout is sometimes opaque.

Pakaḍ—a quintessential phrase of the *rāg*, which captures its key features and syntax. Again, we emulate Bhatkhande's use of commas and spacing in the notation—with the same caveat as above.

Jāti—literally 'class', 'genus' or 'caste'. This is defined by the number of different pitch classes in the ascending and descending scale forms of the *rāg*:

- *Auḍav* = 5-note (pentatonic).
- *Ṣāḍav* = 6-note (hexatonic).
- *Sampūrṇ* = 7-note (heptatonic).

The *jāti* expresses the ascending and descending forms as a pair—for example:

- *Auḍav–ṣāḍav* = five notes ascending, six-notes descending.
- *Sampūrṇ–sampūrṇ* = seven notes ascending and descending.

Ṭhāṭ—literally 'framework' (also used to signify the sitar fret setting for a *rāg*). This identifies the parent scale of the *rāg* according to Bhatkhande's *ṭhāṭ* system, which arranges Hindustani *rāg*s into ten families distinguished by their different permutations of natural, flat and sharp scale degree (see Figure 1.3.1, above).

Vādī—the most salient note in a *rāg*, usually considered in conjunction with *saṃvādī*.

Saṃvādī—the next most salient note, usually four or five steps higher or lower than the *vādī* note. In other words, *vādī* and *saṃvādī* belong to complementary tetrachords of the scale of the *rāg*: one in the lower tetrachord (*pūrvaṅg*), the other in the upper (*uttaraṅg*).

2.5 The *Rāgs*

2.5.1 Rāg Bhairav

Performing time first quarter (*prahar*) of the day.

Āroh (ascending)	***Avroh*** (descending)
S R G M, P D, N Ṡ	Ṡ N D, P M G, R, S

Pakaḍ – S, G, M P, D, P

Jāti – *Sampūrṇ–sampūrṇ* (heptatonic–heptatonic)

Ṭhāṭ – Bhairav

Vādī – Re

Saṃvādī – Dha

(Source: Bhatkhande 1994/1937, II: 162, 164)

Bhairav should be sung at dawn or in the early morning. Its position in the *rāg* time cycle (*samay cakra*) means that it rarely gets heard in live performance, unless perhaps at the end of an all-night concert. But the *rāg* remains alive on recordings and in the early morning practice (*riyāz*) of musicians. It is regarded as one of the major *rāg*s of the Hindustani repertory. Its mood is generally serious and devotional (Bhairav is one of the names of Śiva), though romantic compositions in Bhairav can certainly be found. In keeping with the stillness of twilight, its delivery should be relaxed and unhurried, the tone unforced.

The keys to this *rāg*'s twilight ambience are its śrutis (microtonal tunings) on *komal* Re and *komal* Dha—the flattened 2nd and 6th scale degrees. These most salient tones of the *rāg* (*vādī* and *saṃvādī*) are often executed with a slow *āndolan* (oscillation) which borrows something of the brighter colour of the note above, evoking the hues of dawn. While Re and Dha can be sustained, they rarely stand alone: often decorated by a *kaṇ svar* (grace note) on Ga or Ni respectively, they will typically want to fall to Sā or Pa respectively; or, if approached from below, to continue in ascent.

Motions such as G–M–D are quite common, and can be a poignant way to approach Pa—as at the start of 'Dhana dhana murata', the *bandiś* heard on *Rāg samay cakra* (notated below). Ma, also salient, contributes to the *rāg*'s character and grammar: the *antarā* of 'Dhana dhana murata' sets out from this note and climaxes on it in the higher octave.

Although the *jāti* of Bhairav is commonly *sampūrṇ-sampūrṇ*—seven notes both ascending and descending—in another variant, only five notes are used in ascent: Sā, Ga, Ma, Dha and Ni. This form was sometimes favoured by artists of an older generation. Among the recordings of such doyens, Gangubai Hangal's (1913–2009) rendition of the *vilambit* (slow) composition 'Bālamavā more saīyā̃' (as discussed in Section 4.2) shows how, even in its romantic vein, Bhairav maintains its gravity; after all, early morning is regarded as a time for meditation and prayer.

Performance by Vijay Rajput
(*Rāg samay cakra*, Track 1
https://hdl.handle.net/20.500.12434/8a19270a)

Spoken version of *bandiś* text
(*Rāg samay cakra*, Track 15
https://hdl.handle.net/20.500.12434/7c2a8b8e)

Bandiś: 'Dhana dhana murata'

This is a devotional song to Lord Kr̥ṣṇa, characteristically depicted playing his flute. In this recording, the *antarā* begins with a reference to 'bansī dhuna' ('flute sound'), using the wording of the text taught to VR by his first guru. However, a textual variant 'bansīdhara' ('flute bearer'), is also possible. The former version emphasises the divine sound of Kr̥ṣṇa's flute, the latter his human figure. Sabaraṅg, invoked at the end, is the pen name (*chāp* or *ta<u>kh</u>allus*) of Ustād Bade Ghulam Ali Khan (1902–68), the probable composer of the song.

Sthāī

Dhana dhana murata Kr̥ṣṇa Murāri,	*Blessed the image of Kr̥ṣṇa Murāri,*
sulaksaṇa giridhārī,	*Auspicious the mountain-bearer,*
chavi sundara lāge atī pyārī.	*How beauteous his brilliance, most dear to me.*

Antarā

Bansī dhuna [Bansīdhara] manamohana suhāve,	*Lovely is the flute-bearer, enchanter of the mind,*
bali bali jāũ,	*Again and again I devote myself,*
more mana bhāve, Sabaraṅga dhyāna vicāre.	*Delightful it is to my mind—thereon dwell the thoughts of Sabaraṅg.*

राग भैरव

स्थाई

धन धन मुरत कृष्ण मुरारि

सुलक्षण गरिधारी

छवि सुन्दर लागे, अति प्यारी।

अंतरा

बंसी धुन [बंसीधर] मनमोहन सुहावे

बली बली जाऊँ

मोरे मन भावे, सबरंग ध्यान विचारे॥

Bandiś in Rāg Bhairav: 'Dhana dhana murata'

tīntāl

x				2				o				3			
1	**2**	**3**	**4**	**5**	**6**	**7**	**8**	**9**	**10**	**11**	**12**	**13**	**14**	**15**	**16**

Sthāī

								:G	M	D̲	D̲	P	–	M	M
								Dha-	na	dha-	na	mu-	-	ra-	ta
G	R̲	G	M	ᴳR̲	–	S	– :	S	D̲	–	S	–	S	S	S
Kr̥ṣ-	-	ṇā	mu-	rā-	-	ri,——		su-	la-	-	kṣa-	-	ṇa	gi-	ri-
R̲	–	S	–	S	R̲	G	M	P	P	P	D̲	Ṡ	– ᴺ	D̲	P
dhā-	-	ri,——		cha-	vi	sun-	-	da-	ra	lā-	-	ge——		a-	tī
PD̲	NṠ	ṠṘ̲	ṠN	D̲N	D̲P	MG	M								
pyā-	-	-	-	-	-	rī.——									

Antarā

								:M	–	M	–	P	P	D̲	D̲
								Ban-	-	sī——		dhu-	na	ma-	na-
								[Ban	-	sī-	-	dha-	ra]		
P	D̲	Ṡ	N	Ṡ	–	Ṡ	– :	Ṡ	Ṙ̲	Ṁ	Ġ	Ṙ̲	–	Ṡ	–
mo-	ha-	na	su-	hā-	-	ve,——		ba-	li	ba-	li	jā-	-	ũ——	
N	N	Ṡ	N	D̲	–	P	–	M	M	G	M	P	–	P	P
mo-	re	ma-	na	bhā-	-	ve,——		Sa-	ba-	raṅ-	ga	dhyā	-	na	vi-
PD̲	NṠ	ṠṘ̲	ṠN	D̲N	D̲P	MG	M								
cā-	-	-	-	-	-	re.——									

2.5.2 Rāg Toḍī

Performing time second quarter (*prahar*) of the day.

Āroh (ascending)	***Avroh*** (descending)
S, R̲ G̲, Ḿ P, D̲, N Ṡ	Ṡ N D̲ P, Ḿ G̲, R̲, S

Pakaḍ – Ḍ̲, Ṇ S, R̲, G̲, R̲, S, Ḿ, G̲, R̲ G̲, R̲ S

Jāti – *Sampūrṇ–sampūrṇ* (heptatonic–heptatonic)

Ṭhāṭ – Toḍī

Vādī – D̲h̲a̲

Saṃvādī – G̲a̲

(Source: Bhatkhande 1994/1937, II: 429–30)

Toḍī is an important *rāg* in the Hindustani classical repertoire. It is also known as Miyā̃ kī Toḍī—an attribution to the legendary singer Miyā̃ Tānsen (ca. 1500–89)—although Bhatkhande uses the shorter title. Sung or played in the second phase of the morning, Toḍī draws from the *karuṇ ras*, which is noted for its qualities of pathos, sadness and compassion. Possessing greater gravity than its close relative Gujarī Toḍī, this *rāg* expands slowly in an *ālāp* or *baṛā k̲h̲ayāl*; in a fast-moving *choṭā k̲h̲ayāl* like the one presented here the mood can be lighter and more playful.

All the flattened notes—R̲e̲, G̲a̲ and D̲h̲a̲—should be rendered *very* flat (*ati komal*). Pa needs subtle handling: the beauty and significance of this *svar* should be in inverse proportion to its limited frequency. When Pa does appear, it most usually features in descent, approached by a subtle and carefully timed glide from sustained D̲h̲a̲, probably prefigured by Ni.

In rendering Miyā̃ kī Toḍī, the performer must take care not to create confusion with *rāgs* based on the same scale, such as Multānī or Gujarī Toḍī. Whereas in Multānī, D̲h̲a̲ is only used as a passing note, in Miyā̃ kī Toḍī, this note assumes considerable prominence as the *vādī* note—often in association with Ni. What most obviously distinguishes Miyā̃ kī Toḍī from Gujarī Toḍī is the presence of Pa; and in Miyā̃ kī Toḍī, G̲a̲ rather than R̲e̲ is prominent. (The prominence of R̲e̲ and D̲h̲a̲ in Gujarī Toḍī gives it similar properties to the evening *rāg* Mārvā, causing some to refer to the former as 'subah kā Mārvā'—'morning Mārvā'.)

Although Bhatkhande theoretically includes Pa in his notation of the ascending scale of Toḍī (see the *rāg* specification above), in practice, any ascent to this note would not normally continue to Dha, but would rather reverse direction. In an old form of melodic construction, Pa can form part of an upward motion to D̲h̲a̲ if immediately quitted by descent—for example, Ḿ–P–D̲–Ḿ–G̲—, R̲–G̲–R̲–S.

Performance by Vijay Rajput
(*Rāg samay cakra*, Track 2
https://hdl.handle.net/20.500.12434/21cf4b2b)

Spoken version of *bandiś* text
(*Rāg samay cakra*, Track 16
https://hdl.handle.net/20.500.12434/7b86b9eb)

Bandiś: 'Laṅgara kā̃karīyā'

This famous Toḍī composition is a staple of the khayāl repertoire, and is a perfect example of the 'amorous hassling' song type—to use du Perron's nomenclature (Magriel and du Perron 2013, I: 137–9). The text might refer to a courting practice in which the boy tries to attract the girl's attention by throwing small pebbles at her. Or perhaps he is aiming for the pitcher of water she is carrying on her head—a common image in such songs—and she fears the pebbles will bounce off and hurt her. The girl's anxious reference to her ever-suspicious female in-laws is also typical. The archetypal pair in such stories of amorous teasing is of course Rādhā and Kr̥ṣṇa.

This *bandiś* is usually rendered as a *drut* (fast) *khayāl*, though it might be sung in a not-too slow *madhya lay* (medium tempo). VR's performance here focuses on the numerous ways in which the first line of the *sthāī* and *antarā* can be varied. This brings up the question of which version, if any, is the definitive form of the melody and which are the variants. The song notation attempts to show a possible 'normative' version, but its purpose is, as ever, primarily heuristic.

Sthāī	
Laṅgara kā̃karīyā jīna māro,	*Shameless boy! Don't throw these pebbles at me,*
more aṅgavā laga jāve [jāe].	*They'll hit my body.*
Antarā	
Suna pave morī sāsa nanandīyā.	*My mother-in-law and sister-in-law will hear,*
Dorī dorī ghara āve.	*Quickly, come home.*

राग तोडी

स्थाई

लंगर कॉंकरीया जीन मारो

मोरे अंगवा लग जावे [जाए]।

अंतरा

सुन पावे मोरी सास ननंदीया

दोरी दोरी घर आवे॥

Bandiś in Rāg Toḍī: 'Laṅgar kã̄karīya'

tīntāl

|x				|2				|o				|3				|
1	**2**	**3**	**4**	**5**	**6**	**7**	**8**	**9**	**10**	**11**	**12**	**13**	**14**	**15**	**16**	
Sthāī																
												|:	Ḿ	G	Ḿ	|
													Laṅ -	ga -	ra	
★																
|D	–	–	N	|D	P	P	P	|Ḿ	P	ḾG	–	:|	G	R	S	|
kã̄ -	-	-	ka -	rī -	yā	jī -	na	mā -	-	ro,	—		mo -	-	re	
|S	S	D	–	|Ḿ	–	D	N	|D—	Ḿ	–	GR	|G	R	S	S	|(→★)
aṅ -	ga -	vā	—	—	—	la -	ga	jā -	-	-	ve.	—	Laṅ -	ga -	ra	
								[jā -	-	-	e.]	—				
Antarā																
|: Ḿ	Ḿ	^{D}G	–	|Ḿ	–	D	D	|Ṡ	–	Ṡ	Ṡ	|N	Ṙ	Ṡ	–	:|
Su -	na	pa -	-	ve	—	mo -	rī	sā -	-	sa	na -	nan -	dī -	yā.	—	
|D	Ġ	Ṙ	Ṡ	|–	Ṡ	N	Ṡ	|N	D	N	D	|P	Ḿ	G	Ḿ	|(→★)
Do -	-	rī	do -	-	rī	gha -	ra	ā	-	-	ve.	—	Laṅ -	ga -	ra	

2.5.3 Rāg Śuddh Sāraṅg

Performing time second quarter (*prahar*) of the day.

Āroh (ascending)	***Avroh*** (descending)
S R MR R Ḿ P N Ṡ	Ṡ N ^{D}P M R S

Pakaḍ – S, RMR, P, ḾPDḾP, MRSṆ, ṆḌSṆRS

(Source: VR)

Jāti – *Auḍav–ṣāḍav* (pentatonic–hexatonic)

Ṭhāṭ – Kāfī

Vādī – Re

Saṃvādī – Pa

(Source: Bhatkhande 1993/1937, VI: 155)

While Bhatkhande states that Śuddh Sāraṅg may have both forms of Ni and both forms of Ma, many performers employ only śuddh Ni, while indeed using both *suddh* and *tivra* Ma. It is this latter version that VR adopts on *Rāg samay cakra*, and this is reflected in his specification above for the *āroh–avroh* and *pakaḍ*.

This melodious *rāg* is closely related to other *rāg*s in the Sāraṅg *aṅg* (group). As in Brindābanī Sāraṅg, *śuddh* Ma is frequently heard falling to Re; but in Śuddh Sāraṅg this is complemented by *tivra* Ma which tends towards Pa. Nonetheless, the latter should not be overstated, otherwise the *rāg* will veer towards its relative, Śyām Kalyāṇ.

Dha needs careful handling. It should not be sustained, but rather woven inconspicuously into melodic figures such as ṆḌSṆ, or N^{D}P, or PḾDP—all of which can be heard in the *bandiś* sung here. A characteristic melodic pathway (or *calan*) once Pa is reached, is ḾPN–, NṠ, ṠN^{D}P—DḾPM\R–, RḾPM\R–, MR^{S}Ṇ, ṆḌSṆRS—.

Performance by Vijay Rajput
(*Rāg samay cakra*, Track 3
https://hdl.handle.net/20.500.12434/35382873)

Spoken version of *bandiś* text
(*Rāg samay cakra*, Track 17
https://hdl.handle.net/20.500.12434/a2a052cc)

Bandiś: 'Aba morī bāta'

This composition may originate from Ustād Fayaz Khan (1886–1950) of the Agra *gharānā*—as suggested by the inclusion of his pen name, Prem Pīyā, at the start of the *antarā*. VR learnt it from Prof. Manjusree Tyagi, his one-time mentor.

There are different ways of understanding who is being addressed in the song. In the *sthāī* (first part) the protagonist implores her beloved, while in the *antarā* (second part) she speaks to herself or to a companion, expressing her frustration at the lack of a response.

In this recording, VR experiments with varied repetition of the different lines of the *bandiś*, as well as with the rhythmic placing and decoration of notes. So this is a good example of how a musical realisation may part company from the corresponding notation—or at least from the form of notation used here, which is intended more to communicate the gist of a *bandiś* than to record its potentially inexhaustible nuances in performance.

What is more structural, however, is the way the metre of the composition cuts liltingly across the 4x4 beat *tīntāl* structure. For example, the five-beat figure, 'Aba mori' that opens the song, can be divided into 2+3 beats; while the fourfold repetition of 'vārī', at the end of the *sthāī*, and 'hārī', at the end of the *antarā*, yields a 3+3+3+2 pattern.

Sthāī

Aba morī bāta mānale pīharavā,	*My beloved, now believe what I say,*
jāū̃ tope vārī vārī vārī vārī.	*I sacrifice myself for you, over and over again.*

Antarā

Prema pīyā hama se nahī̃ bolata,	*My loved one makes no answer,*
binatī karata mẽ to hārī hārī hārī hārī.	*And I am wholly spent, exhausted with entreating.*

राग शुद्ध सारंग

स्थाई

अब मोरी बात मानले पीहरवा

जाऊँ तोपे वारी वारी वारी वारी।

अंतरा

प्रेम पीया हम से नहीं बोलत

बिनती करत में तो हारी हारी हारी हारी॥

Bandiś in Rāg Śuddh Sāraṅg: 'Aba morī bata'

tīntāl

x				2				o				3			
1	2	3	4	5	6	7	8	9	10	11	12	13	14	15	16

Sthāī

M |R Ṇ – S |
A - ba mo - - rī

(1st time)

|: Ṇ – – – |Ṇ – Ḍ S – Ṇ |R – S M |R Ṇ – S :|
bā - - - - (bā) - - - - - - ta A - ba mo - - rī

(2nd time)

|R – S R |Ḿ , P – P
- - ta mā - na - le ——— pī - |

|NṠ ṘṠ N – D |PḾP – ḾP DP |M – ⟍ R Ḿ |P NṠ Ṙ Ṡ |
ha - - ra - - - - - - vā, ——— jā - ũ̃ to - - pe

|P Ṡ N Ḿ |– P R M |R Ṇ S
vā - - rī vā - - ri vā - - rī vā - rī.

Antarā

|: P ⟋ Ṡ Ṡ Ṡ |Ṡ – Ṡ Ṡ |
Pre - - ma pī - yā ——— ha - ma

|ṠḾ RḾ Ṙ ⟍ Ṡ |NṠ ṘṠ N ᴰP :| RḾ Ḿ Ḿ |Ḿ P Ḿ P |
se ——— na - hĩ̃ bo - - la - ta, bi-na- tī ka - ra - ta mẽ to

|PN Ṡ N Ḿ |– P R M |R Ṇ S
hā - - rī hā - - rī - rī hā - rī.

2.5.4 Rāg Brindābanī Sāraṅg

Performing time noontime (*madhyan*).

Āroh (ascending)	***Avroh*** (descending)
Ṇ S, R, MP, N Ṡ	Ṡ N̲P, M R, S

Pakaḍ – Ṇ SR, MR, PMR, S

Jāti – *Auḍav–auḍav* (pentatonic–pentatonic)

Ṭhāṭ – Kāfī

Vādī – Re

Saṃvādī – Pa

(Source: Bhatkhande 1995/1937, III: 496)

This *rāg* is also known as Vṛindābanī Sāraṅg, along with other variants of its name (Bhatkhande, for example, has Bindrābanī Sāraṅg). These all invoke the village of Vrindavan—in the present day, a town in Uttar Pradesh—where the historical Kṛṣṇa is said to have spent his childhood.

Brindābanī Sāraṅg is considered by some to be the definitive representative of the Sāraṅg group (*aṅg*). Among this *rāg*'s distinguishing features are its pentatonic *jāti*, which is differently configured in *āroh* and *avroh*: the ascending scale begins on *suddh* Ni, while its descending counterpart incorporates *komal* Ni.

Perhaps most distinctive of all is Re, the *vādī* tone, which is very often approached tenderly from above via Ma. This intimate connection is mirrored by a similar affinity between Pa and N̲i̲.

Bhatkhande discusses the relation of Brindābanī Sāraṅg to other members of the Sāraṅg *aṅg*, in particular Madhma Sāraṅg, distinguished by its more exclusive focus on *suddh* Ni. By contrast, in Brindābanī Sāraṅg, *suddh* and *komal* Ni have equal status. Joep Bor et al. (1999: 52) remind us that Brindābanī Sāraṅg is generally treated as a light *rāg*, with similarities to Megh (also included in this collection) and Deś.

Performance by Vijay Rajput
(*Rāg samay cakra*, Track 4
https://hdl.handle.net/20.500.12434/6f30c285)

Spoken version of *bandiś* text
(*Rāg samay cakra*, Track 18
https://hdl.handle.net/20.500.12434/2ee70bab)

Bandiś: 'Raṅga le manavā'

This is a romantic song for the hot noontime and early afternoon, in which the protagonist, sitting under the flowering mango tree, tells joyfully of the colours and beauty of the scene. It is most appropriately rendered in a leisurely *madhya lay tīntāl.*

Like its Śuddh Sāraṅg forebear, this Brindābanī Sāraṅg *bandiś* nicely illustrates the possibilities of cross-metrical play between text and *tāl.* In the *sthāī,* the opening line, 'Raṅga le manavā bānā', comprises 2+4+4+6 beats; while the second line, 'jhulata bora jhukī', creates a 3+3+2 beat lilt; and the third line, 'koyala saṅga alī umaṅga', creates a 3+3+3+3 beat feel.

Sthāī

Raṅga le manavā bānā,	*Take delight, O my mind, of this lustrous sight,*
jhulata bora jhukī ambuvā kī ḍaliyā,	*The blossom swaying on the bending branch of the mango tree,*
koyala saṅga alī umaṅga nisa.	*Gladdening the cuckoo and the bee alike.*

Antarā

Chāī dopaharī caṛho [caḍhī] sunharī,	*Noon, that now has spread all around,*
kalaśa līai nīja rāja pratāpī.	*Went up with his golden vessel to the glory and brilliance of his own kingdom.*
Nisa ranga kī le ḍubakī hararaṅga le.	*Plunge and bathe yourself in the colour and passion of Hari!*

राग ब्रिंदाबनी सारंग

स्थाई

रंग ले मनवा बाना

झुलत बोर झुकी अंबुवा की डलिया

कोयल संग अली उमंग निस।

अंतरा

छाई दोपहरी चढ़ो [वढी] सुनहरी

कलश लीऐ नीज राज प्रतापी

निस रंग की ले डुबकी हररंग ले॥

Bandiś in Rāg Brindābanī Sāraṅg: 'Raṅga le manavā'

tīntāl

|x 1 2 3 4 |2 5 6 7 8 |o 9 10 11 12 |3 13 14 15 16 |

Sthāī

Ṇ S ★|: R M P N̲ |PN̲ PM RS ṆS |
Raṅ - ga le ——— ma - nu - vā ———

|R – – Ṇ |S – Ṇ S : |
bā - - - - nā, ——— Raṅ - ga
(1st time)

(2nd time)
|S – – |: Ṇ Ṇ Ṇ S |– S Ṇ S |
nā, ——— jhu - la - ta bo - - ra jhu - kī

|R M R M |P N̲ M — P : |P Ṡ N Ṡ |– Ṡ P N̲ |
am - bu - va kī ḍa - li - yā, ——— ko - ya - la saṅ - - ga a - lī

|P N̲ – N̲ |PN̲ PM RS ṆS |(→★)
u - maṅ - - ga nī - sa. Raṅ - ga

Antarā

|: M M M |P P N – |
Chā - ī do - pa - ha - rī ———

|N –Ṡ – Ṙ |N – Ṡ – : |N N N N |Ṡ – Ṡ Ṡ |
ca - - ṛho ——— sun - ha - - rī, ——— ka - la - śa lī - ai ——— nī - ja
[ca - - ḍhī]

|PN ṠṘ NṠ Ṡ |N̲ — P P |P Ṡ N Ṡ |Ṡ — P N̲ |
rā - - ja pra - tā - - - pī. Nī - sa raṅ - ga kī ——— le ———

|P N̲ N̲ – |PN̲ PM RS ṆS |(→★)
ḍu - ba - kī ——— ha - ra - raṅ - ga - [le.]

2.5.5 Rāg Bhīmpalāsī

Performing time third quarter (*prahar*) of the day.

Āroh (ascending)	***Avroh*** (descending)
N S G M, P, N Ṡ	Ṡ N D P M, G R S

Pakaḍ – N S M, MG, PM, G, MGRS

Jāti – *Auḍav–sampūrṇ* (pentatonic–heptatonic)

Ṭhāṭ – Kāfī

Vādī – Ma

Saṃvādī – Sā

(Source: Bhatkhande 1995/1937, V: 561–2)

While Bhīmpalāsī can be rendered at all tempi—from the slowest *baṛa khayāl* to the fastest *tarānā*—its movements are characteristically languid, matching the heat of the early afternoon. Most characteristic is the slow *mīṇḍ* (glide) from Ma to Ga. Ni especially contributes to this *rāg*'s association with the *karuṇ ras*—with its aesthetic of poignancy, compassion and sadness.

As *vādī*, Ma is officially one of the most prominent notes in this *rāg*. Pa is also important even though it should not be overly sustained, which would risk confusion with Rāg Dhanāśrī. Among Bhīmpalāsī's rarely mentioned subtleties is the possibility that *komal* Ni be inflected very slightly sharper when approached from above and very slightly flatter when approached from below. In *avroh*, Ni may move to Dha via a *kaṇ svar* (grace note) on Pa—as in ṠN^{P}DP. Similarly, in the lower tetrachord, Ga may move to Re via a *kaṇ svar* on Sā—as in M\G^{S}RS.

Similar *rāg*s with which Bhīmpalāsī should not be confused include Dhānī (same scale but with no Re or Dha), Patdīp (similar flavour but with *suddh* Ni), and Bāgeśrī (same scale but SGMDNṠ in *āroh*, greater prominence of Dha, and only occasional, specialised use of Pa).

Performance by Vijay Rajput
(*Rāg samay cakra*, Track 5
https://hdl.handle.net/20.500.12434/84443350)

Spoken version of *bandiś* text
(*Rāg samay cakra*, Track 19
https://hdl.handle.net/20.500.12434/d9f0d030)

Bandiś: 'Hamarī kahī mitavā'

This song is a composition by Pandit Vinaychandra Modgal (1918–95), who was Principal of the Gandharva Mahavidyalaya, New Delhi at the time VR studied there. The song bears the pathos of the *karuṇ ras*: the protagonist implores her lover not to leave her side. In the *antarā*, the image of the beloved in a far-away place is another common trope of khayāl songs.

Sthāī

Hamarī kahī mitavā māna le,	*Consider well my words, dear friend,*
bīnatī karata tore paīyā parata hū̃.	*In humble submission I fall at your feet.*

Antarā

Jina jāvo bidesa bālamavā.	*Do not go abroad, O my beloved.*
Tuma bina maikā kala nā parata hai.	*Without you, there is no peace for me.*
Binatī karata tore paīyā parata hū̃.	*In humble submission I fall at your feet.*

राग भीमपलासी

स्थाई

हमरी कही मितवा मान ले

बिनती करत तोरे पईया परत हूँ।

अंतरा

जिन जावो बिदेस बालमवा

तुम बिन मैका कल ना परत है

बिनती करत तोरे पईया परत हूँ॥

Bandiś in Rāg Bhimpalāsī: 'Hamarī kahī mitavā'

tīntāl

x				2				o				3			
1	**2**	**3**	**4**	**5**	**6**	**7**	**8**	**9**	**10**	**11**	**12**	**13**	**14**	**15**	**16**

Sthāī

1	2	3	4	5	6	7	8	9	10	11	12	13	14	15	16
								|:Ṉ	D	P	D	|M	P	G̱	M |
								Ha-	ma-	rī	ka-	hī———		mi-	ta-
|P	–	–	M͜G̱	|M—G̱		R	S :|		G̱ M	P	ᴾM	|G̱	R	Ṉ̣	S |
vā———			ma-	-	na	le,	———		bī-na-tī		ka-	ra-	ta	to-	re
|M	–	M	M	|M	P	G̱	M |								
paī-	-	yā	pa-	ra-	ta	hũ.	———								

Antarā

1	2	3	4	5	6	7	8	9	10	11	12	13	14	15	16
								|:	P	P	P͜Ṉ	|P͜M	G̱	–	M |
									Ji-	na	jā-	-	vo———		bi-
|P	–	Ṉ	Ṉ	|Ṡ	Ṡ	Ṡ	– :|	P	Ṉ	Ṡ	Ġ̱	|Ṙ	–	Ṡ	– |
de-	-	sa	bā-	la-	ma-	vā.———		Tu-	ma	bi-	na	mai-	-	kā———	
|Ṉ	Ṉ	Ṡ	Ṉ	|D	D	P	– |		G̱ M	P	M	|G̱	R	Ṉ̣	S |
ka-	la	nā	pa-	ra-	ta	hai.———			Bī-na-tī		ka-	ra-	ta	to-	re
|M	–	M	M	|M	P	G̱	M |								
paī-	-	yā	pa-	ra-	ta	hũ.	———								

2.5.6 Rāg Multānī

Performing time fourth quarter (*prahar*) of the day.

Āroh (ascending)	***Avroh*** (descending)
Ṇ S, G̲ Ḿ P, N Ṡ	Ṡ N D̲ P, Ḿ G̲, R̲ S

Pakaḍ – Ṇ S, Ḿ G̲, P G̲, R̲ S

Jāti – *Auḍav–sampūrṇ* (pentatonic–heptatonic)

Ṭhāṭ – Toḍī

Vādī – Pa

Saṃvādī – Sā

(Source: Bhatkhande 1991/1937, IV: 171–2)

Bhatkhande suggests that Multānī occupies a transitional place within the diurnal cycle of *rāg*s. It is a *parmel-praveśak rāg*, meaning that it introduces a new *ṭhāṭ* (group of *rāg*s). Leading us away from the Kāfī *ṭhāṭ*—which includes *rāg*s such as Bhīmpalāsī with flat Ga and Ni—Multānī looks towards the Pūrvī *ṭhāṭ*—in which *rāg*s such as Pūriyā Dhanāśrī take flattened Re and Dha, and sharpened Ma. Multānī itself, belonging to the Toḍī *ṭhāṭ*, sits between those other *ṭhāṭ*s and mediates their different qualities. With flattened Ga and Dha, and sharpened Ma, it has properties of both a late afternoon and a twilight (*sāndhi prakaś*) *rāg*. These points, then, provide support for theories of *rāg* performing-time (*samay*) based on scale construction; indeed they are cited by Nazir Jairazbhoy (1971: 63–4) in his own development of Bhatkhande's time theory.

While Multānī shares a scale with Rāg Toḍī, it has a different grammar, which foregrounds Sā, Pa and Ni, and uses R̲e̲ and D̲h̲a̲ only discreetly. In descending patterns, R̲e̲ is commonly approached elliptically from below via a *kaṇ svar* (grace note) on Sā. And G̲a̲ often bears the shadow of *tivra* Ma—hence ḾG̲ is a common figure. These various properties might typically be joined together in a phrase such as P–$^{\text{D̲PḾP}}$Ḿ\G̲^{S}R̲^{Ṇ}S–, which encapsulates Multānī's melodious, flowing character. Its mood is romantic compared with the pathos of Toḍī; but this does not diminish its status as an important *rāg* in the k̲h̲ayāl repertory.

Performance by Vijay Rajput
(*Rāg samay cakra*, Track 6
https://hdl.handle.net/20.500.12434/f49a67f5)

Spoken version of *bandiś* text
(*Rāg samay cakra*, Track 20
https://hdl.handle.net/20.500.12434/25212f2e)

Bandiś: 'Runaka jhunaka'

While technically a *drut khayāl*, this *bandiś* is best sung not too quickly. The scene depicted appears in a number of khayāl compositions (see, for example, Pūriyā Dhanāśrī (Section 2.5.7) in this collection). The female protagonist, discreetly approaching the bed of her loved one, fears that the tinkling of the bells on her anklet and belt might give the game away to her mother- and sister-in-law; perhaps this is as much a topic for the sultry heat of the deep afternoon as it is for the quiet of the night.

Sthāī	
Runaka jhunaka morī pāyala bāje,	*My anklets jingle-jangled,*
bichuā chuma chuma chananana sāje.	*Chum chananana went my toe rings.*
Antarā	
Saija caṛhata morī jhāñjhara hālī,	*I mounted the bed, my anklets shook and trembled,*
sāsa nananda kī lāja.	*My mother-in-law and sister-in-law close by, I felt coy.*

राग मुलतानी

स्थाई

रुनक झुनक मोरी पायल बाजे

बिछुआ छुम छुम छननन साजे।

अंतरा

सैज चढ़त मोरि झांझर हाली

सास ननंद की लाज॥

Bandiś in Rāg Multānī: 'Runaka jhunaka'

tīntāl

x				2				o				3			
1	**2**	**3**	**4**	**5**	**6**	**7**	**8**	**9**	**10**	**11**	**12**	**13**	**14**	**15**	**16**

Sthāī

								:P	Ḿ	G̲	Ḿ	G̲	R̲	S	S
								Ru -	na -	ka	jhu -	na -	ka	mo -	rī
N̲	S	G̲	Ḿ	P	–	Ḿ	G̲ :	G̲	Ḿ	P	N	Ṡ	N	D̲	P
pā -	-	ya -	la	bā -	-	je,	———	bi -	chu -	ā	———	chu -	ma	chu -	ma
Ḿ	Ḿ	P	D̲	P	–	Ḿ	G̲								
cha -	na -	na -	na	sā -	-	je.	———								

Antarā

								:Ḿ	–	P	D̲	P	ḾG̲	Ḿ	P
								Sai -	-	ja	caṛ -	ha -	ta	mo -	rī
N	–	Ṡ	N	Ṡ	–	Ṡ	– :	P	N	Ṡ	Ġ	Ṙ	Ṙ	Ṡ	–
jhañ -	-	jha -	ra	hā -	-	lī,	———	sā -	-	sa	na -	nan -	da	kī	———
P	N	Ṡ	N	D̲	P	Ḿ	G̲								
lā -	-	-	-	-	-	-	ja.								

2.5.7 Rāg Pūriyā Dhanāśrī

Performing time evening twilight (*sandhyākāl*).

Āroh (ascending)	***Avroh*** (descending)
Ṇ R̲ GḾP, D̲P, NṠ	Ṙ̲ ND̲P, ḾG, Ḿ R̲ G, R̲S

Pakaḍ: – ṆR̲G, ḾP, D̲P, Ḿ G, Ḿ R̲G, D̲ ḾG, R̲S

Jāti – *Auḍav–sampūrṇ* (pentatonic–heptatonic)

Ṭhāṭ – Purvī

Vādī – Pa

Saṃvādī – R̲e̲

(Source: Bhatkhande 1991/1937, IV: 341–2)

Pūriyā Dhanāśrī is an early evening *rāg*, which Bhatkhande indicates should be sung at the time known as *sandhyākāl*: the transition between day and night; a time when lamps are lit and prayers are said. VR recounts how his one-time teacher, Pandit M.G. Deshpande similarly numbered Pūriyā Dhanāśrī among the *sandhi prakaś* (twilight) *rāg*s. Prakash Vishwanath Ringe and Vishwajeet Vishwanath Ringe (n.d.: https://www.tanarang.com/english/puriya-dhanashri_eng.htm) assign it to the fourth quarter (*prahar*) of the day.

A related *rāg* is Pūrvī. But Bhatkhande reminds us that while Pūrvī admits both forms of Ma, Puriyā Dhanāśrī has only *tivra* Ma. The latter *rāg*'s characteristic figure PḾGḾR̲G links this *svar* to the *vādī* and *saṃvādī* notes Pa and R̲e̲. Further characteristic movements are GḾD̲NṠ and Ṙ̲ND̲P.

The status of Pa as *vadī* is confirmed by its obvious prominence in performance—for instance, this pitch initiates both the first and second lines of the *bandiś* 'Pā̃yalīyā jhanakāra', sung here. But Bhatkhande's identification of R̲e̲ as *saṃvādī* is more ambiguous, given that this note is never dwelled on. It is likely that his choice here is theoretically driven, since *vadī* and *saṃvādī* should be four or five notes apart. Conversely, Ringe and Ringe cite Sā as *saṃvādī*. Either way, these tones further distinguish Pūriyā Dhanāśrī from Pūrvī, where Ga and Ni are the *vadī* and *saṃvādī*.

> Performance by Vijay Rajput
> (*Rāg samay cakra*, Track 7
> https://hdl.handle.net/20.500.12434/97cee070)

> Spoken version of *bandiś* text
> (*Rāg samay cakra*, Track 21
> https://hdl.handle.net/20.500.12434/3a923b5a)

Bandiś: 'Pā̃yalīyā jhanakāra'

This famous song depicts a canonical scene of Braj Bhāṣā poetry: a young woman who fears that the jingling of her ankle bells will wake her mother- and sister-in-law as she steals away to her lover in the night. As with all good *bandiś*es, this one eloquently captures the key melodic features of the *rāg* (as described above), offering a good guide to its *rūp* or structure. VR's rendition here illustrates the many ways in which the opening lines of the *sthāī* and *antarā* can be varied in performance.

Sthāī	
Pā̃yalīyā jhanakāra morī,	*My ankle bells are ringing,*
jhanana jhanana bāje jhanakārī.	*Jingle-jangle, jingle-jangle, they ring.*
Antarā	
Pīyā samajhāū̃ samajhata nāhī̃,	*If I explain to my beloved, he doesn't understand,*
sāsa nananda morī degī gārī.	*My mother-in-law and sister-in-law will scold me.*

राग पूरिया धनाश्री

स्थाई

पाँयलीया झनकार मोरी

झनन झनन बाजे झनकारी।

अंतरा

पीया समझाऊँ समझत नाहीं

सास ननंद मोरी देगी गारी।।

Bandiś in Rāg Pūriyā Dhanāśrī: 'Pā̃yalīyā jhanakāra'

tīntāl

x				2				o				3			
1	**2**	**3**	**4**	**5**	**6**	**7**	**8**	**9**	**10**	**11**	**12**	**13**	**14**	**15**	**16**

Sthāī

1	2	3	4	5	6	7	8	9	10	11	12	13	14	15	16
								|: P	–	Ḿ	G	|Ḿ	D̲	N	D̲ |
								Pā̃-	-	ya -	lī -	yā ———		jha -	na -
|N	——	D̲ —	P	|–	Ḿ	D̲	P :	|P	P	Ḿ	G	|Ḿ	R̲	G	– |
kā -	-	-	ra ———		mo -	-	rī,	jha -	na -	na	jha -	na -	na	bā -	-
|G	R̲	G	Ḿ	|G	R̲	S	S |								
je ———		jha -	na -	kā -	-	-	rī.								

Antarā

1	2	3	4	5	6	7	8	9	10	11	12	13	14	15	16
								|: Ḿ	Ḿ	G	G	|Ḿ	–	D̲	– |
								Pī -	yā	sa -	ma -	jhā -	-	ū̃ ———	
|Ṡ	Ṡ	Ṡ	Ṡ	|N	Ṙ̲	Ṡ	Ṡ :	|D̲	–	N	Ṙ̲	|N	D̲	P	P |
sa -	ma -	jha -	ta	na -	-	-	hī̃,	sā -	-	sa	na -	nan -	da	mo -	rī
|P	–	Ḿ	G	|GḾ	PḾ	GR̲	S |								
de -	-	-	gī	gā -	-	-	rī.								

2.5.8 Rāg Bhūpālī

Performing time first quarter (*prahar*) of the night.

Āroh (ascending)	***Avroh*** (descending)
S R G P, D, Ṡ	Ṡ, D P, G, R, S

Pakaḍ – S, R, S Ḍ, S R G, P G, D P G, R, S

Jāti – *Auḍav–auḍav* (pentatonic–pentatonic)

Ṭhāṭ - Kalyāṇ

Vādī - Ga

Saṃvādī - Dha

(Source: Bhatkhande 1995/1937, III: 23)

Bhūpālī is found across a range of musical idioms—from folk music and light classical genres such as ṭhumrī, through khayāl (as here), to more heavyweight styles such as dhamār and dhrupad. So, although this seemingly simple pentatonic *rāg* is well suited to beginners, it can also be rendered expansively and with gravity by experienced performers.

While Ga and Dha are the *vādī* and *saṃvādī* notes, Sā and Pa may also be sustained. Re can sometimes be savoured on its way to other notes, but should not be overly dwelled on.

Bhūpālī is associated with the śānt *ras* (Sanskrit: śāntam *rasa*) and its feelings of peace and tranquillity. Related *rāgs* include Deśkār, a morning *rāg* with the same *āroh* and *avroh* but with Dha rather than Ga as the *vādī* note, and greater emphasis on the upper tetrachord.

Performance by Vijay Rajput
(*Rāg samay cakra*, Track 8
https://hdl.handle.net/20.500.12434/b22b83a4)

Spoken version of *bandiś* text
(*Rāg samay cakra*, Track 22
https://hdl.handle.net/20.500.12434/641e5eab)

Bandiś: 'Gāīye Gaṇapatī'

The text of this *bandiś* is by the devotional poet and Hindu saint, Goswami Tulsidas. Commentators variously give his birth date as 1497, 1511, 1532 and 1554; most agree he died in or around 1623. The words of 'Gāīye Gaṇapatī' come from the beginning of his poem *Vinay-Patrikā* ('Letter of Petition'), and are part of a hymn to the elephant-headed god, Gaṇeś (Ganesh).

The language here is in a different poetic vein from the other songs in *Rāgs Around the Clock*. Tulsidas wrote primarily in the Avadhī and Braj languages—eastern and western dialects of Hindi respectively. The version of the song text given below is partly based on a Hindi edition of the *Vinay-Patrikā* edited by Hanuman Prasad Pohar (Tulsidas 2015).

VR was taught this *bandiś* by Pandit M.G. Deshpande while his student at the Gandharva Mahavidyalaya, New Delhi. Numerous other versions of it can readily be found online. The text may also be heard sung to different melodies in other *rāg*s, such as Mārvā, Hansadhvanī and Yaman, often in the lighter style of a bhajan.

Sthāī	
Gāīye Gaṇapatī jag vandanā.	*Sing praise to Gaṇpatī [Gaṇeś] to whom the whole world prays.*
Śaṅkara sumana [suvana] Bhavānī nandana.	*The brilliance of Śaṅkar [Śiva], the son of Bhavānī [Pārvatī].*
Antarā	
Siddhī sadana, gaja vadana, vināyaka.	*The embodiment of spiritual accomplishment, elephant-faced, destroyer of obstacles.*
Kr̥pā sindhu, sundara, saba dāyaka [lāyaka].	*Compassion dwells in him, handsome one, helper of all.*

(Translation adapted by DC from a word-to-word translation in Rasikas 2008.)

राग भूपाली

स्थाई

गाईये गणपती जग वंदना।

शंकर सुमन [सुवन] भवानी नंदन ॥

अंतरा

सिद्धी सदन, गज वदन, विनायक।

कृपा सिन्धु, सुन्दर, सव दायक [लायक]॥

Bandiś in Rāg Bhūpālī: 'Gāīye Gaṇapatī'

tīntāl

x				2				o				3			
1	**2**	**3**	**4**	**5**	**6**	**7**	**8**	**9**	**10**	**11**	**12**	**13**	**14**	**15**	**16**

Sthāī

								: Ṡ	–	D	P	G	R	S	R
								Gā -	-	ī -	ye	Ga -	ṇa -	pa -	tī
G	G	G	P	R	G	–	– :	G	–	G	R	G	P	D	Ṡ
ja -	ga	van -	-	da -	nā. ———			Śaṅ -	-	ka -	ra	su -	ma -	na	Bha -
												[su -	va -	na]	
D	Ṡ	Ṡ	–	D	Ṡ	D	P								
vā -	-	nī ———		nan -	-	da -	na.								

Antarā

								: G	–	P	D	Ṡ	Ṡ	Ṡ	Ṡ
								Si -	-	ddhī	sa -	da -	na,	ga -	ja
Ṡ	Ṙ	Ġ	Ṙ	Ṡ	–	Ṙ	Ṡ	D	Ṡ	–	D	–	P	P	–
va -	da -	na,	vi -	nā -	-	ya -	ka.	Kr̥ -	pā ———		sin -	-	dhu,	sun -	-
D	Ṡ	D	P	G	R	S	S								
da -	ra,	sa -	ba	dā -	-	ya -	ka.								
				[lā -	-	ya -	ka]								

2.5.9 Rāg Yaman

Performing time first quarter (*prahar*) of the night.

Āroh (ascending)	***Avroh*** (descending)
Ṇ R G Ḿ D N Ṡ	Ṡ N D P Ḿ G R S

Pakaḍ – ṆRG; P^{ḾG}RS

Jāti – *Ṣāḍav–sampūrṇ* (hexatonic–heptatonic)

Ṭhāṭ – Kalyāṇ

Vādī – Ga

Saṃvādī – Ni

(Source: VR)

Rāg Yaman exists in more than one version. The commonly adopted form passed down to VR, and thence to his students, has a *jāti* that omits Sā and Pa in ascent—as shown in the specification above. Even though this ascending form eventually leads to upper Sā, making a hexatonic rising scale, the common association within Yaman of figures such as ṆRG and GḾDN adds subtle pentatonic (*auḍav*) hues to its overall *ṣāḍav–sampūrṇ* (hexatonic–heptatonic) *jāti*. By contrast, Bhatkhande describes a different incarnation, whose *jāti* he notes as, simply, '*sampūrṇ*' (heptatonic): he gives the *āroh–avroh* as SRG, ḾP, D, NṠ | ṠND, P, ḾG, RS; and the *pakaḍ* as ṆRGR, S, PḾG, R, S (Bhatkhande 1994/1937, II: 17, 18).

The mood of Yaman is typically calm and romantic, capturing the peacefulness of the time immediately after sunset. The emphasis on Ga and Ni does much to create this mood. Re and Pa are also prominent, and contribute to the *rāg*'s beauty. Indeed, all notes in Yaman are to some degree able to be sustained: while Ḿa and Dha are relatively less prominent, they are more than fleetingly touched upon, contributing significantly to the *rāg*'s colouration.

Although musicians commonly learn Yaman early in their studies, this in no way detracts from its importance in the repertory. It was much loved by Pandit Bhimsen Joshi, who performed it up to the very end of his musical life. As well as being a staple of the Hindustani classical canon, Yaman is also found in light classical and film music.

Performance by Vijay Rajput
(*Rāg samay cakra*, Track 9
https://hdl.handle.net/20.500.12434/5103e2df)

Spoken version of *bandiś* text
(*Rāg samay cakra*, Track 23
https://hdl.handle.net/20.500.12434/a623742d)

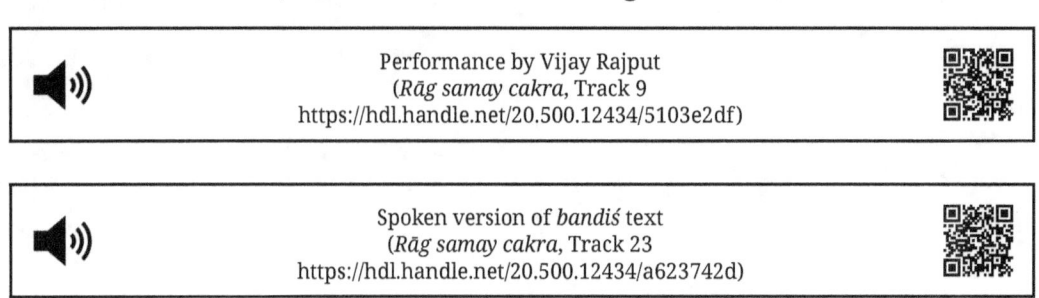

Bandiś: 'Śyām bajāi'

This joyful composition depicts Lord Kṛṣṇa (Śyām) playing his flute, the whole world intently listening. The lyricist would appear to be Manaraṅg (Mahawat Khan of Jaipur, according to Bonnie Wade (1997: 20)), who names himself in a play on words in the text. This *bandiś* was popularised by Bhimsen Joshi, who taught it to VR and numerous other disciples.

Sthāī	
Śyām bajāi āja muraliyā̃,	*Today Śyām [Kṛṣṇa] plays upon his flute,*
ve apano [apane] adharana gunī so.	*On his lips, like a musician.*
Antarā	
Jogī jaṅgama jatī satī aura gunī munī,	*Yogīs, ascetics and saints and good women,*
saba nara nārī mil.	*All men and women come together.*
Moha liyo hai Manaraṅga [man raṅga] ke.	*He has enchanted Manaraṅg [their minds with passion].*

राग यमन

स्थाई

श्याम बजाइ आज मुरलियाँ

वे अपनो [अपने] अधरन गुनी सो।

अंतरा

जोगी जंगम जती सती और गुनी मुनी

सब नर नारी मिल

मोह लियो है मनरंग [मन रंग] के।।

Bandiś in Rāg Yaman: 'Śyām bajāi'

tīntāl

x				2				o				3			
1	**2**	**3**	**4**	**5**	**6**	**7**	**8**	**9**	**10**	**11**	**12**	**13**	**14**	**15**	**16**

Sthāī

|: G – R |S – S |
Śyām—— ba- jā- - i

|Ṇ Ḍ Ṇ R |G R G – :|P – Ḿ G |G Ḿ P – |
ā - ja mu- ra- li- yā̃,—— ve—————— a- pa- no——
[a- pa- ne]

|N D P Ḿ |G R S – |
a- dha- ra- na gu- nī so.——

Antarā

| P – P |P – P P |
Jo- - gī jaṅ- - ga- ma

|G Ḿ G Ḿ |P – P P |Ḿ N ⟍ D N |Ṡ – – – |
ja- tī—— sa- tī—— au- ra gu- ni—— mu- nī,——

|N Ṙ Ġ Ṙ |Ṡ N DP ḾG | G G R |G Ḿ P – |
sa- ba na- ra nā- rī mil.—— Mo- ha li- yo—— hai——

|N D P Ḿ |G R S – |
Ma- na- raṅ- - - ga ke.——
[ma- na raṅ- - - ga]

2.5.10 Rāg Kedār

Performing time first quarter (*prahar*) of the night.

Āroh (ascending)	***Avroh*** (descending)
S M, M P, D P, N D, Ṡ	Ṡ, N D, P, Ḿ P D P, M, G M R S

Pakaḍ – S, M, M P, D P M, P M, R S

Jāti – *Auḍav–sampūrṇ* (pentatonic–heptatonic)

Ṭhāṭ – Kalyāṇ

Vādī – Ma

Saṃvādī – Sā

(Source: Bhatkhande 1995/1937, III: 118)

The warmth of this *śṛṅgār ras* (romantic-aesthetic) *rāg* comes in part from its sensitivity to *śuddh* Ma. Its sensuous entreaties are captured by oblique (*vakra*) motions such as MG-PḾ-DP—as at the opening of the *bandiś* 'Bola bola mose', sung here. Such indirect patterns crucially distinguish Kedār from Bihāg, which likewise has both forms of Ma. While in Bihāg, Ga is prominent (the *vādī* tone), in Kedār, it is Ma that is the *vādī*, and Ga is typically subsumed into it—within figures such as M$^{\backslash G}$P.

These are just some of the subtleties which the performer needs to master in this melodically complex *rāg*. Others include the treatment of Re—absent entirely in *āroh*, and typically prefaced by a *kaṇ svar* (grace note) on Sā in the elliptical descent from Ma—i.e. M–^{S}RS. Handled carefully, *komal* Ni is also very occasionally permitted as a *vivādī* (foreign) note. *Rāgs* that feature similar melodic movements to Kedār include Hamīr and Kamod.

Performance by Vijay Rajput
(*Rāg samay cakra*, Track 10
https://hdl.handle.net/20.500.12434/cd5e11f9)

Spoken version of *bandiś* text
(*Rāg samay cakra*, Track 24
https://hdl.handle.net/20.500.12434/d6bd37e3)

Bandiś: 'Bola bola mose'

Here is a classic devotional song to Lord Kṛṣṇa, addressed—in one of his many alternative appellations—as 'son of Nand'. The setting is his home village of Brij, whose denizens are depicted as ever hungry for their god. Although this *bandiś* is in *drut lay*, the pace should be sufficiently measured to bring out the feelings of entreaty and devotion. VR learnt this song from his former teacher Pandit Vinay Chandra Maudgalya.

Sthāī

Bola bola mose Nanda kũvaravā,	*Talk, talk to me, O son of Nand,*
rasa bharī batiyā̃ lāge madhura torī.	*So sweet to me is your talk, so full of feeling.*

Antarā

Subhaga hātha tore bansī Śyāma sī,	*The flute in your graceful hands,*
brijavāsī nīrakhata naina bharī,	*The people of Braj gaze upon it and fill their eyes,*
nahī̃ aghāta jaise bhūkha bhikhārī.	*Like mendicants ever hungry for more.*

राग केदार

स्थाई

बोल बोल मोसे नंद कुंवरवा

रस भरी बतियाँ लागे मधुर तोरी।

अंतरा

सुभग हाथ तोरे बंसी श्याम सी

बृजवासी नीरखत नैन भरी

नहीं अघात जैसे भूख भिखारी॥

Bandiś in Rāg Kedār: 'Bola bola mose'

tīntāl

x					2				o				3			
1	2	3	4	5	6	7	8	9	10	11	12	13	14	15	16

Sthāī

								:M	–	G	P	–	Ḿ	D	P
								Bo-	–	la	bo-	–	la	mo-	se

M	–	R	S	Ṇ	R	S	– :	S	S	M	G	P	Ḿ	D	P
Nan-	–	da	kũ-	va-	ra-	vā,		ra-	sa	bha-	rī	ba-	ti-	yã̄	

PP	DN	ṠN	D P	Ḿ	P	D	P
lā-	–	–	ge ma-	dhu-	ra	to-	rī.

Antarā

								:P	P	P	Ṡ	–	Ṡ	Ṡ	Ṡ
								Su-	bha-	ga	hā-	–	tha	to-	re

Ṡ	–	Ṡ	Ṡ⌢	N	Ṙ	Ṡ	– :	Ṡ⌢	D	ˢ⌢D	–	Ṡ	–	M	Ṡ
ban-	–	sī	Śyā-	–	ma	sī,		bri-	ja	vā-	–	sī		nī-	ra-

N	Ṡ	ˢ⌢D	–	Ḿ	DP	ᴹᴳM	–	M	M	G	P	–	Ḿ	D	P
kha-	ta	nai-	–	na	bha-	rī,		na-	hī̃	a-	ghā-	–	ta	jai-	se

PP	DN	ṠN	D P	ḾP	DP⌢	M	M
bhū-	–	–	kha bhi-	khā-	–	–	rī.

2.5.11 Rāg Bihāg

Performing time second quarter (*prahar*) of the night.

Āroh (ascending)	***Avroh*** (descending)
| S G, M P, N Ṡ |	| Ṡ, N D P, M G, R S |

Pakaḍ – Ṇ S, G M P, G M G, R S

Jāti – *Auḍav–sampūrṇ* (pentatonic–heptatonic)

Ṭhāṭ – Kalyāṇ/Bilāval

Vādī – Ga

Saṃvādī – Ni

(Source: Bhatkhande 1995/1937, III: 181–2)

Bihāg is an example of a *rāg* whose identity has changed within recent memory. This mutation turns around the subtly increasing status of *tivra* Ma (the sharpened fourth degree), which in Bihāg co-exists with the always more prominent *suddh* Ma (natural fourth). At one time, *tivra* Ma was expressed only fleetingly—perhaps touched on within a descending *mīndh* (gliding motion) between Pa and Ga. Subsequently, *tivra* Ma has become more salient with some performers, though it is still heard only in *avroh* between Pa and Ga or in patterns such as PḾP. Sung with the right kind of inflection, this can bring out the romantic character of the *rāg*. In the later-twentieth century VR was taught the earlier style of the *rāg* by his then guru, Pandit M. G. Deshpande, though he himself now gives greater prominence to *tivra* Ma (as we hear in *Rāg samay cakra*).

The ambiguity around the status of *tivra* Ma is reflected in Bihāg's place in the *ṭhāṭ* system. Ringe and Ringe (n.d.: http://www.tanarang.com/english/bihag_eng.htm), and Patrick Moutal (1997/1991: 101) classify it under the Kalyāṇ *ṭhāṭ*, which has a sharpened fourth. Conversely, Bhatkhande, writing in the earlier twentieth century, places it in the Bilāval *ṭhāṭ* (the natural-note scale), classifying *tivra* Ma as *vivādī*—a note outside the *rāg* yet available as an occasional nuance. He also cautions against overstressing Re and Dha, so as to avoid confusion with Rāg Bilāval itself.

As ever, knowledge of related *rāg*s is important: here the comparators include Kedār, Kāmod and Hamīr. The motion SMG, for example, while allowable in Bihāg (as at the word 'tarapa' in the *bandiś* performed here), should not be over-emphasised, as this figure is more characteristic of Kedār. Meanwhile, Māru Bihāg complements its sibling *rāg* by reversing the dominance of *tivra* Ma and *suddh* Ma (placing the former in the ascendant), and by according much greater prominence to Dha and Re which only have a passing function in Bihāg itself.

Performance by Vijay Rajput
(*Rāg samay cakra*, Track 11
https://hdl.handle.net/20.500.12434/54b5c23f)

Spoken version of *bandiś* text
(*Rāg samay cakra*, Track 25
https://hdl.handle.net/20.500.12434/8c258468)

Bandiś: 'Abahũ lālana'

This is another classic song of longing for an absent lover. In the *antarā*, the natural world and inner world come together in the images of rain clouds and the welling up of tears, of lightning and the trembling heart.

Sthāī	
Abahũ lālana maikā yuga bīta gāe,	*Already now, my love, so many eons have passed for me,*
tumhāre darasa ko tarapa tarapa jīyarā tarase re.	*My heart is tormented, longing endlessly to see you.*
Antarā	
Umaṅgẽ nainā bādarī sī jhara lāge,	*My welling eyes rain forth like clouds,*
jīyarā tarase [larajai],	*My heart trembles,*
dāminī sī kaundha caundha,	*It is as if lightning had dazzled me,*
maiharvā barase.	*The cloud showers forth rain.*

राग बिहाग

स्थाई

अबहुं लालन मैका युग बीत गए

तुम्हारे दरस को तरप तरप जीयरा तरसे रे।

अंतरा

उमंगें नैना बादरी सी झर लागे

जीयरा तरसे [लरजै]

दामिनी सी कौंध चौध

मैहरवा बरसे॥

Bandiś in Rāg Bihāg: 'Abhũ lālana'

tīntāl

x				2				o				3			
1	**2**	**3**	**4**	**5**	**6**	**7**	**8**	**9**	**10**	**11**	**12**	**13**	**14**	**15**	**16**

Sthāī

								: Ṇ	S	G	M	P	–	N	N
								A -	ba -	hũ ———		lā -	-	la -	na
Ṡ	–	N	– –	^{PḾ}P	– Ḿ	G	G :	GM	PḾ	G	M	G	– R	^{ṠN}S	–
mai -	-	kā ————				yu -	ga	bī -	-	ta	gā -	e, ————			
Ṇ	P̣	Ṇ	Ṇ	S	S	S	–	S	M	G	M	G	M	P	P-Ḿ
tum -	hā -	re	da -	ra -	sa	ko ———		ta -	ra -	pa	ta -	ra -	pa	jī -	ya -
G	M	P	M	G	– R	^{ṠN}S	–								
rā ———		ta -	ra -	se ———		re. ———									

Antarā

P	P	Ṡ	–	Ṡ	–	Ṡ	–	Ṡ	–	Ġ	^{ṠN}Ṡ	–	Ṡ	N	N
U -	maṅ -	gẽ ———		nai -	-	nā ———		bā -	-	da -	rī ———		sī	jha -	ra
^{PḾ}P	–	^{P}Ṡ	–	N	– D	^{PḾ}P	–	G	M	P	M	G	R	S	–
lā -	-	-	-	ge, ————				jī -	ya -	rā ———		ta -	ra -	se, ———	
												[la -	ra -	jai]	
Ṇ	–	P̣	S	–	S	S	–	G	S	–	S	N	–	^{PḾ}P	–
dā -	-	mi -	nī ———		sī	kaun -	-	dha	caun -	-	dha,	mai -	-	har -	-
G	– —	P	M	G	– R	S ———									
vā ———		ba -	ra -	se. ————											

2.5.12 Rāg Mālkauns

Performing time third quarter (*prahar*) of the night.

Āroh (ascending)   *Avroh* (descending)

| N̲ S, G̲ M, D̲, N̲ Ṡ | Ṡ N̲ D̲, M, G̲, G̲ M G̲ S |

Pakaḍ – MG̲, MD̲N̲D̲, M, G̲, S

Jāti – *Auḍav–auḍav* (pentatonic–pentatonic)

Ṭhāṭ – Bhairavī

Vādī – Ma

Saṃvādī – Sā

(Source: Bhatkhande 1995/1937, III: 700–1)

Performed in the depths of the night, Mālkauns likewise inhabits the depths of the imagination and cultural memory. Daniel Neuman (1990: 64–6) recounts stories from hereditary Muslim musicians who feared to sing this *rāg* alone after midnight because it might summon up capricious spirits known as *jinn*s. Mālkauns is regarded as a masculine *rāg* belonging to the *vīr ras*, with its connotations of heroism and war; the mood is one of gravity. Unhurried presentation and pervasive use of very slow *mīṇḍ* (gliding motion) are essential to capturing its character.

Omkarnath Thakur (2005: 227) tells us that Mālkauns is a dialect form of the name 'Mālvakausik', and that its correct *prakriti* (mode of delivery) is *śānt* (peaceful) and *gambhīr* (serious). Thakur describes the formal features of Mālkauns using more traditional terminology than does his rival, Bhatkhande. In Thakur's account, Ma has the status of *nyās svar*—a standing or sustained note; Sā and N̲i have the status of *grah svar* (notes used to initiate a phrase) in *ālāp* and in *tān*s respectively; and G̲a and D̲ha are *anugāmī svar* (passing notes). Thakur also draws attention to the significance in this *rāg* of *samvad svar*—notes paired in fourths: Sā–Ma, G̲a–D̲ha, Ma–N̲i.

 Performance by Vijay Rajput
(*Rāg samay cakra*, Track 12
https://hdl.handle.net/20.500.12434/1dcb60b2)

 Spoken version of *bandiś* text
(*Rāg samay cakra*, Track 26
https://hdl.handle.net/20.500.12434/e3fe4456)

Bandiś: 'Koyalīyā bole ambuvā'

This cheerful song makes the point that a *rāg* can encompass a spectrum of moods, and that a *choṭā khayāl* in particular can show facets of the *rāg* other than the dominant one. In this romantic *bandiś* full of natural imagery, the Kokila (Asian Koel) bird—which has similar poetic connotations to the nightingale in western culture—sings from the mango tree, heralding spring (for more on the place of birds in Braj Bhāṣā poetry and Hindustani *bandiś*es, see Magriel and du Perron 2013, I: 146–53). In the *antarā*, the image of the bee playing among the buds could be an allusion to Kṛṣṇa among the cowherds.

Sthāī

Koyalīyā bole ambuvā ḍāra para,	*The sweet Kokila bird gives voice on the branch of the mango tree,*
ṛtu basanta ko deta sandesavā.	*And so heralds for us the arrival of Spring.*

Antarā

Nava kaliyana para gunjata bhãvarā,	*On the new buds the bee buzzes,*
una ke saṅga karata raṅgaraliyā̃,	*In their company he plays his games,*
yahī basanta ko deta sandesavā.	*This is what heralds the Spring.*

राग मालकौंस

स्थाई

कोयलीया बोले अंबुवा डार पर

ऋतु बसंत को देत संदेसवा।

अंतरा

नव कलियन पर गुंजत भँवरा

उन के संग करत रंगरलियाँ

यही बसंत को देत संदेसवा॥

Bandiś in Rāg Mālkauns: 'Koyalīyā bole ambuvā'

tīntāl

x				2				o				3			
1	2	3	4	5	6	7	8	9	10	11	12	13	14	15	16

Sthāī

								|: Ṡ	ṠN̲	Ġ̲	Ṡ	| D̲	M	D̲	N̲ |
								Ko -	ya -	lī -	yā	bo -	le	am -	bu -
| Ṡ	–	–	N̲D̲	| N̲	D̲	M	M :	| G̲	G̲	G̲	MD̲	| N̲Ṡ	N̲	Ṡ	– |
vā———			ḍā -	-	ra	pa -	ra,	ṛ -	tu	ba -	san -	-	ta	ko———	
| G̲	–	M	D̲	| G̲	M	G̲S	– |								
de -	-	ta	san -	de -	sa -	vā.———									

Antarā

								|: G̲	G̲	M	M	| D̲	D̲	N̲	N̲ |
								Na -	va	ka -	li -	ya -	na	pa -	ra
| Ṡ	–	Ṡ	Ṡ	| ṠĠ̲	ṠN̲	Ṡ	– :	| N̲	N̲	N̲	–	| Ṡ	–	Ṡ	Ṡ |
gun -	-	ja -	ta	bhã -	va -	rā,———		u -	na	ke———		saṅ -	-	ga	ka -
				[bhā -	-	ḍā]									
| D̲	M	D̲	N̲	| D̲	D̲	M	–	| G̲	G̲	G̲	MD̲	| N̲Ṡ	N̲	Ṡ	– |
ra -	ta	raṅ -	ga -	ra -	li -	yã,———		ya -	hī	ba -	san -	-	ta	ko———	
| G̲	–	M	D̲	| G̲	M	G̲S	– |								
de -	-	ta	san -	de -	sa -	vā.———									

2.5.13 Rāg Megh

Performing time rainy season (*varṣa r̥tu*).

Āroh (ascending)	*Avroh* (descending)
| S R M P Ṉ Ṡ |	| Ṡ Ṉ P M R S |

Pakaḍ – S^M RP—, ^P Ṉ–P, Ṡ^P ṈPM\R S

Jāti – *Auḍav–auḍav* (pentatonic-pentatonic)

Ṭhāṭ – Kāfī

Vādī – Sā

Saṃvādī – Pa

(Source: VR; Bhatkhande 1991/1937, VI: 242–3)

For all that the rainy season is regarded as a time of romance, this monsoon *rāg* is quintessentially weighty and serious—an old and revered *gambhīr rāg*. Megh draws its gravity from its place in the Malhār group of *rāg*s; indeed it is often known as Megh Malhār or Megh Mallār. It evokes dark storm clouds, the rumbling of thunder, and dramatic lightning flashes. Ringe and Ringe (n.d.: http://www.tanarang.com/english/megh_eng.htm) associate it with the heroic and masculine *vīr ras*.

All this distinguishes Megh from similar but lighter (*cancal*) *rāg*s of the Sāraṅg group—such as Bṛindābanī Sāraṅg and, especially, Madhmād Sāraṅg. The latter superficially resembles Megh through its use of the same scale and similar melodic figures. But Megh plumbs greater depths through its application of slow and heavy *mīṇḍ* (glides) and its more ponderous treatment of *svar* and ornaments. Re is often dwelled on, and is nearly always approached via Ma, which, conversely, is often treated as a *kaṇ svar* (grace note). The use of *āndolan* (oscillation) between these two notes is another point of difference from Madhmād Sāraṅg; and the figure ^M R–P, drawn from Rāg Malhār, is similarly distinctive. (For further details see Moutal 1991: 121–2.)

As with many *rāg*s, it would be unwise to try and pin down too definitive a form of Megh. The specification and description above reflect a synthesis of Bhatkhande's and VR's slightly different understandings. VR makes a pragmatic distinction between Megh itself and Megh Malhār, the latter being distinguished by the subtle inclusion of *komal* Ga; but he admits that it remains moot whether these constitute entirely different *rāg*s. Bhatkhande discusses only Megh Mallār (Megh Malhār) in his *Kramik pustak mālikā*, mentioning that this can sometimes include the note Dha. Walter Kaufmann outlines three possible variants of Megh Mallār (1993/1968: 395–401). Similar ambiguity surrounds the identification of *vādī* and *saṃvādī* tones. Following Bhatkhande, we here give Sā and Pa, while Ringe and Ringe (ibid.), Moutal (1991: 122) and Kaufmann (ibid.: 397) all have Ma and Sā.

Performance by Vijay Rajput
(*Rāg samay cakra*, Track 13
https://hdl.handle.net/20.500.12434/4baf8c20)

Spoken version of *bandiś* text
(*Rāg samay cakra*, Track 27
https://hdl.handle.net/20.500.12434/01b7e65e)

Bandiś: 'Ghanana ghanana'

This *bandiś* evokes the might of an approaching thunderstorm, not only through the meaning of the words (*ghor*—frightful, rumbling; *garajnā*—to thunder, to roar), but also through their sounds; onomatopoeia and cumulative repetition serve both a textual and a musical purpose. These devices are brought out by *gamak* (heavy shakes) and *ākār tāns*.

In the *antarā* the lyricist identifies himself with the pen name (*chāp*) Sadāraṅg—the early eighteenth-century musician, Ni'mat Khan—which may or may not be an authentic attribution. He implies he is drenched not just by the rain but also by love.

VR learnt this composition from his guide and teacher Manjusree Tyagi, and further draws inspiration from historic recorded performances of the *rāg* by Ustād Amir Khan (1912–74).

Sthāī	
Ghanana ghanana ghana ghora ghora,	*Awesome rumbling, cloud on cloud,*
ghora ghora garajata āe.	*Frightful roaring thunder looms.*
Antarā	
Āī ṛītu barakhā bhīje [bhīge] Sadāraṅga,	*The rainy season has come and Sadārang is drenched,*
pavana calata pūravīyā,	*The East wind blows,*
sanana sanana so sananananananana.	*Singing, whistling, thrilling, all the while.*

राग मेघ

स्थाई

घनन घनन घन घोर घोर

घोर घोर गरजत आए।

अंतरा

आई ऋीतु बरखा भीजे [भीगे] सदारंग

पवन चलत पूर्वीया

सनन सनन सो सननननननन॥

Bandiś **in Rāg Megh: 'Ghanana ghanana'**

tīntāl

x				2				o				3			
1	**2**	**3**	**4**	**5**	**6**	**7**	**8**	**9**	**10**	**11**	**12**	**13**	**14**	**15**	**16**

Sthāī

								|: R	R	R	S	| N̲	S	R	S |
								Gha-	na-	na	gha-	na-	na	gha-	na
				(1st time)											
| N̲̣	—	.P	S	| –	S	N̲̣	S : |							
gho-	-	ra	gho-	-	ra,	gha-	na								
				(2nd time)											
				| –	S	Ṡ	–	| Ṡ	ᴾN̲	–	P	| PN̲	PM	RS	N̲S |
				-	ra,	gho-	-	ra	gho-	-	ra	ga-	ra-	ja-	ta
| N̲̣S	RM	RM	PN̲	| PN̲	PM	RS	N̲̣S |								
ā-	-	-	-	-	-	e. ———									

Antarā

								|: M	M	P	P	| N̲	N̲	ᴺP	– |
								Ā-	ī	r̥ī-	tu	ba-	ra-	khā ———	
| Ṡ	–	Ṡ	Ṡ	| Ṙ—	N̲	Ṡ	Ṡ :	| N̲	Ṡ	Ṙ	Ṁ	| Ṙ	Ṙ	Ṡ	Ṡ |
bhī-	-	je	sa-	dā-	-	raṅ-	ga,	pa-	va-	na	ca-	la-	ta	pū-	ra-
[bhī-	-	ge]													
| N̲	Ṡ	N̲Ṡ	ṘṠ	| N̲	—	P	–	| P	P	P	Ṙ	| Ṙ	Ṙ	Ṡ	– |
vī-	-	-	-	-	-	yā, ———		sa-	na-	na	sa-	na-	na	so ———	
| P	N̲	P	M	| R	S	N̲̣	S |							
sa-	na-	na-	na-	na-	na-	na-	na.								

2.5.14 Rāg Basant

Performing time springtime (*Basant*) or final quarter of the night (*rātri kā antim prahar*).

Āroh (ascending)	***Avroh*** (descending)
S G, ḾD̲, Ṙ̲, Ṡ	Ṙ̲ N D̲, P, ḾG, ḾG, ḾD̲ḾG, R̲S

Pakaḍ – ḾD̲, Ṙ̲, Ṡ, Ṙ̲ ND̲P, ḾG, ḾG

Jāti – *Auḍav–sampūrṇ* (pentatonic–heptatonic)

Ṭhāṭ – Pūrvī

Vādī – *Tār* Sā

Saṃvādī – Pa

(Source: Bhatkhande 1991/1937, IV: 371–2)

Basant, which means 'spring', is a seasonal (*mausam*) *rāg*. On the Indian subcontinent, springtime extends from around early February—the time of the Sarasvatī *pūjā*—to around mid-to-late March—the festival of Holī. During this period, Rāg Basant may be performed at any time. Otherwise, it may be heard in the last phase of the night, which has similarly romantic connotations.

Basant is an *uttaraṅg pradhan rāg*: it emphasises the upper tetrachord of the scale. Hence *tār* Sā, the upper tonic, is the principal note (or *vādī*). Like Rāg Purvī, Basant uses both versions of Ma, though *tivra* Ma predominates. Śuddh Ma appears in the characteristic figure S–M–Ḿ–M–G, which draws from the grammar of Rāg Lalit—one of the few *rāg*s to permit two versions of the same note consecutively. While the Lalit *aṅg* (limb) is not compulsory in Basant, its effect can be beautiful if used sparingly; it is typically followed by the figure ᴹᴳN–D̲–P.

A related *rāg* is Paraj. Bor et al. (1999: 30) mention that some musicians do not even distinguish between the two *rāg*s; but Paraj has its own characteristic melodic figures, such as Ṡ–Ṙ̲–S–Ṙ̲–N–D̲–N and G–M–G; and unlike Basant it incorporates Pa in ascent. Moreover Paraj is a *cancal* (light, flowing) *rāg*, while Basant would be classified as a more serious, *gambhīr rāg*—notwithstanding the lively *choṭā k̲h̲ayāl* sung here.

Performance by Vijay Rajput
(*Rāg samay cakra*, Track 14
https://hdl.handle.net/20.500.12434/fd0a0875)

Spoken version of *bandiś* text
(*Rāg samay cakra*, Track 28
https://hdl.handle.net/20.500.12434/1c65157b)

Bandiś: 'Phulavā binata'

This *ektāl* composition can be sung in *madhya lay* (medium tempo) but is most effective in *drut lay* (fast tempo). The notation of the final line of the *antarā* simplifies the *tān* sung by VR in the last six beats on the recorded version. The poem can be read as a conversation between two onlookers, who address each other with the endearing term 'rī'. They admire a daughter of the village of Gokul, which we can presume to be Rādhā, the consort of Lord Kṛṣṇa (in the *antarā*, Kṛṣṇa is identified with the name Nandalāl). The girl's beauty parallels that of the natural world: her face is like the moon, she has eyes like lotus flowers, and is radiant like the sun. This imagery perfectly captures the romantic feel of springtime and the *rāg* that bears its name.

Sthāī	
Phulavā binata ḍāra ḍāra,	*She picks blossoms from every branch,*
Gokula kī sukumārī,	*She the beauteous one of [the village of] Gokul,*
candṛbadana kamalanainī,	*Moon-faced, lotus-eyed,*
bhānu kī laṛiyai rī [laḍīrī].	*The daughter of the sun, O my dear one!*
Antarā	
Ai rī eka sukumārī,	*And while she, that beauteous one,*
calata nā añcala savārī,	*Walks along and takes little care to veil herself,*
āvenge nandalāla.	*The son of Nand [Kṛṣṇa] will come.*
Dekha ke ḍarīyai rī.	*Seeing him she will feel afraid.*

राग बसंत

स्थाई

फुलवा बिनत डार डार

गोकुल की सुकुमारी

चंदृबदन कमलनैनी

भानु की लड़ियै री [लडीरी]।

अंतरा

ऐ री एक सुकुमारी

चलत ना अंचल सवारी

आवेंगे नंदलाल

देख के डरीयै री॥

Bandiś in Rāg Basant: 'Phulavā binata'

ektāl

x		o		2		o		3		4	
1	**2**	**3**	**4**	**5**	**6**	**7**	**8**	**9**	**10**	**11**	**12**

Sthāī

:Ṡ	Ṡ	Ṡ	Ṡ	Ṡ	Ṡ	Ṡ	–	N	Ḿ	–	D̲ :
Phu -	la -	vā	bi -	na -	ta	ḍā -	-	ra	ḍā -	-	ra,
:Ḿ	–	Ḿ	Ḿ	Ḿ	–	Ḿ	G	R̲	S	–	S :
Go -	-	ku -	la	kī———		su -	-	ku -	mā -	-	rī,
M	–	M	M	M	M	M	Ḿ	M	G	–	G
can -	-	dr̥ -	ba -	da -	na	ka -	ma -	la -	nai -	-	nī,
Ḿ	–	Ḿ	D̲	–	D̲	Ṡ	–	–	Ḿ	–	D̲
bhā -	-	nu	kī———		la -	ṛi -	-	-	yai———		rī.
					[la -	ḍī -	-	-	-	-	rī]

Antarā

:Ḿ	–	Ḿ	–	Ḿ	D̲	Ṡ	–	Ṡ	Ṙ̲	–	Ṡ :
Ai———		rī———		e -	ka	su -	-	ku -	mā -	-	rī,
Ṡ	Ṡ	Ġ	Ġ	–	Ġ	Ḿ̇	Ġ	Ṙ̲	Ṡ	–	Ṡ
ca -	la -	ta	nā———		añ -	ca -	la	sa -	vā -	-	rī,
Ṡ	–	–	Ṡ	–	Ṡ	N	Ṡ	N	Ḿ	–	D̲
ā -	-	-	ven -	-	ge	nan -	-	da -	lā -	-	la.
Ḿ	–	Ḿ	D̲	Ḿ	D̲	Ṡ	–	–	Ḿ	–	D̲
De -	-	kha	ke———		ḍa -	rī -	-	-	yai———		rī.

3. EXPLORATIONS AND ANALYSES (I): *RĀG SAMAY CAKRA*

 https://doi.org/10.11647/OBP.0313.03

3.1 Introduction

In the next two parts of *Rāgs Around the Clock*, I (David Clarke, henceforth DC) undertake a close reading of Vijay Rajput's (henceforth, VR) performances on the book's associated albums: *Rāg samay cakra* (here, in Part 3) and *Twilight Rāgs from North India* (in Part 4). While it would have been possible to organise these studies as track-by-track analyses of the albums, I have opted for a different strategy. Sections 3.2 and 3.3 consider in turn the two performance stages on which every track of *Rāg samay cakra* is based: *ālāp* and *choṭā khayāl*. The analyses pull out extracts from across the entire album in order to illustrate the different facets of these two stages (and in so doing also provide commentary on all of the fourteen *rāg*s sung). Following this, Part 4 includes a similarly extended account of the *baṛā khayāl* in Rāg Yaman from *Twilight Rāgs*. Hence, across the two parts, all of the three principal stages of a khayāl performance are investigated. (Other contents of Part 4 are discussed in its own introduction, Section 4.1.)

While these essays are longer reads than the earlier writings in this book, and have a stronger theoretical orientation, I have couched the material in ways that I hope will be accessible to students and lay listeners, as well as being of interest to researchers and professional musicians (I should add that it is not compulsory to read every part of every essay; each section is designed to be, to some extent, freestanding and informative in its own right). Importantly, these inquiries continue to include a pedagogical dimension. A key heuristic strategy is to place the reader in the position of the performer, and ask: what do I need to know in order to sing (and hence also to understand) an *ālāp*, or a *choṭā khayāl*, or—in Part 4—a *baṛā khayāl*?

In asking such questions, I also seek to pull out general truths from the specifics of VR's performances, and speculate on some of the bigger questions raised by khayāl and Hindustani classical music more widely. The answers are often formulated as rubrics that codify the knowledge which musicians and listeners acquire over a long period—musicians in order to perform, listeners in order to become appreciative audience members (*rasika*s) with whom artists can subtly and co-creatively interact in the live event. Ultimately this inquiry leads to the question (also addressed in the book's Epilogue) of what kind of knowledge is constituted by such rubrics, and how this relates to the intrinsically musical knowledge that is passed down through successive generations of performers—more bluntly, the perennial question of the relationship between theory and practice.

3.2 How Do You Sing an *Ālāp*?

Preamble

Ālāp is a fundamental principle of Indian classical music. It is the quintessential means through which a performer brings *rāg* into being: as musicologist Ashok Ranade reminds us (paraphrasing the medieval scholar Śārṅgadeva (1175–1247)), the Sanskrit word *ālapti* means 'to express or elaborate *raga*' (Ranade 2006: 176).

In order to distil this melodic essence, *ālāp* loosens its bonds with rhythm—with *tāl* and *lay*. Hence, during the *ālāp* that opens practically every Hindustani classical performance, the accompanying drum—tabla or pakhāvaj—is silent. Alone under the spotlight, the vocal or instrumental soloist is able to extemporise and explore a *rāg* at their own pace, free from any manifest pulse or metre—a condition known as *anibaddh*. Vocalists are also largely liberated from the constraints of text, instead singing non-semantic syllables.

*Ālāp*s vary enormously in length—in contemporary practice, lasting anything from about a minute to over an hour. They also vary in form, according to whether the soloist is a vocalist or instrumentalist; according to genre (for example, khayāl, dhrupad); according to *gharānā* (stylistic school); and according to performance circumstances. Audio Example 3.2.1 illustrates *ālāp* in the context of khayāl and the circumstances of the album *Rāg samay cakra*, in which *rāg* performances are compressed to an average of just five minutes; here we have the opening track, in which Vijay Rajput sings the dawn *rāg*, Bhairav.

Audio Example 3.2.1 Rāg Bhairav, *ālāp* (*RSC*, Track 1, 00:00–02:01)
https://hdl.handle.net/20.500.12434/54b2530c

We might describe this unaccompanied, prefatory stage of a *rāg* performance as the *ālāp* 'proper'. But—importantly—the principles of *ālāp* often also manifest in the subsequent stages of a performance. In khayāl, a soloist often returns to this manner of singing during the subsequent *bandiś* (composition), alongside the tabla which now sustains the *tāl*. In such passages, *nibaddh* (metred) and *anibaddh* (unmetred) states co-exist as the *rāg* is further developed—a process sometimes known as *vistār*; I examine this matter further in my discussions of *choṭā khayāl* principles (Section 3.3) and *baṛā khayāl* principles (Section 4.3). In instrumental performance, and in vocal performances in the dhrupad style, the *ālāp* proper may be followed by two further stages, *joṛ* and *jhālā*, which invoke a pulse, though not yet the metrical rhythmic cycle of *tāl* (and usually still without drum accompaniment). While these stages are also considered part of the *ālāp* process, I do not extensively discuss them here, as they are not directly relevant to khayāl, my main topic of inquiry.

Given the significance of *ālāp* to Indian classical music, learning how to improvise in this fashion is paramount for a student. Indeed, this goes hand in hand with learning a *rāg*. The latter involves the student imitating phrases sung or played to them by their teacher in rhythmically free form, from simple to more complex, from lower register to higher register and back, so as gradually to internalise the characteristic behaviour of each *svar* and the *rāg*'s repertory of melodic formations. In effect, this is the same process as fashioning an *ālāp*.

Just about every musician will affirm that learning mimetically like this is the only way truly to acquire such skills. They will probably also recommend close listening to performances and recordings by the great masters and other professional artists (increasingly possible in an internet age, and an opportunity afforded by the albums accompanying the present volume). While this wisdom is unimpeachable, it is also true that pedagogy is not entirely uninformed by theory, including the legacy of the *śāstras*—the historical Indian treatises on music and performing arts. For example, in one of the most thoroughly researched accounts of *ālāp* in anglophone musicology, Ritwik Sanyal and Richard Widdess (2004: 144–52) show a continuity between rubrics for *ālapti* set out in Śārṅgadeva's thirteenth-century treatise, *Saṅgīta-ratnākara* (2023/1993: 199–201), and *ālāp* performances by present-day *dhrupadiyās*—findings not without relevance to *k͟hayāliyās*. While Widdess's investigation (with which I dialogue below) analyses Sanyal's own *ālāp* practice against the background of this wider historical context, my approach here is more inductive, seeking to channel rubrics for performing a k͟hayāl-style *ālāp* from VR's renditions on *Rāg samay cakra* and from my own experience of learning from him. Nonetheless, this will also reveal a degree of consistency with historic formulations; and I will also seek to draw out some generalisable theoretical principles from my analysis.

I approach my question, How Do You Sing an *Ālāp*?, through three explorations, each involving close musical analysis. In effect, these are self-contained essays that could be read in any order. In the first and longest, I consider *ālāp* formation: how does a performer shape an *ālāp*, both across its entire span and from phrase to phrase? In the second, I undertake an empirical analysis of duration and proportion in an *ālāp*: how long should an *ālāp* last, both in absolute terms and relative to its place in a *rāg* performance as a whole? And in the third exploration, I broach the under-examined issue of what it is that k͟hayāl singers sing instead of words in an *ālāp*: how do they select and combine non-lexical syllables?

Exploration 1: *Ālāp* Formation

Although an *ālāp* is improvised, and approaches to it vary between artists and *gharānās*, this does not mean that anything is possible. An *ālāp* must take a coherent shape, beyond mere *rāg*-based noodling. 'What is your plan?', VR once provocatively asked me in a lesson, after I sang him a rather formless *ālāp*. Listen to any of the *ālāp*s on *Rāg samay cakra* and it is clear that he always has a plan, even if an unconscious one. How, then, does a performer shape an *ālāp*—give it form, and in the process elicit a *rāg*? In this exploration, I approach this question through two stages of inquiry. First, I explore VR's *ālāp* in Rāg Bhairav in its entirety as a case study. In the second stage, I widen the discussion, selecting extracts from *Rag samay cakra* as a whole, in order to explore variants of this and other principles identified in the case study.

Key to Exploration 1 are a number of theoretical terms that encapsulate certain essential processes of an *ālāp* and its melodic materials. Some of these terms come from explanations VR has given me verbally in class; others are adapted from western music theory; and yet others I have devised myself. Although I introduce these concepts individually as the account proceeds, I also summarise and further explain them at the end of Exploration 1. Readers may want to consult that passage for reference as they work through the analysis below.

Case Study: An Ālāp in Rāg Bhairav

Since every performer needs to know how to begin their performance, and since we have already listened to VR's Bhairav *ālāp* in its entirety (Audio Example 3.2.1), let us now consider how he creates the sense of an opening—as extracted in Audio Example 3.2.2.

Audio Example 3.2.2 Rāg Bhairav, *ālāp*: opening (establishing phase)
(*RSC*, Track 1, 00:00–00:37)
https://hdl.handle.net/20.500.12434/94dce8a1

What do we hear in this passage? To begin with, the omnipresent drone of the tānpurā and just a hint of the *rāg* to come as harmonium player Mahmood Dholpuri discreetly touches *komal* Re in the background. But the first main event is VR's entry at 00:07, where he sustains Sā, centring himself in his *svar*, the felt inner life of the note. *Svar* begins to mutate into *rāg*, and this single tone into a phrase, as he moves from Sā to Re; and he allows us to hear just a little flash of Ga, as a grace note (*kaṇ*), before descending back to Sā. These details are notated in Figure 3.2.1, phrase (i).

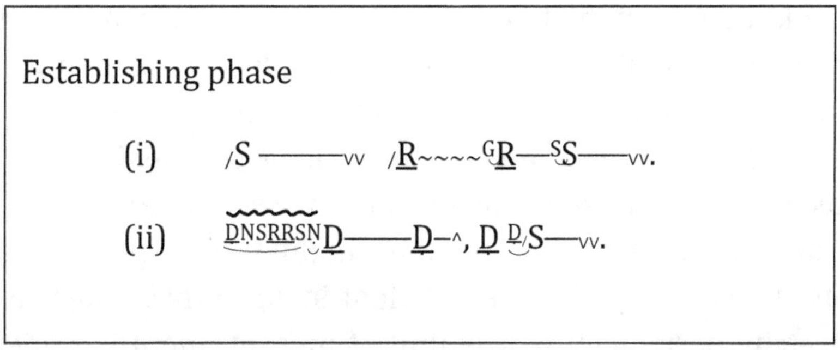

Fig. 3.2.1 *Ālāp* in Rāg Bhairav: opening (establishing phase), transcription. Created by author (2024), CC BY-NC-SA.

This transcription also includes VR's next phrase, (ii), which begins with a rapid flourish of notes—the ornamental figure known as *murkī*—and then sustains *komal* Dhā in the lower octave; following this, as before, we return to Sā.

From even this tiny amount of material, there is already much we can glean about how to perform an *ālāp*. First, as we have already begun to observe, what VR sings is more than a plain sequence of pitches. The sustained tones—notated (approximately to scale) with extended lines in Figure 3.2.1—are variously approached, enlivened, or ended by various kinds of ornamentation (*alaṅkār*). The more explicit decorations, such as *kaṇ* and *murkī*, are indicated with superscripted *sargam* letters. Below this threshold are other embellishments that would be distractingly cumbersome to spell out: instead, the initial approach to Sā from an unspecified pitch space and the subsequent glide (*miṇḍ*) up to Re are shown with an oblique (/); continuous oscillation (*āndolan*) (as applied here to Re) is shown with a string of tildes (~~~), while a shake or mordent at the end of a note (one possible understanding of the term *kampit*) is indicated with one or more wedge or inverted wedge symbols (for example, ^, vv); the application of *gamak* (a wide shake), is shown with a wavy line. Meanwhile, other microscopic fluctuations are left for discerning ears to savour. (For more on ornamentation see Section 1.8.)

For the performer, there is a careful balance to be struck between sustained notes and decoration. 'Just relax', VR might advise; 'take your time, don't make it too busy'. Indeed one of the distinguishing features of Hindustani classical music is the prevalence of sustained notes during *ālāp*—as compared with its Karnatak counterpart, which places ornamentation much more in the foreground. VR sometimes refers to the sustained (or 'standing') notes in khayāl with the older śāstric term, *nyās svar* (see Jani 2019: 24; Ranade 2006: 233). As is so often the case, the meaning of this Indic term is mutable: *nyās* can also mean the note on which a phrase or a *rāg* ends—which may or may not be the same as any of its sustained notes. Ambiguities aside, such notes provide a crucial melodic focus to each phrase; hence I sometimes also refer to them below as 'organising pitch' or 'goal pitch' (the latter borrowed from Sanyal and Widdess (2004: 145)).

The second point we should infer from this opening phase of VR's Bhairav *ālāp* is his projection of the *rāg*'s grammar. Which notes can be sustained, which ones have a more decorative role, and in what fashion, will depend on the *rāg*. In this example in Bhairav, VR sustains the *vādī* tone, Re, in the first phrase, and the *saṃvādī* tone, Dha, in the second. In fact, in Bhairav, most pitches—with the qualified exception of Ni—can be sustained in some manner, as we will eventually hear.

Thirdly, we should note how the two short phrases transcribed in Figure 3.2.1, form a balanced pair—evidence of a plan. Each begins and ends on Sā; the first phrase *ascends* to the *vādī* tone and the second *descends* to the *saṃvādī*, as already noted. The first phrase begins to explore the middle octave (*madhyā saptak*), the second the lower octave (*mandra saptak*). And while the first phrase is longer than the second (around seventeen seconds compared to around twelve seconds), the two might still be perceived as durationally equivalent because they are relatively equivalent in substance. There is elasticity in the equivalence, a stretchy periodicity whose unit of measurement is something closer to a breath rather than a beat. (This observation complements Widdess's identification of a subliminal pulse in the *ālāp* practice of Sanyal (Sanyal and Widdess 2004: 176–80).)

All the material we have considered so far constitutes what I term the *establishing phase* of an *ālāp*. This is, in turn, part of a larger *phase schema* for the *ālāp* as a whole—a notion explored below. Introducing another theoretical concept, adapted from western music theory, we can say that the establishing phase starts to map out *svar space* (pitch space) around Sā. By voicing *vādī* and *saṃvādī*, and their associated *āndolan*, VR introduces those colours fundamental to the *rāg*'s identity. Above all, the establishing phase confirms Sā as the embracing tonic—as *the* key reference point, and ultimate point of departure and return. While there is no single way to execute the establishing phase, the structure that VR adopts here is classic, and can be summarised in the following simple rubrics:

1. Sustain Sā.
2. Explore the *svar* space slightly above and return to Sā.
3. Explore the *svar* space slightly below and return to Sā.

What next? In a nutshell, over the course of the rest of the *ālāp*, VR fully establishes the *rāg* by: (i) fashioning a series of similarly well-formed phrases that gradually ascend to *tār* (upper) Sā; and then (ii), in a somewhat shorter timescale descend back to *madhya* (middle) Sā. In this, we see how, behind the music's surface, the basic *āroh–avroh* contour of the scale of the *rāg* provides a structuring framework (as it does for just about every other facet of musical material in a performance). I refer to these complementary trajectories as the *ascending phase* and *descending phase* of the *ālāp*.

In our Bhairav example, VR ascends to *tār* Sā between 00:38 and 01:32, and returns to *madhya* Sā between 01:32 and 01:59. However, his ascent is made indirectly: in an *intermediate ascending phase*, he gets some way towards the goal, but breaks off with a descent back to Sā; then, in a *concluding ascending phase*, he resumes his ascent, this time completing the journey to *tār* Sā. Let us consider these individual phases in more detail.

The intermediate ascending phase is extracted in Audio Example 3.2.3 and notated in Figure 3.2.2. In phrase (iii), VR improvises around Ga, picking up from the highest pitch of the establishing phase. Next, in phrase (iv), he rises to Ma and reinforces it—for Ma has structural salience in Bhairav. Then, in phrase (v), he quits the ascent and returns to *madhya* Sā, lingering on the *vādī* tone, R̲e, whose significance and character are highlighted by the decorative *murkī* that leads into it and the *āndolit* (microtonal oscillation) that prolongs it.

 Audio Example 3.2.3 Rāg Bhairav, *ālāp*: intermediate ascending phase
(*RSC*, Track 1, 00:38–01:01)
https://hdl.handle.net/20.500.12434/b95cf025

Intermediate ascending phase

(iii)   S̆R̆S̆G————R̲,

(iv)   GG̲M————ᵥᵥ, M–ᵥᵥ,

(v)   ͞M͞G͞P͞M͞MG\R̲~~~~~~R̲S——.

Fig. 3.2.2 *Ālāp* in Rāg Bhairav: intermediate ascending phase, transcription. Created by author (2024), CC BY-NC-SA.

The concluding ascending phase is captured in Audio Example 3.2.4, and notated in Figure 3.2.3. The initial organising pitch, in phrase (vi), is Pa, which terminates with a momentary deflection back to Ga. The next two pitches on VR's trajectory, voiced in phrases (vii) and (viii), are D̲ha and Ni; in the latter phrase they are heard in conjunction, illustrating the acute sensitivity between them in Bhairav. On the one hand, Ni strongly implies upward resolution to *tār* Sā, the goal of this phase; on the other, D̲ha also points downward to Pa, suggesting another deflection from the ultimate goal of the passage. However, this time, VR sees the implied ascent through to its conclusion and in phrase (ix) rises from D̲ha to *tār* Sā—another way in which D̲ha may behave under the *rāg* grammar of Bhairav (and in any case here catching Ni again in an ornamental *kaṭhkā* on the way). Such decisions

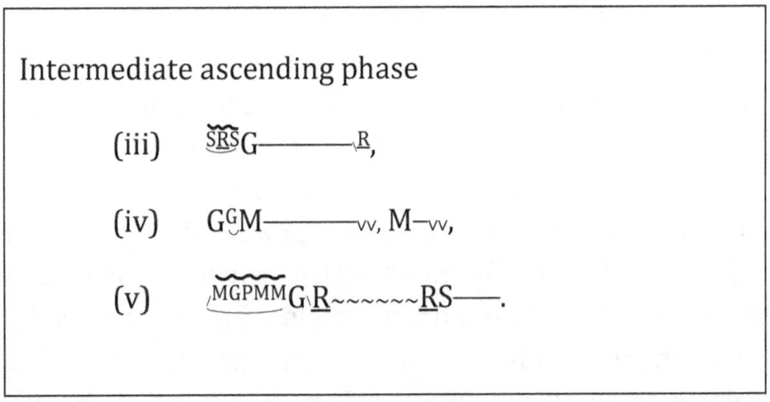

can retrospectively change our understanding of what we heard prior to them. It is only because VR chooses to proceed to *tār* Sā that we hear this passage as the *concluding phase* of the ascent; had he chosen to reverse course after phrase (viii) and returned from Ni to *madhya* Sā—a stylistically available option—the whole passage would have instead been be perceived as a second *intermediate* phase. (For more on the changing significance of *ālāp* material in real time, see Clarke 2017: paras. 6.1–6.5.)

Audio Example 3.2.4 Rāg Bhairav, *ālāp*: concluding phase of ascent to *tār* Sā (Track 1, 01:02–01:32)
https://hdl.handle.net/20.500.12434/121ba272

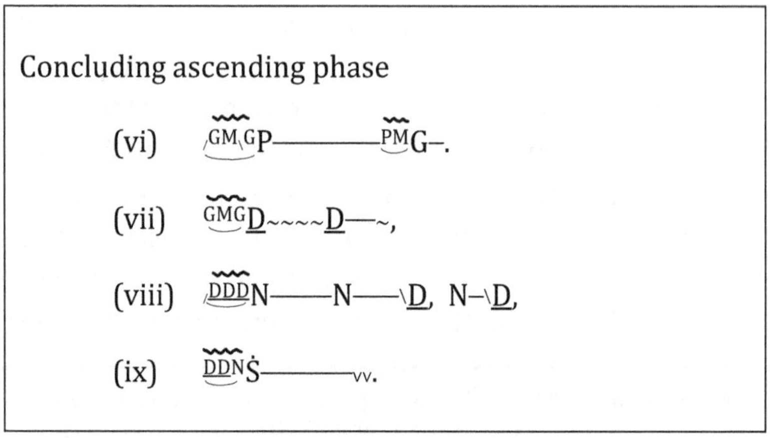

Fig. 3.2.3 *Ālāp* in Rāg Bhairav: concluding ascending phase, transcription. Created by author (2024), CC BY-NC-SA.

Having achieved *tār* Sā, VR now embarks on the descending phase of his *ālāp*. Following convention, this is accomplished in considerably less time than the ascending phase (I discuss the question of the relative duration of *ālāp* phases in Exploration 2, below). The descent is executed in a single span from *tār* Sā to *madhya* Sā, though the pathway has its twists and turns—as can be heard in Audio Example 3.2.5, and seen in Figure 3.2.4. In phrase (x), VR echoes the preceding coupling of Dha and Ni; in phrase (xi), he approaches sustained Pa elliptically via Ma, and follows it with a drop to Ga. Behind the ornamentation, the overall trajectory of these two phrases yields the pattern N–D–M–P–G—a *vakra* (crooked) formation congenial to Bhairav. In the final gesture of the descent, phrase (xii), VR exploits the particular qualities of Re in this *rāg*. Paralleling the association between Ni and Dha in the upper tetrachord, Re is here approached via Ga, which creates a longing for continuation to, and closure on, Sā. Initially, that implication remains unfulfilled while VR repeats the G–R motion three more times, stretching out the moment, until finally resolving to Sā.

Audio Example 3.2.5 Rāg Bhairav, *ālāp*: descending phase (return to *mahdya* Sā) (*RSC*, Track 1, 01:32–02:01)
https://hdl.handle.net/20.500.12434/aa9037cd

> Descending phase
>
> (x) ṄṠṚṠṄṠN\D———ᴺ⌣D~~~~.
>
> (xi) ᴾᴹᴳM–M̃M̃P———ᴹ⌣G–.
>
> (xii) ᴿᴳᴹᴾᴹᴾᴹG\R–~~, ᴳ⌣R~~, ᴳ⌣R~, ᴳ⌣R\S———.

Fig. 3.2.4 *Ālāp* in Rāg Bhairav: descending phase, transcription. Created by author (2024), CC BY-NC-SA.

By way of summary, we can extrapolate from the particulars of VR's performance some rubrics for how to execute the ascending and descending phases of the *ālāp* (this list continues the one given above for the establishing phase):

4. Maintaining a balance between sustained and ornamental tones throughout, improvise a series of phrases, progressing steadily through the *āroh* scale of the *rāg*; continue until you reach *tār* Sā. This creates the *ascending phase*.

5. You may interrupt the ascending phase partway along by a return to Sā, to form an *intermediate phase* of the ascent.

6. If you take this option, you should next resume the ascending phase. You do not need to begin again at *madhya* Sā, but can pick up either from where you left off or in the space between Sā and that point.

7. On reaching *tār* Sā, return to *madhya* Sā, using the *avroh* scale. This creates the *descending phase*, which should be shorter than ascending phase.

8. Throughout, ensure the *rāg* grammar is projected; stay mindful of the *vādī* and *saṃvādī* tones, of other *nyās* (sustainable) *svar*s that are important to the *rāg*, and of melodic motions salient to the ascending or descending phases. Not all of these features need to be projected equally prominently, but attending to at least some of them will help you convey the salient qualities of the *rāg*.

Phase Schema: Variations

At this juncture, we need briefly to pause to absorb the following points: the rubrics sketched out above are primarily *heuristic*; they do not represent universally applied principles, but offer pragmatic guidelines for what *may* take place in an *ālāp*; variants of them are possible, and indeed common. For example, the complete *ālāp* schema—establishing, ascending and descending phases—is often abbreviated in order to proceed more directly to the entry of the *bandiś* (which is always felt to be waiting in the wings). In the ensuing section I will consider some of the ways in which the duration and ambit of a khayāl *ālāp* can be expanded or contracted, and its content elaborated, simplified or nuanced. Looking ahead to later sections, we should also note that what a performer does or does not do in their *ālāp* may well have an impact on the succeeding khayāl stage of the performance, and vice versa. For example, a *choṭā khayāl* may resume the uncompleted

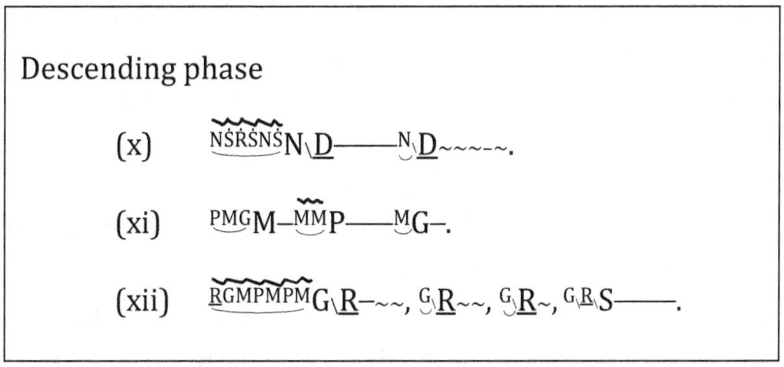

āroh trajectory of an abbreviated *ālāp* in a series of rising *bol ālāp* passages (discussed in Section 3.3). And a *baṛā khayāl* often requires only the most perfunctory *ālāp*, since it may assimilate the contour of the entire *ālāp* phase schema into its own initial process—as manifested in the staged ascent of its *baṛhat* phase to *tār* Sā, and the eventual descent of the culminating *antarā* back to *madhya* Sā (discussed in Section 4.3).

But for now, let us consider some inflections of the rubrics derived from our case study, in order to get a sense of the wider spectrum of possibilities for an *ālāp* in the khayāl style. The supplementary rubrics below pick up from the ones above, and are each followed by an explanatory gloss. Rubrics 9–15 consider the construction of phases, rubrics 16–19 the formation of phrases. My examples draw largely from subsequent tracks on *Rāg samay cakra*, so also offering a wider window onto the album as a whole.

9. While *madhya* Sā is usually the organising pitch of the establishing phase, you do not have to make this the very first note you sing (cf. rubric 1).

   A theoretical distinction from the śāstras—one also made by VR—is useful here. This is between *grah svar*, a note on which you may begin a phrase, and *nyās svar*, a note which you may sustain, or which may act as a goal (as discussed above). Hence, while Sā functions as the *nyās svar* of the establishing phase, any other note appropriate to the *rāg* may serve to initiate it.

   For example, on *Rāg sama cakra*, Track 2, VR begins Rāg Toḍī by dwelling on Re and Ga before falling to Sā (Audio Example 3.2.6, 00:25–00:51). This is consistent with the *rāg* grammar for Toḍī, in which Ga is the *saṃvādī* tone and Re can also be given prominence in conjunction with it. Following this (00:52–01:13), VR steps back up to Ga from *mandra* Dha, the *vādī* of the *rāg*, before once again returning to Sā. All this underwrites the particular importance of the *vādī* and *saṃvādī* in this *rāg*, which at times rival Sā.

   Audio Example 3.2.6 Rāg Toḍī, *ālāp*: establishing phase (*RSC*, Track 2, 00:00–01:13)
   https://hdl.handle.net/20.500.12434/9d62934f

10. In the establishing phase, when exploring the space below Sā, do not normally go any lower than the upper tetrachord of the lower octave (cf. rubrics 2 and 3).

    While it is possible in principle to go all the way down to *mandra* Sā in an extended *ālāp*, in a shorter khayāl *ālāp* one would not normally explore more than four or five notes below Sā—in other words, confining oneself largely to the upper tetrachord (*uttaraṅg*) of the lower octave (*mandra saptak*). In *Rāg samay cakra* the deepest VR goes in his lower-octave explorations is to *mandra* Ma—most notably, in Rāg Mālkauns, as heard in Audio Example 3.2.7. Here Ma is the *vādī*; the opening up of *svar* space between it and Sā prolongs the establishing phase, capturing the particular gravity of this *rāg*.

    Audio Example 3.2.7 Rāg Mālkauns, *ālāp*: establishing phase (*RSC*, Track 12, 00:18–01:37)
    https://hdl.handle.net/20.500.12434/eec80b4b

11. You may create more than one intermediate ascending phase; this/these should be each based around successively higher notes within the *rāg*, according to its grammar (cf. rubric 5).

    While, in our case study, VR includes just one intermediate ascending phase, further additional stopping-off points are possible. These should focus on successively higher pitches—those that are allowed to be sustained within the *rāg* grammar. Each intermediate ascent should return to *mahdya* Sā.

    This principle is an important means of growing an *ālāp* and appears to be historically consistent with Śārṅgadeva's division of his *ālapti* framework into gradually ascending phases, termed *svasthāna* (Śārṅgadeva 2023/1993: 199–200, also discussed by Sanyal and Widdess (2004: 145).

12. The ascending phase can go beyond *tār* Sā (cf. rubric 4).

    As we can hear on several tracks of *Rāg samay cakra*, VR follows through on the accumulating intensity of the ascending phase to rise to *tār* Re or Ga. In longer performances it would be possible to go even further, and in fact VR touches just momentarily on *tār* Ma at the peak of the ascending phase in Brindābanī Sāraṅg (Track 4, 01:30–01:52). As ever, such moves follow the grammar of their respective *rāg* and serve to bring out its particular emotive properties (*ras*). The following instances are illustrated by the respective excerpts in Audio Example 3.2.8:

    a. In Multānī, VR fleetingly sings *tār* G̱a and *tār* Ṟe as decorations of *tār* Sā, within the figure N–Ṡ–ᴳṞˢNṠ—. This does not disturb the prominence of Sā as the *saṃvādī* of the *rāg*.

    b. In Toḍī, by contrast, VR voices *tār* G̱a much more fulsomely after he has reached *tār* Sā. In this passage, he also emphasises *komal* Ga's connection with *komal* Dha (as *saṃvādī* to *vādī*), as he did in the lower register (cf. Audio Example 3.2.6). This plangent rendering of upper G̱a evokes the *karuṇ ras*, which is associated with this *rāg*.

    c. In Pūriyā Dhanāśrī, VR moves to *tār* Ṟe before he settles on *tār* Sā, in a phrase that can be distilled as G–Ḿ–Ḏ–N—, N–Ḏ–N–Ṙ–N–Ḏ–P—. Shortly afterwards, we hear *tār* Ṟe again, this time following the attainment of *tār* Sā; once again the higher note is touched on elliptically via Ni, in a movement that skirts around *tār* Sā. All these figures help create the particular expressive colouristic palette of this *sandhi prakāś* (twilight) rag.

 Audio Example 3.2.8 Ascents beyond *tār* Sā:
(a) in Multānī (*RSC*, Track 6, 00:59–01:14)
(b) in Toḍī (*RSC*, Track 2, 01:57–02:18)
(c) in Pūriyā Dhanāśrī (*RSC*, Track 7, 01:19–01:59)
https://hdl.handle.net/20.500.12434/bc05c226

13. The ascending phase does not have to go all the way up to *tār* Sā (cf. rubric 4).

    Whereas rubrics 11 and 12 showed how the notional phase schema can be expanded, here we consider ways in which its elements can be contracted, or even simply not applied.

Foreshortening of the ascending phase is common when an *ālāp* needs to be concise. Often this is the case prior to a *baṛā khayāl*, where an overly developed *ālāp* would upstage the following *khayāl*, which, after all, is meant to be the main focus of the performance. For example, in both *ālāp*s on the *Twilight Rāgs* album, VR takes the ascending phase only as far as Pa.

But brevity—actual or relative—is only one factor. In VR's *ālāp* in Rāg Śuddh Sāraṅg (Track 3), where the ascending phase stops at Pa (Audio Example 3.2.9, 00:00–01:03), we can assume brevity not to be top priority, because he then allows himself a second ascent to the same pitch (Audio Example 3.2.9, 01:03–01:34).

Audio Example 3.2.9 Rāg Śuddh Sāraṅg, *ālāp* (*RSC*, Track 3, 00:00–01:35)
https://hdl.handle.net/20.500.12434/64f47f8d

VR's motive for stopping at Pa is more likely not to overshadow the generally low profile of the first line of the following *bandiś*. When I asked him about this, he replied that this was not a conscious decision, though, interestingly, he did affirm a wider principle: 'you must let the *khayāl* influence your *ālāp*; the *ālāp* is not just your creation, but is influenced by lots of things. You have to know the meaning of the *bandiś* and match its style in your *ālāp*'.

This point is further illustrated by a presentation in Rāg Bhairav on the *Music in Motion* (AUTRIM Project) website (Rao and Van der Meer n.d.: https://autrimncpa.wordpress.com/bhairav/, 01:06–02:10). Here, vocalist Padma Talwalkar progresses the ascending phase of her *ālāp* only as far as Dha; on the return journey to Sā she pauses on Ga. These prominent tones prepare the *svar* space for the same pitches in the opening of the *bandiś* 'Jāgo mohan pyāre', which flows on almost seamlessly in a beautiful transition into the *khayāl* that obviates any further exposition of the *ālāp*. This example nicely illustrates the point made at the opening of this section, that the ascending phase of an *ālāp* is often curtailed in order not to overly delay the entrance of the *bandiś*.

In other circumstances, it may be possible to dispense with the ascending and descending phases of the *ālāp* altogether. Many khayāl performances present only the establishing phase of an *ālāp*—enough to affirm Sā and indicate the essential characteristics of the *rāg* which are then fully explored in the ensuing *khayāl*. In such cases, this is usually a *baṛā khayāl*, and the prescinded form of the *ālāp* resembles the form known as *aucār*. Examples include Gangubai Hangal's (1913–2009) recording of Rāg Bhairav (1994) or Kumar Gandharva's (1924–92) rendition of Mālkauns (1993).

14. In certain *rāg*s, it can be appropriate to begin with the descending phase.

Some *rāgs*, known as *uttaraṅg pradhan rāg*s, emphasise the upper tetrachord. In such contexts, phrases may be oriented around *tār* Sā rather than *madhya* Sā, taking this higher pitch as their starting point and/or ultimate goal. One such *rāg* is Basant, whose *vādī* is identified by Bhatkhande as, explicitly, *tār* Sā (see Section 2.5.14).

This characteristic can be heard in the *bandiś* 'Phulavā binata', which VR chooses for this *rāg* (Track 14). Its opening sets out from *tār* Sā; and so, accordingly, does the *ālāp* which prefaces it. Here, then, VR is true to his maxim that what you do in your *ālāp* should relate to the content of your *khayāl*. Indeed, the phase schema of this *ālāp* unusually comprises *two* descending phases, both beginning on *tār* Sā, with no prior establishing or ascending phase. The first descent (Audio Example 3.2.10), pauses on Pa, then Ga. VR then momentarily drops further to *mahdya* Sā, but only as a jumping off point to sing the so-called Lalit *aṅg*, which involves both *suddh* and *tivra* versions of Ma sung adjacently—a figure that draws on the idiosyncratic grammar of Rāg Lalit. This motion resolves onto Ga, which could be heard as the goal tone of this first, intermediate descending phase.

Audio Example 3.2.10 Rāg Basant, *ālāp*: first descending phase (*RSC*, Track 14, 00:00–00:29)
https://hdl.handle.net/20.500.12434/136bbc82

VR next steps back up through Ḿa and Dha to regain *tār* Sā; he redoubles this motion, touching on *tār* Re, and then curves back to begin the second descending phase (Audio Example, 3.2.11). This is initially modelled on the first descent; again, Pa and Ga function as intermediate goal tones. From Ga, VR makes a delightful rising deflection, Ḿ–N, before completing the descent to *madhya* Sā. This ends the *ālāp* and leads directly to the following *drut ektāl khayāl*, launched from the same *uttaraṅg* register.

Audio Example 3.2.11 Rāg Basant, *ālāp*: second descending phase, leading to opening of *bandiś* (*RSC*, Track 14, 00:29–01:06)
https://hdl.handle.net/20.500.12434/5aa5f800

(As a codicil to these observations, we should also note the complementary type of *rāg*, *pūrvaṅg pradhan*, which focuses on the lower tetrachord. Some *rāg*s are often considered in complementary pairs that exhibit similar scale forms and qualities but privilege opposite tetrachords. Well-known examples include Darbārī Kānaḍā and Aḍānā, which are *pūrvaṅg* and *uttaraṅg pradhan rāg*s respectively; and, similarly, Bhūpālī and Deśkār.)

15. The elements of the phase schema are not radically discrete; they should flow from one another as a continuous process; their identities may sometimes blur. Phrases do not always map onto phases.

These points are a reminder that the phase schema which we extrapolated from VR's Bhairav *ālāp* is more an implicit, notional framework behind the music's surface than an explicit, empirical structure that manifests on every occasion. The actually sung *phrases* do not always align with the theoretical *phases* of the schema.

We can hear this by revisiting the extract from Pūriyā Dhanāśrī, discussed under rubric 12, above—Audio Example 3.2.8(c). In the elliptical turn around *tār* Sā the ascending phase blends seamlessly into the descending phase within a single sung phrase. Here, phase boundary and phrase boundary do not coincide. Contrast this with the equivalent point in Rāg Yaman—Audio Example 3.2.12. Here, after ascending from Ni to *tār* Sā, VR sustains this goal pitch, winds joyful variants of the decorative figure N–D–N–Ṙ around it, then takes a short breath; this phrase and the ascending phase are both over. In a new phrase (at 00:25 on the audio example), he sings *tār* Sā again, and begins the descending phase. Here, then, phrase and phase *are* in alignment. Even so, there is no change of idiom at the turning point; we still sense continuity between the successive ph(r)ases.

Audio Example 3.2.12 Rāg Yaman, *ālāp*: turn from ascending to descending phase (*RSC*, Track 9, 02:19–02:56)
https://hdl.handle.net/20.500.12434/4b7e18e3

In VR's realisation of Bhīmpalāsī, we find a subtle blurring of identity between all the elements of the *ālāp*'s phase schema, none of which precisely aligns with the manifest phrases—as we can trace in Audio Example 3.2.13. In the establishing phase (00:00–00:18), VR merges the motion below and above the initially sustained Sā into a single phrase: S—, .P–N̲–S–G̲—R–S. Already this elicits an ascending tendency beyond the immediate *svar* space around Sā, to Ga; and this blends into the trajectory of the subsequent intermediate ascending phase, to Ma, to Pa, to N̲i̲ (00:19–00:43)—before returning to Sā (00:44–01:00). This non-alignment of the phase framework with the phrase structure continues in the concluding ascending phase (begins 01:00), where the attainment of *tār* Sā (at 01:21) melts into the beginning of the descending phase back to *madhya* Sā, all within a single arc.

Audio Example 3.2.13 Rāg Bhīmpalāsī, *ālāp* (*RSC*, Track 5, 00:35–02:26)
https://hdl.handle.net/20.500.12434/31b570eb

A similar compression of establishing, ascending and descending phases can be heard in VR's *ālāp* for Rāg Bihāg (Audio Example 3.2.14). Striking here is the way practically all phrases are drawn magnetically to Ga, the *vādī* of the *rāg* and a recurrent goal pitch (*nyās svar*) whose force of attraction becomes a key organising principle, working in productive tension with the phase schema.

Audio Example 3.2.14 Rāg Bihāg, *ālāp* (*RSC*, Track 11, 00:00–01:34)
https://hdl.handle.net/20.500.12434/3de48f10

The phrases discussed in these examples are so fluidly conjoined that it may seem arbitrary to conceptually separate them into different phases at all. Nonetheless the phase schema remains discernible, even if, in these circumstances, it is sensed as a more abstract presence behind the sensory formation of actual phrases. This tells us that these discrete but interacting principles are both part of an *ālāp*'s organisation. And it also tells us that the way successive phrases are conjoined is an important aspect of how to sing an *ālāp*. It is to this matter that we turn next, in a further set of rubrics.

Phrase Formation and Succession

16. In each phrase of the ascending phase, do not generally go higher in your melodic elaborations than its organising pitch or goal tone. However, you may subtly allude to the organising pitch of the next phrase as you approach the end of your present one.

    The sustained organising pitch (*nyās svar*) of a phrase represents a kind of ceiling. The musical elaborations that decorate this pitch should normally come from below—from the *svar* space that you have already begun to open up—so as to deepen the impression of the *rāg* as so far unfolded, rather than steal the thunder of what is coming up. However, this is more of a general principle than an abstract rule, and may sometimes be relaxed. In particular, it can be appropriate to give a discreet hint of the *nyās svar* of the next phrase as you reach the end of your present one. To illustrate this, let us briefly revisit the intermediate ascending phase of VR's *ālāp* in Rāg Bhairav—as captured in Audio Example 3.2.3 and Figure 3.2.2. Here the goal tone is Ma, attained and sustained in phrase (iv); and it is approached from Ga, sustained in phrase (iii). Within each of these phrases, the sustained tones are elaborated by notes no higher than themselves. Nonetheless, once he reaches Ma, VR turns back to Sā with a *murkī* that fleetingly touches on Pa: for those with sharp ears, this anticipates the organising pitch of the next phase.

17. You don't have to begin a phrase on its organising pitch.

    Just as an *ālāp* does not have to begin on Sā (rubric 9) so any phrase can begin on a note other than its organising pitch. To reiterate the terminology of the historical treatises, there is a distinction between *grah svar*, a note on which you can begin, and *nyās svar*, a note which you can hold. (Of course, in order to comply with rubric 16, the former must not be higher than the latter.) This is clearly illustrated in the extract from Bhairav just considered.

18. You don't have to end a phrase on its organising pitch.

    Even though the sustained, organising pitch of a phrase is usually perceived as its goal, it does not have to be sustained right to the phrase's end. We can see examples of such behaviour in Figure 3.2.5, which notates the ascending and descending phases of VR's Bhūpālī *ālāp*, as heard in Audio Example 3.2.15 (I do not consider the establishing phase here). We can readily note that in phrases (i) and (ii) the respective organising pitches Pa and Dha—shown in bold—are approached from Ga, below (cf. rubric 16), *and are then quitted with a drop back to Ga.* While not compulsory, this return helps keep the *svar* space below each goal pitch (indeed also the *vādī svar*) alive as VR progresses through the ascending phase.

Audio Example 3.2.15 Rāg Bhūpālī, *ālāp*: ascending and descending phases (*RSC*, Track 8, 00:34–01:30)
https://hdl.handle.net/20.500.12434/15d329f8

Ascending phase

(i) G^{G}R**P**——^{P}G——v.

(ii) ^{P}GP**D**——v, GDP^{P}G——.

(iii) ^{P}GP$^{\dot{S}}$D, **Ṡ**—————…

Descending phase

(iv) …$^{\dot{S}}$D Ṡ$^{\dot{S}}$D^{D}P^{P}**G**—.

(v) G–^{G}RP–^{P}**G**—.

(vi) G–^{G}R, G**R**–,

(vii) S^{S}RG^{G}RS^{S}Ḍ**S**—v.

Fig. 3.2.5 *Ālāp* in Rāg Bhūpālī: ascending and descending phases, transcription. Created by author (2024), CC BY-NC-SA.

19. The *svar* spaces of successive phrases can (and usually do) overlap.

We can note a related property in the same Bhūpālī *ālāp*—namely that successive phrases often start by revisiting part of the earlier *svar* space, creating a *svar*-space overlap. For example, in Figure 3.2.5 while phrase (i) reaches Pa, phrase (ii) begins on Ga below it, before attaining Dha; phrase (iii) also starts on Ga, before ascending even higher, to *tār* Sā.

Svar-space overlaps may occur in the opposite direction. In the descending phase of the Bhūpālī extract, phrase (iv), dropping from *tār* Sā, has Ga as its goal; Ga remains the goal tone of the next phrase, (v), which backfills the previous pitch space by recapturing Pa, even as it also alludes to an impending descent by touching on Re. Similarly, the final phrase, (vii), begins on, and is organised around, Sā; but the phrase recoups the higher space of its forebear, in the motion **S**^{S}RG^{G}R–, before mapping out new pitch space in the lower octave—…S^{S}Ḍ**S**—.

The purpose of such overlaps is to foster connectivity between phrases and to keep the entire *rāg* alive and growing even when the focus is on specific organising pitches. This makes the point that it is the nurtured *rāg* itself—rather than the more abstract principles of the phase schema—that is the living heart of the music.

Summary: Terminology and Key Principles of Ālāp Formation

To conclude this Exploration, I here recapitulate and re-gloss some of the main technical terms used above, along with their associated principles. This is principally by way of summary, but it also points to the possibility of a formalised theory of <u>kh</u>ayāl-style *ālāp*—a potential future project.

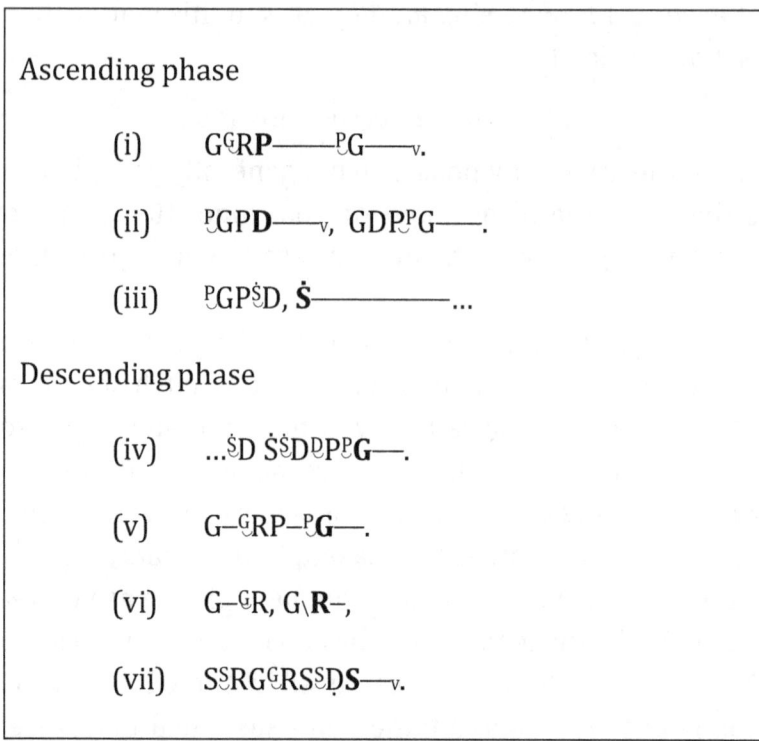

- *Ālāp*s progress through several *phases*: typically an *establishing phase*, an *ascending phase* (which may be subdivided into *interim* and *concluding* phases), and finally a *descending phase*. In this, my own nomenclature, I have preferred the word 'phase' to 'section' since it captures the essentially fluid nature of *ālāp*s and the way they shape time. I use the term *phase schema* to signify this sequence as a whole.
- *Ālāp*s comprise a succession of *phrases*. Pragmatically, we may describe a phrase as a short unit of melodic material articulated by a breath, pause or some other marker. While it is possible to make a theoretical distinction between different phrase levels (for example, 'phrase', 'sub-phrase'), this has not been essential to our present purpose (for a formalised investigation of phrase grammar in *ālāp*, see Clarke 2017). A more useful distinction, pursued above, is that between the phrases and phases of an *ālāp*, which, significantly, do not always map onto each other.
- Phrases are usually organised around one or more *sustained tones* or *standing notes*—or, to use the śastric term for this, *nyās svar*, meaning a note which can be held or sat on. Eligible notes include the *vādī* and *saṃvādī* tones of a *rāg* but need not be confined to these. *Nyās* can also mean the note on which a phrase (or a *rāg*) concludes—which may or may not be the same as any of its sustained notes. In similar vein, *goal pitch* refers to an emphasised note within a given stage of an *ālāp* (Sanyal and Widdess 2004: 145). Depending on context, I have used all these terms, with their overlapping shades of meaning, as well as the general descriptor, *organising pitch*. It should also be clear that I have used 'note', 'tone' and 'pitch' largely interchangeably, none of which fully captures the meaning of the Hindavi term *svar*.
- The sustained, organising pitch of a phrase is usually embellished by various kinds of ornament (*alaṅkār*) which bring the *svar* to life. In the notation of individual phrases, I have not shown every microscopic detail of these, as important as they are, since my aim has usually been to foreground what is melodically structural.
- I have invented the term *svar space* (adapting the western theoretical term *pitch space*) to refer metaphorically to the compass of pitches available to decorate a sustained note. As an *ālāp* unfolds, and the *rāg* opens up, so the bandwidth of this space gradually increases. In the ascending phase, the available *svar* space lies primarily below the current sustained note. In the descending phase, because the *svar* space has already been fully opened up, there is somewhat freer movement through it. Perceptually, *svar* space is embedded as a trace in the memory, subtly regenerated as we pass through the *ālāp*, deepening the *rāg*.

Exploration 2: Duration and Proportion

One question that faces any soloist as they begin a *rāg* performance is, how long shall I make my *ālāp*? The possibilities are elastic. Musicians often nostalgically recount a mythological heyday (I have heard VR do this) when famed artists performed *ālāp*s lasting up to two hours, making it possible to penetrate the true depths of a *rāg*. At the other extreme, an *ālāp* may last under a minute: accomplished performers know how to present a *rāg*'s essence in just a few phrases when necessary.

An *ālāp*'s duration—in both relative and absolute terms—is dependent on genre and performing context. Figure 3.2.6 considers several exemplary Hindustani classical genres, indicating typical proportions of their *ālāp* stage (shaded) relative to their composition-based stage (unshaded). These representations are highly schematic—approximate indications of events which may be variously extended, contracted, omitted or compounded, according to circumstance. The same *rāg* is of course performed continuously throughout.

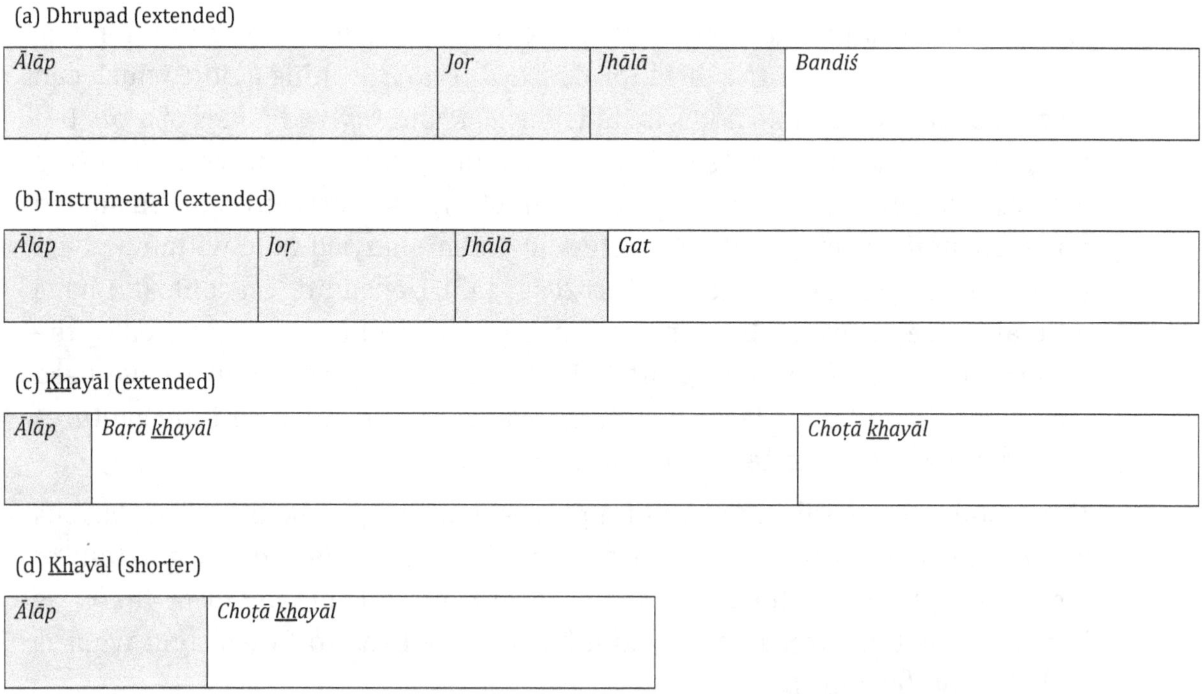

Fig. 3.2.6 Relative duration of *ālāp* and composition stages in Hindustani classical genres. Created by author (2024), CC BY-NC-SA.

In part (a) we see how, in an extended dhrupad performance (whether vocal or instrumental), *ālāp* is the predominant feature. Even under present-day concert constraints and audience expectations, *ālāp*s lasting between thirty and forty-five minutes are not uncommon; these will often include *joṛ* and *jhālā* sections, extending the *ālāp* proper, and invoking a regular rhythmic pulse, but not the full metrical apparatus of *tāl* (and usually without drum accompaniment). The succeeding *bandiś* (with pakhāvaj accompaniment) is proportionally much shorter—in absolute terms commonly lasting up to around ten to fifteen minutes, which still gives scope for extemporisation and development. In variants of this schema (usually in subsequent, lighter items of a programme), the *ālāp* stage may be less extensive, perhaps dispensing with *joṛ* and *jhālā*, and re-balancing the proportional relationship with the succeeding *bandiś*.

Instrumental *rāg* performances likewise often begin with an extended *ālāp*, typically lasting between fifteen and forty minutes, and also including *joṛ* and *jhālā*—as mapped in Figure 3.2.6(b). The composition (*gat*) section that follows (accompanied by tabla) is likely to be commensurably substantial. It may involve more than one composition, the first in a relatively slow (*vilambit*) *lay* or in *madhya lay*, the subsequent one(s) in *drut lay*. In lighter renditions, both *ālāp* and *gat* may be briefer, with *joṛ* and *jhālā* omitted.

In a k͟hayāl performance, an *ālāp*'s duration depends to a large extent on what follows it. At the beginning of a programme, an *ālāp* is likely to preface a slow, extended *baṛā k͟hayāl*, followed by a faster *choṭā k͟hayāl*, the former imparting an aesthetic gravity comparable to dhrupad (a topic I discuss at greater length in Section 4.3). Paradoxically, this requires the *ālāp* to be radically shorter than is the case with dhrupad—compare parts (a) and (c) of Figure 3.2.6—since the opening stage of the *baṛā k͟hayāl* itself draws on the *anibaddh* (unmetred) ethos of an *ālāp*. The *ālāp* proper is accordingly often reduced to just a few phrases, though it can be longer (as in VR's *ālāp*s on the *Twilight Rāgs* album, which last around three minutes). In subsequent or shorter concert items, the *baṛā k͟hayāl* may be omitted, leaving just the *ālāp* and *choṭā k͟hayāl*; this allows the *ālāp* scope for expansion—see Figure 3.2.6(d). Even so, there remains the question of proportion: it would be unusual for an *ālāp* to be longer than the succeeding *choṭā k͟hayāl*.

All the tracks on *Rāg samay cakra* follow the simpler, *ālāp–choṭā k͟hayāl* schema shown in Figure 3.2.6(d). The album format and the pre-requirement to keep each *rāg* performance to an average of around five minutes serve as creative constraints at every level. At the level of the album as a whole, VR plays with the duration of tracks on either side of the mean length. This is demonstrated in Figure 3.2.7, which provides track data and a related column chart. Here we see significant variation in the length of performances, with Rāg Kedār at the shortest extreme (3'48"), Pūriyā Dhanāśrī at the longest (7'39"), and Bihāg lasting exactly the mean duration of the entire series (5'33"). These variations create a subtle ebb and flow in the large-scale pacing, which is tracked by the trendline mapped onto the column chart; this is based on a three-period moving average (i.e. the average duration of successive sets of three *rāg*s—of Tracks 1–3, then 2–4, then 3–5 etc.).

Track durations

1. Bhairav	00:05:06
2. Toḍī	00:05:47
3. Śuddh Sāraṅg	00:05:12
4. Brindābanī Sāraṅg	00:03:53
5. Bhīmpalāsī	00:05:15
6. Multānī	00:04:45
7. Pūriyā Dhanāśrī	00:07:39
8. Bhūpālī	00:07:03
9. Yaman	00:07:22
10. Kedār	00:03:48
11. Bihāg	00:05:33
12. Mālkauns	00:06:57
13. Megh	00:04:32
14. Basant	00:04:47
Average duration	**00:05:33**

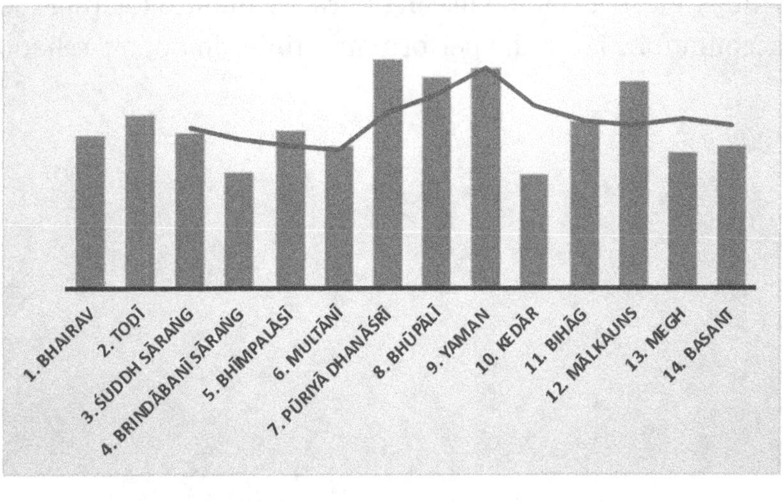

Fig. 3.2.7 *Rāg samay cakra*: track durations. Created by author (2024), CC BY-NC-SA.

Figure 3.2.8 shows how VR varies the absolute and relative lengths of individual components—*ālāp* and *choṭā khayāl*—across performances. The durations of *ālāp*s, range from 0'56" (Basant) to 3'27" (Pūriyā Dhanāśrī); with Bhairav, at 1'59", clocking in close to the mean duration of 2'01". (Instrumental introductions, whose lengths are also somewhat variable, are not analysed separately here, but rather included in the *ālāp* duration.) Similarly for *choṭā khayāl* durations: these range from 1'45" (Brindābanī Sāraṅg) to 5'19" (Pūriyā Dhanāśrī), with Mālkauns, at 3'30", close to the mean of 3'32". But interestingly, while *ālāp* and *khayāl* sometimes increase or decrease their three-period moving average length in step, at other times the trends proceed in contrary motion. We see flexibility in every dimension.

	***Ālāp* duration**	***Choṭā khayāl* duration**
1. Bhairav	00:01:59	00:03:07
2. Toḍī	00:02:42	00:03:06
3. Śuddh Sāraṅg	00:01:33	00:03:39
4. Brindābanī Sāraṅg	00:02:08	00:01:45
5. Bhīmpalāsī	00:02:25	00:02:50
6. Multānī	00:01:19	00:03:26
7. Pūriyā Dhanāśrī	00:02:20	00:05:19
8. Bhūpālī	00:01:28	00:05:35
9. Yaman	00:03:14	00:04:08
10. Kedār	00:01:23	00:02:25
11. Bihāg	00:01:30	00:04:01
12. Mālkauns	00:03:27	00:03:30
13. Megh	00:01:48	00:02:44
14. Basant	00:00:56	00:03:51
Average duration	**00:02:01**	**00:03:32**

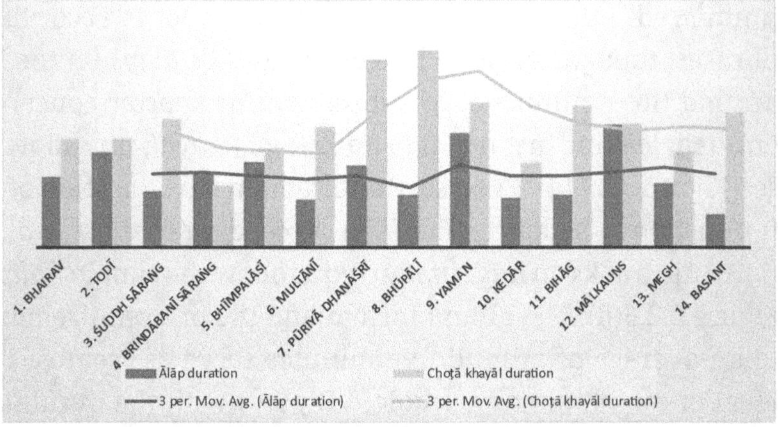

Fig. 3.2.8 *Rāg samay cakra: ālāp* and *choṭā khayāl* durations. Created by author (2024), CC BY-NC-SA.

These relativities are shown in another way in Figure 3.2.9, which charts *ālāp* length as a percentage of the overall performance duration. For example, in Bhūpālī and Basant, the *ālāp* only accounts for some 20% of the overall duration, whereas in Yaman this figure is 44%. And, unusually, in the cases of Mālkauns and Brindābanī Sāraṅg, the *ālāp* lasts half of the performance or more (50% and 55% respectively). If these seem relatively long durations, they remain acceptable because of the context: a sequence of many short performances, which would not be the norm in a live concert. Here, in the interests of creating a satisfying whole, VR seems to be teasing norms without violating them: the *ālāp*s, which on average account for 37% of the performance time, do not overshadow the *khayāl*s.

	Ālāp as % of duration	**Ālāp duration**	**Performance duration**
1. Bhairav	39	00:01:59	00:05:06
2. Toḍī	46	00:02:42	00:05:47
3. Śuddh Sāraṅg	30	00:01:33	00:05:12
4. Brindābanī Sāraṅg	55	00:02:08	00:03:53
5. Bhīmpalāsī	46	00:02:25	00:05:15
6. Multānī	28	00:01:19	00:04:45
7. Pūriyā Dhanāśrī	31	00:02:20	00:07:39
8. Bhūpālī	21	00:01:28	00:07:03
9. Yaman	44	00:03:14	00:07:22
10. Kedār	36	00:01:23	00:03:48
11. Bihāg	27	00:01:30	00:05:33
12. Mālkauns	50	00:03:27	00:06:57
13. Megh	40	00:01:48	00:04:32
14. Basant	20	00:00:56	00:04:47
Average:	**37**	**00:02:01**	**00:05:33**

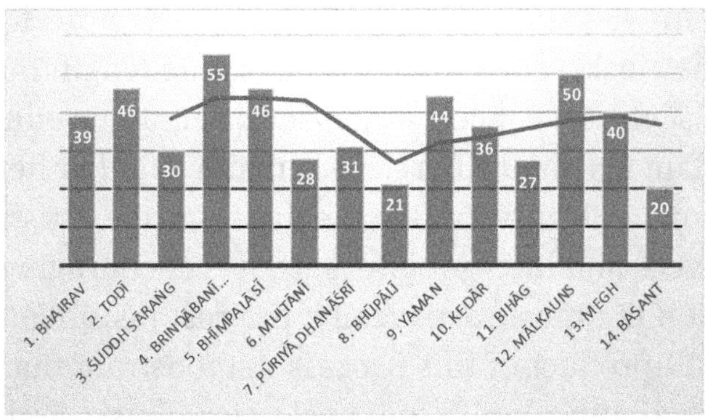

Fig. 3.2.9 *Rāg samay cakra*: *ālāp* durations as percentage of track durations. Created by author (2024), CC BY-NC-SA.

Finally, Figure 3.2.10 analyses duration *within ālāps*. This measures the periods before and after the arrival on *tār* Sā, a key goal in the phase schema (as discussed in Exploration 1). In the case of Rāg Śuddh Sāraṅg, which only ascends as far as Pa, I have taken the second ascent to this note as the point of measurement; and Basant is omitted from the data, because, as an *uttaraṅg pradhan rāg*, it begins on *tār* Sā and hence has no ascending phase as such (see rubric 14, above). As would be expected, this analysis shows the period prior to *tār* Sā (or equivalent highest note) to be significantly the longer, accounting for on average 77% of the overall *ālāp* duration. This is approximately the inverse proportion of the ratio of overall *ālāp* duration to overall performance duration shown in the previous figure.

	Duration up *tār* Sā*	**Duration after *tār* Sā***	**Pre-*tār* Sā as % of ālāp**
1. Bhairav	00:01:27	00:00:32	73
2. Toḍī	00:01:47	00:00:54	66
3. Śuddh Sāraṅg*	00:01:11	00:00:22	76
4. Brindābanī Sāraṅg	00:01:32	00:00:36	72
5. Bhīmpalāsī	00:01:57	00:00:28	81
6. Multānī	00:01:03	00:00:16	80
7. Pūriyā Dhanāśrī	00:01:47	00:00:33	76
8. Bhūpālī	00:00:59	00:00:29	67
9. Yaman	00:02:27	00:00:47	76
10. Kedār	00:01:14	00:00:09	89
11. Bihāg	00:01:11	00:00:19	79
12. Mālkauns	00:02:35	00:00:52	75
13. Megh	00:01:39	00:00:09	92
Average:	**00:01:36**	**00:00:30**	**77**

(* or highest goal tone)

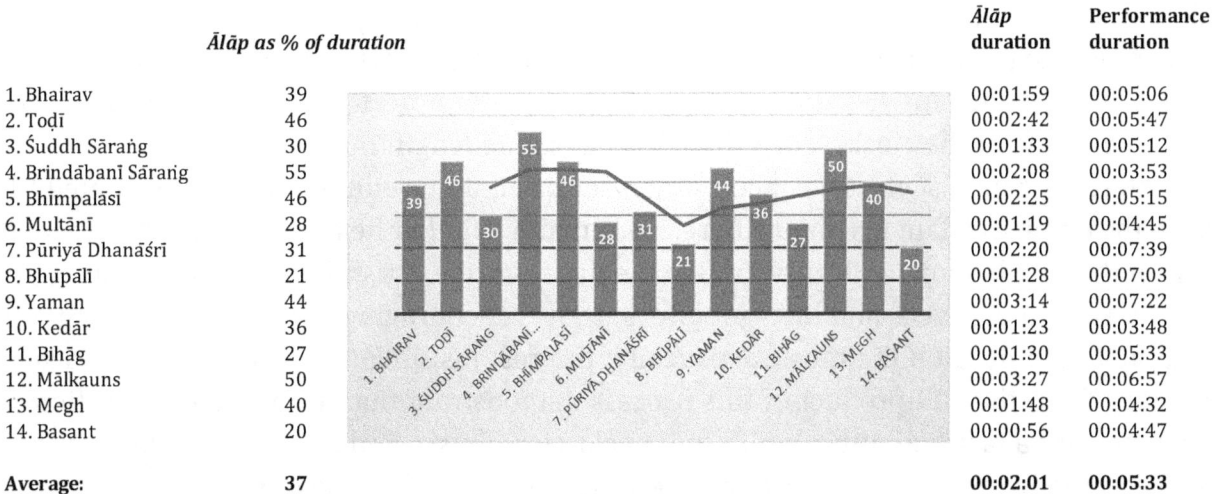

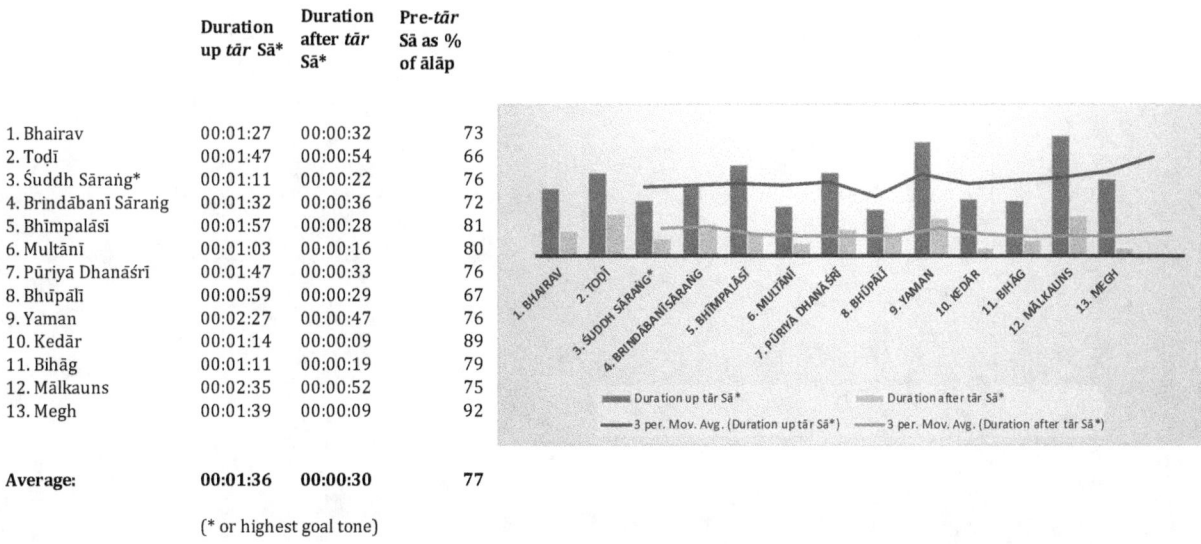

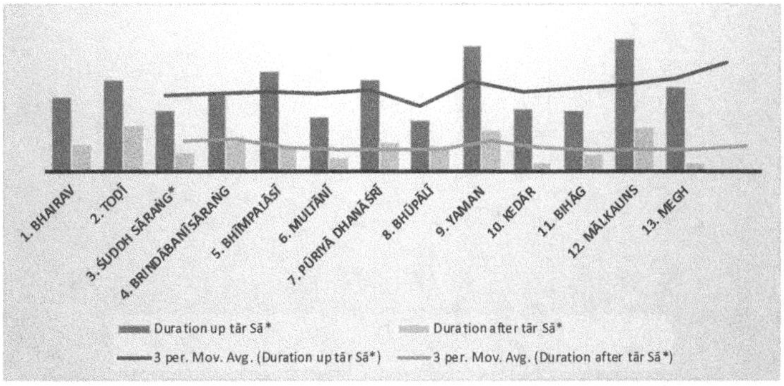

Fig. 3.2.10 *Rāg samay cakra*: durations before and after reaching *tār* Sā within *ālāp*. Created by author (2024), CC BY-NC-SA.

In summary, these analyses illustrate the extent to which the relative and absolute durations of an *ālāp* and its internal elements can be varied within a given performance context. The approach here is empirical—measurement based—and could be suggestive of a wider programme of analysis comparing, say, artists, *gharānās* and genres from similar standpoints across a wide corpus. But there is also the question of the performer's phenomenology—of how duration is *felt* and judged in experience. This question has practical relevance for the student, since the pacing of a performance cannot be learnt just by looking at the clock—even though its absolute length may well be determined by an external agency, such as a concert organiser or album producer. Having presented VR with the empirical data assembled here, I asked him whether he had consciously intended any of the trends shown. He answered in the negative: the artists had begun recording the earlier *rāgs* in the cycle, and then got into a groove, encouraging each other through their interaction to develop the music artistically; the rest just followed. The data empirically evinced from the end-product of this process demonstrate that durational proportion is as important a factor as any other in Indian classical music, and can be similarly nuanced and creatively fashioned—indeed at several levels. But, like those other factors, this one also has to be internalised through a long period of practice and accumulated experience.

Exploration 3: *Ālāp* Syllables

Among the least explained aspects of khayāl are the non-lexical vocables—syllables without a meaning—that vocalists use when fashioning an *ālāp*. For all that this matter is barely talked about, these sounds are crucial, since a singer cannot sing without singing *something*, and the introductory *ālāp* of a *khayāl* does not, as a general principle, use any text. (This changes during a *bandiś*, when a singer may use the technique of *bol ālāp*, that is, *ālāp*-style passages which deploy words from the song text.) So, if you are singing a prefatory *ālāp*, what vocables should you use?

Two options might be *sargam* syllables and *ākār* (singing to the vowel 'ā')—as in the case of *tāns*. But, while your teacher may encourage you to sing *sargam* syllables while you are learning *ālāp* (to stay aware of what you are singing and the direction you are going in), it is less common to do so in an actual performance. Conversely, one might indeed use 'ā'—but often this would be one of only several syllables. In practice, a large range of vocables is available: a sample taken from the *ālāp*s VR sings on *Rāg samay cakra* includes 'ā', 'a', 'nā', 'mā', 'e', 're', 'de', 'ī', rī, and 'nū'—a syllabary typical of many khayāl singers. I spell these as if they were transliterated from Hindi, Urdu or Sanskrit, to reflect possible linguistic backgrounds, even though, in an *ālāp*, such syllables are non-lexical (they do not form parts of actual words) and non-semantic (they carry no conventional meaning).

When and how does a singer deploy such vocables? And, more speculatively, what is their source, and what logic governs their combination? In the following discussion, I will explore both these dimensions—the practical and theoretical—since each has a bearing on the other.

To begin with the practical, let us revisit VR's *ālāp* in Rāg Bhairav, listening again to Audio Example 3.2.1, and giving particular attention to the syllables sung. Figure 3.2.11 transcribes these for each phase of the *ālāp*, in a layout corresponding to that of the *sargam* transcriptions in Figures 3.2.1–3.2.4.

Audio Example 3.2.1 [repeated] Rāg Bhairav, *ālāp* (*RSC*, Track 1, 00:00–02:01)
https://hdl.handle.net/20.500.12434/54b2530c

Establishing phase (00:00–00:37)

Nā—, Nu>ā—nā.

Nā nā— nu>ā—, re nu>ā—.

Intermediate ascending phase (00:38–01:01)

Ā—(n)a,

ā—, ā—,

ā—(n)a nā—.

Concluding ascending phase (01:02–01:32)

Ā— (m)ā—.

Ā— nā—,

nā— nā—>e, e,

nā—.

Descending phase (01:32–01:59)

Nā—, nu>ā—.

Nu>ā ā—(n)a.

E—>ā—, nu>ā—, nū, nū>e—.

Fig. 3.2.11 Rāg Bhairav, *ālāp*: syllable sequence. Created by author (2024), CC BY-NC-SA.

It is clear from Figure 3.2.11 that the two most common syllables in this *ālāp* are 'nā' and 'ā'. The prevalence of 'ā' confirms *ākār* as an implicit underlying principle for *ālāp* singing. 'Nā' could be interpreted as an inflection of this which adds a soft dental consonant that focuses the initial articulation and tuning of *svar*—especially important in the establishing phase. In the ascending phase, VR uses 'ā' and 'nā' in full chest voice as he approaches *tār* Sā, to give a strong open sound—appropriately to this serious *rāg*. As he descends back to *mahdya* Sā, he returns to 'nā' and its variants, giving this performance a general symmetry. Prominent among these variants is 'nu>ā'—which should be read as 'nu' morphing into 'nā'. Initially, 'nu' is only briefly touched on, concentrating the beginning of the sound envelope at the front of the mouth before opening up to 'ā' at the back. At the end of the descending phase, VR more explicitly voices 'nū' as a vocable in its own right, before morphing it to 'e'. A related tendency is his subtle shaping of the envelope of a vowel with a half-articulated 'm' or 'n'—notated with parentheses in the Figure—which gives a subtle rhythmic nudge to the sustained vowel.

The syllabary in this *ālāp*, then, is carefully controlled: the overall selection is relatively confined; adjacent syllables are usually related; and contrasting ones—such as 're'—or less regular ones—such as 'nū'—are used sparingly and/or at strategic moments. The penchant for morphing sounds is a more individual aspect of VR's *gāyakī*; indeed, in the next track,

Rāg Toḍī, we find an even more idiosyncratic application. VR's *ālāp* in this *rāg* can be found complete in Audio Example 3.2.16; and its syllable sequence is notated in Figure 3.2.12, following the conventions used above.

Audio Example 3.2.16 Rāg Toḍī, *ālāp* (*RSC*, Track 2, 00:00–02:42)
https://hdl.handle.net/20.500.12434/a8532369

Establishing phase (00:25–01:12)

(R)a—,

ra>e nā—, a>ā>e—.

Da re da nā— e—,

nā— re— e re nu>ā—.

Ascending phase (01:13–02:11)

Dā—,

de re—,

nā—(n)ā—ā—>e— e—.

Nā—,

ā—, nā—,

e— [*tār* Sā] — (m)a(v)e(m)a(d)uā—.

Nā—(n)a>e(v)e.

E—he—(n)ā—.

Descending phase (02:11–02:41)

Ā—(h)e—he-e-e—, nā—.

Nā—>a—(n)ā—,

re—e—(h)e he, nu>ā—.

Fig. 3.2.12 Rāg Toḍī, *ālāp*: syllable sequence. Created by author (2024), CC BY-NC-SA.

Syllables such as 'da', 'de', 're' and 'nā', provide a sonic contrast to those VR deployed in his Bhairav *ālāp*. Sung in close succession, the initial consonants lend a forward impulse to the musical progression. While these sounds would be recognised as part of a khayāl syllabary, the morphing phonetic string that VR sings after reaching *tār* Sā, '(m)a(v)e(m)a(d)uā—', is more idiosyncratic, as are the succeeding sequences, 'E—he—(n)ā—' and 'Ā—(h)e—he-e-e—'. What is the intent here? We might surmise that, in the imaginative spirit of khayāl, VR is pushing a little beyond the orthodox syllabary in order to intensify a peak expressive moment in a *rāg* associated with the *karuṇ ras*, whose qualities are pathos, sadness and compassion. He brings emotional expression to the brink of actual words, but holds back from crossing the boundary, as this would destroy the very effect of yearning for the ineffable that is so essential here.

But, in any case, who decides what is or is not permissible? The question of who or what determines orthodoxy for *ālāp* syllables in khayāl remains moot. Historical writings offer some guidance, though the lessons may be equivocal. For example, Hakim Karam Imām's treatise of 1856–7, *Ma'adan ul-musīqī*, lays down a distinct orthodoxy about which syllables may or may not be used in an *ālāp*, and in what combinations (Imām 1959: 11–13; for a commentary on the socio-historical significance of this work see Qureshi 2001: 324–35). Imām roots his maxims in mythological prehistory, invoking 'Mahadeo' (Śiva) and 'the inhabitants of the Nether world' as the source of the originating syllables 'ā', 'nā', 'tā' and 'rā' (Imām 1959: 11–12). But his authority for how this syllabary can be extended (to include, for example, 're', 'nām', 'tom'), and its elements combined into *bol*s (such as 'ta-nā', 'ni-rī'), comes from the historically sanctioned practice of the *kalāvant*s—elite singers whose pedigree goes back to the court of Akbar the Great (r. 1556–1605). Yet Imām is here discussing the *kalāvant*s as exponents of dhrupad, not khayāl; conversely, he tells us that the *qavvāl*s, among whom 'the singing of *Khayal* has been prevalent', 'do not have *Alap*. Instead they begin with words of *Tarana*' (ibid: 11).

On the one hand, then, Imām's rubrics would seem not to bear on present-day khayāl practice, since contemporary *khayāliyā*s indeed do sing *ālāp*s, unlike their *qavvāl* forebears, but in a different way from *dhrupadiyās*/*kalāvant*s. On the other hand, a comparison between the syllables sanctioned by Imām and those used by present-day *khayāliyā*s reveals some overlaps and connections. So it is worth considering the extent to which the non-lexical syllabaries of tarānā and dhrupad bear on khayāl—even if indirectly—given that these remain current in Hindustani music.

Tarānā syllables are familiar to most khayāl singers because this genre remains part of khayāl practice—a *tarānā* would optionally be sung at the *end* of a *rāg* performance as a virtuosic follow-on (or alternative) to a *choṭā khayāl*. The syllables used—such as 'tā', 'nā', 'de', 're', 'dim', 'nūm'—facilitate rapid vocal articulation and lively cross-rhythmic play (*laykārī*). They are believed to have their origins in the Persian language—which would be consistent with the cultivation of this form by the Sufi *qavvāl*s. Complementing this, the syllabary of dhrupad, often termed *nom tom*, is held to have its roots in Hindu *mantra*s, quintessentially '*oṃ ananta nārāyaṇa hari oṃ*', from which syllables such as 'ā', 'nā', 'ta', 'ra', 'rī' and 'nūm' are argued to be derived (Sanyal and Widdess 2004: 156–7). Such syllables, along with related ones such as 'te' and 'tūm', are key to the life force of dhrupad *ālāp*—appropriately also known as *nom tom ālāp*.

While in both tarānā and *nom tom ālāp*, syllables can be permutated in many ways, there are also implicit conventions governing their combination. This takes us back to the orthodoxy reinforced by Imām, even though he gives no systematic rationale for which combinations are desirable and which are circumscribed. By contrast, Sanyal and Widdess (2004: 154–6) successfully sketch out an explicit syntax for the combination and ordering of dhrupad syllables, even though the authors acknowledge that their formula may not be rigorously followed in practice; and Widdess develops some of these ideas further in a subsequent analysis (2022).

All this sheds light on khayāl. On the one hand, most syllables used in a khayāl *ālāp* can also be found in the syllabaries of dhrupad, tarānā, or both (given that there are some overlaps). The fact that syllables such as 'do', 'mī' or 'to' would sound eccentric in a khayāl *ālāp* is probably related to the fact that they would not be sanctioned in dhrupad or tarānā either. For khayāl singers, then, these genres—with which most are familiar—might act as an unconscious regulating presence in the background. And, for some, their influence might be more conscious. When I discussed this matter with VR, he confirmed that dhrupad is a subtle influence on his *ālāp* style, and reminded me that he had spent several months learning dhrupad with Ustād Wasifuddin Dagar; indeed, his own guruji Pandit Bhimsen Joshi (1922–2011), also studied dhrupad. When singing an *ālāp*, VR told me, he holds the mantra (or its devotional spirit) in his head as would a dhrupad singer, even though he may not literally be voicing its syllables.

On the other hand, part of what characterises the use of syllables in khayāl *ālāp* is its self-differentiation from those other genres. For one thing, not all their syllables seem equally available—VR once reprimanded me for using 'te', presumably because it too strongly connotes dhrupad. But it is also a question of delivery style: not at all like *tārānā*, with its rapid-fire syllables that fully engage with *tāl*, and different too from dhrupad *ālāp*, which is considerably less melismatic than its khayāl relative. In khayāl the enunciation of syllables may be fuzzy, and the rules for how they go together are most definitely so, compared with the quasi-syntactic constraints that Sanyal and Widdess identify for dhrupad. Even so, there are implicit understandings of appropriateness that are more elusive to define—more of an ethos than a syntax. In sketching some of these conventions below, I return from theory to practice, and to a more specific response to a student's question, 'What syllables should I sing, and when?'

1. Vowels such as 'ā' and 'e' are commonly sung; 'ī' is also possible, though less frequent.
2. These can also be sung with an initial consonant, giving options such 'nā' and 're' (more common), and 'de' and 'rī' (less common, but still appropriate); this helps focus tuning, and perhaps also alludes to more formalised syllabaries, such as that of dhrupad.
3. Syllable choice may be conditioned by register. Hence 'ā' and 'nā' tend to be more congenial to the lower register, 'e' to the middle, 'ī' to the higher; but this is not to say that any of these syllables cannot be used in other registers.
4. Carefully measured variety among syllables can help underscore the flow and direction of melodic invention; but don't have too big a selection at any one time—it is undesirable to draw attention to the syllables themselves.
5. Rarer syllables should be used sparingly and in strategic places. For example, 'nū' might best be used at or towards the end of a phrase to indicate closure (as would be the case with 'nūm' in dhrupad).

As our brief look at VR's *ālāp* renditions has shown, much is also dependent on the expressive context—this is khayāl after all, a genre noted for its range of expression and creative imagination. For example, when singing *tār* Sā, 'rī' is a congenial syllable, since it focuses *svar*, constrains the airflow, and hence can be sustained for a long time; on the other hand, the same note can be sung in full chest voice to a syllable such as 'nā' if a certain robustness is appropriate—as in VR's Bhairav *ālāp*. What seems particularly important to his *gāyakī*—no doubt an aspect of his grounding in the Kirānā *gharānā* and his affinities for dhrupad—is the intimate connection between syllable and *svar*. On any given *svar*, changing the syllable will change its formant—the relative strength of overtones within the note, and hence its tone colour. This perhaps explains VR's calculated penchant for morphing vowels and blurring syllables.

Thus, the salience of a particular note within a *rāg*, the expressive connotations of *ras*, and the colouring one accordingly seeks to give it, can all be affected by the syllable chosen. This is not to say that these things are invariably consciously calculated—more probably they are imbibed through an intuitive absorption of style. Compared with dhrupad and tarānā, the syllabary of a khayāl *ālāp* is more open, flexible, and personal. While some artists and *gharānā*s may choose to keep to a circumscribed syllable set, we have seen that, for VR, a measure of play within this parameter is part of the rich expressive world afforded by khayāl.

Conclusion

The preceding explorations have examined some key principles that bear on how one sings an *ālāp*. In the process I have sought also to illuminate VR's *ālāp* renditions on *Rāg samay cakra*, and to illustrate aspects of his *gāyakī*. Throughout, I have allowed a tension to play out between providing pragmatic rubrics for practice and developing these into a theory of *ālāp* in its own right. To that extent I have allowed my text somewhat to exceed what would have been strictly necessary for a purely practical primer.

The tendency to theorise here is no doubt a response to the far-reaching nature of *ālāp* in Indian classical music; *ālāp* carries with itself a complex story that asks to be told. But what is also at the heart of the matter, is the way a beautiful, or touching, or searching *ālāp* may exceed or qualify any theoretical rubrics that can be written for it. This is not to dismiss the role of theory—whose own essence is a kind of reflection and exploration (not unlike an *ālāp*). But it is to note that theory and practice are rightly not identical—a point honoured in the *śāstras*, which sought to codify and recount past practices while also acknowledging their evolution in the present. Theory—whether communicated orally or set down in practice—will always try to capture the riches of practice and pass these on to future generations. Practice will always pull at the moorings of theory, and sometimes slip them, especially if your search is to touch the divine. Perhaps the orally transmitted and improvised nature of *rāg* music makes any kind of comprehensive theory of *ālāp* fundamentally impossible. Any claim that the rubrics I have tried to draw out here might make to universality is countervailed by a practice that nudges all such formulations towards the status of heuristics—of rules of thumb.

VR draws attention to a strongly pragmatic and contingent dimension to performing an *ālāp*, when he says, 'everything affects your *ālāp*, not just the *rāg*, but the composition that follows it, the accompanists, the audience, the room you're singing in, your mood'. These things would have had an impact on the performances recorded on *Rāg samay cakra*, involving particular people, in a particular place, on a particular day. Nonetheless, what we have been able to explore through that album is something that also exceeds those contingencies. Its *ālāp*s connect with those performed by countless other musicians, and, as we have glimpsed, have resonances with treatises going back through a long and rich history. My hope is to have conveyed from the intense specifics of the performed moment something of that bigger picture and abundant culture.

3.3 How Do You Sing a *Choṭā Khayāl*?

Introduction: Song and Its Elaboration

In Indian classical vocal music, *ālāp* finds its complement in song. *Ālāp*—free from the constraints of text and metre—explores *rāg* in purely musical terms. Song—animated by words and rhythms—grounds music in images and ideas. And while it may be a truism to say that song is vital to all Indian vocal types (whether khayāl, dhrupad, ṭhumrī, bhajan, ghazal, varṇam, kirtan, filmi, and so on), what distinguishes genres at the classical end of the continuum is the way they embed song into a process of improvised musical development.

In the vocabulary of Hindustani classical music, one word for song is *cīz*, though the more commonly used term is *bandiś*. The equivalent in instrumental music is *gat*, though instrumentalists also talk about playing a *bandiś*, especially if this also happens to be a song melody, as is not uncommonly the case. Significantly, *bandiś* carries the meaning of 'binding' (Ranade 2006: 71–4). A *bandiś* is bound to, and bound together by, the underlying *tāl* framework: it belongs to the *nibaddh* (metred) stage of the performance; by contrast, an *ālāp* belongs to the prior, *anibaddh* (unmetred) stage. *Bandiś*, *gat* and *cīz* are also often translated as 'composition'—though this differs from the western understanding of the word, since this one fixed element of a performance is only a few lines or phrases long, and usually lasts not much more than a minute. This is why considerable musical extemporisation around a *bandiś* is needed to make a fully-fledged performance. The *bandiś*, used as a reference point throughout, is what binds the elaborated passages into a larger whole.

Here, I use the concepts improvisation, extemporisation and elaboration somewhat interchangeably. I do not intend these terms in any transcendental sense, to imply the continuous, spontaneous generation of utterly novel ideas. Rather, Hindustani performers internalise a large stock of phrases, formulae, gestures, shapes and schemata through many hundreds of repetitions over thousands of hours of *riyāz*, which they then combine and permutate during a performance—sometimes predictably, sometimes unexpectedly, often engagingly, occasionally breathtakingly. (More detailed de-mystifications of the process include Napier 2006, Nooshin and Widdess 2006, Zadeh 2012.)

To present and improvise around a *bandiś* in the khayāl style is what is meant by 'singing a *khayāl*'. In this book, I use italics to denote performance in this vein, and upright font for the genre itself; hence, also, in dhrupad one sings a *dhrupad*, and in ṭhumrī one sings a *ṭhumrī*. In fact, khayāl singers sing two types of *khayāl*: the slow-tempo *baṛā khayāl*, and the medium- or fast-tempo *choṭā khayāl*. A full-length performance includes both types, while a shorter performance is more likely to feature just the *choṭā khayāl*—which means 'small *khayāl*' or 'short *khayāl*'. In this section, I focus on the latter type, which, while less weighty than a *baṛā khayāl*, has its own complexities and presents its own challenges for the performer (I consider *baṛā khayāl*—'large *khayāl*'—later, in Section 4.3).

How, then, do you sing a *choṭā khayāl*? In the first instance, I explore this question with examples from Vijay Rajput's album *Rāg samay cakra*, on which all the *khayāl*s are *choṭā khayāl*s. I take his performance of Rāg Bhairav (Track 1) as an initial case study, and then widen the canvas with further empirical analyses of extracts from the entire album, examining the full range of elaborative techniques he employs. In a second approach to the question—a more formally theoretical account—I draw the threads of these analyses together into an extensive series of rubrics for performance; ultimately, I speculate whether what underpins the flow of a *choṭā khayāl* might be something like a grammar. All this amounts to quite a journey; if its latter stages push beyond the everyday discourse of musicians, I nonetheless continue to make the pragmatics of practice my touchstone. Readers are of course at liberty to tarry with the parts that interest them most.

Case Study: A *Choṭā Khayāl* in Rāg Bhairav

The *choṭā khayāl* in Rāg Bhairav heard on Track 1 of *Rāg samay cakra* is among the simplest of the cycle, and hence a good starting point for analysis. Here, VR demonstrates that even a minimal set of ingredients—the relatively straightforward delivery of a *bandiś* together with a few simple *tāns*—can make an aesthetically satisfying performance. We hear him in Audio Example 3.3.1; a notation of the *bandiś*—'Dhana dhana murata'—can be found above, in Section 2.5.1.

Audio Example 3.3.1 Rāg Bhairav, *choṭā khayāl* (*RSC*, Track 1, 02:00–05:06)
https://hdl.handle.net/20.500.12434/14d9ee1a

For this *bandiś* in *tīntāl*, VR chooses a stately medium tempo (*madhya lay*)—about 105 beats per minute (bpm)—which matches the sober, devotional mood of Bhairav. Typically of many a *bandiś*, this one does not begin on *sam*, the first beat of the *tāl*, but with a lead-in from several beats earlier—in this case from *khālī*, beat 9. Also typical is the way tabla player Athar Hussain Khan delays his own entrance until beat 13 (he might have held back longer, until *sam*). VR presents the *sthāī*, the first part of the *bandiś*, according to convention—repeating the first line, singing the remaining lines just once, and then returning to the first line, which thus begins to function as a refrain. This opening portion can be heard in Audio Example 3.3.2.

Audio Example 3.3.2 Rāg Bhairav, *sthāī* (*RSC*, Track 1, 02:00–02:45)
https://hdl.handle.net/20.500.12434/6a84bef3

Having reached this point, VR has the option of sticking with the *sthāī* and extemporising around it. However, on this occasion he goes down another stylistically sanctioned path: he segues into the *antarā*, the second part of the composition (Audio Example 3.3.3), thus giving us the *bandiś* complete before any elaboration begins. In the *antarā*, as in the *sthāī*, he repeats the first line as per convention; and because the *antarā* cannot stand alone—it is a contrasting episode—once its final line is sung, VR segues back to the first line of the *sthāī*.

Audio Example 3.3.3 Rāg Bhairav, *antarā* (with lead in) and return to *sthāī*
(*RSC*, Track 1, 02:43–03:30)
https://hdl.handle.net/20.500.12434/b85e0604

Already this structure, with its various levels of repetition and contrast, begins to imbue the *choṭā khayāl* with shape and form. While VR keeps the execution simple, he does not lose the opportunity to add judicious embellishments to the melody, especially when material is repeated. Most notably, he applies the technique of *gamak*—a wide shake—to create expressive intensity at salient points in the composition. Several instances are captured in Audio Example 3.3.4: (a) on the last line of the *sthāī* (on the word 'pyārī'), which already has a *tān* like form; (b) on the equivalent line of the *antarā* (on 'vicārī'), which echoes its forebear and rhymes with it; and (c) on the repetition of the first line of the *antarā* (at 'mohane suhave') in figuration that fills the gap between Dha and *tār* Sā, immediately followed (at the climactic 'bālī bālī') by a gesture that similarly fills the gap between *tār* Re and *tār* Ma. Entirely suited to the steady *madhya lay*, these inflections add gravity and substance.

Audio Example 3.3.4 Rāg Bhairav: *gamak* inflections (*RSC*, Track 1):
(a) 02:28–02:36
(b) 03:11–03:20
(c) 03:02–03:12)
https://hdl.handle.net/20.500.12434/508d4c4a

Having completed his exposition of the *bandiś*, VR now needs to extend his performance. On this track, he does this quite simply, by presenting a series of short, eight-beat *tāns*—melodic runs—that succeed the first half-line of the *sthāī*. As the latter also lasts eight beats, each statement and its associated *tān* in total lasts one *āvartan* of the sixteen-beat *tīntāl* cycle. Three such iterations—captured in Audio Example 3.3.5 and notated in Figure 3.3.1—are enough to create contrast and move the proceedings forward.

Audio Example 3.3.5 Rāg Bhairav: *sargam tāns* (*RSC*, Track 1, 03:20–03:59)
https://hdl.handle.net/20.500.12434/dfa21ef6

tīntāl

o				3				x				2			
9	**10**	**11**	**12**	**13**	**14**	**15**	**16**	**1**	**2**	**3**	**4**	**5**	**6**	**7**	**8**
G	M	D	D	P	–	M	M	ṠN	DP	–D	MP	GM	P	P	–
Dha -	na	dha -	na	mu -	-	ra -	ta								
G	M	D	D	P	–	M	M	SR	GM	PD	NṠ	–N	DP	MG	RS
Dha -	na	dha -	na	mu -	-	ra -	ta								
G	M	D	D	P	–	M	M	ṠN	DP	MP	DP	MP	DP	MG	M
Dha -	na	dha -	na	mu -	-	ra -	ta								

Fig. 3.3.1 Rāg Bhairav: *sargam tāns*, notated. Created by author (2024),

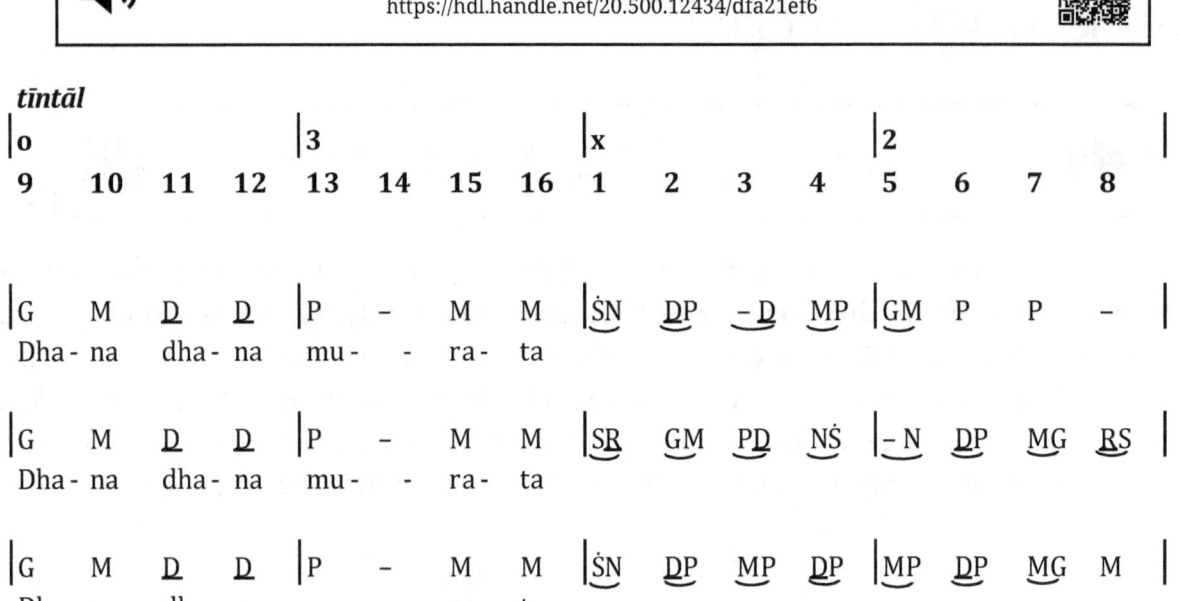

These are *sargam tāns*—i.e. *tāns* sung to *sargam* syllables (we will consider other types of *tān* below). Such examples can be readily emulated by students, and are often recorded in their notebooks, either dictated by their teacher, or invented by themselves. Repeating *tāns* many times over in one's *riyāz* helps build a stock of fixed ideas that can be dissected and permutated in ever-new variations in the moment of performance—as discussed in the preceding reflections on improvisation. VR has often reminded me that there is no shame in drawing from memorised, pre-composed materials on stage: 'even guruji [Pandit Bhimsen Joshi] used to do it', he has told me more than once: 'the first few *tāns* were always composed. Once you get settled in, then you can improvise.'

As it happens, VR holds back from extended *tān* work in this opening track—we will hear more elaborate ones later. In the final stages of this *choṭā khayāl* (from 01:58 of Audio Example 3.3.1), VR simply returns to the *sthāī*, reprising it in its entirety, and including a repetition of the first line that has a slight variation at 'Kr̥ṣṇa murāri'.

Practically all Indian classical performances end with a *tihāī*—a figure repeated three times—and this one is no exception. As we hear in Audio Example 3.3.6, VR's strategy is again straightforward, and in fact typical of the Kirānā *gharānā* (stylistic school), which is not preoccupied with excessive rhythmic complexity. Having reprised the *sthāī*, VR takes its first half-line, 'dhana dhana murata' and sings it three times, so that the last iteration ends on *sam* with the word 'Kr̥ṣṇa'. On cue, the tabla stops playing, and VR winds down the performance, improvising a brief, unmetred continuation of the phrase in the vein of an *ālāp*, which brings us home to Sā.

Audio Example 3.3.6 Rāg Bhairav, *choṭā khayāl*: concluding *tihāī* (*RSC*, Track 1, 04:32–05:06)
https://hdl.handle.net/20.500.12434/d4dc3447

By way of a coda, it is worth pointing out that a well-written *bandiś* provides an excellent encapsulation of the grammar and melodic behaviour of a *rāg*. As George Ruckert puts it (2004: 54), 'The fixed compositions carry the maps of the *rāgs*—the balances of the notes, the moods, the typical phrases, the proper way to begin and end—in short, the lore of the *rāgs*'. And so it is the case with the present composition, which exemplifies many salient features of Bhairav, some of which were noted in Section 2.5.1. A useful exercise is to note which pitches are used to begin and end each phrase, and which can be dwelled upon. The *bandiś* can suggest material for improvisation: taking several adjacent notes of a composition (such as G–M–D, or GRGM^{G}R), slowing them down, singing them non-metrically while preserving their relative prominence, and applying discreet decoration can, for example, yield suitable phrases for an *ālāp*.

Having narrated VR's progress through a single *rāg* performance, I now take a complementary look across *Rāg samay cakra* as a whole, highlighting particular techniques VR uses to extend a *choṭā khayāl*. In what follows, I discuss typical vehicles of musical expansion, such as *bol ālāp*, *tāns* and *behlāvā*. But I first consider how VR exploits the potential of the *bandiś* itself for extending a performance.

Treatments of the *Bandiś*: Simplicity and Repetition

Although VR sometimes keeps things simple for didactic purposes (as in his Bhairav performance), his purpose is also to show that this can still be musically satisfying. Simplicity can be a creative option when placed on a continuum encompassing more elaborate treatments. Across the course of *rāg samay cakra*, we find several rising waves of complexity which fall back to simpler formations—peaks and troughs broadly commensurate with the length of tracks, as mapped in Figure 3.2.7. For example, one of the most developed workings of material comes mid-way through, in Rāg Pūriyā Dhanāśrī (Track 7), followed by relatively straightforward treatments of Kedār and Bihāg (Tracks 10 and 11).

Most straightforward of all is Track 4, Brindābanī Sāraṅg. At 1'45", the *choṭā khayāl* on this track is the shortest on the album—shorter even than its prefatory *ālāp*. The *khayāl* focuses exclusively on the *bandiś*: we do not find even the handful of *tān*s heard in Bhairav. This perhaps reflects the fact that the *bandiś* is relatively long: the *sthāī* and the *antarā* each have three lines (Audio Example 3.3.7). The *bandiś* also has an interesting cross-metrical structure (for details, see the *rāg* description in Section 2.5.4). As if to help us savour this feature, VR repeats the second line of the *sthāī* in addition to the more usual repetition of the first. There is also a nice *enjambement* between the last line of the *antarā* and the return to the first line of the *sthāī*. By dispensing with any further development, VR allows the flowing elegance of the *bandiś* to speak for itself.

Audio Example 3.3.7 Rāg Brindābanī Sāraṅg, *sthāī* and *antarā* (*RSC*, Track 4, 02:09–03:25)
https://hdl.handle.net/20.500.12434/ea3867fd

In Rāg Bhīmpalāsī (Track 5), VR applies repetition intensively throughout the *bandiś* (see Section 2.5.5 for the notation). Here the *sthāī* has just two lines. He sings the first line three times, the second twice; returns to the opening line, again singing it three times; goes back to the second line, again sung twice, then back to the first. The first line of the *antarā* is similarly intensified, in this case being sung four times; the second and third lines are both sung twice. The complete sequence of events is shown line-by-line in Figure 3.3.2, which should be read in conjunction with Audio Example 3.3.8; time codes in the figure (and in the discussion below) are given for both the album track itself and for this audio example respectively.

Audio Example 3.3.8 Rāg Bhīmpalāsī, *choṭā khayāl* (*RSC*, Track 5, 02:26–05:20)
https://hdl.handle.net/20.500.12434/7ecc7207

Sthāī (02:26/00:00)

1st line x 3

2nd line x 2

1st line x 3 (* varied 2nd time)

2nd line x 2

1st line x 1.5

Harmonium interlude (03:36/01:10) for 1.5 *āvartans*

Antarā (03:44/01:18)

1st line x 4 (* varied 3rd time)

2nd line x 2 (* varied 2nd time)

3rd line x 2

Sthāī (04:33/02:09)

1st line x 2 (tabla *tihāī* 2nd time)

2nd line

1st half-line x 3 (= final *tihāī*)

Fig. 3.3.2 Rāg Bhīmpalāsī, *choṭā khayāl*: repetition structure. Created by author (2024), CC BY-NC-SA.

Again, there is no *tān* work in this *choṭā khayāl*; repetition is virtually the sole means of expansion. But this is never monotonous, thanks to various subtleties that are also traces of the performers' own enjoyment and invention. These include the short harmonium interlude by Mahmood Dholpuri at 03:36/01:10, which picks up where VR breaks off, halfway through the first line of the *sthāī*, and artfully foreshadows the second line of the upcoming *antarā*. Then there are variants of individual lines—indicated with asterisks in Figure 3.3.2. VR is careful not to overdo this: he needs only one variant to complement several iterations of the original. Added to these variants are numerous subliminal inflections to the rhythmic and textual delivery of the ostensibly non-varied lines, and other elements such as tabla player Athar Hussain Khan's *tihāī* a few seconds after the reprise of the *sthāī* at 04:33/02:09.

Here, then, we get a strong sense that VR is *composing with the composition*. Out of the small form of the *bandiś* he creates something bigger. The *bandiś* need not simply serve as a foil for improvisatory episodes, but can itself act as a basis for musical expansion. We can hear a similar approach in Rāg Śuddh Sāraṅg (Track 3, from 01:34; notation in Section 2.5.3). The *choṭā khayāl* extends itself through substantial repetition within the *bandiś* (especially the *sthāī*); and it is only in the last minute or so of the track that VR begins to apply other techniques of expansion, such as *bol ālāp* and *tāns* (devices I discuss below).

First-line Accumulation

The technique of expansion-through-repetition finds its epitome in a process I term *first-line accumulation.* While the first line of both *sthāī* and *antarā* is normally repeated once, or possibly twice, sometimes—most notably in fast-tempo *khayāl*s—it can be repeated repeatedly, to the point where a listener might lose count of how many times. And this is the point: in such a context, the first line's role as a formal element in a balanced poetic structure is temporarily suspended as it becomes a point of intrinsically musical focus—a kind of time loop. The aforementioned performance of Rāg Śuddh Sāraṅg, where VR at one point repeats the first line of the *sthāī* five times (Track 3, 02:34–03:04), verges on this category. But for an archetypal example in *Rāg samay cakra* we should consider Rāg Yaman (Track 9; *bandiś* notation in Section 2.5.9). VR launches this *choṭā khayāl* by singing the *sthāī*'s opening line, 'Śyām bejāi āja moraliyā̃', a total of eleven times—as excerpted in Audio Example 3.3.9 and transcribed in Figure 3.3.3.

Audio Example 3.3.9 Rāg Yaman, *sthāī*: first-line accumulation (*RSC*, Track 9, 03:10–04:01)
https://hdl.handle.net/20.500.12434/da6343d4

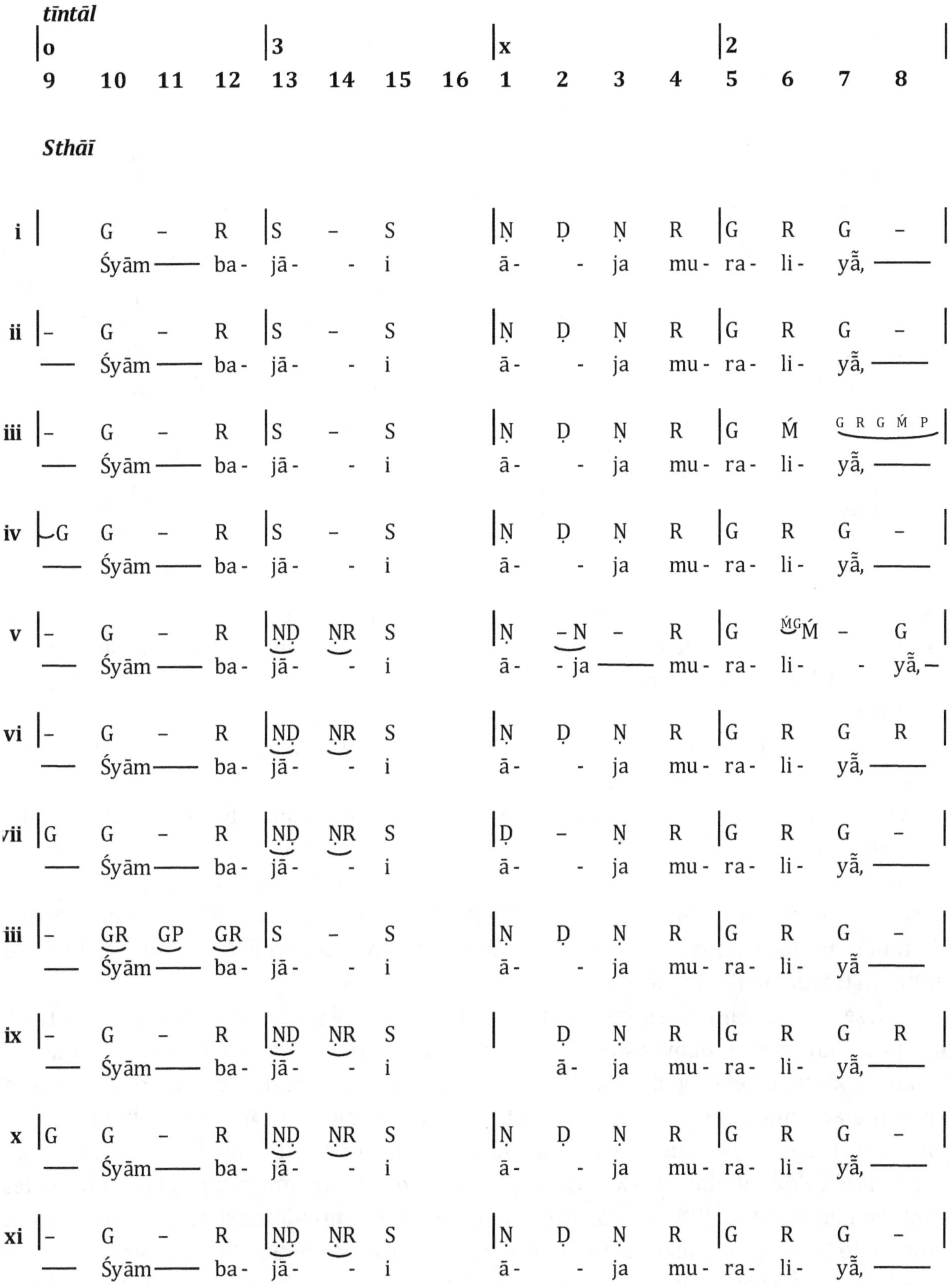

Fig. 3.3.3 Rāg Yaman, *sthāī*: first-line accumulation. Created by author (2024), CC BY-NC-SA.

I will return to this passage presently, but first let us consider a couple of further examples. In Rāg Toḍī (*bandiś* notation in Section 2.5.2), the opening line, 'Laṅgara kā̃karīya jīna māro', is heard eight times, and then four times more after a brief deflection to the second line, 'more aṅgavā'—so, twelve times in total (Audio Example 3.3.10(a)). This intensification is reflected in the *antarā*, whose opening line, 'suna pave morī', is heard five times (Audio Example 3.3.10(b)).

Audio Example 3.3.10 Rāg Toḍī: first-line accumulation:
(a) *sthāī* (*RSC*, Track 2, 02:41–03:50)
(b) *antarā* (ibid., 04:14–04:46)
https://hdl.handle.net/20.500.12434/9f9b9514

In Rāg Basant, VR sings the opening line of the *sthāī*, 'Phulavā binata ḍāra ḍāra', nine times in succession, and that of the *antarā*, 'Ai rī eka sukumārī', seven times (Audio Example 3.3.11 (a) and (b); *bandiś* notation in Section 2.5.14). The process in fact seems endemic across this *khayāl*: more unusually, it is applied to the third line of the *antarā*, 'āvenge nandalāla', which is sung five times, a gesture perhaps unconsciously triggered by its resemblance to the opening of the *sthāī* (Audio Example 3.3.11 (c)).

Audio Example 3.3.11 Rāg Basant: repetition–accumulation:
(a) *sthāī* opening line (*RSC*, Track 14, 00:57–01:25)
(b) *antarā* opening line (ibid., 02:03–02:28)
(c) *antarā*, third line (ibid., 02:29–02:46)
https://hdl.handle.net/20.500.12434/607ffe9f

As can be heard from these several examples, such intensive repetition is an occasion for melodic and rhythmic variation. The process needs discreet handling—as illustrated in Figure 3.3.3, which transcribes the opening of the *sthāī* from Rāg Yaman (cf. Audio Example 3.3.9, above). Here, the variation process does not begin until the end of iteration iii, with a melodic flourish on the last syllable, after which the fourth statement is sung 'straight'. In iteration (v), VR decorates the second *vibhāg* to create what is in effect a little *bol tān* (ṆḌ ṆR) on the last two syllables of 'bajāi'. Subsequently, this figure virtually becomes a fixture, being subtly voiced in every iteration except for the eighth, which instead makes a short *tān* out of the content of the first *vibhāg*. (Such morphing of identity perhaps also gives an indication of how *bandiś*es mutate over time.) We can also note tiny rhythmic displacements after *sam* in iterations (v) and (ix), which add further life and unpredictability to the sequence.

If these are the manifest characteristics of such intensive repetition, what is its function? In *choṭā khayāl*s that follow extended and intensive *baṛā khayāl*s, first-line accumulation creates a kind of clearing of the air; gives the soloist a chance to mentally re-group; and gives the accompanists, especially the tabla player, a chance to move into the limelight for a short period—as can be heard at the onset of the *choṭā khayāl* in Rāg Yaman on the *Twilight Rāgs* album, Track 6. On *Rāg samay cakra*, first-line accumulation provides contrast between the different *rāg* renditions, as well as providing didactic exemplars of how to do it in any context. As the name suggests, the aesthetic effect of such intensive repetition is *accumulative*. Rather than stalling the proceedings, the process actually creates momentum, tension and excitement by generating the expectation of moving on, while withholding change. We might see this as a melodic embodiment of the principle of *tāl*: a ceaseless cycling which nevertheless is also part of a directional drive. Subtle variations of the kind analysed in Figure 3.3.3 underwrite this tendency: their succession creates an expansion of content, a localised sense of development, the whole becoming greater than the sum of the parts.

Even though a *bandiś* can serve as its own resource for extending a performance, sooner or later, a soloist will reach a point where they have to do something else in order to create contrast and further expansion. In the following sections, I will consider some of the available techniques for doing so.

Bol Ālāp/Vistār

Musical development can flow quite naturally out of the *bandiś*. A technique that facilitates this is *bol ālāp*, in which the soloist improvises in the manner of an *ālāp* using the words—*bols*—of the composition, over the continuing *tāl*. In Rāg Multānī (Track 6), VR sings a *bol ālāp* after completing the opening *sthāī*—as we hear in Audio Example 3.3.12 and see transcribed in Fig 3.3.4 (for a notation of the complete *bandiś* see Section 2.5.6).

Audio Example 3.3.12 Rāg Multānī: *bol ālāp* (*RSC*, Track 6, 01:45–02:22)
https://hdl.handle.net/20.500.12434/e0623666

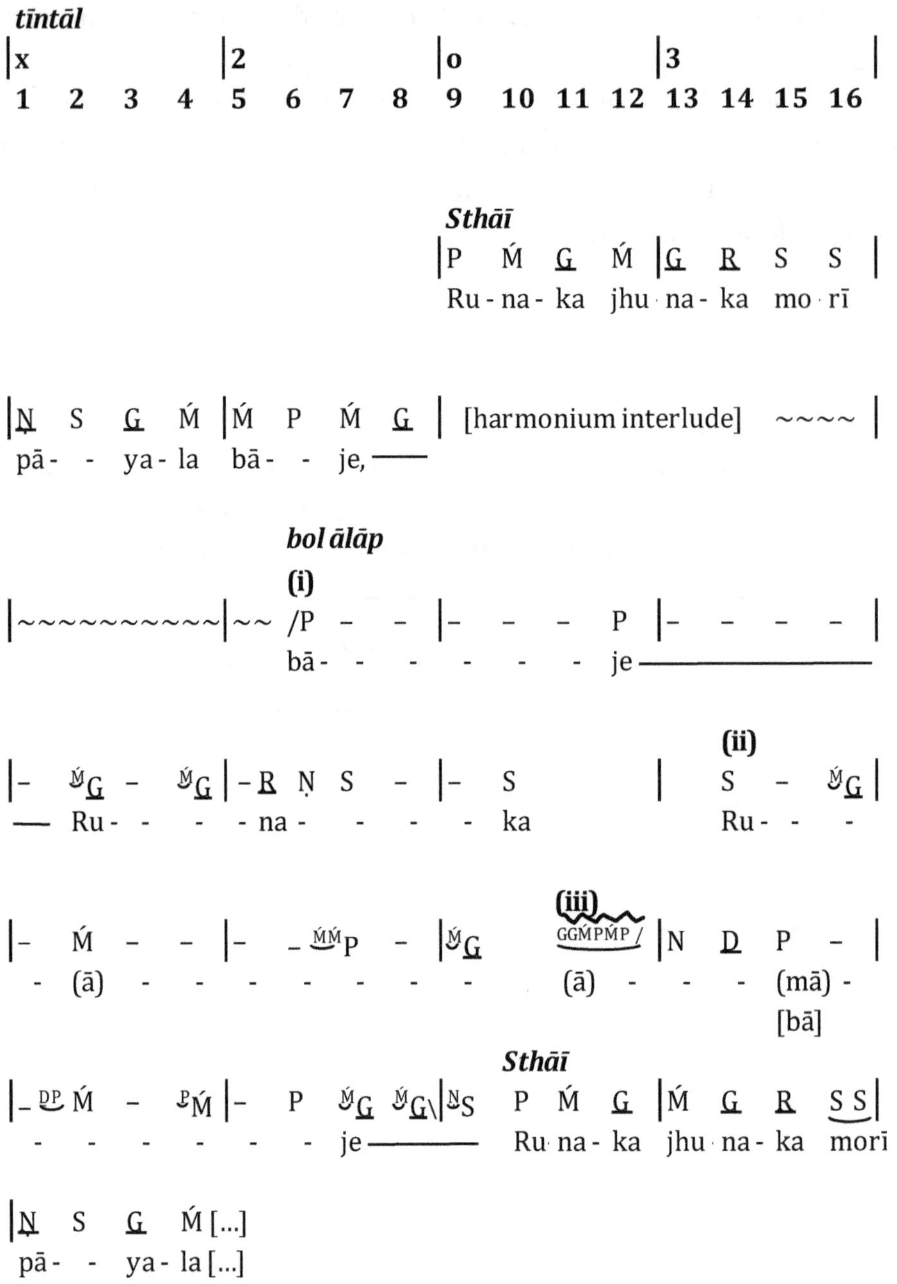

Fig. 3.3.4 Rāg Multānī: *bol ālāp*, transcription. Created by author (2024), CC BY-NC-SA.

The transcription includes essentials of melodic ornamentation without seeking to be too granular. Similarly, it locates the rhythmic position of notes in the *bol ālāp* only approximately in relation to the metrical *tīntāl* grid indicated at the top of the notation. This is partly for technical reasons, but also because, paradoxically, paying too much attention to precise rhythmic positioning would be contrary to a singing style whose spirit is to detach itself from precise rhythmic positioning: while the character of the *tāl* is *nibaddh* (bound—metrical), the melody gravitates towards the opposite condition, *anibaddh* (unbound—non-metrical).

The notation remains sufficiently sensitive to capture these qualities. It clearly reflects how, in contrast to the *sthāī*, VR's *bol ālāp* melody is melismatic (several notes to one syllable) rather than syllabic; and how the soloist begins his phrases on non-structural points of the metrical framework—in this case on (or around) beats 6, 14 and 11 (the three episodes are labelled with roman numerals). This positioning is probably less the result of conscious calculation and more the outcome of intuitive avoidance of key metrical markers, such as the beginning of *vibhāg*s. Even so, a soloist has to keep one ear open for the *tāl*. Phrase (iii) ends directly on *khālī*—which means that when VR resumes the *sthāī* it is initially shunted one beat 'to the right', and he has to compress the two syllables of 'morī' into a single beat, so that the second half of the first line (beginning 'pāyala') is correctly aligned on *sam*.

Melodically, VR begins phrase (i) of his *bol ālāp* by sustaining Pa, and ends it by falling to Sā. Following this, Pa remains the organising tone, though now as a goal rather than a point of prolongation: in phrase (ii) it is approached from below with the motion S–$^{\acute{M}}$G–Ḿ, and in phrase (iii) from above with N<u>D</u>P. All the while, there is subtle melodic decoration appropriate to the supple contours of Multānī. We should recall from our prior discussion of *ālāp* (Section 3.2) that the term *ālapti* means 'to express or elaborate *raga*'; as he gradually expands the compass of his free melodic explorations, this is just what VR is doing here.

In the expressive flow of *bol ālāp*, a vocalist may also loosen ties to the text itself—choosing just one or two words and even re-ordering them; sometimes phonetic integrity also falls away as text syllables dissolve into sustained vowels. Figure 3.3.4 reveals how, in phrase (i), VR selects just two words—'baje' and 'runaka'—from the *bandiś*, dislocating them from their surrounding text and reversing their original order. In phrase (ii), which would begin with 'runaka', the first vowel, 'u', soon morphs into 'ā', on which VR fashions a long melismatic melody. Rather than completing the word (with '-naka') he ends the melody with '-je', the second syllable of 'baje', thus conflating the fragments of the original two words. Clearly, there is a shift of aesthetic priorities in this semantic and phonetic dissolution, away from the syntax and storytelling of the *bandiś*, and towards the general feelings engendered by it and the *rāg* itself.

It is only a short step from these conditions to using this *anibaddh* technique without words at all—instead using *ākār* (singing to the vowel 'ā') or other non-semantic syllables. This happens in VR's *choṭā <u>kh</u>ayāl* for the monsoon *rāg* Megh (Track 13), captured in Audio Example 3.3.13. As before, these *anibaddh* passages flow from statements of the first line of the *bandiś* ('Ghanana ghanana ghana ghora ghora'). The first has a strong focus on the pitch Re (prominent in Megh), and begins with the syllable 'gho-', taken from 'ghor' in the *bandiś* text. But 'o' quickly shifts to 'a', and then to 're' and 'nā'—non-semantic syllables often used in an *ālāp* (see Section 3.2, Exploration 3). Something similar happens in the second *anibaddh* passage, which uses the syllable sequence 'gho-', 'ā', 'dā', 'nā', in a melodic ascent to *tār* Sā. Aesthetically, there is no discernible difference between this style of delivery and that of *bol ālāp* (which uses actual words), even though any contact with the *bandiś* text is highly attenuated.

Audio Example 3.3.13 Rāg Megh: *bol ālāp/vistār* (*RSC*, Track 13, 2:15–03:09)
https://hdl.handle.net/20.500.12434/f3efbb6b

Do we need a different name for a *bol ālāp* without *bols*? The question prompts a brief digression on the vicissitudes of Indian music terminology. Pragmatically, VR tends to describe this type of wordless elaboration simply as '*ālāp*' (even though, in this context, a *tāl* is also present). Alternatively, some commentators might apply the term *vistār*, meaning 'expansion' (for example, Ruckert 2004: 57–9)—though, *vistār* is also sometimes used interchangeably with another term, *baṛhat*, meaning 'increase' (Clayton 2000: 137–8). For some, *baṛhat* has the more specific connotation of a systematic process of *ālāp*-style elaboration over a *tāl*, gradually rising through the scale degrees of a *rāg*—a procedure that dominates a *baṛā khayāl*, but may also be intermittently encountered in a *choṭā khayāl*. But then others also understand *vistār* this way; while yet others use *baṛhat* to mean a more generalised process of growth and acceleration across a *rāg* performance (Ruckert 2004: 57). My own preferences in this book are to reserve the term *ālāp* for the unaccompanied *ālāp* 'proper' that opens a performance; to use *vistār* for *bol ālāp*-style passages without words in a *choṭā khayāl* (as discussed above), or sometimes even as a synonym for *bol ālāp* itself; and to reserve *baṛhat* for the more thorough expansion process of a *baṛā khayāl* (as discussed in Section 4.3).

As well as knowing *how* to sing *bol ālāp* or *vistār*, there is also the question of *when* to do so. As with much else in a *choṭā khayāl*, there are seemingly no completely hard and fast rules for this, only certain conventions that can be expressed heuristically and then applied and adapted according to mood and circumstance. Some possible models are shown in Figure 3.3.5—schematised respectively from VR's renditions of Rāgs Multānī and Megh, as already discussed, and Yaman, discussed below.

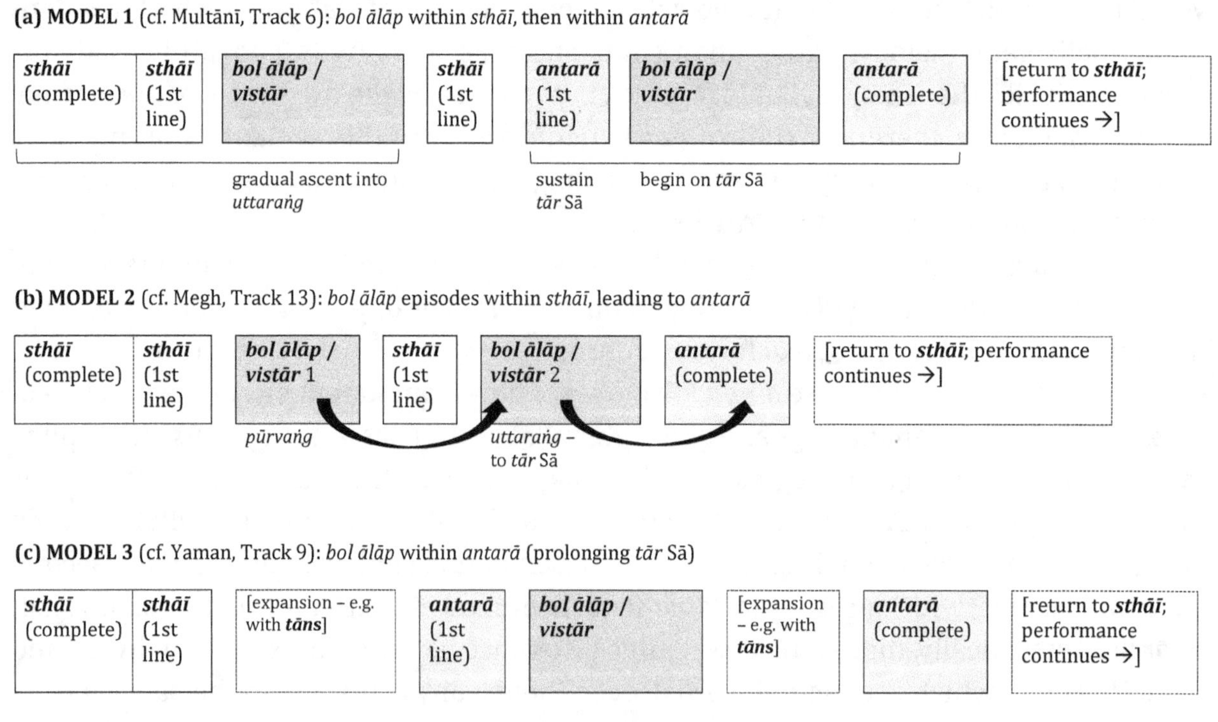

Fig. 3.3.5 Models for timing of *bol ālāp/vistār* within a *choṭā khayāl* (not drawn to scale). Created by author (2024), CC BY-NC-SA.

Model 1 proposes one answer to the question, when do you sing *bol ālāp* or *vistār*? You can sing it after the *sthāī* and at the start of the *antarā*. But note that it is conventional to have sung the *sthāī* in its entirety first, because this provides stable ground from which the more expansive *vistār* episodes flow. After this, you may initiate your *bol ālāp* or *vistār* (shown in dark shading in the graphic). As we heard in VR's Multānī performance (Audio Example 3.3.12), this might involve several phrases which successively expand the ambit of the *rāg*, gradually ascending into the *uttaraṅg* (upper tetrachord) of its scale. A fall back to *madhya* Sā and a reprise of the first line of the *sthāī* close off this episode. Next, from several possible avenues of continuation, VR elects to sing the *antarā*, and this generates another occasion for *vistār* (the entire passage can be heard between 02:28 and 03:34 of Track 6). Characteristically, this episode is sparked by the arrival on *tār* Sā in the first line of the *antarā*: VR sustains that pitch for a while before he begins his *vistār* (in this instance, he also morphs into another singing style, *behlāvā*, discussed below; but *vistār* or *bol ālāp* would be the norm). Only when he has completed his extemporisation does he sing the *antarā* complete, and this leads back to the *sthāī* and further development. Under this model, then, the *bol ālāp* episodes are embedded into their discrete performance stages, as shown by the braces under the graphic of Model 1.

Model 2 shows another option. It is possible to sing two or more *vistār* passages after the initial *sthāī*, each prefaced by the *sthāī* refrain, and each rising higher than the last, until *tār* Sā is reached, which then launches the *antarā*. This is the model VR adopted in his performance of Megh, as discussed above and heard in Audio Example 3.3.13: first, *vistār* in the lower tetrachord (*pūrvaṅg*); then back to the first line of the *sthāī*; then another *vistār*, this time in the upper tetrachord (*uttaraṅg*), reaching *tār* Sā; finally the *antarā*, sung complete. The arrows in Model 2 indicate the overall goal-directed tendency of the individual *vistār* episodes.

The overarching ascending trajectory here could be understood to reflect the conventions of an *ālāp* 'proper'—or indeed the staged rising profile that some call *baṛhat*. And we could interpret the ensuing *antarā*, whose initial melodic focus is *tār* Sā and descends back to *madhya* Sā, as similarly mirroring the subsequent descending phase of an *ālāp*. What all this suggests is that the overall process and its *āroh–avroh* vector can underpin a performance in different guises at different times (it is also lies implicitly behind Model 1, for that matter).

In their different ways, the *vistār* passages of Models 1 and 2 help promote continuity between *sthāī* and *antarā*; but it may also be possible to use the technique to create a contrast. This option is represented in Model 3, which is based on VR's *choṭā* <u>*kh*</u>*ayāl* in Rāg Yaman. Here, as in Model 1, *bol ālāp* is used as a means of expanding the *antarā*. However, unlike Model 1, there is no prior *bol ālāp* passage associated with the *sthāī*. Instead, expansion in the *sthāī* phase is achieved initially through first-line accumulation—as already discussed (see Figure 3.3.3 and Audio Example 3.3.9, above)—and then through an energetic series of *tāns*. These last are heard at the beginning of Audio Example 3.3.14, and are followed by a short harmonium interlude. VR then sings the first line of the *antarā*—'Jogī jaṅgama jatī satī aura gunī munī'—pausing on the last word, sustaining *tār* Sā, and—only now—giving time for an expansive *bol ālāp* episode, which contrasts with the previous, more metrically oriented material. After several *bol ālāp* phrases, VR seems poised to sing the *antarā* complete—but not yet: the emotion behind this burgeoning melodic expression first explodes into a dazzling, extended ākār *tān* whose energy finally takes us there.

Audio Example 3.3.14 Rāg Yaman: *antarā* and *bol ālāp*, with lead-in (*RSC*, Track 9, 04:32–05:45)
https://hdl.handle.net/20.500.12434/fdff71b5

There is no single model, then, for when and how to sing *bol ālāp/vistār*—the examples given here are by no means exhaustive. Although the technique, with its reflective sensibility, is commonly applied before moving to more virtuosic *tān* work, this need not always be the case—as we saw in Model 3. In a *choṭā khayāl*, anything is in principle possible within the available stylistic conventions and constraints, as long as the performance is coherent in its concept and convincing in its execution. I will return to the wider question of how we might codify those conventions and constraints in the later stages of this section. But first let us consider some more of the available devices for expansion of a *khayāl*.

Tāns

Tāns—melodic runs and flourishes—are as important a device for extending a performance as anything else a khayāl singer has in their armoury. *Tāns* are a hallmark of the style; neither dhrupad nor ṭhumrī—related Hindustānī vocal styles—use them. There are essentially four basic types of *tān* that khayāl singers use on a regular basis:

- *Sargam tāns*—sung to *sargam* syllables.
- *Ākār tāns*—sung to the open vowel 'ā'.
- *Bol tāns*—incorporating words from the *bandiś*.
- *Gamak tāns*—incorporating a wide melodic shake or oscillation around each note.

Not all types will be equally prominent in any given performance. This may depend on the *gharānā*(s) with which a singer identifies, and on their personal skill set. However, *ākār tāns* usually feature particularly strongly, given that they are most conducive to flights of invention. They are certainly favoured by VR, who is a virtuoso of rapid *tān* work (as was his late guru, Bhimsen Joshi). Hence, there are plenty of examples of *ākār tāns* on *Rāg sama cakra*; but the other types of *tān* are also heard. Let us consider all four in turn.

Sargam Tāns

Sargam tāns are normally the first form of *tān* a student learns. We have already considered some simple examples in our earlier account of Bhairav, but to amplify the principles, we can also consider the latter part of VR's *choṭā khayāl* in Rāg Bihāg (Track 11)—as captured in Audio Example 3.3.15 and notated in Figure 3.3.6.

Audio Example 3.3.15 Rāg Bihāg: *sargam tāns* (*RSC*, Track 11, 03:47–04:47)
https://hdl.handle.net/20.500.12434/7f3f16b8

tīntāl

	o				3				x				2			
	9	**10**	**11**	**12**	**13**	**14**	**15**	**16**	**1**	**2**	**3**	**4**	**5**	**6**	**7**	**8**
i	Ṇ	S	G	M	P	–	N	N	SP	ḾP	GM	GP	ḾP	GM	GR	S
	A -	ba -	hũ——		lā -	-	la -	na								
ii	Ṇ	S	G	M	P	–	N	N	ṆS	GM	PM	GM	PM	GM	GR	S
	A -	ba -	hũ——		lā -	-	la -	na								
iii	Ṇ	S	G	M	P	–	N	N	GM	PN	ṠN	DP	ḾP	GM	GR	S
	A -	ba -	hũ——		lā -	-	la -	na								
iv	Ṇ	S	G	M	P	–	N	N	PṠ	ṠN	DP	– D	ḾḾ	PG	GM	PS
	A -	ba -	hũ——		lā -	-	la -	na								
	GM	PṆ	SG	MP	MG	MP	N –	Ṡ –	ĠṘ	ṠN	DP	ḾP	G	MG	RS	
v	Ṇ	S	G	M	P	–	N	N	ṆS	GM	PN	ṠĠ	ĠṘ	ṠN	ṠṘ	ṘṠ
	A -	ba -	hũ——		lā -	-	la -	na								
	ND	PḾ	PṠ	ṠN	DP	PN	ND	PḾ	PD	DP	ḾP	GM	MG	RS	ṆS	

Fig. 3.3.6 Rāg Bihāg: *sargam tāns*, notation. Created by author (2024), CC BY-NC-SA.

We can draw several general principles of *tān* construction from this example, which may apply equally to other types of *tān*:

1. The *tāns* alternate with the first line, or first half-line, of the composition (*sthāī* or *antarā*, depending on the stage of the performance).
2. The *tāns* subdivide each *mātrā*, so intensifying the level of rhythmic activity.
3. Several *tāns* are performed in succession; they loosely relate together.
4. The *tāns* vary in length; as the sequence proceeds, they tend to get longer.
5. *Tāns* often have an underlying *āroh–avroh* contour; as the sequence progresses, their compass tends to get wider; profiles may vary from *tān* to *tān* to avoid predictability.

To elaborate on these general principles as VR applies them in this specific *tān* sequence, as notated in Figure 3.3.6:

1. The first half-line of the *sthāī* ('Abahũ lālana') occupies beats 9–16 of the *tīntāl* cycle; this is then followed by either an 8-beat or 24-beat *tān*, beginning on *sam* and concluding on beat 8, ready for the next iteration on *khālī*.

2. In general, the *tāns* proceed at a rate of two notes per beat, though in *tān* (iv) there are some longer notes or short gaps which create rhythmic play (*laykārī*).
3. Here we have a sequence of five *tāns* that begin simply and become more complex. We can hear linkages between them: the first three end similarly; *tāns* (iv) and (v) spend more time in the higher register intimated by *tān* (iii); the figure GM PN ṠN DP ḾP at the beginning of *tān* (iii) is developed as the figure PṠ ṠN DP –D ḾḾ P at the beginning of *tān* (iv); and the all-encompassing *tān* (v) captures fragments from all the preceding ones (for example, ṆS GM P; GM PN Ṡ; PṠ ṠN DP).
4. VR opts for just two lengths of *tān* in this particular passage. The earlier ones last eight beats, the later ones twenty-four. *Tāns* of other durations would also have been possible, though for durations divisible by sixteen it is necessary to sing the entire first line of a *tīntāl* composition to ensure it returns at the right place in the *tāl* cycle. In principle, *tāns* of any length are possible in any *tāl*. But for beginners (and even experts) simplicity has its place, especially in the first stages of improvising a *tān* sequence.
5. Regarding contour and compass: *tāns* (i) and (ii) suggest an *āroh–avroh* contour by ascending to Pa within the first few beats and falling back to Sā in the last three beats. *Tān* (iii) does this by ascending directly from Ga to *tār* Sā, and then returning slightly elliptically to *madhyā* Sā. In *tān* (iv), the *āroh–avroh* pattern only emerges about halfway through, after an early descent from *tār* Sā; this avoids predictability. *Tān* (v) opens with a steep ascent to *tār* Ga and uses the remaining twenty beats to wind gradually back to *madhyā* Sā. This happens to be a *palṭā* that VR often teaches his students—a practice phrase that encapsulates key melodic features of a *rāg* (this one also works for Rāg Bhīmpalāsī, which has the same *āroh–avroh* structure as Bihāg). Such phrases serve as storehouses of ideas for improvisation.

Although *sargam tāns* are common enough, they beg the question, why spell out the names of the notes one is singing? Is such musical self-referentiality not a little odd, tautologous even, compared to *bol tāns* which use words from the *bandiś* text, or *ākār tāns* which free the performer from verbal constraints altogether? One possible answer is historical: singers sing *sargam tāns* because that is simply the way it has been done by previous generations; by continuing to do so, one upholds tradition—*paramparā*. Other reasons are didactic: singing *tāns* to *sargam* syllables encourages students to communicate to themselves a terminology for pitch in Indian music in the very act of singing it—a unified moment of theory and practice. Practically speaking, *sargam tāns* are easier to sing at a steady tempo than is the case for *ākār tāns*; the presence of a consonant at the start of a note makes it easier to sing in tune.

While these features facilitate behind-the-scenes learning, they can also be attractive in a performance. The articulation of *tāns* with *sargam* syllables can imbue them with life and playfulness, and audiences can also find enjoyment in subliminally identifying the syllables with the notes—affirming that they too are in the know. *Sargam tāns* can be particularly effective at faster tempos in a demonstration of vocal flair. We hear this in a later stage in VR's performance of Rāg Pūriyā Dhanāśrī, captured in Audio Example 3.3.16. Here a short sequence of *sargam tāns* contributes to an extended process of musical development that also includes *ākār tāns*, instrumental *tāns* and, beyond the excerpt, much more. When the performers are seeking to pull out all the stops like this, *sargam tāns* afford a valuable additional resource.

Audio Example 3.3.16 Rāg Pūriyā Dhanāśrī: *sargam tāns* in a developmental context (*RSC*, Track 7, 05:03–06:03)
https://hdl.handle.net/20.500.12434/66d7d267

Ākār Tāns

In principle, any *sargam tān* can also be sung in *ākār*, provided the tempo is fast enough to let the *tān* flow freely, which is their essence. The reverse is also true: any *ākār tān* could also be sung in *sargam* provided the tempo is not tongue-twistingly rapid. What these observation point to is the intimate connection between *tān* and *lay*. *Ākār tāns* are particularly suited to *drut lay*, where they contribute to rhythmic drive. They feature abundantly in VR's up-tempo performance of Rāg Yaman: Audio Example 3.3.17(a) illustrates a passage after the reprise of the *sthāī*, when, following an interlude from the accompanying instrumentalists, he surfs across the *tāl* in strings of melismatic *tāns*, two notes per *mātrā*. The entry of the *tāns* builds on energy generated in the instrumental interlude; as in the previous audio example, from Pūriyā Dhanāśrī, we find ourselves in the thick of an extended developmental process at a climactic point in the performance, and it feels like the music is free from any formulaic confines. A similar pattern of events can be heard in Audio Example 3.3.17(b), taken from the latter part of Rāg Basant, in *drut ektāl* (Track 14). We first hear harmonium player Mahmood Dholpuri mirroring VR's *tān* style, which VR picks up on in further *tāns* of his own, finally returning to the *bandiś*. In both these examples, then, we hear how *tāns* contribute to rhythm: they channel the burgeoning forward flow of the music and help expand time within a wider interplay of ideas and techniques.

Audio Example 3.3.17 *Ākār tāns* in a developmental context:
(a) in Rāg Yaman (*RSC*, Track 7, 05:03–06:03)
(b) in Rāg Basant (*RSC*, Track 14, 03:40–04:08)
https://hdl.handle.net/20.500.12434/a68e6cde

Even in less rapid tempos, VR finds opportunities for virtuosic displays of *ākār tāns* in the later, more developmentally oriented stages of the performance. In such cases, he sings *tāns* at a rate of *four* notes per *mātrā*. Audio Example 3.3.18 extracts moments from his *choṭā khayāls* in Śuddh Sāraṅg and Bhūpālī.

Audio Example 3.3.18 Four-note-per-*mātrā ākār tāns*:
(a) in Rāg Śuddh Sāraṅg (*RSC*, Track 3, 04:15–04:37)
(b) in Rāg Bhūpālī (*RSC*, Track 8, 04:08–04:26)
https://hdl.handle.net/20.500.12434/3006861d

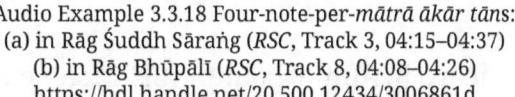

Bol Tāns

Bol tāns are similar in style to *ākār tāns*—only with words from the *bandiś* text rather than purely with vowels (analogously to *bol ālāp*). On *Rāg samay cakra*, VR uses this device sparingly, usually applying it to repetitions of a *bandiś* in order to create variety. In Audio Example 3.3.19, two very brief extracts illustrate this usage in contrasting ways. In (a), from Rāg Multānī, VR sings a *bol tān* to the words 'pāyala bāje', following the opening half-line of the *sthāī*: it displaces the second half-line of the melody with a different profile. Conversely, in (b), from Rāg Bhūpālī, the function of a *bol tān* sung to 'gāīye' is to *decorate* the first half-line melody with a flourish: it maintains the original profile.

Audio Example 3.3.19 *Bol tāns*:
(a) in Rāg Multānī (*RSC*, Track 6, 03:41–03:50)
(b) in Rāg Bhūpālī (*RSC*, Track 8, 02:11–02:19)
https://hdl.handle.net/20.500.12434/8b90ff4f

Not uncommonly, we hear VR move from *bol tāns* to *ākār tāns* in close proximity, demonstrating that to some extent these devices are interchangeable. Revisiting Audio Example 3.3.11(a), at the inception of the *choṭā khayāl* in Rāg Basant, we hear both forms of *tān* as comparable ways of varying the many iterations of the first line of the *bandiś*; it is as if the *ākār tāns* realise an emancipation from the *bandiś* implied in the earlier *bol tān*. Revisiting Audio Example 3.3.10(b) (from 01:12), we again hear *bol tāns* judiciously adding variety to a period of first-line accumulation—in this case in the *antarā* of Rāg Toḍī.

Gamak Tāns

As *ākār tāns* may be fostered by the drive of a *drut khayāl*, so *gamak tāns* are prompted by steadier *lays*. Their shaking style adds colour and character, bringing *tāns* in slower tempos to life. *Gamak* is unquestionably a difficult technique to master, involving a single, wide oscillation around each note that at its extreme may make the actual *svar* almost unidentifiable to the listener—though not to the performer (for a more detailed account, including spectrographic analysis see Sanyal and Widdess 2004: 164–6). While *gamak* is a technique cultivated in dhrupad, it is no stranger to khayāl, its heavy style being especially appropriate to *gambhir rāgs*—*rāgs* of gravity. We have already commented on its application in the *tān*-like elements of VR's *bandiś* in Rāg Bhairav (Audio Example 3.3.4); in Audio Example 3.3.20 we can hear examples of actual *gamak tāns* in Rāg Mālkauns.

Audio Example 3.3.20 Rāg Mālkauns: *gamak tāns* (*RSC*, Track 12, 04:47–05:15)
https://hdl.handle.net/20.500.12434/1a8ac27b

Behlāvā

A related technique can be heard in Audio Example 3.3.21: an extraordinary *vistār* passage in the *antarā* of Rāg Multānī, where VR extemporises widely in a style that hybridises *bol ālāp* and *gamak*. He explained to me that this is a rare technique called *behlāvā*, peculiar to the Gwalior *gharānā*. This provenance is confirmed by Nicolas Magriel, who describes it as 'an emotive "calling out" voice quality' (Magriel and DuPerron 2013, I: 60). Sandeep Bagchee also acknowledges the Gwalior origins, stating that *behlāvās* 'develop the *rāga* through *swar-vistār* in *ākār*' (1998: 123)—a description consistent with the way VR sings in this passage.

Audio Example 3.3.21 Rāg Multānī: *behlāvā* (*RSC*, Track 6 , 02:34–03:20)
https://hdl.handle.net/20.500.12434/8a41a687

Bol Bāṇṭ, Lay Bāṇṭ

A further way to extend a khayāl performance is through *laykārī*—an umbrella term that encompasses various techniques of rhythmic elaboration or variation (see Clayton 2000: 153–4). One such technique is *bol bāṇṭ* ('word division'), which draws out the rhythmic potential of the song text by repeating words or re-arranging their order. Although this device is more a feature of dhrupad than khayāl, we do find occasional instances in VR's *gāyakī*—for example, during his *baṛā khayāl* in Rāg Bhairav on the *Twilight Rāgs* album (Track 2, 12:22–12:55). A related device, also associated with dhrupad, is *lay bāṇṭ*—defined by Martin Clayton as 'a special technique involving diminution of the *bandiś* to double, triple, and/or quadruple speed within an unchanging *tāl* structure' (2000: 159). VR provides us with an example of this in his *choṭā khayāl* in Rāg Kedār (*Rāg samay cakra*, Track 10)—as captured in Audio Example 3.3.22, and notated in Figure 3.3.7. In this extract, he sings the *bandiś* first at normal speed (*ekgun*) and then at double tempo (*dugun*), while the underlying *lay* in *tīntāl* remains constant. Strictly speaking, in *lay bāṇṭ*, the *bandiś* melody would remain unchanged under such rhythmic diminution, whereas here VR creatively re-composes it; but he arguably invokes the spirit if not the letter of the technique.

Audio Example 3.3.22 Rāg Kedār: *lay bāṇṭ* and *laykārī* (*RSC*, Track 10, 02:30–03:12)
https://hdl.handle.net/20.500.12434/d2efe16c

Fig. 3.3.7 Rāg Kedār: *lay bāṇṭ* and *laykārī*, notation. Created by author (2024), CC BY-NC-SA.

Already in its original form, the *bandiś* is rhythmically playful. The opening words, 'bola bola mose', group the eight beats from *khālī* to *sam* into a 3+3+2 pattern that cuts liltingly across the 4+4 arrangement of the *vibhāg*s—as indicated by braces over line (i) of the notation. In his *lay bāṇṭ* treatment of the *bandiś*, transcribed in lines (ii) and (iv), VR not only delivers the words at double speed, but also recomposes the melody. Although this does not break up the text (as it would under *bol bāṇṭ*), it does intensify the syllabic cross-accentuation: the 3+3+2 figure of the *bandiś* gets condensed into the first *vibhāg*, creating a lively syncopated feel. This compression creates space to fit the second line of the *bandiś* ('rasa bharī batiyā̃ ...') into the same *āvartan*; it is again presented in *dugun* and again re-composed, this time as a torrent of syllables. While these variations keep the text intact, they nevertheless direct our attention towards its phonetic and rhythmic properties—towards what is musical in the poetry. After a further *ekgun* statement of the first line of the *bandiś* (Figure 3.3.7(v)), VR sings a *sargam tān* (vi), which, slightly syncopated, maintains the previous *laykārī* feel. Midway, at *sam*, he introduces a new figure lasting five beats (M— MM P—, highlighted with a brace in the notation), and repeats it. This has the effect of shifting the melody's accentuation out of line with the *tīntāl* structure, so that the first line of the *bandiś* begins a beat late and has to be compressed in order to reach *sam* at the right point (vii).

Lay Increase

The introduction of *tān*s and *lay bāṇṭ* increases *rhythmic density*: the level of activity per *mātrā* or beat (see Clayton 2000: Chapter 6). A further option is to increase the rate of the *lay* itself. While not compulsory, one or more upward tempo shifts are quite common in longer performances (conversely, drops in tempo are extremely rare). Even though the *choṭā khayāl*s on *Rāg samay cakra* are all short, three of the longest ones—in Rāgs Pūriyā Dhanāśrī, Yaman and Mālkauns—include *lay* increases. The several moments where these step changes occur can be found in Audio Example 3.3.23.

Audio Example 3.3.23 *Lay* increase:
(a) Rāg Yaman (*RSC*, Track 9, 06:20–06:49)
(b) Rāg Mālkauns (*RSC*, Track 12, 05:48–06:14)
(c) Rāg Pūriyā Dhanāśrī (*RSC*, Track 7, 04:41–05:11)
(d) Rāg Pūriyā Dhanāśrī (ibid., 05:54–06:32)
https://hdl.handle.net/20.500.12434/6faac6c1

Performers must stay mindful of the relationship between the character of the *bandiś* and the *lay* in which they perform it; and they must ensure that any acceleration of the *lay* is justified—that it either issues out of already intensifying activity or facilitates it. In the Yaman example, the *bandiś* is well suited to *drut lay*: the exuberant picture painted by the words would be less effectively conveyed if the *lay* were slower. So, VR sets out at around 270 bpm; the gradual acceleration to 290 bpm heard in Audio Example 3.3.23(a) arises logically after a passage of *ākār tān*s that very slightly nudges the tempo forward, as if the performers were previously straining at the leash.

While this takes us from *drut* to *ati drut* (very fast) *lay*, the tempo increase in the Mālkauns extract (Audio Example 3.3.23(b)) takes us from 165 bpm—only a little faster than *madhya lay*—to 225 bpm—clearly *drut*. This enables VR to diversify the types of *tān* he can include: *gamak* in the earlier phase (cf. Audio Example 3.3.20); *ākār* in the final minute. If the former type reflects the *gambhīr* character of the *rāg*, the latter is perhaps a response to the joyful poem about springtime.

In the Pūriyā Dhanāśrī examples—(c) and (d)—we find a *bandiś* that can sit comfortably at either end of the *drut* spectrum—a point evidenced by *two* tempo increases. Both of these are associated with the extended developmental process heard in this performance. The first tempo uplift (c) accelerates the *lay* from 165 to 225 bpm. It comes once VR has completed an exposition of both *sthāī* and *antarā* and turns to expand his presentation: reprising the *sthāī*, he now embarks on a series of *sargam tān*s (discussed above in conjunction with Audio Example 3.3.16). The second tempo increase (Audio Example 3.3.23(d)) follows intensive engagement with the accompanists, and takes us to around 260 bpm for the climactic closing stages. VR initially takes advantage of this even faster *lay* not to inject further *tān*s (these will come later), but to sing an expansive *bol ālāp* passage which takes him well into the upper octave. In other words, the faster *lay* sustained by the tabla is initially accompanied by a radical drop in rhythmic density from the soloist, who instead increases melodic intensity. This makes the point that *lay* accumulation is not a one-dimensional strategy.

Putting It All Together: A Scheme of Rubrics

In the next stage of this investigation, I seek to synthesise all the above observations into a theoretical schema for the event sequence of a *choṭā khayāl*. In more extended form, this revisits the question we examined earlier in respect of *bol ālāp*: not only what do you sing, but also when (and how) do you sing it?

In truth, musicians do have a kind of mental road map through which to navigate their journey through a *khayāl*. This is very clear in the case of a *baṛā khayāl*, as I discuss in Section 4.3; but, paradoxically, although (or because) a *choṭā khayāl* is less weighty, the number of possible routes through it is greater, and in this respect it is more complex. Its particular challenge to the singer—mirrored in the enjoyment of a knowledgeable listener—is to decide at every juncture, which way now? Student performers are likely to be advised by their teacher to plan their route in advance and keep it simple—as in our opening Bhairav example. But as they gain in skill and confidence, musicians may increasingly leave their options open. The ideal is a state of spontaneity and aliveness, where, in the moment of delivery, even the performers do not know exactly what will happen next.

Of course, while much of this creative decision-making may be unconscious, and while the ineffable may play its part, the process is firmly underpinned by convention, even though this permits considerable flexibility. Is it possible systematically to capture such conventions in words, and to organise their presentation in such a way as to reflect that flexibility? Would we even want to? Clearly, khayāl singers are eminently capable of practicing their art, and listeners are capable of enjoying it, without consulting theory books. However, while the kind of theoretical description to which these questions steer us takes us beyond what is strictly necessary for performance, it also makes conscious a yet more compelling image of what is at stake when performers perform; and potentially all parties—students, listeners, researchers and professional artists—have investment in such knowledge.

As in my analysis of *ālāp* in Section 3.2, I here proceed by assembling a schema of rubrics. As before, these do not represent axiomatic, final principles, but rather heuristic guidelines for possible actions in live performance. The rubrics are arranged below in three groups. The first—termed *event sequence rubrics*—focuses on the overall ordering of events. The second group—*musical elements*—explores options for executing different techniques and types of musical material within that sequence. And the third group—*global rubrics*—has a more generalised bearing on a performance over and above the sequence itself. Each rubric has its own label, comprising one or more letters, and there is frequent cross-referencing: the quasi-algebraic style reflects an intention to keep descriptions rigorous, parsimonious and systematic. Nonetheless, I have tried to think from a performer's perspective throughout; hence, I express the rubrics as if directed to a student performer—which is also to invite the identification of non-performers with the soloist's situation in the moment.

Event Sequence Rubrics

So, let us first consider those rubrics that relate to the order of what happens. Beneath the surface of the musical events, it is possible to discern a beginning–middle–end sequence, whose components I term *opening phase, elaboration phase* and *closing phase.* The bulk of a *choṭā khayāl* is usually oriented around the elaboration phase, but in any case, like the phase schema of an *ālāp,* the phases here are not discrete 'sections' as such. Rather, they succeed one another almost imperceptibly; they are more correlates of the artist's disposition at each stage of the performance: 'now I'm beginning'; 'now I have to grow the core of my performance'; 'now it's time to end'. Each phase is described below under its own rubric; its components are in turn cross-referenced to the rubrics for *musical elements* (indicated in parentheses).

O – Opening phase

- Sing the *sthāī* of your chosen *bandiś* in its entirety (S), either in simple mode (s) or extended mode (e).
- You may optionally sing the entire *sthāī* (S) a second time.
- You may optionally follow the *sthāī* with the *antarā* (A) in simple mode (s).
- After you have sung the *sthāī* (and *antarā,* if you elect to do so) you should normally sing a reprise of its—the *sthāī*'s—first line (S^1), which from here on acts as a refrain, or *mukhṛā.*
- Next, proceed to the elaboration phase (E).

  NOTES:

  - A complete second statement of the *sthāī* immediately following the first is less commonly made, but is not unusual. (On *Rāg samay cakra,* VR applies it in the *choṭā khayāl*s for Toḍī, Śuddh Sāraṅg, Bhīmpalāsī, Pūriyā Dhanāśrī, Yaman, Kedār and Mālkauns.)
  - The *antarā* is quite commonly deferred until the elaboration phase, where there are additional options for its delivery.

E – Elaboration phase

You have several options for what to sing next. You can mix and match from the following:

- *Bol ālāp/vistār* (V).
- *Tān*s (T).
- *Antarā* (A).
- *Laykārī* (L).
- Reprise of the entire *sthāī* (S).
- *Lay* increase (LI).
- Instrumental interlude (Int).

NOTES:

- *Vistār* and *tāns* are the most common vehicles for musical expansion, and normally begin to be heard earlier in the elaboration phase.
- Not all these elements are compulsory, though all are in principle available. There is some mutability regarding order, but the *antarā* (unless already sung in the opening phase) is not likely to appear before passages of *vistār* and *tāns* have begun to do their work of expansion. Similarly, *laykārī* techniques, and especially any *lay* increase, make most sense once some developmental momentum has already been achieved.
- In principle, all the above elements may be executed more than once. Indeed, this would be strongly expected in the case of *vistār* and (especially) *tāns*, which occur frequently and are often linked together in series. Other features, such as the *antarā*, are likely to be revisited at most once.
- Between episodes of each type of material, and often within them, it is customary to interpolate the first line of the *sthāī* as a refrain (S^1).
- A reprise of the complete *sthāī* (S) within the elaboration phase tends to re-focus the musical direction after a period of growth involving *tāns* and/or *vistār*. As in its initial statement, a reprise of the *sthāī* may take simple or extended form, including first-line accumulation (S^1A). This may also be associated with an increase in *lay* (LI).
- Some principles of instrumental interludes (Int) are outlined under 'global rubrics', below.
- Once you have executed the elaboration phase to your (and your audience's) satisfaction, proceed to the closing phase (C).

C – <u>Closing phase</u>

- Your performance should normally end by first returning to the *sthāī*, or at least the first line (S/S^1).
- The first line or half-line of the *sthāī* may then be used as the basis for a final *tihāī* (Th) which leads to closure on *sam*, whereupon the tabla stops playing.
- You, the soloist, should keep going for a few seconds more with a concluding *bol ālāp* phrase (Cba) that finally comes to rest on *madhya* Sā.

  NOTE:

  - The first step of the closing phase (S or S^1) may also serve as the final step of the elaboration phase, thus creating an elision (→) between the two phases.

Musical Elements

The following rubrics are glosses on the musical elements and gestures referenced in the event sequence rubrics above. The rubrics below include options—and hence decisions that have to be made—regarding each kind of material.

S – Complete statement of *sthāī*

Either:

(s) Simple presentation: the *sthāi* is sung in its entirety, the first line normally repeated once, the other lines less likely to be repeated—see rubric BH (*bandiś* hierarchy), below. This is followed by a return to the first line of the *sthāī* (S^1).

Or:

(e) Extended presentation: the first line is subjected to several repetitions, creating first-line accumulation (S^1A), before the whole *sthāī* is delivered. Subsequent lines may also be repeated once (analytically notated as S^2R, S^3R etc.), though this is less common.

NOTES:

- Option (s) is more usual in a freestanding *choṭā khayāl*, i.e. without a prior *baṛā khayāl*.
- Option (e) often occurs when the *choṭā khayāl* follows a *baṛā khayāl*.
- The greater the level of repetition within the *sthāī*, the greater the need for variation or decoration of the melody in order to sustain musical interest.

S^1 – *Sthāī*, first line as refrain

The first line of the *sthāī* acts as a refrain throughout a *choṭā khayāl*; in this guise it is sometimes referred to as the *mukhṛā*. This gesture commonly punctuates the end of events and actions, and/or acts as a launchpad to succeeding ones. This principle is built into the specification of many rubrics, but even where it is not, its operation may be assumed. Here are the most common places you might apply it:

- Following entire statements of the *sthāī* (S).
- Following (or preceding) individual *vistār*/*bol ālāp* episodes (V), individual *tāns* (T) and individual *laykārī* episodes (L).
- Following the final line of the *antarā* (A).

NOTE:

- You may also treat the first line of the *antarā* in a similar, more localised way (A^1) once you get there—for example, as a launching-off point for *tāns*, *vistār* and other developmental techniques in the upper register around *tār* Sā before singing the *antarā* complete (A).

S[1]A – *Sthāī*, first-line accumulation

The first line of the *sthāī* may be repeated several or many times as a means of accumulating intensity. There are two contexts where this rubric may normally be applied:

- In the opening phase, as part of the extended delivery of the *sthāī* (S(e)); this is more likely when the *choṭā khayāl* follows a *baṛā khayāl*.
- In the elaboration phase, where it may also be associated with an increase in *lay* (LI).

NOTE:

- The first line of the *antarā* may be similarly treated (A[1]A)—see next.

A – *Antarā*

It is usual to sing the *antarā* at least once in a performance. Essentially, there are three possibilities:

(s) Simple presentation: sing the *antarā* in its entirety, usually repeating the first line once.

(e) Extended presentation: sing the first line of the *antarā* one or more times (A[1]), then sustain *tār* Sā (which is normally the goal tone of the first line); extemporise around this pitch, rising higher if you feel this is appropriate (*tār* Sā is most commonly prolonged by *vistār*/*bol ālāp*, but *tān*s are also possible). Once this work is done, you may either: (i) sing the complete *antarā*; or (ii) first repeat the entire process to build further intensity.

(d) Delayed presentation: the first line is subjected to first-line accumulation (A[1]A) before the whole *antarā* is sung; or the first line is treated as a localised refrain (A[1]) with several intervening episodes of *vistār* or *tān*s before the entire *antarā* is sung; or there may be some blending of these processes.

NOTES:

- Option (s) is usually applied when the *antarā* is sung as part of the opening phase, though it may be delivered this way in the elaboration phase too.
- Option (e) is normally associated with the elaboration phase, and occurs quite commonly. Its elaborations around *tār* Sā create localised development, as well as contributing to the larger tendency of growth.
- Option (d) is less common and usually occurs in the elaboration phase. Its essence is a spirit of play around the moment of arrival of the complete *antarā*. Its orientation is towards the future.
- The *antarā* itself is usually composed with a built-in return to the lower register and *madhya* Sā, which prompts a return to the first line of the *sthāī* (S[1]) or possibly all of it (S).
- In principle, it is possible to sing the *antarā* a second time, following an intervening period of development (for example, VR does this in the *choṭā*

khayāl of Rāg Mālkauns). However, this is not common: if you wish to take this option, you should bear rubric BH in mind (see below).

V, T – *Vistār, tāns*

Vistār and *tāns* are the main techniques for musical expansion and development in a *choṭā khayāl*. Because they often interact, I here treat them together.

- *Vistār* is used to expand the expressive reach of the *bandiś* and the *rāg*. The term is used in this rubric to mean either a passage of wordless *ālāp* (V(a)) or a passage of *bol ālāp* (V(b))—sung independently of the *tāl* maintained by the tabla.
- *Tāns* have a contrasting function: they 'bring out ... the decorative possibilities within a *rāga*' (Mittal 2000: 121). They normally take one of the following forms:

  T(s) *sargam tāns*

  T(a) *ākār tāns*

  T(b) *bol tāns*

  T(g) *gamak tāns*

NOTES:

  - It is common to present one or more episodes of either or both techniques during the elaboration phase.
  - Each instance of either technique is normally preceded and followed by the *mukhṛā* (S^1 or A^1, depending on the context).
  - You may proceed directly from one technique to another, or interpolate these with S^1/A^1.
  - Which technique to use when is partly a question of whether it is desirable to increase or lower rhythmic density at any given point: *tāns* will increase it, *vistār* will lower it. This is related to whether you wish to step up the intensity or introduce a period of contrast after a period of busy activity—cf. rubric AI, below.
  - Although *sargam* and *ākār tāns* are most commonly heard among the *tān* types, and the former may more likely be sung before the latter, there are no hard and fast principles regarding ordering.

L – *Laykārī*

Although the term can encompass 'any technique intended to develop or vary rhythm' (Clayton 2000: 153), for this rubric I use *laykārī* to signify techniques of rhythmic play or intensification that are not listed in other rubrics, notably:

- L(bb) *bol baṇṭ*.
- L(lb) *lay baṇṭ*.

NOTES:

- These techniques are more commonly associated with dhrupad, and not extensively used in their own right in k͟hayāl. But their cross-rhythmic, syncopated style may sometimes be applied to variations of the *bandiś* or within the delivery of *tān*s.
- *Laykārī* techniques are more likely to be introduced later in the elaboration phase.
- Other *laykārī* devices listed under separate rubrics include *lay* increase (LI), and *tihāī* (Th)—see next.

LI – *Lay* increase

As the elaboration phase proceeds, you have the option of increasing the *lay*. This may be associated with an episode of first-line accumulation (S^1A/A^1A). The decision to increase the *lay*, as well as when to do so, should be made with regard to the overall accumulation of intensity (AI).

Th – *Tihāī*

While most Indian classical performances end with a *tihāī*—a phrase repeated three times—this rhythmic device can be introduced anywhere to create musical interest. Usually a *tihāī* will end either on *sam* or at the beginning of S^1 or A^1. *Tihāī*s can create cunning cross-rhythmic play; they can even be compounded into a *cakradār*—a *tihāī* within a *tihāī* within a *tihāī*, though this device is more usually deployed in instrumental music. In the Kirānā *gharānā*, where melodic invention is more important than rhythmic, *tihāī*s are normally kept simple. At the very least, a k͟hayāliyā needs to know how to employ a *tihāī* in the closing phase (C) of their performance.

Int – *Interlude*

Occasionally, as the lead artist, you may want to signal an interlude, giving one or more of the accompanying team a little time in the limelight. This is an effective way to create contrast and/or to give yourself a moment to re-group physically and mentally. As always, timing needs to be judicious, as does duration. An interlude is most likely to be effective some way into the elaboration phase, once you have established your presence as soloist. Too long a break from centre stage will detract from the main focus of the performance: yourself and your own invention. A similar foregrounding of one of the accompanists might happen at the beginning of a *choṭa* k͟hayāl (S(e)) when this follows an extended *baṛā* k͟hayāl.

Global Rubrics

The following rubrics do not apply to any specific phase of the performance, nor, usually, to any specific type of musical material; rather they condition the performance as a whole.

AI – Accumulation of intensity

Practically every Hindustani classical performance is shaped by one or more arcs of mounting intensity at local and global levels. This principle (AI) is engineered through the combination and permutation of a number of elements, including:

- Ascending register, for example, across episodes of *vistār* and *tān* work.
- Increasing length of such episodes.
- Increasing *lay* (LI).
- Increasing *lay* density—i.e. level of rhythmic activity per *mātrā, āvartan*, etc.
- Increasing complexity of invention, including level of interaction with accompanists.
- Increasing volume.

  NOTE:

  - AI is usually not manifested as a single uninterrupted gradient, but as a series of rises and falls within an overall ascent. The choice of techniques, and the manner of their application, should be made with this in mind.

BH – *Bandiś* hierarchy

The overall performance is conditioned by an assumed hierarchy within the different components of the *bandiś*:

a) The *sthāī* is superordinate to the *antarā*. It is presented first, and it or its elements (notably the first line) should preponderate. While the *antarā* is quite often sung only once (and may very occasionally be omitted entirely), it would be unthinkable to treat the *sthāī* this way. The *antarā* is always followed by a return to the *sthāī*.

b) The first line of both *sthāī* and *antarā* have greatest salience within their respective portion of the *bandiś*. In the case of the *sthāī*, the first line is usually repeated, sometimes cumulatively (S^1A); and it operates as a refrain, or *mukhṛā*, across the entire performance (S^1), helping bind it together. The first line of the *antarā* is often similarly repeated, and may similarly operate as a reference point while that stage holds sway (A^1, A^1A).

c) Other lines of the *sthāī* and *antarā* may be repeated, but this is rarer. Overstating them would violate (a) and (b). For example, it would be highly unusual to repeat the last line of the *antarā*, since it tends to have the composed-in function of leading back to the *sthāī*.

NOTES:

- At one extreme of the hierarchy we have the first line of the *sthāī*, which could be seen to stand synecdochally for the *bandiś* as a whole; and at the other we have the last line of the *antarā*, which may be heard only once in the entire performance.
- This rubric matters because it regulates the balance of the different elements across the performance as a whole. For example, if, after a period of development, you decide to introduce the *antarā* a second time, you need to ensure that you give comparably greater attention to the *sthāī*, so that the latter is not eclipsed. For the same reason, you would be less likely to sing the *antarā* a third time.

→ Merge/elision

Not all the categories of musical material outlined above remain discrete at all times. *Bol ālāp* may merge into wordless *ālāp* (*vistār*), or, as it becomes more rhythmically energised, morph into *tān* singing or *laykārī*. Similarly, as you begin singing the *sthāī* or its *mukhṛā*, you may want to hand over to one of the accompanists, hence transitioning into an interlude. A late statement of the *sthāī* may simultaneously round off the elaboration phase and initiate the closing phase, creating an elision between them. These and other examples of merging or elision are represented in this account with an arrow symbol between the components, for example, V(a)→T(a) (= *vistār*/wordless *ālāp* merging into ākār *tān*s).

Does a *Choṭā Khayāl* Have a Performance Grammar?

If the above schedule of rubrics looks surprisingly complicated, this is because the options for singing a *choṭā khayāl* actually *are* complicated—or can be. What this schema implies is that beneath a performance there may lie something not unlike a grammar that can generate realisations on a continuum from the simple to the complex. If the above rubrics are correctly formulated, they should in principle be able to model any *choṭā khayāl* performance. While fully testing this hypothesis would be a long-term project, we can consider a complementary pair of instances here as initial proof of concept.

At the simpler end of the spectrum, Figure 3.3.8(a) presents a second analysis of VR's Bhairav *choṭā khayāl*, in the form of an *event synopsis*. This re-description applies the rubrics developed above to the performance events in tabular form. The first column gives the track time code for the inception of each event. The second indicates the *āvartan* in which the event begins: *āvartan*s are numbered successively, and beat numbers are indicated with superscripts—which confirm that virtually all the events in this *tīntāl* performance begin on *khālī*, beat 9. (The final *āvartan*, 19, is shown in brackets since this is not a complete instance at all: the *tāl* dissipates as soon as the final *sam* is articulated.) The third and fourth columns respectively show the performance phase and constituent musical elements, using rubric codes from the schema. The fifth column provides a concise generic description of the elements, and is supplemented by the sixth which comments on features specific to the performance.

Choṭā khayāl in Rāg Bhairav

(a) Event synopsis

1 Time code	2 *Āvartan no.*	3 Perf. phase	4 Elements	5 Description	6 Comments
02:01	0^9	**O**	S(s)	*Sthāī* complete (simple mode).	
02:36	4^9		S^1	1st line of *sthāī* (*mukhṛā*).	
02:45	5^9		A(s)	*Antarā* complete (simple mode).	
03:21	9^9		S^1	1st line of *sthāī* (*mukhṛā*).	
03:29	10^9	**E**	T(s)	*Sargam tāns.*	3 x 8 beat *tāns*, preceded by 1st half-line of *sthāī* as *mukhṛā*.
03:56	13^9	**E→C**	S(s)	*Sthāī* complete (simple mode). Creates elision with closing phase.	
04:33	17^9	**C**	Th(S½)	*Tihāī*, based on 1st line of *sthāī*.	
04:46	[19...]		Cba	Closing *bol ālāp*.	
05:00				[Ends]	

(b) Event string

O: S(s), S^1, A(s), S^1

E: T(s)

E → C: S(s)

C: Th(S½), Cba.

Fig. 3.3.8 Rāg Bhairav, *choṭā khayāl*: (a) event synopsis; (b) event string. Created by author (2024), CC BY-NC-SA.

This synoptic analysis makes the straightforwardness of the performance transparent. It shows how the opening phase (O) prevails for half the total duration (nine *āvartans* out of eighteen); how the elaboration phase (E) essentially comprises a simple sequence of *tāns*; and how it elides with the closing phase (E→C) as the *sthāī* is reprised in its entirely before the final *tihāī*.

Part (b) of the figure extracts this information more concisely still. This *event string* arranges the sequences of musical elements linearly by performance phase. It is this notation that suggests the possibility of some form of quasi-grammatical underpinning.

Choṭā khayāl in Rāg Pūriyā Dhanāśrī

(a) event synopsis

1	2	3	4	5	6	7
Time code	***Āvartan* no.**	**Perf. phase**	**Elements**	**Sub-elements**	**Description**	**Comments**
02:21	0^{10}	**O**	S(e)	S^1A	Complete presentation of *sthāī*, in extended mode: first-line accumulation.	First line 4x.
02:46	4^9			S^2R	Second line of *sthāī*, repeated.	
02:59	6^{10}		S(e)	S^1A	Further complete presentation of *sthāī*. First-line accumulation (*sthāī*).	First line 4x. Overall pattern same as preceding.
03:25	10^{10}			S^2R	Second line of *sthāī*, repeated.	
03:38	12^{10}		S^1		First line of *sthāī* used as refrain (*mukhṛā*).	
03:44	13^{10}	**E**	A(e)	A^1	*Antarā* (first line).	Extended mode.
03:50	14^{10}			A^1→V(b)	First line of *antarā*, merging into *vistār* (*bol ālāp*).	Ends with short *tān*.
04:15	18^9			A^1A	1st-line accumulation (*antarā*).	First line 4x.
04:41	22^{10}			A^2	2nd line of *antarā*.	Concludes *antarā*.
04:47	23^{10}	**E2**	S^1A+LI		First-line accumulation (*sthāī*), with *lay* increase.	First line 3x. LI begins during 2nd statement.
05:06	27		T(s)		*Sargam tāns*.	3 *tāns*, with 1st half of S^1 as *mukhṛā*.
05:18	29^9		S^1→Int		First line of *sthāī* merging into harm. interlude.	
05:28	31^9		T(a)		*Ākār tān*.	Single, short *tān* lasting ½ *āvartan*.
05:31	32		Th($S^{1/4}$) →S^1 →Int		*Tihāī* based on first quarter-line of *sthāī*; elides with first line, merging into harm. interlude	
05:46	35		T(a)		*Ākār tān*.	Single, longer *tān* lasting 1.5 *āvartans*.
05:53	36^{10}		S^1→Int →S^1		First line of *sthāī* merging into interlude, merging back into first line of *sthāī*.	
06:07	39^9	**E3**	S^1R+LI →Int		First line of *sthāī*, repeated, with *lay*	

					increase, merging into harm. interlude.	
06:17	41^{13}		V(b)		*Vistār* (*bol ālāp*).	Segue into following *tans*.
06:32	45^{9}		T(a)		*Ākār tāns*.	Climactic, accumulative. S^1 (or fragments) as *mukhṛā*.
06:58	52^{2}		Th(S¼) →S^1→		*Tihāī* based on first quarter-line of *sthāī*, merging into 1st line, merging into ...	
07:04	53^{9}	C	S(s)		reprise of *sthāī* (complete).	
07:12	55^{10}		Th(S½)		*Tihāī*, based on 1st half-line of *sthāī*.	
07:18	[57...]		Cba		Closing *bol ālāp*	Returns to *madhya* Sā.
07:36					[Ends.]	

(b) Event string

O: S(e){S^1A, S^2R}, S(e){S^1A, S^2R}, S^1

E: A(e){A^1, A^1→V(b), A^1A, A^2}

E2: S^1A+LI, T(s), S^1→Int, T(a), Th(S¼)→S^1→Int, T(a), S^1→Int→S^1

E3: S^1R+LI→Int, V(b), T(a), Th(S¼)→S^1→

C: S(s), Th(S½), Cba.

Fig. 3.3.9 Rāg Pūriyā Dhanāśrī, *choṭā khayāl*: (a) event synopsis; (b) event string. Created by author (2024), CC BY-NC-SA.

The elements are arranged syntagmatically, i.e. in a meaningfully related chain; and they elaborate principles implicit in the performance-phase rubrics.

Before reflecting further on the validity of the grammatical conceit, let us first apply the above model to a more complex example of a *choṭā khayāl* performance. This one is in Rāg Pūriyā Dhanāśrī, from Track 7 of *Rāg samay cakra*. The event synopsis of VR's rendition is shown in Figure 3.3.9(a). It follows the format of the previous figure, except that it contains an additional column, 5, which shows sub-elements of musical elements where appropriate; this is necessitated by the greater complexity of the performance, the longest on the album. We can see in column 4 that VR elects to open with the *sthāī* in its extended mode (S(e)), whose sub-elements are a period of first-line accumulation (S^1A), in which the first line is heard four times, and a repeated second line (S^2R). As if this were not repetition enough, VR then repeats the entire sequence—S^1A, S^2R—followed by a reprise of the first line of the *sthāī* (S^1) which henceforward acts as a *mukhṛā* or refrain. Such pervasive repetition requires imaginative delivery, and VR obliges with subtle variations of the first line throughout—as captured in Audio Example 3.3.24.

Audio Example 3.3.24 Rāg Pūriyā Dhanāśrī: opening phase (*sthāī* in extended mode) (*RSC*, Track 7, 02:20–03:43)
https://hdl.handle.net/20.500.12434/6f80a1fb

Audio Example 3.3.25 Rāg Pūriyā Dhanāśrī: beginning of elaboration phase (*antarā* in extended mode) (*RSC*, Track 7, 03:43–04:49)
https://hdl.handle.net/20.500.12434/43bc8b34

The *antarā* is likewise presented in extended mode (A(e))—heard in Audio Example 3.3.25 and summarised in Figure 3.3.9(a). The *antarā*'s position, immediately following the *sthāī*, initially suggests that it might be a continuation of the opening phase. However, mid-way through a repeat of the first line, VR pauses on *tār* Sā and morphs this into an extended period of *vistār* (*bol ālāp*)—(A^1→V(b)). By this point it is clear that we have moved into the elaboration phase (see column 3)—an impression confirmed by a subsequent period of first-line accumulation (A^{1}A). This mirrors the opening treatment of the *sthāī* (S^{1}A) and retrospectively suggests that even the opening phase had something of the quality of an elaboration phase. Moreover, the event synopsis shows how the elaboration phase 'proper' dominates the performance; column 3 interprets it as compounded into three stages—E, E2 and E3—the latter two being articulated by *lay* increases (LI).

As was the case with the Bhairav analysis, Figure 3.3.9(b) distils this information into an event string, one line per performance phase. Sub-elements are notated within curly brackets, as subsets of their respective elements; these in turn are presided over by the rubric code for the respective performance phase—shown in bold. This concise notation facilitates comparison between performances: even a superficial glance reveals something of the significantly greater complexity of the performance compared with its precursor. While the algebraic style looks abstract, the compressed encryption of rubrics is in fact an apt metaphor for the near-instantaneous decision-making demanded of a performer in the live moment: each letter symbolises a commitment to a musical action that subsequently unfolds with full expression (and often passion) in real time. And, even more than the last example, this encoding is suggestive of an underlying grammar that might have generated it. But in what sense might we understand this notion?

Conclusion

The event-string representation suggests a grammar because it reflects the way elements of musical material are chained together under repeatable and combinable principles that are understood by those making and hearing the music; it reflects how a potentially infinite number of combinations can be generated from a finite number of conventions. However, the notation is not yet a formal description of the putative grammar itself, but rather of its outputs. To model the underlying principles of the grammar per se would need a yet further level of formalisation: one able algorithmically to express the options for the combination and succession of rubrics, perhaps in the form of a flow diagram, perhaps mutating quasi-algebra into actual algebra. A properly formalised grammar would also need to find a systematic and rigorous way to express the probability of options within the schema, which in this account I have only indicated informally with modal verbs such as 'should', 'can' or 'may', or with adverbs such as 'usually' or 'not commonly'.

Such a grammar would also need to contend with the fact that a *choṭā khayāl* is both *hypotactic* and *paratactic*. To explain: hypotaxis refers to the way language may structure ideas in terms that are mutually dependent—for example, the embedding of sub-clauses within a main clause. Parataxis refers to a sequence of ideas whose order is mutable and does not subordinate any one to any other. We can see hypotaxis operating within the hierarchic conditions described in global rubric BH—for example, the first line of the *sthāī* as superordinate to the following lines. Hypotaxis is also visible in the event-string notation, which shows several nested levels: a line for each performance phase, presided over by a governing rubric (indicated in bold); the linking of elements so governed with commas; and the representation of their sub-elements inside curly brackets, as subsets. However, many of those same elements also function *paratactically*, thus manifesting a countervailing, anti-hierarchic tendency. For example, S^1 and S^1A may occur at various points; and devices such as *tāns* and *bol ālāp* operate under similarly loose conditions, with considerable flexibility as regards order. Thus, hypotaxis and parataxis intermingle, with an attendant challenge for grammatical modelling—or even for the notion of grammar as such. I do not intend to pursue these matters further here, but signal that these are some of the issues that any future programme of analysis along such lines would need to address.

Finally, does any of this matter? I think it does. While on the one hand, the written schema of rubrics, and the implicit grammar to which its formal organisation points, exceeds what practicing musicians consciously need to know, on the other hand, the rubrics are closely related to performance: they codify the guidance communicated orally by gurus and internalised by students over many years of practice until it takes the form of intuition. The notion of a performance grammar may be apposite because, as Harold Powers put it in a classic article, 'few musics are as much like language as Indian music is'; and in Indian classical music, 'spontaneous and flexible musical discourse is as essential and almost as easy for the trained musician as speech for the fluent speaker of a language' (1980: 38, 42). At the back of my own mind in attempting such a theoretical distillation of practice has been the historically remote example of the classical grammarian Pāṇini, who, between the sixth and fourth centuries BCE, codified Sanskrit into a compact number of algorithms (Kiparsky 1993). I speculate about this connection not to aggrandise my own findings, but to throw light on what such frameworks proffer in their abstraction. Significantly, they model unconscious collective knowledge that lies deep beneath everyday discursive utterances. And, as I have attempted to show in this analysis, they make the orally transmitted artistry of Hindustani classical culture—in all its complexity and sophistication—legible to us.

4. EXPLORATIONS AND ANALYSES (II): *TWILIGHT RĀGS FROM NORTH INDIA*

Performers:

Dr Vijay Rajput (khayāl vocalist)

with

Ustād Shahbaz Hussain (tabla)

Ustād Fida Hussain (harmonium)

https://doi.org/10.11647/OBP.0313.04

4.1 Introduction

In contrast to *Rāg samay cakra*, an album comprising concise renditions of fourteen *rāg*s in an extended sequence, *Twilight Rāgs from North India* presents extended accounts of just two *rāg*s, Bhairav and Yaman. These concert-length performances by Vijay Rajput (henceforth VR) and accompanists exemplify the wider and deeper reaches of *rāg* music. Each begins with an *ālāp*, followed by a weighty *baṛā khayāl* (also termed *vilambit khayāl*) and a fully developed *choṭā khayāl* (also termed *drut khayāl*). This form of *rāg* performance launches many a modern-day classical Hindustani vocal recital, after which the soloist usually moves on to shorter and lighter items, including some in semi-classical vein, such as bhajans and *ṭhumrī*s, or sometimes even folk- and filmi-derived songs.

Two factors drew us towards Bhairav and Yaman. First, bearing in mind the theme of our anthology, these *rāg*s mark especially evocative performing times (*samay*). They are associated with the awakening and ending of the day respectively—just after sunrise and just after sunset: times of stillness conducive to contemplation. Second, the *rāg*s have a core place in the Hindustani canon. They are usually learnt early in a student's training, and remain touchstones throughout an artist's career. This is especially true of Yaman—often the first *rāg* a student might learn, yet not disdained by the great artists either. VR tells of how his late guruji, the feted Bhimsen Joshi (1922–2011), never stopped exploring this *rāg*; he was especially fond of the *drut bandiś* 'Śyām bajāi', which VR sings as a tribute on both albums of *Rāgs Around the Clock*.

As the specifications and descriptions for Bhairav and Yaman were outlined in the supporting materials for *Rāg samay cakra* (Section 2.5.1 and Section 2.5.9), there is no need to repeat that content here. Rather, this part of *Rāgs Around the Clock* has two main objectives. First, Section 4.2 provides notations, transliterations, translations and commentaries relating to VR's Bhairav performance on Tracks 2 and 3. Second, Section 4.3 examines the principles of a *baṛā khayāl*, taking VR's Yaman rendering on Track 5 as a case study; this complements (and completes) the analysis initiated in Part 3, which looked at the *ālāp* and *choṭā khayāl* stages of performances from *Rāg samay cakra*.

Twilight Rāgs from North India was recorded at Newcastle University in April 2006 and released the same year in CD format (with slightly different orthography in the title). The sound engineer was John Ayers, and David Clarke (henceforth DC) was the producer. Work published elsewhere (Clarke 2013) provides contextual background to the album.

4.2 Rāg Bhairav: Texts, Notations and Commentaries

Aims

The subject under the spotlight in the present section is VR's performance of the first *rāg* on the *Twilight Rāgs* album, Bhairav. One priority is to provide details of the texts and notations of the *bandiśes*, in the interests not least of students who want to add them to their repertoire. A further aim is to consider the issues raised by these materials and their associated performances. Hence, in the first part of this section, I consider the mutable identity of the *baṛā khayāl bandiś* 'Balamavā more saīyā̃', alongside alternative versions sung by doyens of the Kirānā *gharānā*. And, in the second part, I analyse the subtleties of the *drut bandiś* 'Suno to sakhī batiyā', and the ways in which VR works it into an extended *choṭā khayāl*. With this last analysis, I conjecture further about the possibility of an underlying performance grammar, as first raised in Section 3.3. As I have already considered general principles of *ālāp* in Section 3.1, I will not discuss that stage of VR's performance here (for an analysis of his Yaman *ālāp* from the album, see Clarke 2017).

Baṛā Khayāl: 'Bālamavā more saīyā̃'

Characteristically, VR chooses a *baṛā khayāl* in *vilambit* (slow) *ektāl* for his performance. The text of the Bhairav composition, given below, is characteristically ambiguous as to whether the object of the lyricist's longing and devotion is earthly or divine, or both:

Rāg Bhairav—Baṛā Khayāl

Sthāī	
Bālamavā more saīyā̃ sadā raṅgīle.	*My beloved, my lord, is always resplendent.*
Antarā	
Hũ to tuma bīna, tarasa gaai,	*Without you, I have been pining.*
Darasa bega dīkhāo.	*Quickly, show yourself.*

राग भैरव—बड़ा ख़याल

स्थाई

बालमवा मोरे सईयाँ सदा रंगीले |

अंतरा

हुँ तो तुम बीन, तरस गऐ

दरस बेग दीखाओ | |

Audio Examples 4.2.1 and 4.2.2 extract the *sthāī* and *antarā* respectively from VR's performance on Track 2 of the album; typically, the former is heard at the very outset, while the latter comes some way in, around 11:20. These extracts can be followed in conjunction with their respective musical transcriptions in Figure 4.2.1 (a) and (b).

Audio Example 4.2.1 Rāg Bhairav: *baṛā khayāl*, *sthāī* (*TR*, Track 2, 00:00–01:09)
https://hdl.handle.net/20.500.12434/4abe0d02

Audio Example 4.2.2 Rāg Bhairav: *baṛā khayāl*, *antarā* (*TR*, Track 2, 11:20–12:20)
https://hdl.handle.net/20.500.12434/90345685

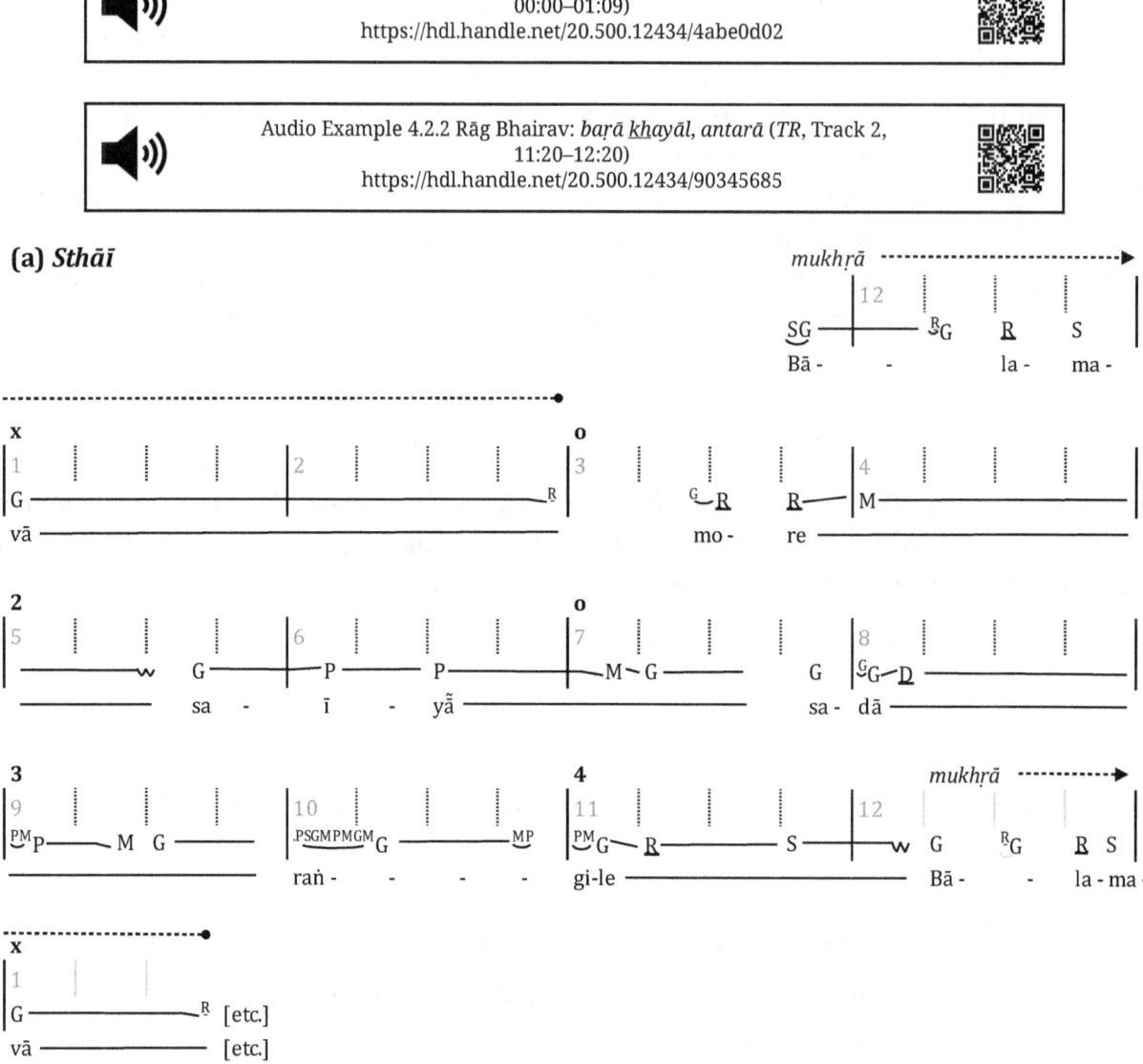

(a) *Sthāī*

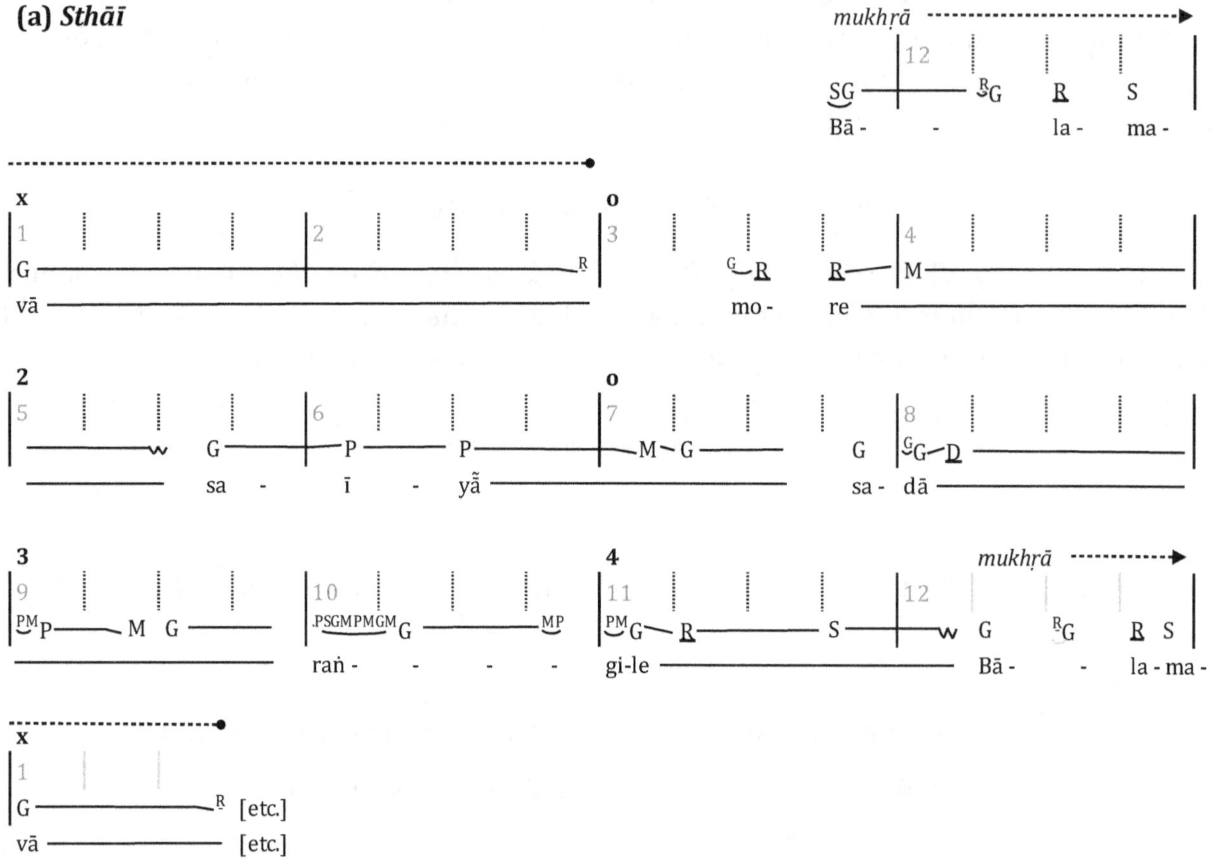

(b) *Antarā*

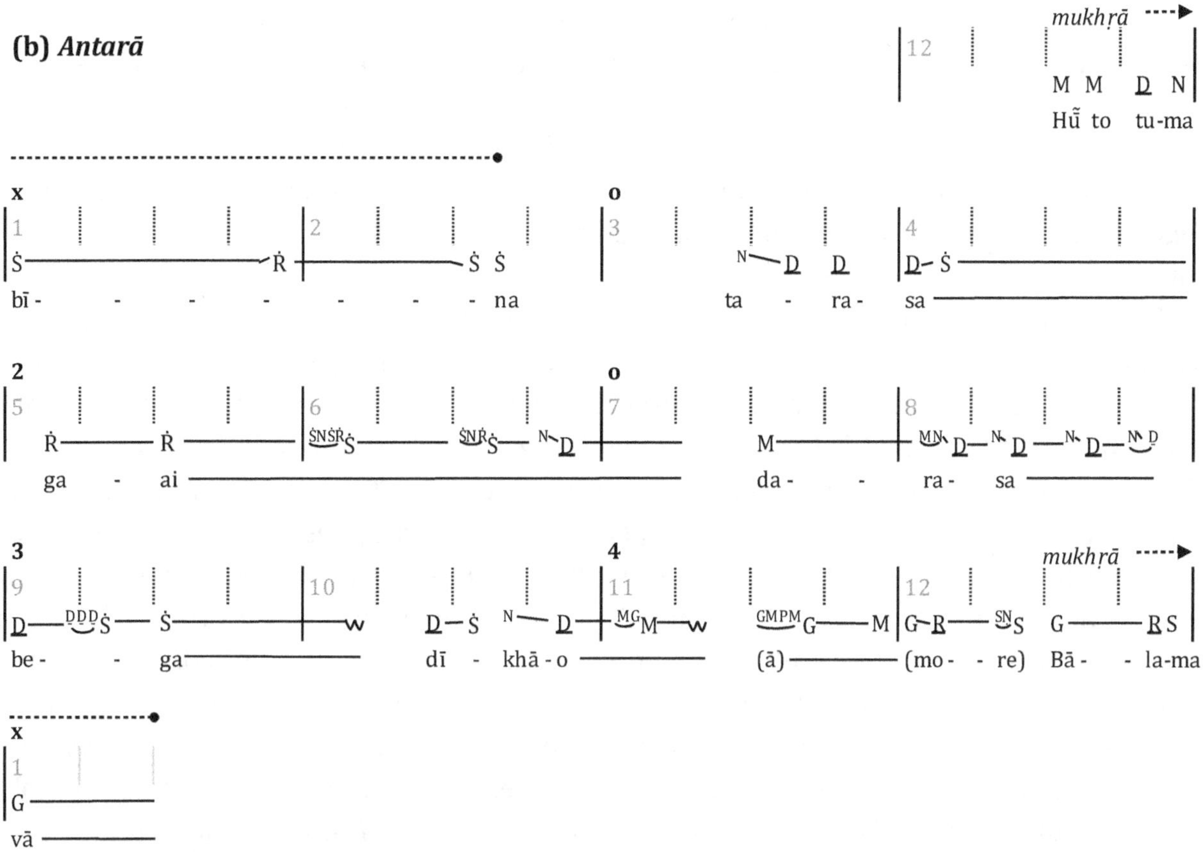

Fig. 4.2.1 Notation of *baṛā khayāl*, 'Bālamavā more saīyā̃': (a) *sthāī*; (b) *antarā*. Created by author (2024),

Notating the composition of a *baṛā khayāl* has its own complications. This is because the form it takes is closer in style to an *ālāp* than to the metrically organised song of a *choṭā khayāl*; it has only a loose connection with the *tāl* framework. Attempting to set down its somewhat amorphous contours in any definitive notated form runs even more against the grain than is the case with a *choṭā khayāl*—a matter I explore in greater depth in Section 4.3. In the present notation of VR's Bhairav *bandiś*, I have sought to render the composition in a reasonable approximation of how he actually sings it—in Charles Seeger's (1886–1979) terminology, this would be *descriptive* music writing (Seeger 1958; see also Section 2.3). Because VR does not overly elaborate the slowly unfolding melodic arc of the composition, or significantly depart from what one might imagine to be its underpinning archetype, this version may also act as a model for emulation by students—in Seeger's parlance, it also serves as *prescriptive* music writing. This is provided students bear in mind that, in any actual performance, the timing of notes in relation to each *mātrā* of the *tāl* is mutable. Although I have notated the pitches here (as closely as the software permits) in the positions at which VR sings them on this particular occasion, the duration, decoration and location of notes do not have to be—indeed should not be—reproduced exactly this way every time.

Such flexibility can be illustrated by comparing VR's different executions of the *mukhṛā*—the head motif that begins the composition and that is used as a refrain throughout the performance. Notionally, the beginning of this figure ('bālama-') should fit within the final beat (beat 12)—of the slow *ektāl* cycle, more or less locking on to its four sub-beats; the final syllable, '-vā' lands on *sam* and extends some way into the beginning of the first complete *āvartan*. But Figure 4.2.1(a) shows how VR already allows himself some metrical leeway, extending the initial prolonged Ga by a beat, so that the whole figure lasts five sub-beats rather than four. Conversely, when he reiterates the *mukhṛā* at the end of the *sthāī* (bottom of Figure 4.2.1(a)), he begins it later in beat 12, compressing it into three sub-beats and holding the final Ga on the following *sam* for a shorter duration than before. Further variations can be heard at the end of every *āvartan*; one such is notated near the end of Figure 4.2.1(b), where, after completing the *antarā*, VR further compresses the *mukhṛā* into the last two sub-beats of the cycle.

The indeterminate identity of a *baṛā khayāl bandiś* means not only that an artist might subtly vary it each time they perform it, but also that even greater differences occur between artists. Interestingly, on commercially released performances of 'Bālamavā more saīyā̃' by Bhimsen Joshi (2016) and Gangubai Hangal (1994), the *sthāī* is so different from VR's version that it could be regarded as a different composition, even though the text is essentially the same. Most saliently, the *mukhṛā* in their versions establishes an altogether different trajectory, taking Dha as the initial goal tone—as shown in Figure 4.2.2 which notates the first three phrases of Gangubai's account. The prominence of Dha reflects the *saṃvādī* status of this pitch in Bhairav; and I will call this the '*dhaivat* version' of the song. (The salience of Ma at the beginning or ends of phrases here is another characteristic of Bhairav, and another point of contrast between this version and the one sung by VR.) Bhimsen Joshi sings the *dhaivat* version a little differently from Gangubai—most notably his rendition is in *vilambit tīntāl* while hers is in *vilambit ektāl*—but the same underlying *bandiś* is discernible behind both performances. Given that both artists belonged to the same branch of the Kirānā *gharānā*—both were disciples of Sawai Gandharva—we might infer a single line of transmission.

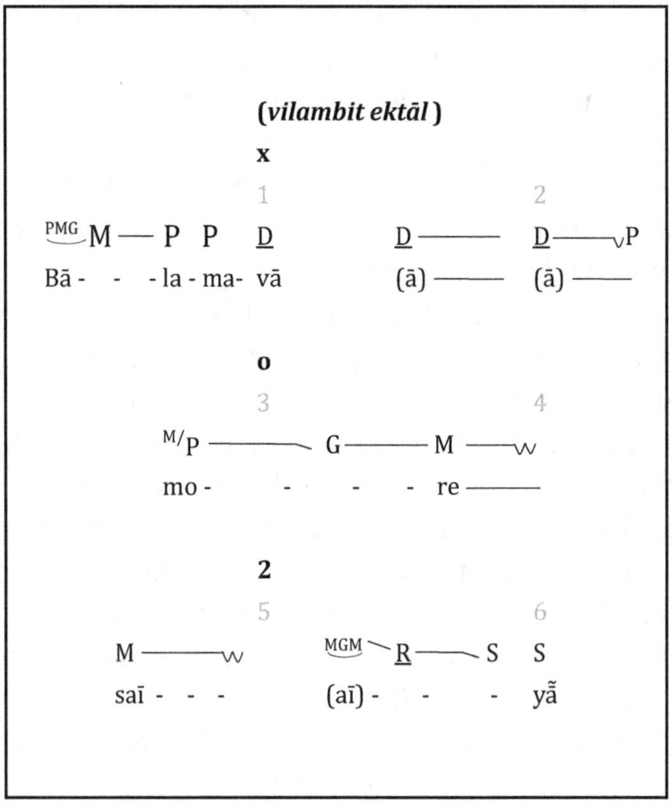

Fig. 4.2.2 Opening of 'Bālamavā more saīyā̃', as performed by Gangubai Hangal (1994: Track 1). Created by author (2024), CC BY-NC-SA.

I have referenced commercially available CDs here, but of course these recordings can also be found in online uploads on streaming platforms such as YouTube by using the artist, *rāg* or *bandiś* name as search terms. Searches also throw up yet further variants of the *dhaivat* version—not only by the same artists, but also by singers of younger generations, such as Manali Bose and Richa Shukla. This suggests the continuing transmission of the *dhaivat* version, and possibly its emerging status as the canonical melody for this text.

Yet the version sung by VR on *Twilight Rāgs*—which we can term the '*gāndhār* version', because Ga is the salient pitch of its *mukhṛā*—can also be found with a little assiduous online searching. Two different performances by Bhimsen Joshi are captured on YouTube (Sangeetveda1 2017: https://www.youtube.com/watch?v=p18MARsM92g&ab and Nadkarni 2022: https://youtu.be/gXT3VEKCZRk). As would be expected, there are differences of contour, pace, melodic segmentation and text underlay between Joshi's version and VR's; but they are recognisably the same *bandiś*, with the foregrounding of Ga in the *mukhṛā* as a salient shared feature. The very sweetness of Ga brings out the romantic aspect of the text, as compared with the gravity of the *dhaivat* version, which foregrounds <u>Dha</u>; we might interpret the *gāndhār* version as invoking the *śṛṅgār ras*, and the *dhaivat* version the *karuṇ ras*. Across the spectrum of recordings available both commercially and online, the contrast is greatest between VR's rendering of the *gāndhār* version—the heartfelt performance of a younger man—and Gangubai's more austere performances of the *dhaivat* version—documents of a much later stage in an artist's life. I make this point not to set these very different accounts in opposition, but rather to point to how they reveal complementary aspects of the *rāg*, its sheer range of expressive possibility. This also underscores the importance of the *Twilight Rāgs* recording as a dissemination channel for the rarer, *gāndhār* version of the *bandiś*, and of VR as one of its bearers within the Kirānā *gharānā*.

Drut <u>kh</u>ayāl: 'Suno to sakhī batiyā'

On Track 3 of *Twilight Rāgs*, we have a quintessential example of a *<u>kh</u>ayāl* in *drut ektāl*. This rapid twelve-beat cycle has a distinctive momentum, owing to successive stresses (*tālī*) on its last two metrical subdivisions (*vibhāg*s), which drive towards *sam*. This particular *drut <u>kh</u>ayāl* is based on a fine *bandiś* in Rāg Bhairav taught to VR by Pandit Madhup Mudgal at the Gandharva Mahavidyalaya in New Delhi. The text is given below in the original language and in translation, and its musical setting is notated in Figure 4.2.3. Audio Examples 4.2.3 and 4.2.4 extract the *sthāī* and *antarā* from VR's performance.

Rāg Bhairav—Drut Khayāl

Sthāī

Suno to sakhī batiyā Ghanaśyāma kī rī	*Listen, my companion, to words about Ghanaśyāma [Kṛṣṇa].*
bīta gaī sagarī raina	*The whole night has passed,*
kala nā parata āve caina	*I have no repose, no peace of mind.*
sudha nā līnī āna kachu dhāma kī rī.	*You did not remember the place, and did not come at all.*

Antarā

Bhora bhaī mere āe	*Dawn has come, and you have come to me,*
pāga peca laṭapaṭāai	*Your curly hair all dishevelled,*
atahī alasāne naina	*Your eyes all bleary—*
tadarā mukha veta naina	*Your eyes evasive.*
bāta karata mukha rijhāta	*As you talk, your face is alight*
pagavā dharata ḍagamagāta	*But you can't walk straight.*
juṭhī sau nā khāta dilā Rām kī rī.	*Don't swear vainly on the name of Rām.*

राग भैरव—द्रुत ख़याल

स्थाई

सुनो तो सखी बतिया घनश्याम की री

बीत गई सगरी रैन

कल ना परत आवे चैन

सुध ना लीनी आन कछु धाम की री।

अंतरा

भोर भई मेरे आए

पाग पेच लटपटाऐ

अतही अलसाने नैन

तदरा मुख वेत नैन

बात करत मुख रिझात

पगवा धरत डगमगात

जुठी सौ ना खात दिला राम की री॥

Audio Example 4.2.3 Rāg Bhairav: *drut khayāl, sthāī* (*TR*, Track 3, 00:41–01:09)
https://hdl.handle.net/20.500.12434/35cb29ec

Audio Example 4.2.4 Rāg Bhairav: *drut khayāl, antarā* (*TR*, Track 3, 04:26–05:03)
https://hdl.handle.net/20.500.12434/0904280d

(a)

ektāl

	x		o		2		o		3		4	
	1	**2**	**3**	**4**	**5**	**6**	**7**	**8**	**9**	**10**	**11**	**12**
Sthāī												
S1	|: N	D̲	P	–	M	P	G	M	P	–	G	Ḿ :|
	Su-	no	to	———	sa-	khī	ba-	ti-	yā	———	Gha-	na-
S2	D̲	–	–	–	P		N‿Ṡ	Ṙ̲‿N	Ṡ	–‿N	D̲	P
	śyā-	-	-	-	ma		kī———	———	———	———	rī———	———
S3	D̲	–	D̲	D̲	P	–	P	M	P	M	–	M
	bī-	-	ta	ga-	ī	———	sa-	ga-	ri	rai-	-	na
S4	G	G	G	R̲	G	P	M	G	M	R̲	–	S
	ka-	la	nā	pa-	ra-	ta	ā-	-	ve	cai-	-	na
S5	S	S	Ḏ̣	S	G	M	P	–	P	P	G	–
	su-	dha	nā	lī-	-	nī	ā-	-	na	ka-	chu———	———
S6	D̲	–	–	–	D̲		N‿Ṡ	Ṙ̲‿N	Ṡ	–‿N	D̲	P
	dhā-	-	-	-	ma		kī———	———	———	———	rī.———	———

(b)

ektāl

	x		o		2		o		3		4	
	1	2	3	4	5	6	7	8	9	10	11	12
Antarā												
A^1	:M	–	M	M	D̲	–	N	Ṡ	N	Ṡ	–	Ṡ :
	Bho -	-	ra	bha -	ī———		me -	-	re	ā -	-	e
A^2	D̲	–	D̲	Ṡ	–	Ṡ	N	N	Ṡ	N	–	D̲
	pā -	-	ga	pe -	-	ca	la -	ṭa -	pa -	ṭā -	-	ai
A^3	D̲	D̲	P	–	M	P	P	M	P	M	–	M
	a -	ta -	hī———		a -	la -	sā -	-	ne	nai -	-	na
A^4	G	G	G	R̲	G	M	R̲G	MP	M	R̲	–	S
	ta -	da -	rā———		mu -	kha	ve -	-	ta	nai -	-	na
A^5	M	G	M	D̲	D̲	D̲	N	Ṡ	N	Ṡ	–	Ṡ
	bā -	-	ta	ka -	ra -	ta	mu -	kha	ri -	jhā -	-	ta
A^6	D̲	D̲	P	Ṡ	N	Ṡ	N	N	Ṡ	ᴺD̲	–	P
	pa -	ga -	vā	dha -	ra -	ta	ḍa -	ga -	ma -	gā -	-	ta
A^7	D̲	–	D̲	P	–	D̲	P	M	P	G	M	–
	ju -	-	ṭhī	sau———		nā	khā -	-	ta	di -	lā -	-
A^8	D̲	–	–	–	D̲		NṠ	ṘN	Ṡ	– N	D̲	P
	Rā -	-	-	-	ma		kī———				rī.———	

Fig. 4.2.3 Notation of *drut khayāl*, 'Suno to sakhī batiyā': (a) *sthāī*; (b) *antarā*. Created by author (2024), CC BY-NC-SA.

What is immediately apparent in all these forms of capture, is that this is a long *bandiś*. The *sthāī* and *antarā* respectively comprise six and eight phrases, each phrase lasting one *āvartan*—numbered S^1, S^2 etc., A^1, A^2 etc. in Figure 4.2.3; interestingly, the *antarā* in effect has two strophes, the second beginning at 'bāga karata' (phrase A^5). In a spontaneous moment, VR sings the sixth phrase ('pagavā dharata') four times, enhancing it with *lāykārī*.

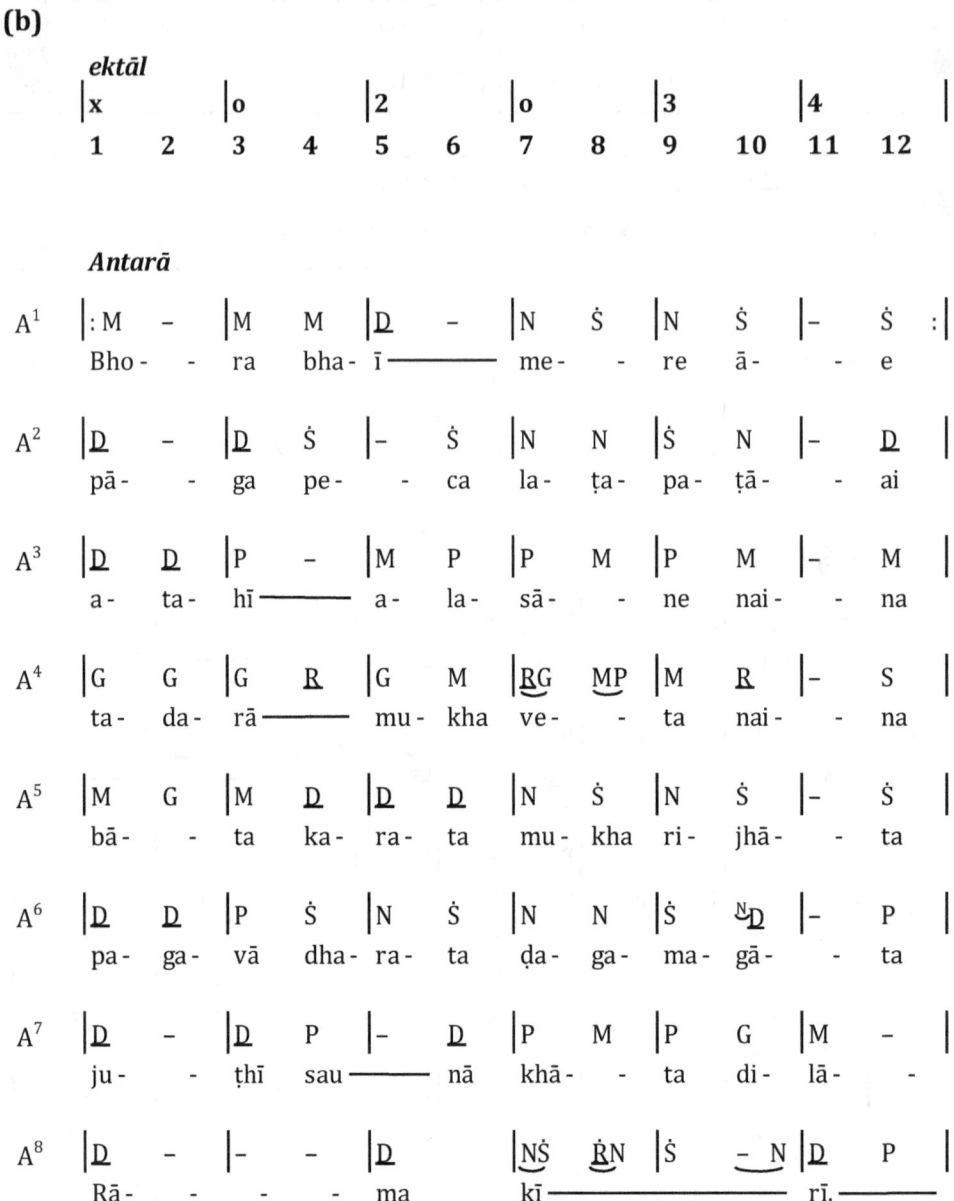

The text tells yet another tale of the *gopī* (cowherd) Rādhā being stood up by her divine lover, Kṛṣṇa. She recounts to her companion (*rī*) how she spent the whole night waiting for him; how she said to him when he finally appeared at dawn, your eyes are bleary, your hair's dishevelled, your footing's unsteady; don't take the name of Ram in vain [by lying to me about where you've been]. For all that such a scene is a classic trope of khayāl poetics (cf. Magriel and du Perron 2013, I: 139–42), the text does not rely on formulaic Braj Bhāṣā phrases typical of so many *bandiś*es. Rather, it has its own distinctive language and construction. For one thing, it is underlaid with a metrical sophistication mirrored in the musical setting and amplified by various internal cross-correspondences within the melody. Figure 4.2.4 shows how textual and musical rhyming reinforce each other: (a) between phrases S², S⁶ and A⁸; (b) between S³ and A³; and (c) between S⁴ and A⁴; equivalences are shown with a mix of horizontal alignment, boxes and braces.

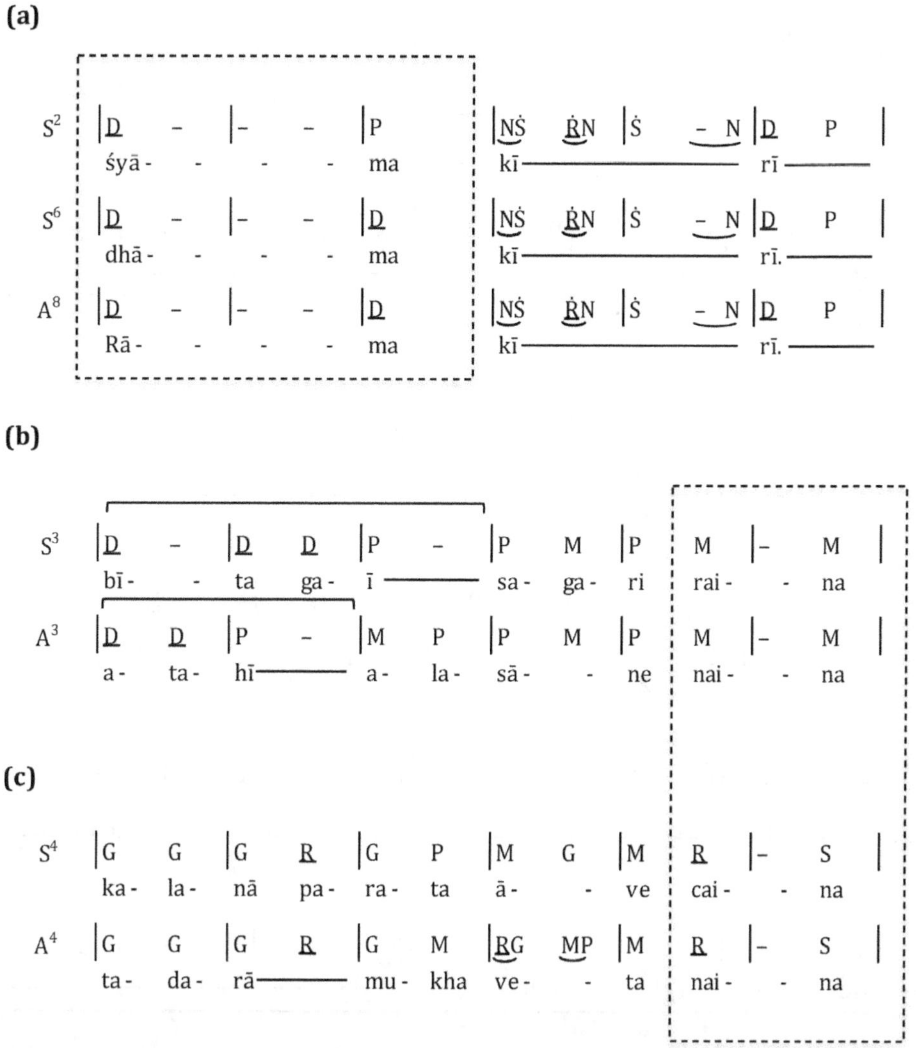

Fig. 4.2.4 'Suno to': musical and textual rhyme patterns. Created by author (2024), CC BY-NC-SA.

There are further subtleties. Focusing on the *sthāī*, Figure 4.2.5 illustrates the imaginative ways the metre of the song variably reinforces or counterpoints the metre of the *tāl*. In S¹, the poetic metre divides the twelve beats of *ektāl* into three groups of four—which is congruent with the *tāl*'s 6x2-beat clap pattern (shown at the top of the figure). By contrast, in S² and S⁶, the main impulses fall on beats 1 and 7, creating two groups of six beats; here the emphasis on beat 7 contradicts the unstressed, second *khālī* of the *tāl* cycle. Sometimes complementary groupings take place *within* an *āvartan*. In S³ and S⁴ the beats are arranged in a (2+2+2)+(3+3) pattern; while S⁵ reverses the grouping to form (3+3)+(2+2+2). These several patterns are generated through their various combinations of melodic and textual stresses and saliences. Their cross-metrical play creates a sense of cut and thrust that conveys the ambivalent feelings recounted in the text, and that imbues the song with life and energy.

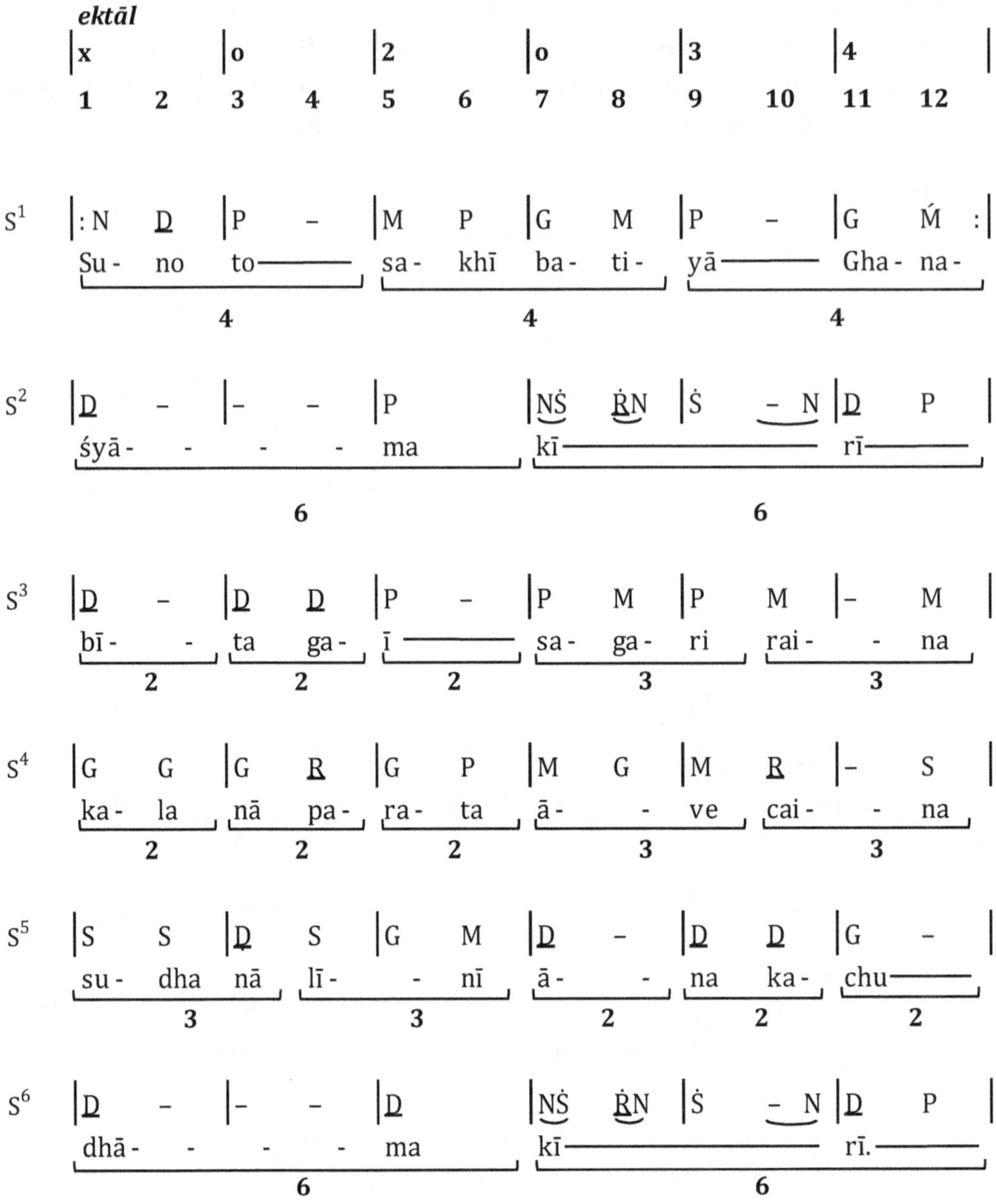

Fig. 4.2.5 'Suno to': metrical play. Created by author (2024), CC BY-NC-SA.

Performing a *bandiś* stylishly is one thing, but a khayāl singer's artistry also lies in extemporising around it to create a full-length performance. Always an issue for the improvising soloist—and especially in such a fast *lay*—is the ever-pressing question of what to do next. Figure 4.2.6 graphically summarises the elaborate chain of events that VR generates in response to this imperative. Shadings highlight the different kinds of materials deployed: the *sthāī* (in its complete form), the *antarā*, passages of *bol ālāp*, and *tāns*. Unshaded areas principally signify the first line of the *sthāī* (S^1) when sung independently from the whole and functioning as a refrain or *mukhṛā*; perhaps because of the rapid tempo, this function is often performed by joining statements of S^1 in pairs, sometimes in a relay from voice to harmonium. White space also indicates occasional rests and fills. The 248 *āvartans* of the *drut khayāl* are numbered underneath each line and are supplemented by time codes cross-referenced to Track 3 of the album. Readers are invited to follow this graphic while listening to the entire track.

Drut khayāl in Rāg Bhairav: 'Suno to sakhī batiyā'

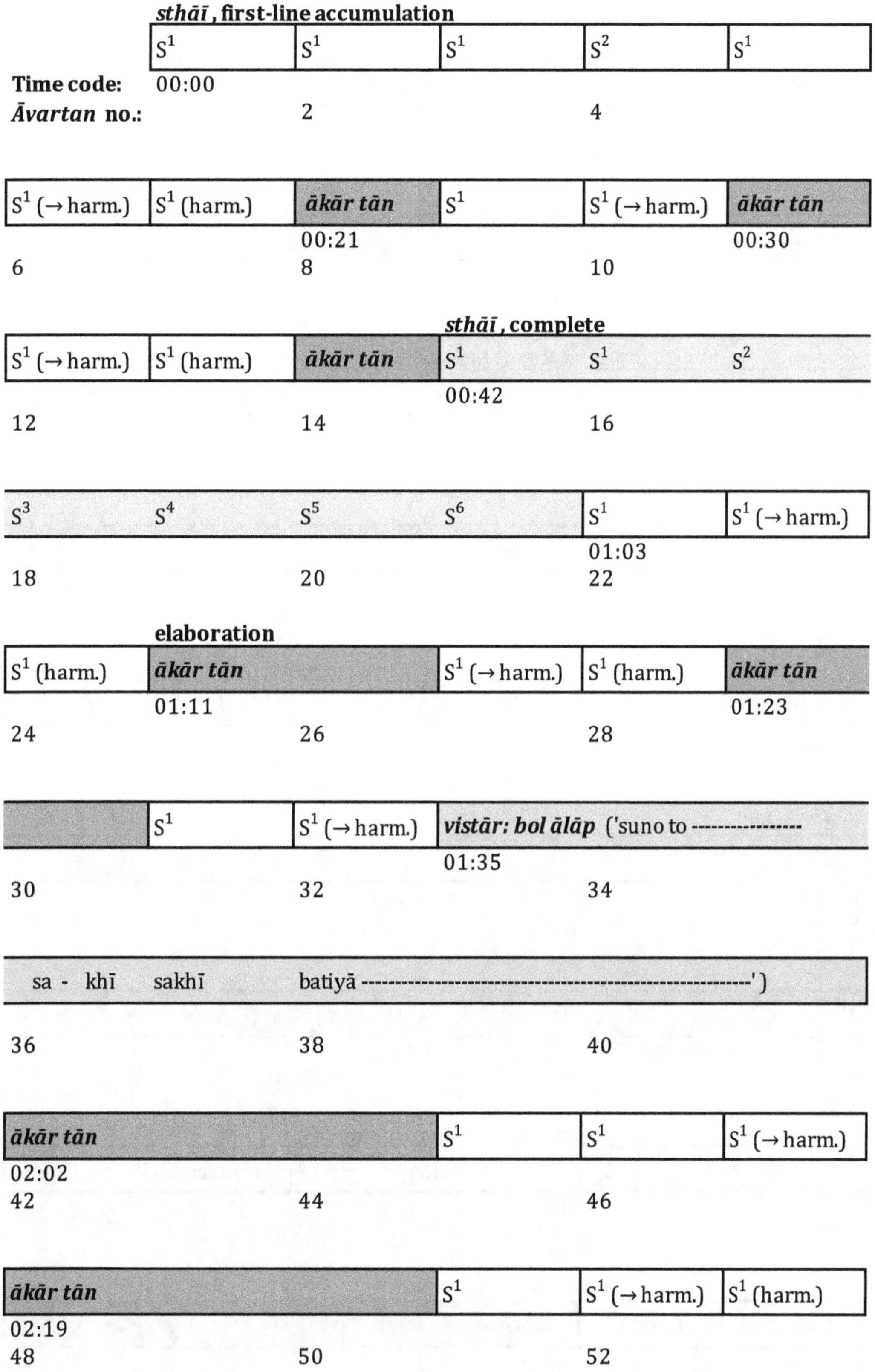
sthāī, first-line accumulation
S1
S1
S1
S2
S1
Time code:
00:00
Āvartan no.:
2
4
S1 (→ harm.)
S1 (harm.)
ākār tān
S1
S1 (→ harm.)
ākār tān
00:21
00:30
6
8
10
sthāī, complete
S1 (→ harm.)
S1 (harm.)
ākār tān
S1
S1
S2
00:42
12
14
16
S3
S4
S5
S6
S1
S1 (→ harm.)
01:03
18
20
22
elaboration
S1 (harm.)
ākār tān
S1 (→ harm.)
S1 (harm.)
ākār tān
01:11
01:23
24
26
28
S1
S1 (→ harm.)
vistār: bol ālāp ('suno to ----------------
01:35
30
32
34
sa - khī sakhī batiyā --')
36
38
40
ākār tān
S1
S1
S1 (→ harm.)
02:02
42
44
46
ākār tān
S1
S1 (→ harm.)
S1 (harm.)
02:19
48
50
52

Fig. 4.2.6 'Suno to': event sequence in graphical form. Created by author (2024), CC BY-NC-SA.

bol tān ('su... no...')		S^1	S^1 (→ harm.)	***ākār tān***	
02:36				02:48	
54		56		58	

	***sthāī*, part**				
	S^1	S^1	S^2 (→ harm. Int)		
	02:57				
60		62		64	

				***sthāī*, first-line accumulatio**	
ākār tān				S^1	S^1
03:11				03:22	
66		68		70	

		***antarā*, inception**	**→**	**elaboration**	
S^1	S^1 (→ harm.)	A^1	A^1	***vistār*: (*bol*) *ālāp*** ('rī ------	
		03:34		03:40	
72		74		76	

------------------	------------------	------------------	-------------	bho - - - - - - - ra')	
78		80		82	

			***antarā*, inception**		
→ ***bol tān*** ('bho. - - - - - - ')			A^1	A^1 / *bol tān*	→ A^1 (harm.)
04:02			04:11		
84		86		88	

elaboration			***antarā*, complete**		
ākār tān			A^1	A^2	A^3
04:19			04:28		
90		92		94	

A^4	A^5	A^6	A^6 (*laykārī*)	A^6 (*laykārī*)	A^6
	04:39		04:45		
96		98		100	

		***sthāī*, first-line accumulation**			
A^7	A^8	S^1	S^1	S^1 ***lay* increase**	S^1
		05:00			
102		104		106	

		elaboration			
S^1 (→ harm.)	S^1 (harm.)	***ākār tān***			
		05:16			
108		110		112	

Fig. 4.2.6 (cont'd) 'Suno to': event sequence in graphical form. Created by author (2024), CC BY-NC-SA.

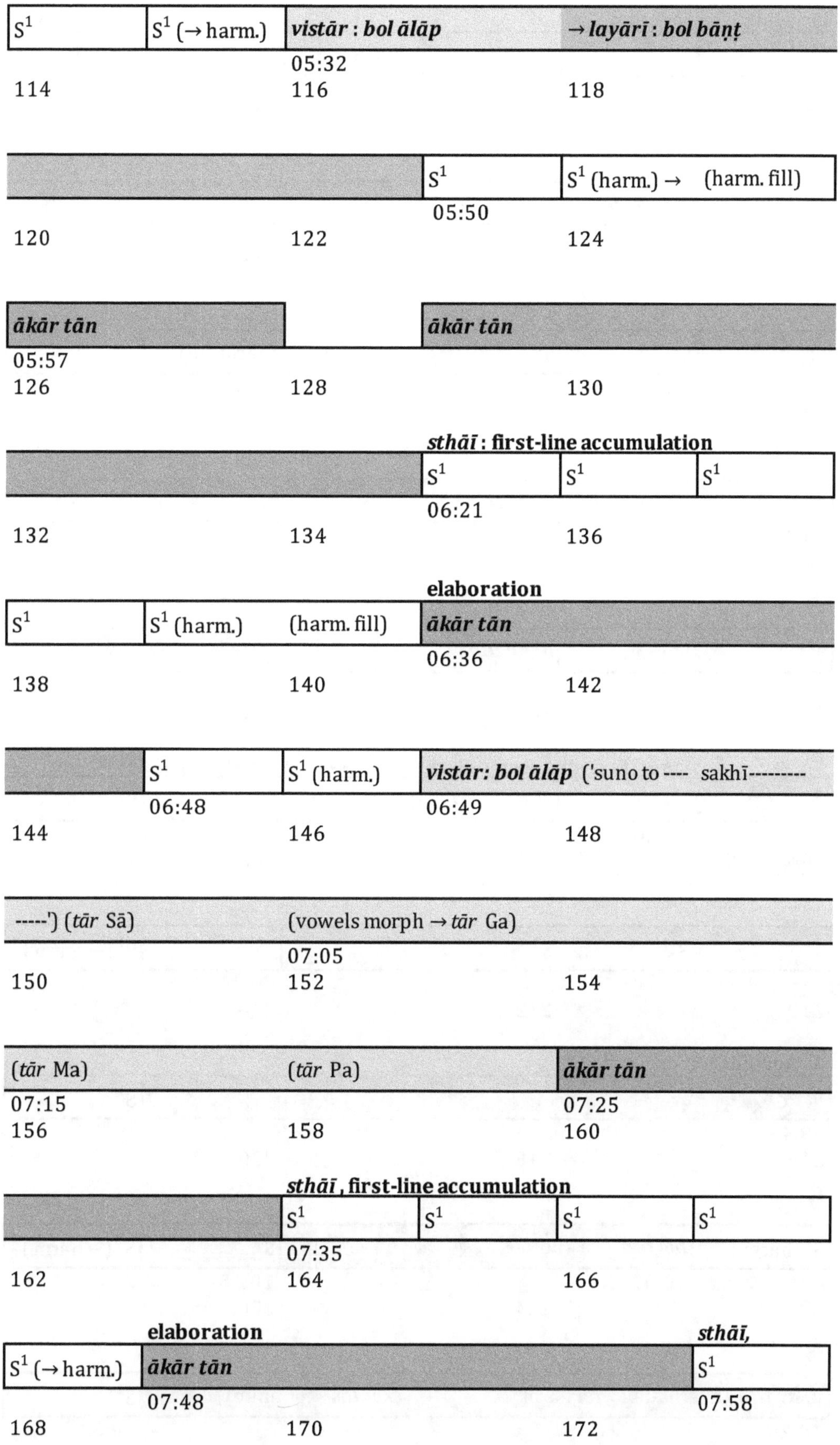

Fig. 4.2.6 (cont'd) 'Suno to': event sequence in graphical form. Created by author (2024), CC BY-NC-SA.

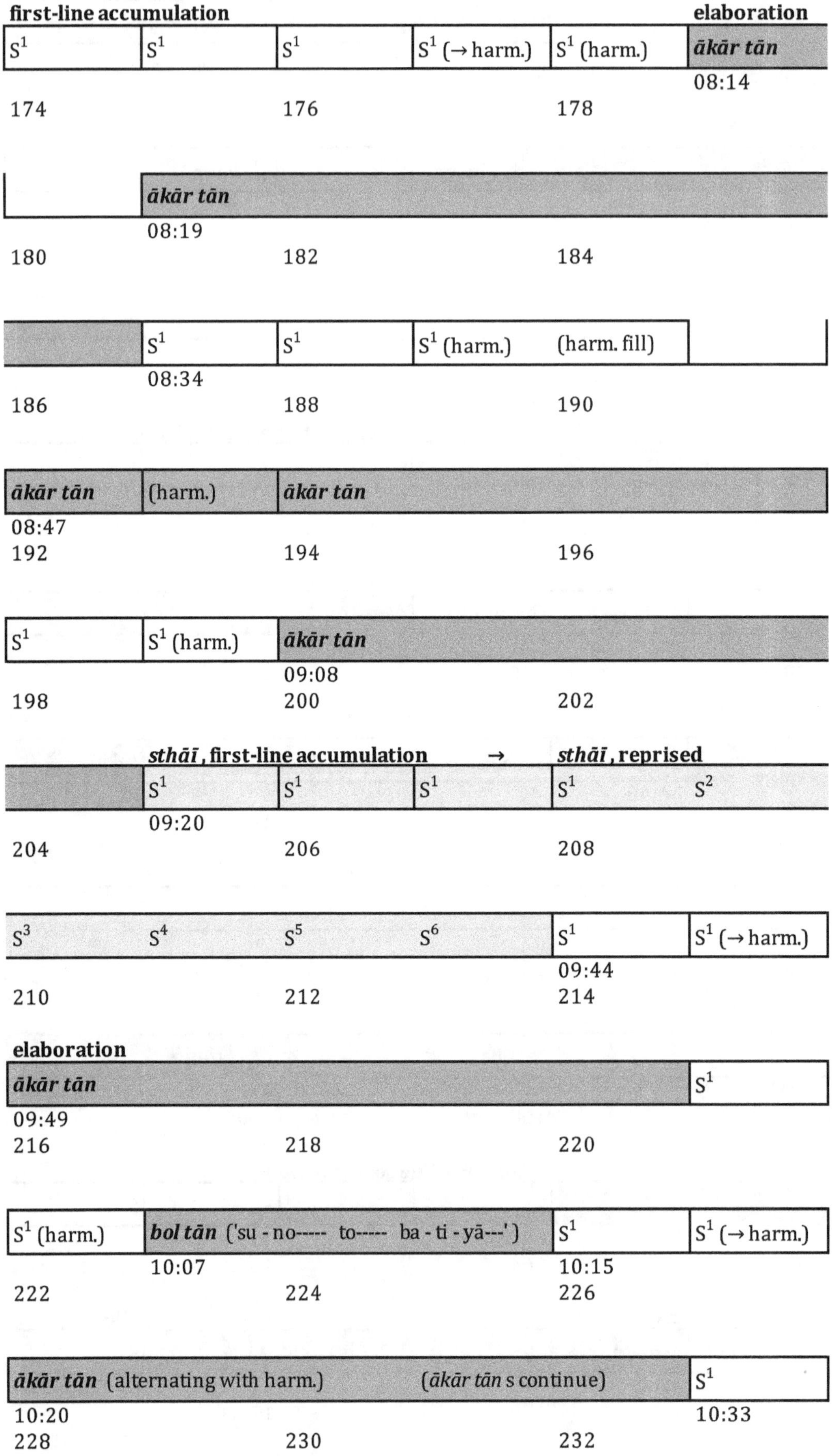

Fig. 4.2.6 (cont'd) 'Suno to': event sequence in graphical form. Created by author (2024), CC BY-NC-SA.

S^1 (→ harm.)	**ākār tān**			**ākār tān**	
				10:46	
234		236		238	

	***sthāī*, reprised**				
5	S^1	S^1	S^2	S^3	S^4
	10:54				
240		242		244	

		final *tihāī* →	**closing *bol ālāp***		
S^5	S^6	S^1 ('suno to')	(descent to madhya Sā ...)		
		11:12	11:15		
246		248	[249 ...]		

Fig. 4.2.6 (cont'd) 'Suno to': event sequence in graphical form. Created by author (2024), CC BY-NC-SA.

What this empirical representation makes clear is that, while statements and repetitions of the first line of the *sthāī* (S^1) are prevalent, accounting for over a quarter of the total performance time, statements of the complete *sthāī* are rare. It is not heard in full until the fifteenth *āvartan*, having been deferred by a period of first-line accumulation interjected with *tāns*; after that it is heard complete only twice more, in the closing stages of the performance at *āvartans* 205 and 241. Even more selectively, the complete *antarā* is sung only once, at *āvartan* 93 (though its inception can be traced back to *āvartans* 74 and 87). These components of the *bandiś*, then, function as stand-out moments against the more loosely ordered *tān* and *bol ālāp* passages that prevail for so much of the rest of the time.

Tāns in fact represent the predominant means of musical extension. Their virtuosic execution here is appropriate to the climactic *drut lay*, and no doubt also reflects VR's predilection for effusive *tān* singing. As already noted, he interjects them into the *drut*'s opening period of first-line accumulation—a gesture that would be premature in a freestanding *choṭā khayāl*, but is fitting following a *baṛā khayāl*, which has already done much of the exegetical work. In total, *tāns*—principally *ākār tāns*—account for about a third of the *drut khayāl*'s performance time. Like the less-prevalent *bol ālāp* or *vistār* passages which complement them, the appearance of these musical gestures feels more contingent and fungible than the nested phrase structure of the *sthāī* and *antarā*. To put it technically, their organisation is *paratactic*—i.e. not dependent on any particular ordering: a *tān* here could be replaced by a *bol ālāp* there; either could in principle be longer or shorter, or come earlier or later. This complements the *hypotactic* organisation of the *sthāī* and *antarā*, which convey a strong sense of internalised narrative direction, due not only to the presence of a text, but also to a corresponding musical syntax that organises the succession of their several phrases into a larger, integrated whole.

That a *choṭā khayāl*, blends hypotactic and paratactic principles is a point I discussed in Section 3.3, where I evaluated the possibility of an actual or virtual grammar underpinning a performer's choices in the moment. It is worth re-visiting this issue here, for VR's *drut khayāl* is a performance both richly spontaneous and subconsciously conditioned by a set of culturally understood conventions. Alongside hypotaxis and parataxis, what further principles might govern the dynamics between the immediate moment and the constantly evolving whole?

Because any larger organising principle or grammar for extemporisation must by definition exist *ex tempore*—that is, outside the time of any actual performance that it generates—we will need momentarily to pull back from the empirical surface of the music as graphed in Figure 4.2.6 if we want to define it. To this end, Figure 4.2.7 distils that information into an *event synopsis*, following the model adopted in Figure 3.3.8 and Figure 3.3.9. In column 4 of this table, each musical element, and its rubric for performance, is encoded with one or more letters, glossed in column 5 (a full schedule of rubrics can be found in Section 3.3); column 6 gives additional information specific to the performance.

Drut khayāl in Rāg Bhairav

1	2	3	4	5	6
Time code	***Āvartan* no.**	**Perf. phase**	**Elements**	**Description**	**Comments**
00:00	1	**O**	S^1A /T(a)	*Sthāī*, first-line accumulation, interspersed with *ākār tāns*.	Harmonium sometimes takes over first line. *Tans* only short at this stage (1 *āvartan*).
00:42	15		S	*Sthāī*, complete.	
01:03	22	→	S^1R	*Sthāī*, 1st line, repeated as refrain (*mukhṛā*). Merges with elaboration phase.	Harm. takes over *mukhṛā*.
01:11	25	**E**	T(a)	*Ākār tāns*.	Interpolated with S^1R (*mukhṛā*).
01:35	33		V(b)	*Vistār* (*bol ālāp*).	
02:02	42		T(a)	*Ākār tāns*.	Interpolated with S^1R (*mukhṛā*).
02:36	54		T(b)	*Bol tān*.	Followed by S^1R (*mukhṛā*).
02:48	58		T(a)	*Ākār tān*.	
02:57	61		S^1R, S^2→Int	*Sthāī*, line 1 (repeated) & line 2, merging into interlude.	Interlude on harm.
03:11	66		T(a)	*Ākār tān*.	Followed by repeats of S^1
03:22	70		S^1A	*Sthāī*, first-line accumulation.	(Slight hint of *lay* increase.)
03:34	74		A(e, ii)	*Antarā* (extended mode, option. ii) – comprising:	
03:34	74		A^1R	1st line repeated;	Inception.
03:40	76		V(a)→(b)	*Vistār* (*ālāp* merging into *bol ālāp*);	
04:02	84		T(b)	*Bol tān*;	
04:11	87		A^1R	1st line repeated;	Inception: 3 statements, varied first with *bol tān* then by harm.
04:19	90		T(a)	*Ākār tān*;	
04:28	93		A	*Antarā*, complete.	Full statement.
05:00	104		S^1A+LI	*Sthāī*, first-line accumulation, with *lay* increase.	*Lay* increase at 106.
05:16	110		T(a)	*Ākār tān*.	Followed by S^1R (*mukhṛā*).
05:32	116		V(b)→L(bb)	*Vistār* (*bol ālāp*) merging into *laykārī* (*bol bāṇṭ*).	
05:50	123		S^1R→Int	S^1R (*mukhṛā*), merging into harm. fill.	
05:57	126		T(a)	*Ākār tāns*.	
06:21	135		S^1A	*Sthāī*, first-line accumulation.	Merging into harm. fill at 140.

Fig. 4.2.7 'Suno to': event synopsis. Created by author (2024), CC BY-NC-SA.

06:36	141		T(a)	*Ākār tān.*	Followed by S^1R (*mukhṛā*).
06:49	147		V(b)	*Vistār* (*bol ālāp*).	Climactic (to *tār* Pa).
07:25	160		T(a)	*Ākār tān.*	
07:35	164		S^1A	*Sthāī*, first-line accumulation.	
07:48	169		T(a)	*Ākār tān.*	
07:58	173		S^1A	*Sthāī*, first-line accumulation.	
08:14	179		T(a)	*Ākār tāns.*	Extended episode, interpolated with S^1R, sometimes on harmonium
09:20	205		S^1A→S	First-line accumulation merging into complete statement of *sthāī.*	4 initial statements of S^1.
09:44	214		S^1R	*Sthāī*, 1st line, repeated as refrain (*mukhṛā*).	Harm. takes over *mukhṛā.*
09:49	216		T(a)	*Ākār tān.*	Followed by S^1R (*mukhṛā*).
10:07	223		T(b)	*Bol tān.*	Followed by S^1R (*mukhṛā*).
10:20	228		T(a)	*Ākār tāns*	Initially alternating with harm.; interpolated with S^1R (*mukhṛā*).
10:54	241	**C**	S	*Sthāī* (complete) reprised	
11:12	248		Th	Final *tihāī*	
11:15	[249 ...]		→Cba	Closing *bol ālāp*	
11:40				[Ends]	

Fig. 4.2.7 (cont'd) 'Suno to': event synopsis. Created by author (2024), CC BY-NC-SA.

Two larger principles of organisation are made legible in this synopsis. First, it conveys the saliency of the complete statements of the *sthāī* and *antarā* by carrying over their shading from the previous graphic. The highlighting of the *antarā* in particular draws attention to its presentation in extended mode, with several subcomponents preceding its complete statement at *āvartan* 93. Even though those components include such features as *bol ālāp* and *tāns*, they are here mobilised hypotactically under the auspices of the *antarā* itself (they fall within its orbit), and hence are also shaded in the synopsis.

The second organisational principle is shown in column 3, which identifies the different phases of the performance: the opening phase (O), elaboration phase (E), and closing phase (C) (an arrow signifies a transitional overlap between the opening and elaboration phases). In a previous analysis (Figure 3.3.9) we saw how the elaboration phase accounted for by far the greater part of the performance. This is even more true here, where it extends across *āvartans* 25–240. If we further extract the information from columns 3 and 4 into a linear *event string*—as in Figure 4.2.8(a)—we are left in no doubt about just how many events are concatenated into the elaboration phase (E). (When listening to the performance in conjunction with this string notation it should be noted that a single symbol such as 'T(a)' might signify an entire episode of several *ākār tāns*, and also imply statements of the *mukhṛā* (S^1) interpolated between them but not separately indicated.)

(a)

O: S^{1}A /T(a), S

→ S^{1}R

E: T(a), V(b), T(a), T(b), T(a), S^{1}R, S^2→Int, T(a), S^{1}A, A(e, ii){A^{1}R, V(a)→(b), T(b), A^{1}R, T(a), A}, S^{1}A+LI, T(a), V(b)→L(bb), S^{1}R→Int, T(a), S^{1}A, T(a), V(b), T(a), S^{1}A, T(a), S^{1}A, T(a), S^{1}A→S, S^{1}R, T(a), T(b), T(a)

C S, Th→Cba.

(b)

O: S^{1}A /T(a), S

→ S^{1}R

E: T(a), V(b), T(a), T(b), T(a), S^{1}R, S^2→Int, T(a)

E2: **S^{1}A**, A(e, ii){A^{1}R, V(a)→(b), T(b), A^{1}R, T(a), A}

E3: **S^{1}A**+LI, T(a), V(b)→L(bb), S^{1}R→Int, T(a)

E4: **S^{1}A,** T(a), V(b), T(a)

E5: **S^{1}A**, T(a)

E6: **S^{1}A**, T(a)

E7: **S^{1}A**→S, S^{1}R, T(a), T(b), T(a)

C **S**, Th→Cba.

Fig. 4.2.8 'Suno to': (a) event string; (b) event substrings. Created by author (2024), CC BY-NC-SA.

Although the very long event string of the elaboration phase captures the ceaseless experience of 'keeping going' typical of a *drut khayāl*, it does beg the question of whether there might not be divisions or undulations within it that make the performance more than an experience of just one thing after another. In response, Figure 4.2.8(b) surmises a third possible principle of organisation. Here, instances of first-line accumulation of the *sthāī* (S^{1}A) are posited as salient points of orientation that divide the main event string of the elaboration phase into several substrings, labelled E2–E7. This modelling may to some extent reflect the empirical experience of both performer and listener. Even so, it would be erroneous to regard the substrings as explicitly articulated formal sections like those found in, say, western rondo form.

There are other salient features that additionally mark out waystations in our perception of the larger flow. For example, it could be valuable to integrate the already-noted salience of complete statements of the *sthāi* and *antarā* into this picture. To this end, Figure 4.2.9 maps those events onto the previous pattern of substrings by showing them in larger type. The same convention is also applied to the *lay* increase (LI) that reinforces the first-line accumulation (S^{1}A) at around the half-way point. (For the sake of visual clarity, the figure drops the performance-stage indications.) With its superimposition of several organisational principles, this analysis perhaps represents a closer match between theoretical modelling and the empirical experience of the performance.

S^1A /T(a)

S

S^1R, T(a), V(b), T(a), T(b), T(a), S^1R, S^2→Int, T(a)

S^1A

A(e, ii){A^1R, V(a)→(b), T(b), A^1R, T(a), A}

S^1A+LI, T(a), V(b)→L(bb), S^1R→Int, T(a)

S^1A, T(a), V(b), T(a)

S^1A, T(a)

S^1A, T(a)

S^1A→S, S^1R, T(a), T(b), T(a)

S, Th→Cba.

Fig. 4.2.9 'Suno to': event substrings/salient moments. Created by author (2024), CC BY-NC-SA.

Further to the three organisational principles so far identified, we need to recall a fourth: the principle of accumulating intensity (AI) described under 'global rubrics' in Section 3.3. This has an effect on elaborative materials such as *tāns*, which, across the course of the performance, exhibit a principle of growth. For example, in the opening phase, prior to the first complete statement of the *sthāī*, the interjected *tāns* last just one *tāl* cycle—*āvartans* 8, 11 and 14; but after this point, they extend to two *āvartans* (25–6, 29–30), then to three (42–4, 48–50), then to four (66–9, 110–13), and ultimately to six (181–6). Although there are intermittent periods of contraction and expansion within this tendency, the tendency obtains nonetheless. This tells us that even though there is a paratactic dimension to the timing of *tāns*, they also manifest a discontinuous hypotaxis through this larger cumulative tendency.

Something similar applies to episodes of *bol ālāp*, of which there are essentially three, beginning at *āvartans* 33, 76 and 147 (another, at 116, soon mutates into *bol bāṇṭ*). Across these discontinuous passages, all of which initially focus on *tār* Sā, we can hear a gradual lifting of the registral ceiling: the first pushes gently upwards to *tār* Re, the second to *tār* Ga, and the third to *tār* Pa. The climactic character of the final episode might also qualify it as an addition to the strongly salient passages of this performance. The staged process of ascent and growth here is another connotation of the term *vistār*, which is often used (as in this book) as a close synonym for *bol ālāp* or its wordless counterpart. *Vistār*, in this guise could be considered a fifth principle of organisation within *khayāl*.

Additionally, we might introduce a sixth principle. In live performance, decisions about what to do next would also be conditioned by the performer's judgement of audience response: do they want more; are they getting bored; do they need some contrast? Even a studio performance such as this would involve an internalised imagining of such factors, based on years of live performance experience, as well as actual interaction between lead artist and accompanists.

Collectively, these principles neither conclusively affirm nor definitively refute the operation of a grammatical or syntactic process behind the build-up of a khayāl performance. Instead, in their heterogeneity, they suggest a possible epistemic messiness. However, rather than tidy things up in a quest for some overriding unifying principle (a motive which has driven much western music theory), we might ponder—on this occasion at least—the merits of living with a little chaos. For, in one sense, that is just what the performer has to do. I want to conjecture whether what goes on in their inner experience might not be something like the *multiple drafts* model of consciousness proposed by Daniel Dennett in his 1991 volume, *Consciousness Explained.*

Among other things, Dennett relates this notion to the inner logistics of speech production—which, I would suggest, may not be unrelated to the production of musical utterances. To summarise a complicated argument, Dennett dismisses the idea of any unifying centre of consciousness, and, by analogy, of any central 'meaner' or any central process of generating meaning when human beings create sentences. His memorable image for speech production is of an inner pandemonium, operating at a pre-conscious level, of 'word-demons' and 'content-demons' that spontaneously and simultaneously generate bits of vocabulary, morsels of syntax, fragments of sentences, and so on, some of which coagulate and eventually get voiced as meaningful utterances (1991: 237–52). Dennett posits that '[f]ully fledged and executed communicative intentions—meanings—could emerge from a quasi-evolutionary process of speech act design that involves the collaboration, partly serial, partly in parallel, of various subsystems none of which is capable on its own of performing—or ordering—a speech act' (1991: 239). Substitute 'quasi-evolutionary' with 'cultural', and 'speech act' with 'musical gesture', and we can see how this could apply to performing khayāl. While for some musicians, ideas may be lining up in their minds in an orderly queue waiting to be executed (I have heard reports of such claims), I suspect that for many others, especially in *ati drut lay*, looking into their mind would reveal a ferment of vying possibilities—like the following:

> now sing a *tān* / sing the *antarā* / don't get too intense yet / keep the audience engaged / go higher in this *bol ālāp* than the last time / merge this with something else / let the harmonium player take over for a bit / don't repeat that idea, you sang it a while ago / do it for longer this time / just repeat the first line till something happens / surprise them, break off, go in a different direction / savour this *svar* / don't stop yet, let them guess how long ...

This is not to say that the singer would be literally thinking these thoughts as such—since the whole process is going on below consciousness and as much in parallel as in succession. Rather, I use these words as a conceit to signify pre-conscious intentions, or what Dennett calls 'content-demons': a host of dispositions looking for proto-materials which are similarly looking for desired content. Such materials (which Dennett would call 'word-demons', but which we could here term 'musical ideas') would include memories of musical materials, figures, shapes, patterns, actions and gestures, stored over years of practice and waiting to be triggered by the content demons—the whole pandemonium a buzz of parallel, emerging, collaborating possibilities some of which will eventually manifest as musical gestures—less through conscious decision-making than through a stacking of the odds according to the accumulating circumstances of any given moment. To adapt Dennett (1991: 238, substituting 'singer' for 'speaker'): 'In the normal case, the [singer] gets no preview; he and his audience learn what the [singer's] utterance is at the same time'.

What all this means is that the various organisational principles described and graphed above may all be operating simultaneously in a performance, and that none has any greater privilege over the others as *the* organising model. It may even mean that the rubrics for musical material and behaviour specified in Section 3.3 might represent the maximum level of formalisation possible for any putative performance grammar. This is not to say that some form, or indeed several forms, of syntax might not be operating, since there is a clear difference between a well-timed, elegantly executed musical gesture and a random-sounding or botched one. Nonetheless, if Dennett is right, it could be that such principles operate in an inner cognitive environment that is not entirely free of chaos. Such speculations about the phenomenology, the lived experience, of a performance are important. They suggest, once again, that the musical event of khayāl is a complex and perhaps not entirely tidy admixture of theoretical rubrics and the material contingencies of a real time and place. The creative aim is to produce neither a great work, nor even an interesting piece, but a compelling, indeed memorable performance: a coming together of people, music and imagination.

4.3 How Do You Sing a *Baṛā Khayāl*? Performance Conventions, Aesthetics, Temporality

Preamble: Time Is of the Essence

A *baṛā khayāl* lies at the heart of a full-length khayāl performance. Here is where an artist is able (and expected) most fully to display their artistry—not only their technical prowess, but also their ability to explore the deeper reaches and subtleties of a *rāg*. Learning how to present a *baṛā khayāl* is so essential to the khayāl singer's art that no treatment of Hindustani classical music would be complete without considering it; for audience members too, knowledge of its conventions is invaluable for more rewarding listening.

Paradoxically, while a *baṛā khayāl* is more expressively searching than its *choṭā khayāl* counterpart, pathways through it are generally clearer cut, with fewer likely forks in the road and more time to make decisions. Hence, while the inner game of what to sing next remains an issue, my greater concern in this section is with the aesthetic principles of a *baṛā khayāl* and the way these are implicated in the singer's shaping of musical time. My case study is taken from Vijay Rajput's performance of Rāg Yaman on the album *Twilight Rāgs from North India*. And since I don't want to exclude feelings, sensations and lived experience from this discussion, readers would be repaid by listening to the recording (Track 5), before going further; those wanting a preliminary thumbnail of performance conventions can consult Section 1.7.

The expressive possibilities of a *baṛā khayāl* are afforded by its extended duration ('*baṛā*' means 'large') and by its spacious tempo (an alternative name is *vilambit khayāl*, meaning slow *khayāl*). Time is of the essence here in a different way from how we have so far considered it: while we previously focused on *samay*, the principle of performing a *rāg* at its given time, in this essay I consider time as actually *experienced* through the course of a performance, from the standpoint of both singer and listener. These concerns resonate with Martin Clayton's book-length study, *Time in Indian Music* (2000), though my emphases differ; in particular, I will focus on the subtle tension between non-metrical and metrical principles (*anibaddh* and *nibaddh*) that permeates a *baṛā khayāl*—a tension that conditions other experiential aspects of the music, including pedagogy and aesthetics.

Evidence tells us that in the late nineteenth and earlier twentieth centuries, vocalists such as Amir Khan (1912–74), influenced by Abdul Wahid Khan (1871–1949) of the Kirānā *gharānā*, began to perform ever slower and more spacious *baṛā khayāls* in a quest to broaden expressive horizons (Clayton 2000: 50–1; Deshpande 1987: 64–5; Van der Meer 1980: 61–2). And while artists such as Veena Sahasrabuddhe (1948–2016) counsel that 'one hears much slower vilambit tempi today than our tradition recommends' (Clayton and Sahasrabuddhe 1998: 15), it is not uncommon to find *ati vilambit* (very slow) *khayāls* being adopted almost as a norm in present-day practice.

Sahasrabuddhe also reminds us that the appropriate tempo is a question of both the temperament of the singer and the character of a *bandiś*. Some, more lilting *baṛā khayāl* compositions are best sung in *madhya lay* spread out over two *āvartans*. However, in an *ati vilambit khayāl* (like the one discussed here), the tempo is slow enough to accommodate the *bandiś* within a single capacious *āvartan*, and this duration then becomes the basic yardstick for improvisation. The latter vein tends to be the one favoured by many contemporary artists, especially those, such as VR, who belong to the Kirānā *gharānā*—a stylistic school known for its inclination towards purity of *svar* rather than its cultivation of *lay* (see Deshpande 1987: 41–5). It is this *baṛā khayāl* idiom that I principally discuss here.

Although a *baṛā khayāl* does not feature in every *rāg* performance, when it does, it supplies the expressive centre of gravity, being flanked by a short introductory *ālāp* and one or more succeeding, brisker *choṭā khayāls*. Figure 4.3.1 illustrates how VR models his Yaman performance in just this fashion. This graphic (drawn approximately to scale) reveals his *baṛā khayāl* to be about six times the length of his prefatory *ālāp* and about twice as long as his final *choṭā khayāl*.

Ālāp [3:14]	**Baṛā khayāl** **(or *vilambit khayāl*)** [19:39]	**Choṭā khayāl** **(or *drut khayāl*)** [10:30]

Fig. 4.3.1 Elements of a typical full-length *khayāl* performance, with durations from VR's Yaman recording (*TR*, Tracks 4–6). Created by author (2024), CC BY-NC-SA.

In fact, at just over three minutes, the *ālāp* here is of relatively generous length. Not uncommonly, *ālāp*s prefacing a *baṛā khayāl* might not last much more than a minute or two (indeed, the most succinct form of introduction, known as *aucār*, lasts just a few phrases). The reason for such curtailment is that in the first stage of a *baṛā khayāl*, the vocalist tends to continue in the unmetred style of an *ālāp*; hence there is no need to over-extend the *ālāp* proper, since this would steal the thunder of what follows. Nonetheless, what crucially distinguishes a *baṛā khayāl* from an actual *ālāp* is that the former additionally incorporates a slow *tāl* cycle supplied by the tabla. At the heart of a *baṛā khayāl*, then, is the simultaneous presence of the non-metrical (*anibaddh*) principle of *ālāp* and the metrical (*nibaddh*) principle of *tāl*.

Clayton (2000: 51) remarks on how the historical 'deceleration of the *tāl* [in a *baṛā khayāl*], coupled with the expressive and melismatic singing style, broke down the conventional model of rhythmic organization. Indeed the changes brought about were so radical that it is remarkable that this type of music is still performed in *tāl*'. But another way to consider the situation is to note the scope for creative play that lies in the confluence of *anibaddh* and *nibaddh* principles. For much of the time, the vocalist avoids locking on to the *mātrā*s (beats) of the *tāl* while all the while remaining conscious of it, moving fluidly into and out of metrical synchronisation. In an *ati vilambit khayāl* each radically expanded *mātrā*—what I here term a macro-beat—is divided into four sub-beats, made audible by the tabla; so, in *vilambit ektāl*, used in both *baṛā khayāl*s on our *Twilight Rāgs* album, the slow twelve-beat cycle can also be heard as a faster-moving forty-eight-beat one. The point is to feel these two metrical levels simultaneously; their co-presence creates depth of field and further space for creative exploration.

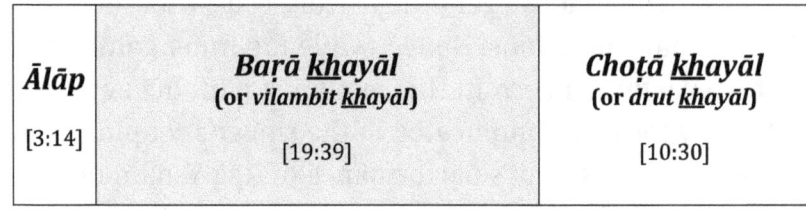

Like much else in Hindustani classical music, a *baṛā khayāl* is largely improvised, albeit with reference to well-established conventions. Its typical sequence of events is mapped out in Figure 4.3.2 (the graphic again cross-references these to their realisation in VR's performance, using track time codes). Even so, it does not feel quite appropriate to consider a *baṛā khayāl* as a 'form' and its different stages or phases as 'sections'—as in, say, western classical sonata form. For those terms carry static, architectural connotations that would belie the felt flow that is of a *baṛā khayāl*'s essence. To be sure, flow is an aspect of western music (and many other musics) too. But perhaps what makes this Hindustani version of the big musical utterance distinctive has something to do with its non- (or very limited) investment in musical notation. A practitioner of western classical music wanting to perform a sonata, for example, would learn 'the piece' from a fully notated score; indeed in western music, pieces of such substance could not have been generated without the technology of writing. Conversely, a practitioner of Hindustani classical music wanting to perform a *baṛā khayāl* would have nothing more in their mind—rather than on the page—than a version of the event sequence sketched in Figure 4.3.2; a knowledge of stylistic and improvisation conventions based on *rāg* and *tāl*; plus a short *bandiś* (composition) lasting no more than a couple of minutes in a chosen *rāg*, around which to improvise at length. Here, substance is generated in a different way.

First part [begins 0:00]	*Sthāī* [0:00]
	Baṛhat – expansion: exploring and developing the *rāg* and composition (*bol ālāp*) [1:25]
	Antarā [8:56]
Second part [begins 11:19]	Further development using a range of techniques, such as: • *bol bāṇṭ* [not used in this performance] • *laykārī* [11:24] • *sargam tāns* [12:27] • *gamak tāns* [13:27] • *bol ālāp* [15:31] • *ākār tans* [16:35]

Fig. 4.3.2 Typical event sequence of a *baṛā khayāl*, with time codes of their occurrence in VR's Yaman recording (*TR*, Track 5). Created by author (2024), CC BY-NC-SA.

In the ensuing commentary, then, I seek not only to illustrate what happens and in what order (which is certainly important for students and listeners to know), but also to convey the various ways in which a *baṛā khayāl*'s ambiguous temporality and related interplay between the fixed and the free, the formal and the informal, permeate the performance ethos and contribute to the experience of musical depth. This also relates to the question of how a *baṛā khayāl* gets taught; as elsewhere in *Rāgs Around the Clock*, my account here includes insights gleaned directly from learning with my own guruji, VR.

Bandiś: 'Kahe sakhī kaise ke karīe'

It will repay us to begin our exploration by examining the *bandiś* VR sings on this recording—'Kahe sakhī kaise ke karīe'—since this encapsulates many of the essential, ultimately temporal, properties of the entire performance. I will focus on two such properties:

1. *Resistance to notation as resistance to metre*: as the only (relatively) fixed or composed aspect of the musical material, the *bandiś* is the feature that most invites being set down in musical notation—not least when being transmitted from teacher to student. Yet at the same time (and even more than is the case in a *choṭā khayāl*), a *baṛā khayāl* composition will want not to be bound by any notational straitjacket—in the same way that its *anibaddh* spirit will seek to elude capture by the *nibaddh* essence of *tāl*.
2. *Eventfulness*: another characteristic of the *bandiś* is that its two components, *sthāī* and *antarā*, are experienced not just as musical content but as musical *events*; and this eventfulness is a further dimension of a *baṛa khayāl*'s temporality, complementing its flux.

Let us now explore each of these properties in turn.

Resisting Notation

Conventionally, the *bandiś* of a *baṛā khayāl* is transmitted orally, directly from guru to *śiṣyā* in the real time of learning, being imitated over and over again by the student until committed to memory. In modern-day practice, however, the process may be a little more complicated, with notation playing at least some kind of role. Even so, the reifying effect of writing—its tendency to turn evanescent invention into a fixed thing—continues to be resisted.

For example, the learning process I have evolved with VR entails writing down only the text of a *bandiś*, adopting the above-described repetitive procedure for acquiring its melody, and also recording my teacher's rendition of the composition on my smartphone. I refer to this recording after the lesson in order to consolidate my learning; it provides a virtual version of my guruji continuing the living work of oral transmission. In the spirit of this approach, I supply the text of the Yaman *bandiś* 'Kahe sakhī kaise ke karie' below—in Romanised transliteration, in English translation (by my fellow student, Sudipta Roy), and in Devanāgarī script (as supplied by VR). In the poem, the lyricist speaks to their most intimate confidant ('sakhī') of the pain of separation from their lover—a classic trope of khayāl poems (see Section 2.2). The text can be read in conjunction with Audio Examples 4.3.1 and 4.3.2, which extract the *sthāī* and *antarā* portions of the *bandiś* from VR's performance.

Rāg Yaman—baṛā khayāl

Sthāī

Kahe sakhī kaise ke karīe	*Dearest friend, what should one do with oneself*
bharīe dina aiso lālana ke saṅga.	*The whole while, when one has such a lover?*

Antarā

Suna rī sakhī mẽ kā kahu to se	*Listen, dearest friend, what more can I say?*
una hī ke jānata dhaṅga.	*Only he would know this longing.*

राग यमन—बड़ा ख़याल

स्थाई

कहे सखी कैसे के करीए

भरीए दिन ऐसो लालन के संग ।

अंतरा

सुन री सखी में का कहु तो से

उन ही के जानत ढंग ॥

Audio Example 4.3.1 Rāg Yaman: *baṛā khayāl, sthāī* (*TR*, Track 5, 00:00–01:24)
https://hdl.handle.net/20.500.12434/4b0f83db

Audio Example 4.3.2 Rāg Yaman: *baṛā khayāl, antarā* (*TR*, Track 5, 10:04–11:20)
https://hdl.handle.net/20.500.12434/39b002c2

Musical notation might be incorporated into the learning process. Some teachers, adapting Vishnu Narayan Bhatkhande's (1860–1936) system, lay out the song in *sargam* notation on a spatial grid representing the *tāl*. (In the present volume, I have used this kind of notation for the *choṭā khayāl*s of the *Rāg samay cakra* album.) However, since a *baṛā khayāl* tends to avoid any systematic attachment to the *tāl*, the student would eventually need to unlearn this metricised version of the composition, unlocking it from the beats and relaxing it into something more fluid. A more congenial approach—again one which I have evolved in my lessons with VR—is to notate a sketch of the *bandiś* using a kind of proportional notation to represent note lengths, in order better to capture the *anibaddh* feel of the delivery. This is illustrated in Figure 4.3.3, which in parts (a) and (b) presents the *sthāī* and *antarā* respectively of this Yaman *bandiś* in simplified form.

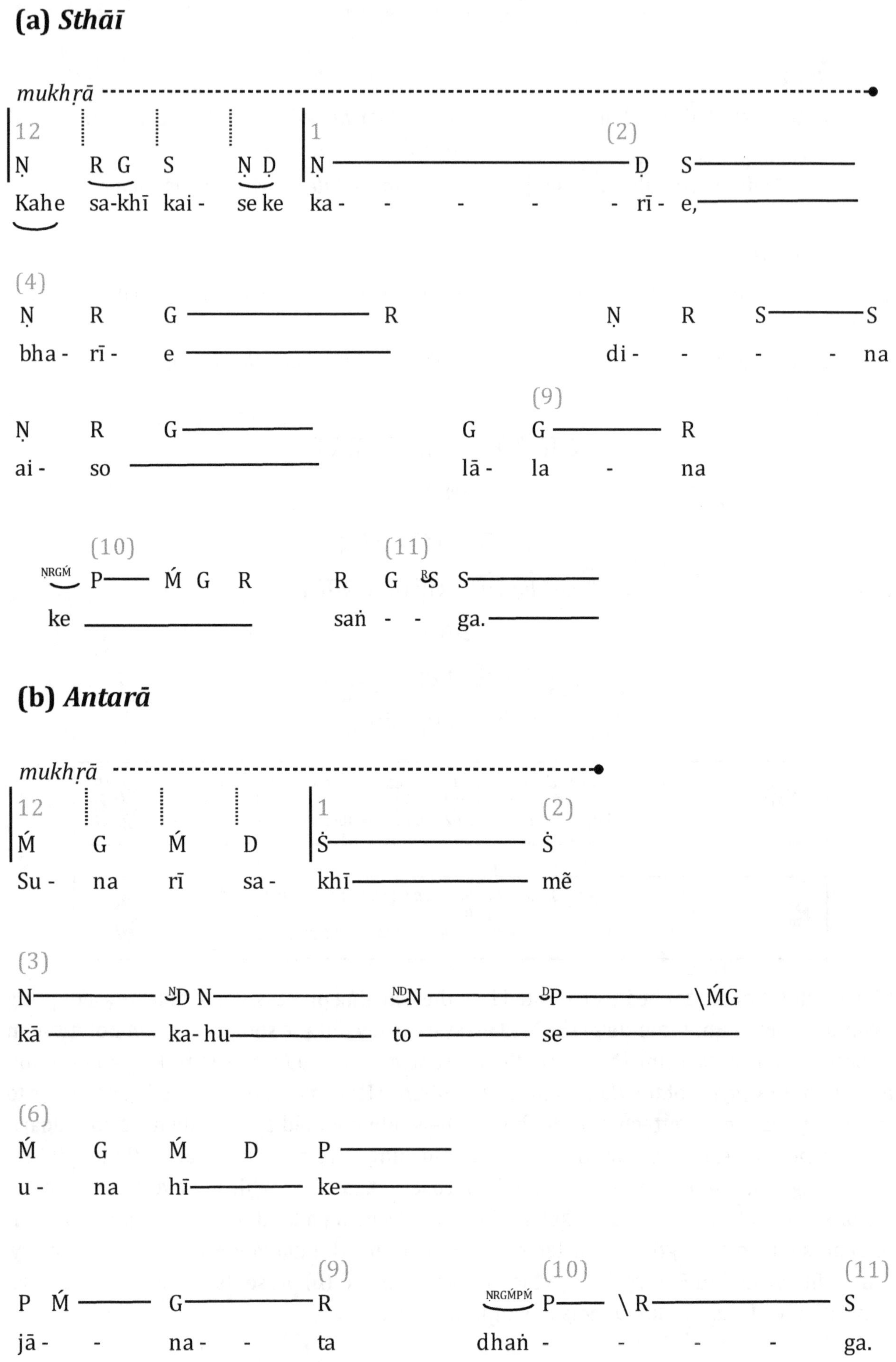

Fig. 4.3.3 Heuristic notation of *bandiś*: (a) *sthāī*; (b) *antarā*. Created by author (2024),

In this style of notation there is only minimal reference to the metrical framework of the *tāl* (the exception being the *mukhṛā*, to be discussed shortly). The composition and its text are laid out phrase by phrase, showing the approximate relative duration of each pitch in *sargam* notation. Only when I have learnt this basic shape of the composition will I then seek to sing it accompanied by the tabla *ṭhekā* (which these days can be supplied digitally on an app for practise purposes), taking care to avoid too closely adhering to the individual *mātrās*. In learning how to fit the material into a single *āvartan* of the *tāl*, I have to listen out for salient points in the *ṭhekā* as approximate cues for where to begin or end a phrase. Such cues are indicated with parenthetical beat numbers in Figure 4.3.3. For example, beginning the second phrase around beat 4 of the *sthāī* (having taken a break after beat 2) avoids having to rush later on. And in an *ektāl* composition such as this, it helps to keep an ear open for beat 9—where the larger drum of the tabla returns to prominence—and beat 10—where the tabla plays the salient *tirakaṭa* pattern—in order to coordinate the later phrases around these points.

The most important point of interlock between *bandiś* and *tāl*—and the only significant point of departure from the *anibaddh* feel—is the *mukhṛā*. This is the head motif of the *bandiś*, which, unlike the rest of the composition, maps relatively directly onto the metrical underlay of the *tāl*. In an *ati vilambit khayāl*, it usually begins on or around the last macro-beat, and fairly explicitly marks out the sub-beats, creating a strong macro-up-beat to *sam*, after which it continues for another macro-beat or two, gradually relaxing the attachment to the metre. The *mukhṛās* for both *sthāī* and *antarā* are indicated in Figure 4.3.3(a) and (b), at which moments (and only these moments) a metrical grid is included for the approach to *sam*. It is important for the performer to have completed the *sthāī* (or, later on, whatever material they are inventing in any given *āvartan*) in time to sing the *mukhṛā* in its correct place in the lead-up to *sam*. Here this means completing the prior material by (or during) beat 11, so that the *mukhṛā* can re-emerge at beat 12.

This form of notation, then, is not intended as a literal transcription of what VR sings in the performance. Rather, it represents the general shape of the composition: the musical knowledge that a performer holds in their memory and which they will subtly differently realise on each occasion of performance. We might say that, commensurably with the fluid and ambiguous quality of time and form in a *baṛā khayāl*, the identity of the *bandiś* is essentially *fuzzy*: there is no definitive version, and it is likely to morph over time. Hence the ambivalent nature of musical notation, which runs counter to this spirit, but which can nonetheless be helpful provided one sees it for no more or less than what it is.

And 'what it is', in this context, might be something like Seeger's (1958) conception of 'prescriptive music writing': a set of instructions for the performer. However, it would be more accurate to describe this as a *heuristic* version of the composition (cf. Section 2.3): it provides a pragmatic approximation—the gist of a structure—from which a student can get started with learning. But on any actual occasion of performance, the material will be decorated with ornaments (*alaṅkār*); and phrases might be elongated or contracted, or change their melodic contour. Even in this heuristic version, a few indications of ornamentation are warranted when, paradoxically, these are felt as integral to a musical gesture.

It is instructive to compare this heuristic version with Figure 4.3.4, a transcription of VR's actual rendering as heard in Audio Example 4.3.1. This transcription would conform to Seeger's category of 'descriptive music writing' (ibid.)—an as accurate as possible record of what is actually heard on a particular occasion. It includes the complete metrical framework of the *tāl*, which only makes more explicit how VR generally fashions his material so as *not* to coincide with individual *mātrās* (except for the *mukhṛā*). Also evident are the many decorations of the melody, generally shown as superscripted additions to the original outline (for more on ornamentation, see Section 1.8). These include *kaṇ* (a lightly touched grace note), and *kaṭkhā* or *murkī* (a rapid cluster of notes leading to a main note); oblique lines indicate *mīṇḍ*, an upward or downward glide. Perhaps most striking of all is the injection of significant additional material in the *antarā* after beat 6—a point to which I will return later.

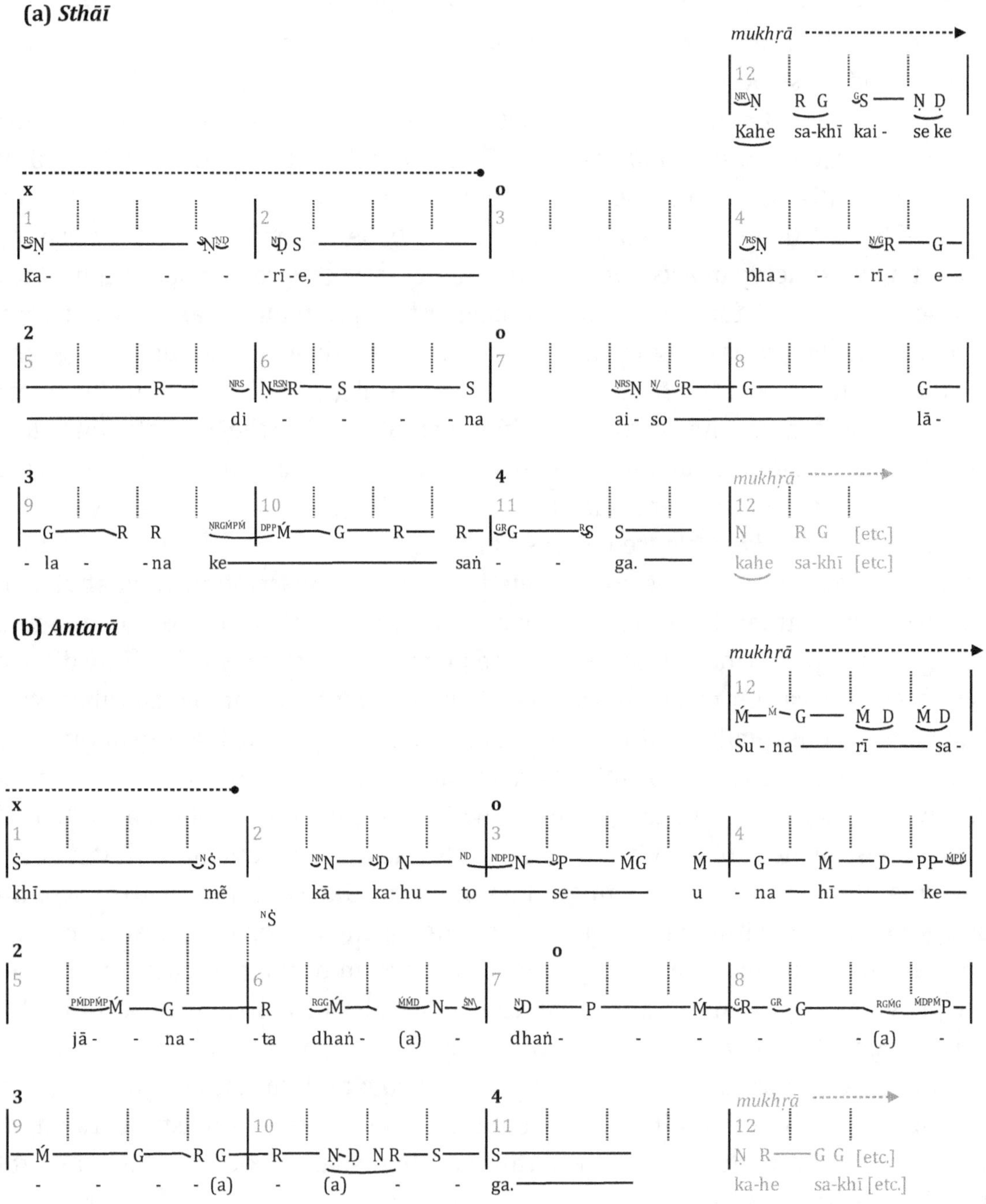

Fig. 4.3.4 Transcription of *bandiś*: (a) *sthāī*; (b) *antarā*. Created by author (2024), CC BY-NC-SA.

In both versions of its notation, we can discern how the *bandiś* typically embodies the salient features of its *rāg*. The *mukhṛā* of the *sthāī*, for example, begins on Ṇi and rises to Ga (on the word '*sakhī*'), which are Yaman's most prominent notes—*saṃvādī* and *vādī* respectively. And the melodic elaborations around these pitches (Ṇ– RG, S– ṆḌ Ṇ—) are likewise characteristic of the *rāg*. The *sthāī* as a whole also conforms to convention by occupying the lower–middle range. After the initial focus on lower Ni, it sustains the *vādī* tone Ga for much of its duration, rising briefly to Pa in its final phrase before returning to the *mukhṛā* (incidentally, VR foreshadows this overall melodic ambit in the preceding *ālāp*, as heard on Track 4 of the album). Complementing this, the *antarā* foregrounds the upper vocal register, initially focusing on *tār* Sā.

To summarise our account so far: by resisting notation, the *bandiś* asserts itself as a subjectively felt flow in which its identity can morph; and this is of a piece with the braided interplay of *nibaddh* and *anibaddh* temporalities of a *baṛā khayāl* more generally. To this we now need to add a further temporal notion: a *baṛā khayāl* punctuates this flow with a series of artfully timed *events* that shape its larger structure. Let us consider this evental property in more detail.

Sthāī and Antarā as Event

In a different context, Mark Doffman (2019) invokes the Greek rhetorical terms *chronos* and *kairos* to characterise a distinction between temporal *process* and *event* respectively. As Doffman puts it, *chronos* 'considers time as durational and cyclical', while *kairos* 'invokes the singularity and heterogeneity of temporal experience'. *Chronos* is 'processual': it 'relates to the sense of a sequentially structured flow'. *Kairos* is 'eventful': it 'projects the idea of a timely or singular moment' (2019: 171). Doffman is writing with jazz in mind, but it would not take a great stretch of the imagination to apply these notions to the Hindustani context. Having already considered a *baṛā khayāl* as 'a sequentially structured flow' (its *chronic* aspect), what can we say of its 'eventfulness' (its *kairic* aspect)? Again, the *bandiś* contains the essence, since the statements of its two discrete components, *sthāī* and *antarā*, clinch decisive structural events.

The very first event of a *baṛā khayāl* is a complete statement of the *sthāī*. Its *mukhṛā* feels especially portentous, marking simultaneously the onset of the *sthāī*, the *bandiś* and the *baṛā khayāl* itself. Furthermore, this moment of inception is dramatised by the entry of the hitherto silent tabla. The tabla player takes his cue from the vocalist, who uses the *mukhṛā*—the only part of the composition that is sung metrically—to indicate the tempo. Following this lead, the tabla player enters on *sam*. Or, indeed, just a moment before: in Audio Example 4.3.3 we hear how, in VR's Yaman performance, Shahbaz Hussain enters with his own, rhythmic *mukhṛā* halfway through the last sub-beat of the vocal *mukhṛā*—a stylistically typical rhetorical flourish that galvanises time, intensifies the lead-in to *sam*, and signals that the *baṛā khayāl* is now underway.

Audio Example 4.3.3 *Mukhṛā* of the *sthāī*, with tabla entry (*TR*, Track 5, 00:00–00:08)
https://hdl.handle.net/20.500.12434/44de6bac

Two further ways in which the *bandiś* is delivered suggest time in the aspect of *kairos*. First the *antarā* is delayed until around halfway through the performance (see Figure 4.3.2); the timing of its arrival becomes an issue for the performer: it is dramatised, and in this way becomes a major structural event (I shall elaborate further on this below—significantly, when the time comes). Secondly, both *sthāī* and *antarā* are usually heard only once in their entirety. After the *sthāī* has been sung in the first *āvartan* we can expect never to hear it sung complete again; and after the *antarā* has been sung complete (much further down the line) we reach another turning point in the performance. Each of these factors defines these moments as unique, and hence as events. Meanwhile, the component that assuredly *is* reiterated is the *mukhṛā* of the *sthāī*, which is sung at the end of practically every successive *āvartan* as a bridge to the next. Acting as a refrain, the *mukhṛā* causes just about every arrival on *sam* to feel like an event (*kairos*) on a localised level; while on the bigger canvas its appearances act as a temporal yardstick with which to calibrate the long-term temporal flux (*chronos*) of the performance.

Given that the composed material of the *bandiś* lasts little more than a couple of minutes, the big question for the vocalist, as ever in this classical tradition, is how to generate the rest of the performance. After the *sthāī*, what next? How does one get to the *antarā*? And then what? As Figure 4.3.2 indicated, there is a cognitive road map available to help the performer navigate this journey. However, the travelling still has to be done in real time; so in the remainder of this essay I will consider how this is managed, looking at the processes and events of the two main stages in turn.

Baṛhat: Analysis of a Process

Following the opening statement of the *sthāī* comes a staged series of improvised elaborations of the *rāg*—a process often termed *baṛhat*, derived from the Hindi verb *baṛhānā*, 'to increase' (Magriel and du Perron 2013, I: 409; Ranade 2006: 195–6). Some (for example, Ruckert 2004: 58–9) also use the word *vistār* ('expansion') to describe this process, though in this book I tend to reserve that term for more episodic appearances of *bol ālāp* in a *choṭā khayāl*. Regardless, this stage of the performance is a process of development—but of what: the *bandiś* or the *rāg* itself? The answer is characteristically ambiguous. Already we have alluded to the fuzzy form of the *bandiś*—due to a combination of its one-off appearance and its mutable, notation-eluding identity. Going further, we might claim that the *bandiś* and *rāg* represent far less distinct categories of musical material in a *baṛā khayāl* than they do in a *choṭā khayāl*. If the *rāg* is embedded in the DNA of the *bandiś* (I have already described how the *bandiś* projects the structure of the *rāg*), the genome of the *bandiś* is in turn detectable throughout the *baṛhat*. Hence, to the extent that the *bandiś* and the *rāg* are of a piece, this slowly expanding exposition of the *rāg* also implies a development of the composition. And although the *sthāī* does not re-emerge complete after its initial exposition, its presence in the *baṛhat* phase is upheld in two ways: first via the refrain function of the *mukhṛā*, in which the part stands for the whole (indeed, there are anecdotal accounts of listeners mistaking a *mukhṛā* for a composition); and second via the continuing presence of the text, which the soloist freely incorporates into his or her extemporisations—though rarely in its entirety, and not necessarily at every point, since sometimes *sargam* syllables or *ākār* might be employed.

Audio Example 4.3.4 illustrates these various points. This picks up the performance at the close of first *āvartan*, where VR concludes the *sthāī*, sings the *mukhṛā*, and begins the second *āvartan*. At this early stage in the proceedings, he still models his material quite closely on the *sthāī*, but now repeats the words 'karīe' and 'bharīe', dwells on lower Ni and middle Sā, then moves via Re to Ga as he sings 'aiso lālana', and finally presents an elaborated version of the *mukhṛā* as he approaches and begins the next *āvartan*.

Audio Example 4.3.4 *Baṛhat*: development of *sthāī* from end of *āvartan* 1 to beginning of *āvartan* 3 (*TR*, Track 5, 00:55–02:31)
https://hdl.handle.net/20.500.12434/5391708b

Performers sometimes describe what they do in the *baṛhat* as simply '*ālāp*', or *bol ālāp* (given that the text is present for much of the time)—which points to the prevailing *anibaddh* feel. But a larger-scale process is also going on: one of subtle long-term intensification, through increasing rhythmic activity, increasingly ornate elaborations, and a gradual rise in vocal register (in Sections 3.3 and 4.2, I referred to this with the shorthand 'AI'—accumulation of intensity). This last aspect, registral ascent, is charted for VR's performance in Figure 4.3.5 (by way of comparison, see Nicolas Magriel's highly systematic analysis of the *baṛhat* of a 1981 performance by khayāl singer Ustād Niaz Ahmed Khan (Magriel 1997)). In my analysis, successive *āvartans* are numbered in the leftmost column, and are correlated in the next column (2) with the time code of their onset (*sam*). Column 3 indicates the final pitch of the *mukhṛā*, which straddles *sam* and closes around beat 2, and, like everything else, is subject to variation. Hence, although Figure 4.3.3(a) and Figure 4.3.4(a) show how, in the *sthāī*, the *mukhṛā* closes on Sā, once the *baṛhat* is under way, this terminus may change to mirror the overall ascending trajectory (for example, Ga in *āvartans* 4–6). But the main, and most systematic, traces of this long-term ascent are found in the main body of the improvised material, whose pitch content is abstracted in columns 4 and 5 of Figure 4.3.5. Column 4 pinpoints the 'standing note' or *nyās svar* which VR makes his focal point in each *āvartan*—a way of providing structure to his improvisation. Reading down the column, we see how these successive standing notes manifest a gradual ascent through the scale of the *rāg*, *āvartan* by *āvartan*—from middle Sā in *āvartan* 2 to upper Sā in *āvartan* 9, coterminous with the beginning of the *antarā*.

1	2	3	4	5
***Āvartan* no.**	**Onset time (*sam*)**	***End note(s) of mukhṛā***	**Standing note (and neighbour)**	**Content / elaboration of standing note(s)**
	0:00			***Sthāī*** begins (*mukhṛā*) ...
1	0:05	S	S	***Sthāī*** concludes (see Fig. 4.3.4 (a)).
2	1:12	S	S (Ṇ)	-S-----; --Ṇ--, -Ṇ--, ṆS---; ---G-R---S.
3	2:17	GRS	G (Ḿ)	--G--, -G----, G----, -Ḿ--G, Ḿ---G, ḾG---RS-.
4	3:24	G	G (Ḿ)	-G--; -Ḿ----G; GḾ-G----Ḿ, -ḾG, -GP--------ḾG; GRS-.
5	4:31	G	P (Ḿ)	--P---------Ḿ, -P------Ḿ-G; GḾGPḾG, -PR-S---.
6	5:37	G	P	-P----------; -P-------; --DP--------RS-.
7	6:44	S	P (D)	-P--, -P-------G; -D----P-------; -DPR, -PR-S-.
8	7:53	Ṇ	N (→ Ṡ)	---N------, -N----^{D}P-; -N-, -N---Ṡ---------. At beat 12: ***antarā*** begins (*mukhṛā*)
9	9:01	Ṡ	Ṡ (N)	- Ṡ --N, - Ṡ------N-; -- Ṡ--------Ṙ--Ṡ----.
10	10:09	Ṡ	Ṡ (→ S)	***Antarā*** concludes (see Fig. 4.3.4 (b)). At beat 12: return to *mukhṛā of* **sthāī**.

Fig. 4.3.5 *Baṛā khayāl* in Rāg Yaman: stages of *baṛhat*. Created by author (2024), CC BY-NC-SA.

Not every note of every *rāg* can be sustained in this way—this will depend on the individual *rāg* grammar. In Yaman, the available *nyās svar*s are Sā, Ga, Pa and Ni; nonetheless, Re, Ḿa and Dha are also permitted some prominence as salient neighbours to the standing notes, to which they will eventually fall or rise. Such examples of 'helping notes' are shown in parenthesis in column 4 next to their respective *nyās svar*. This shows, for example, how VR subtly gives prominence to Ḿa in three successive *āvartans*: as a yearning upper neighbour to Ga in *āvartans* 3 and 4; and as a lower-neighbour elaboration of Pa in *āvartan* 5. This judicious handling of Ḿa helps effect a transition from Ga to Pa, blending the colours of these three different tones.

Even allowing for the inclusion of such adjunct *svar*s, the contents of column 4 remain highly abstract. They model the kind of schema a soloist will likely have in their mind to help them pace their progress through an extended performance. Nevertheless, there is the question of how to put flesh on these bare bones. Column 5 of Figure 4.3.5 shows the traces of such a process. For each *āvartan*, it indicates how the focal *nyās svar* is elaborated between the opening and closing statements of the *mukhṛā*. For example, in *āvartan* 4—Audio Example 4.3.5—Ga and its supporting neighbour, Ḿa, are presented in the following sequence of phrases (other, decorative notes are not shown):

[*mukhṛā*] -G--; -Ḿ----G; GḾ-G----Ḿ, -ḾG, -GP--------ḾG; GRS-. [*mukhṛā*]

Audio Example 4.3.5 *Āvartan* 4 (with opening and closing *mukhṛās*): elaboration of Ga and Ḿa (*TR*, Track 5, 03:19–04:33)
https://hdl.handle.net/20.500.12434/eac11010

I am using the term 'phrase' here in quite a loose sense, the minimum criterion for which is a brief break in the musical flow. This means that some of the elements in this analysis—those followed by a comma—might more correctly be termed sub-phrases. Others have relatively greater closure, and are shown with semi-colons. The last phrase falls to Sā, before the onset of the *mukhṛā*, and is shown with a full stop. The punctuation marks here are in one sense metaphorical: VR sometimes uses this idea with me to think about how to build successive phrases of an *ālāp* into a larger one, to create a coherent 'sentence' rather than formless noodling. This is a heuristic pedagogical strategy; but it also reflects the theoretical point that the melodic structure of a *rāg* performance, and indeed the principles of *rāg* itself, can be construed syntactically (see Clarke 2017).

The dashes featured in the notation of column 5 also contain coded information. They indicate the relative prolongation of the *svar* with which they are associated—one dash represents approximately one sub-beat's duration. 'Prolongation' can mean that the *svar* in question is itself sustained, or it can mean that it is decorated by other notes and figuration during this time span (either before or after the *nyās svar*). It would, in principle, be possible to illustrate these manifold decorations through the kind of detailed transcription shown in Figure 4.3.4 for the *bandiś*. But my purpose here is different. The information shown in column 5 of Figure 4.3.5 is intended as a reductive 'gist' of how each *nyās svar* in column 4 is elaborated—revealing the structure behind the elaboration. It stops short of notating the decorative minutiae, which are audible enough in the recording and can be savoured against this middle ground.

For most of the duration of an *āvartan* the standing note shown in column 4 is also the highest note. It acts as a kind of limiter on the pitch bandwidth, which helps the soloist pace their progression through the *baṛā khayāl*. (This principle derives from the extemporisation of an *ālāp*—see my discussion of '*svar* space' in Section 3.2, Exploration 1.) It is, however, permitted to relax this constraint towards the end of an *āvartan*, in order briefly to suggest the (higher) main note of the next—a kind of sneak preview. Column 5 shows how this happens at the end of *āvartan* 2, which, focusing on Sā neighboured by lower Ni for most of its duration, rises to Ga in the concluding phrase, before descending via Re back to Sā. This foreshadowing is sometimes also echoed at the close of the succeeding *mukhṛā*. For example, at the beginning of *āvartan* 3, the *mukhṛā* also ends Ga–Re–Sā (see column 3), rather than closing directly on Sā as originally heard in the *sthāī*.

In its slow and gradual working through the background grammar and foreground subtleties of the *rāg*, the *baṛhat* phase takes the form of a 'sequentially structured flow'. Here, then, we experience time in the guise of *chronos*. The overall trajectory of this process—as shown in Figure 4.3.5, column 4—is towards *tār* Sā and the onset of the *antarā*. This is a key event in the larger-scale structure; hence time at *that* moment is experienced as *kairos*. Typically, *chronos* and *kairos* become blended in the approach to this structural moment, as the soloist teases the listener regarding the actual time of arrival of *tār* Sā. In Audio Example 4.3.6, we can hear how VR does this in *āvartan* 8 (cf. Figure 4.3.5, column 5) through an extensive and intense prolongation on Ni. Repeated iterations of this pitch push all the while towards upper Sā which is eventually attained and sustained in the final phrase. And this moment triggers the onset of the *antarā*, whose own *mukhṛā*, sung to the words 'Suna rī sakhī mẽ', is heard on beat 12 of the slow *ektāl* cycle (see Figure 4.3.4(b)), and leads us into *āvartan* 9.

Audio Example 4.3.6 *Āvartan* 8: prolongation of Ni, leading to *tār* Sā (*TR*, Track 5, 7:52–09:10)
https://hdl.handle.net/20.500.12434/5b15b94c

At this point, there is a further delaying tactic. Rather than launch into the complete *antarā*, VR follows the *baṛā khayāl* convention of presenting at least one further *āvartan* of *bol ālāp* before the *antarā* begins. In principle it is possible to extend this process for two or more *āvartans*, moving further into the upper octave; but commonly, as in VR's performance here, just one proleptic *bol ālāp* is enough. This can be heard in Audio Example 4.3.7; the pitch content is again outlined in Figure 4.3.5, column 5, *āvartan* 9. VR makes an extended extemporisation around *tār* Sā to the word 'sakhī', after which the *antarā* is then heard complete in *āvartan* 10. Hence, while the main part of the *baṛhat* process *follows* the *sthāī*, the *baṛhat* associated with the *antarā* is *anticipatory*—it is filled with expectancy. The *antarā* functions as the climax of the *baṛhat* process—its outcome, even.

Audio Example 4.3.7 *Āvartans* 9 and 10: prolongation of *tār* Sā leading to *antarā* sung complete (*TR*, Track 5, 08:51–11:22)
https://hdl.handle.net/20.500.12434/317c01e1

Across the course of a single *āvartan*, the *antarā* typically follows a descending path from *tār* Sā to *mahdyā* Sā. This is discernible in the heuristic notation of Figure 4.3.3(b) which also shows the stopping-off points in this process. The first phrase ('Suna rī sakhī mẽ') intensely voices *tār* Sā; the second ('kā kahu to se') emphasises Ni before falling to Pa; the third ('una hī ke) also winds around Pa and rests there; the fourth ('jānata') falls from Pa to Re; and the final phrase ('dhaṅga') echoes this shape but continues to the concluding *madhya* Sā, deploying a characteristic Yaman cadential figure, P–R–S.

This, at least, is the notional outline. The contingencies of live performance, however, might take the vocalist along other byways—as can be seen by comparing Figure 4.3.3(b) with Figure 4.3.4(b), the transcription of what VR actually sings. This most obviously shows how he weaves various beautiful decorations into the heuristic form; but another difference also transpires: he concludes the penultimate phrase ('jānata') early in the cycle, at beat 6. Its pregnant final Re strongly implies the ultimate descent to Sā—but there are still five long beats to go before the *mukhṛā*. In the hands of an experienced performer, such contingencies can be readily absorbed within the elasticity of the form. On 'dhaṅga', VR recoups the upper register, rising from Ḿa to Ni; restates the first syllable as he slowly re-treads his steps down to Ga across beats 7 and 8; then with a flamboyant *kaṭhkā* regains Pa at the end of beat 8 and gradually descends once again, reaching *mahdya* Sā at beat 11 via an elliptical movement to *mandra* Ni and Dha in beat 10. This spontaneous moment of invention is as good an illustration as any of the blurred boundary between *bandiś* and *bol ālāp* in a *baṛā khayāl*.

The *antarā*'s descending trajectory is a mirror image of the *baṛhat* as a whole, which in essence rises from *Madhya* Sā to *tār* Sā. Over the course of just one *āvartan*, the *antarā* captures and then releases the intensity of that process. But given that the preceding *baṛhat* has taken so much longer, it would feel premature to end the *baṛā khayāl* here. And indeed, this moment, followed by a return to the *mukhṛā* of the *sthāī*, heralds the beginning of a new phase.

Laykārī

The emphasis now turns towards various forms of rhythmic variation, or *laykārī* (for a detailed discussion of this notion, see Clayton 2000: chapter 10). Henceforward we hear VR making a more explicit engagement with the pulse and metre of the *tāl*, changing the feel from *anibaddh* to *nibaddh*, and from introversion to extraversion. It is common, though not compulsory, for the tempo now to move up a gear: in the *baṛā khayāl* in Rāg Bhairav on the *Twilight Rāgs* album, VR indeed increases the *lay* (Track 2, 12:15); whereas at the equivalent point in the Yaman *baṛā khayāl* (Track 5, 11:23) he maintains the same pulse. Despite the change of delivery style, the *muhkṛā* of the *sthāī* remains a presence, articulating *sam*, marking out the *āvartans* and maintaining continuity and unity.

***Āvartan* no.**	**Onset time (*sam*)**	**Content**
11	11:17	*Laykārī* (*sargam*)
12	12:21	*Sargam tāns*
13	13:22	*Gamak tāns*
14	14:24	*Ākār tāns*
15	15:27	*Bol ālāp, ākār tāns*
16	16:32	*Ākār tāns* (in upper octave)
17	17:36	*Ākār tāns*
18	18:37	*Ākār tāns*
(19...)	19:38	Ends (19:40)

Fig. 4.3.6 Second part of *baṛā khayāl*: *laykārī* etc. Created by author (2024), CC BY-NC-SA.

As in the *baṛhat* phase, the aim is now carefully to build the intensity over the course of several *āvartans*. The soloist has a variety of techniques at his disposal, and Figure 4.3.6 details how VR deploys them in this performance. One common device is *bol bāṇṭ*, in which the song text is manipulated and treated syllabically, creating syncopation and/or cross-accentuation. VR uses this technique in his Bhairav *baṛā khayāl* (Track 2, 12:22–12:55) but not in its Yaman counterpart. Instead, in *āvartan* 11, he creates a similar *laykārī* effect using *sargam*—as captured in Audio Example 4.3.8.

Audio Example 4.3.8 *Āvartan* 11: *laykārī* (*TR*, Track 5, 11:20–12:04)
https://hdl.handle.net/20.500.12434/7006ea70

The momentum engendered by this *laykārī* treatment continues in *āvartan* 12, where VR launches an array of *sargam tāns*—melodic runs sung to *sargam* syllables (Audio Example

4.3.9). The switch to this technique helps the *baṛā khayāl* progress incrementally, retaining the previous use of *sargam* syllables but now eliciting these in a steady rhythmic stream, four syllables to a sub-beat (sixteen to a macro-beat). Throughout, VR injects various twists and turns into the melodic flow, and further resists uniformity by briefly teasing the metrical constraints (at 00:37 of the audio example), and by momentarily morphing *sargam* into ākār/ekār/ikār *tāns*—'ga-a-a, re-e-e, ni-i' (at 00:43).

Audio Example 4.3.9 *Āvartan* 12: *sargam tāns* (*TR*, Track 5, 12:26–13:24)
https://hdl.handle.net/20.500.12434/b910582b

In *āvartan* 13, VR presents several strings of *gamak tāns*, illustrated in Audio Example 4.3.10. With this change of technique he again creates a sense of progression: he continues the preceding *tāns* at the same speed, but now transforms the style of delivery; *gamak tāns* involve making a wide oscillation around each note (a technique key to the dhrupad vocal style). Then, in *āvartan* 14, these become pure *ākār tāns* (i.e. sung to the vowel 'ā'), as VR moves into the higher register (Audio Example 4.3.11). In the third and fourth of five runs he uses a head voice as he ascends to *tār* Ga and *tār* Ḿa respectively. What also compounds the intensity here is a ratcheting up of rhythmic complexity. Listeners with sharp ears (or access to appropriate software) will spot that VR rolls out his *tāns* at a rate of five notes per sub-beat (or twenty notes per macro-beat), and that their melodic grouping does not coincide with the beats but rather cuts unpredictably and ambiguously across them. This is a characteristic *laykārī* technique (Clayton 2000: 159–66), and points forward to a *tour de force* of *tān* work with which VR ends this *baṛā khayāl*.

Audio Example 4.3.10 *Āvartan* 13: *gamak tāns* (*TR*, Track 5, 13:25–13:47)
https://hdl.handle.net/20.500.12434/8d84f54c

Audio Example 4.3.11 *Āvartan* 14: *ākār tāns* (*TR*, Track 5, 14:23–15:28)
https://hdl.handle.net/20.500.12434/d63ecad9

But we are not at this point yet, and, as if to remind us of the fact, VR begins the next *āvartan* (15) with an extended passage of *bol ālāp*, focusing on the word 'sakhī' and the note *tār* Sā (rising to *tār* Re at 00:37 of Audio Example 4.3.12). In doing so, he creates contrast with the prevailing singing style while maintaining intensity. This also enhances the unity of the performance by recalling the *baṛhat* phase of the *baṛā khayāl*. However, the reversion to *bol ālāp* is only temporary, and shortly before the ninth macro-beat (at 0:46 of the audio example) VR resumes singing *ākār tāns*, deferring the *mukhṛā* until the last two sub-beats, where it is sung at double speed (*dugun*).

Audio Example 4.3.12 *Āvartan* 15: return to *bol ālāp* singing style (*TR*, Track 5, 15:23–16:35)
https://hdl.handle.net/20.500.12434/15e225ea

Having re-entered *ākār tān* mode (his self-confessed specialism), VR stays there, sustaining a plateau of intensity for the final three *āvartans* with a dazzling display of invention and virtuosity. Typically, he makes no single consummating final gesture, since the *baṛā khayāl* is by no means the end of the performance. Instead, after the final *mukhṛā*, he segues into the up-tempo *choṭā khayāl*, 'Śyām bejāi'.

Conclusion

Through the preceding account we have journeyed with VR through the course of a *baṛā khayāl* performance. We have considered how the conventions of Hindustani classical music in general—the grammar of *rāg*, the ordering framework of *tāl*—and those of a *baṛā khayāl* in particular—its ground plan of events, its dialectic between the metrical and non-metrical—come together to make this a quintessential form of extended *rāg* performance. Practised and internalised over many years, these conventions become absorbed in a musician's consciousness until they become second nature: not merely theoretical but also *experiential* knowledge, absorbed into his or her mind and body over many performances, developing as an ever-more refined ability to fashion the temporal unfolding of a *baṛā khayāl*'s two large-scale waves of mounting intensity.

It is probably not coincidental that the evolution of a *baṛā khayāl* over the course of the twentieth century into its now-archetypal guise is coeval with India's own negotiation with modernity. As Hindustani classical music increasingly became a secular concert practice, its leading musicians sought to develop its forms and conventions to allow more aesthetically substantial statements which, intentionally or otherwise, compare in magnitude to those of western classical traditions. As ever, this process has been conducted on the subcontinent's own terms, leading to a canon not of great works and great composers, but of great exponents and pedagogical lineages (*gharānās*), and legendary performances. Many of these have been captured by contemporary recording technology and globally disseminated, including, in the present day, over the internet.

This is *paramparā*: the weight of tradition, of long lines of illustrious forebears, of conventions and codes of performance. This is what bears on every musician as they sit down alongside their fellows and before often highly knowledgeable audiences—as they centre themselves within the resonance of the tānpurās and begin to sing or play. This is what is reborn in every moment of a performance. And, on a personal note, this is what was tangible on the day in 2006 when VR, Shahbaz Hussain and Fida Hussain sat down in a recording studio at Newcastle University to record *Twilight Rāgs from North India*. Each track was captured in a single take with only minimal post-production editing (and with impeccable sound engineering by John Ayers). The album stands as a record of this event and as a document of VR's role as a bearer of the legacy of his several teachers, most notably Pandit Bhimsen Joshi, and the Kirānā *gharānā*.

Epilogue: *Laya/Pralaya*

On a chilly October morning, I'm sitting in a café in a leafy suburb of Newcastle upon Tyne with my fellow khayāl student Sudipta Roy. In her day job, Sudipta is a professor of electrochemical engineering, but like me (David Clarke), she is also a *śiṣyā* of Vijay ji; in the *guru-śiṣyā* scheme of things, that makes her my *guru-bahan* (guru-sister) and me her *guru-bhāī* (guru-brother). We sometimes take our vocal class together, and have on numerous occasions shared a stage as performers. Over the years, Sudipta and I have spent many hours in our favourite coffee shops and eateries sharing our thoughts on academic life, Indian music, and the experience of learning from our guruji. If learning khayāl over some two decades has inadvertently become an extended piece of fieldwork for me, Sudipta, as well as being a good friend and ally, has been a key cultural interpreter on this ethnographic journey, sharing with me insights into Indian culture that have enriched and complemented Vijay's musical tutelage.

On this occasion, I'm updating her on how things are going with *Rāgs Around the Clock*. I've just completed a draft of the chapter on *baṛā khayāl*, and over brunch we compare notes on what it feels like to actually sing one—on how you fit the loose and shifting rhythmic profiles of the *sthāī* and *antarā* into a *tāl* cycle.

'I don't really think of this like a *bandiś* in the normal sense', Sudipta says. 'It's not rhythmically tied down like in a *choṭā khayāl*—it's more like an *ālāp*. But in any case, we Bengalis, we don't really use the term *ālāp*, even for an actual *ālāp*—we'd just say *anibaddh*, you know, "unmeasured". And for a "normal" *bandiś*, like in a *choṭā khayāl*, we'd say *nibaddh*, "measured". *Bandiś* means to bind, right? In a *choṭā khayāl* the song's bound to the *lay*, the rhythm, but in a *baṛā khayāl* it isn't like that, really'.

I nod. That's my experience too, I say: the composition in a *baṛā khayāl* does similar work to the *bandiś* of a *choṭā khayāl*, but it just doesn't feel the same on account of its ambiguous relationship with metre. And now that I think about it, I've sometimes felt myself equivocating around the word *bandiś* when talking about *baṛā khayāl*s (oddly, the English word 'composition', which doesn't have the connotation of 'binding', feels OK).

And then, almost in passing, Sudipta goes on to mention something that opens up our dialogue onto something altogether more fundamental.

'This is just a personal thing', she says, 'I've never heard anyone else put it like this—but in my mind, the whole question of *lay* is different. For me *lay* isn't just a case of rhythm: the way I make sense of it is in relation to its opposite in Sanskrit, and that's *pralaya*—which kind of means "chaos". So, when you're creating *laya*, you're creating order, something that opposes *pralaya*'.

I've never heard *lay* (Sanskrit, *laya*) described quite like this—musicians usually talk about it purely in musical terms, to mean tempo or rhythm. But Sudipta seems to be pointing to something in her cultural memory of that word that looks more philosophical, even metaphysical. Her description of singing a *baṛā khayāl* as being like walking a tightrope between order and chaos rings true. It's a dramatic image that captures what it can actually feel like when you're improvising.

This is all part of what musicians do in their conversations: tell stories, come up with images and ideas that help them make sense of their practice—*khayāl*: imagination. But the scholar in me wants to know chapter and verse. So we finish our coffees, pay the bill, and drive back to Sudipta's house. There, she takes down her copy of Bandopadhyay's Sanskrit–Bengali dictionary from the shelf, I take out my laptop, and we sit down at the kitchen table.

Sudipta finds the page. 'Here, it is; look. Under *laya* they give related words like *gīt* and *tāl*; and as the antonym they give *pralaya*'. Now she looks up that entry: 'Aha: *"pralaya*, destruction, end of time"!'

Next, I log on to the Cologne Digital Sanskrit Dictionaries website (n.d.), which gives ready access to Monier-Williams' Sanskrit–English dictionary in its second, 1899 edition—a monumental work of scholarship. Under *laya* (लय), Monier-Williams gives a wealth of meanings extracted from a wide historical corpus of texts. Among these, I find the definition that musicians are familiar with: 'time (regarded as of 3 kinds, viz. *druta*, "quick", *madhya*, "mean or moderate", and *vilambita*, "slow")'. (Following this up later, I confirm a similar definition of *laya* by Bharata Muni (2006/1989), in chapter 31 of his *Nāṭyaśāstra*, from the early centuries CE, even though this isn't listed among Monier-Williams' sources.) But it's the non-musical meanings in Monier-Williams' definition of *laya* that are so intriguing—including: 'the act of sticking or clinging to'; also 'rest, repose' and 'melting, dissolution, disappearance or absorption in'; shading further into 'extinction, destruction, death'. And the entry for *pralaya* (प्रलय) goes further along the same semantic axis, to include 'dissolution, reabsorption, destruction, annihilation' and, most finally, 'the destruction of the whole world, at the end of a Kalpa'.

I look up at Sudipta: 'Amazing. We started out chatting about what it's like to sing a *baṛā <u>kh</u>ayāl*, and here we are looking at *laya* on the most cosmic timescale!' What this foray has also shown is that *laya* and *pralaya* aren't necessarily opposites: in Monier-Williams' entry, the eschatological meaning of *pralaya* is already implicit in *laya*, in its sense of 'dissolution, disappearance or absorption'.

Stand back a little, and you can see that there are in fact many ways of thinking and talking at work in this narrative. There's the free-ranging chat of musicians in coffee shops (or at roadside chāī stalls, or on car journeys, or in the green room). There's the discourse of ethnographers, who would want not just to recount such conversations but also to read them for their wider cultural significance; and, for that matter, of autoethnographers, who would want to pull out the bigger cultural meanings of their own experiences (as, of course, I'm attempting to do here). There's the discourse of music theory, which wants to describe with some rigour what it is that musicians do in idioms such as a *baṛā <u>kh</u>ayāl* (as I have sought to do in the later stages of *Rāgs Around the Clock*). There's the discourse of scholarship more widely, including the achievements of Monier-Williams, whose dictionary stands on the shoulders of its even more monumental forebear, the Petersburg Sanskrit–German dictionary of 1855–75 by Otto Böhtlingk and Rudolph Roth—in complicated ways (see Steiner 2020). Then there are the kinds of discourse referenced in those dictionaries themselves—musical, literary, theological, mythological and so on. And waiting in the wings are the discourses of cultural historians and socio-political commentators, who would urge us to stay awake to the colonial dimensions of those nineteenth-century scholars' work, and to appropriations of Sanskrit as a part of a nationalist cause in India's present-day polity (which doesn't mean there can't be more salutary applications, as here).

Under the weight of so many discourses, one might begin to crumple. But I enumerate them partly to indicate, in this book's final paragraphs, the range of ways of thinking that have given the work its general complexion; and partly to regulate what can be claimed with this particular closing tale. For the imaginative re-thinking of musical *lay* in light of the wider range of meanings of the Sanskrit term *laya* and its relative, *pralaya* is probably not something you would encounter in any wider theoretical corpus. And yet, there remains something powerfully suggestive in the *laya/pralaya* idea, on hermeneutic, i.e. interpretive, grounds: that to improvise a *baṛā khayāl* is to tap into *lay* in the sense both of the metrically organised unfolding of musical time (*nibaddh*) and of its dissolution (*anibaddh*). We might read this as a metaphor that conveys something of the gravity that an individual performer needs to summon up in the immensity of a slowly unfolding *ati vilambit tāl* cycle—in order to draw out *rāg*-based material that reposes in *lay* and yet tries to dissolve previous musical ideas; to bring the ever-new into being, and let it fall away again.

While a *baṛā khayāl* represents the epitome of this situation thus dramatised, it would be plausible also to claim that the same process operates across khayāl as a whole (often playfully so), and, even more widely, across Indian classical music in general. Moreover, this productive tension between the rigour of a metric and the play of an individual subject's invention resonates with another notion that has become thematised in this book: the interplay between theory and practice; the way the culturally transmitted conventions of the latter invite codification, rubric, terminology and taxonomy, yet ultimately go beyond them. When all the thinking and writing is done, we come back to the creative fashioning of sound, nurtured within relationships between *people*—between guru and *śiṣyā*, between fellow students, between performers and audiences, between community members, and down generations of practitioners. Sounds formed creatively out of living human and cultural relationships, resonating in history: all in all, not a bad definition of music.

Glossary of Terms Used in Hindustani Classical Music

Ākār	Singing to the vowel 'ā' (lit. 'doing ā').
Ākār tān	Virtuosic melodic run sung to the vowel 'ā'.
Alaṅkār	(i) Ornament or decoration. (ii) Exercise based on ascending and descending sequential repetition of a short phrase; cf. *palṭā*.
Ālāp	Unmetred, quasi-meditative opening section of a classical Indian music performance, used to establish the *rāg*.
Ālapti	The expression or elaboration of *rāg*.
Āndolan	Slow, microtonal oscillation around a note.
Aṅg	(i) A group of *rāgs*. (ii) A characteristic phrase of a single *rāg* within a hybrid *rāg* (lit. 'limb').
Anibaddh	Unmetred (as in an *ālāp*); cf. *nibaddh*.
Antarā	Second part of a composition (*bandiś* or *gat*), usually in middle-to-upper register; cf. *sthāī*.
Āroh	Ascending form of a scale; cf. *avroh*.
Aucār	Very short unmetred introduction to a *rāg* performance, lasting just two or three phrases (like a short *ālāp*).
Auḍav	Five-note (pentatonic); see *jāti*; cf. *ṣāḍav*, *sampūrṇ*.
Āvartan	Cycle of a *tāl*.
Avroh	Descending form of a scale; cf. *āroh*.
Bandiś	Vocal or song composition (lit. 'bound'); cf. *gat*.
Baṛā khayāl	Lit. 'large *khayāl*': slow opening metred section of an extended *khayāl*; also known as *vilambit* ('slow') *khayāl*.
Baṛhat	Lit. 'increase': staged, *ālāp*-style development of a *rāg*, in presence of *tāl*; see also *bol ālāp*, *vistār*.
Bāyā̃	(Larger) left-hand drum of the tablā; cf. *dāyā̃*.
Behlāvā	Technique of melismatic melodic development associated with the Gwalior *gharānā*.
Birādarī	Wider family group of musicians connected by marriage ties; cf. *khāndān*.

Bol	Name given to a tablā stroke (lit. 'word').
Bol ālāp	*Ālāp*-style passage (in presence of *tāl*) using words of the *bandiś*; cf. *baṛhat, vistār*.
Bol bāṇṭ	Improvised rhythmic play with the words of a composition (*bandiś*)—a technique of musical development; cf. *lay bāṇṭ*.
Bol tān	Melodic run using the words of a composition (*bandiś*).
Calan	Lit. 'movement', 'conduct': series of phrases illustrating the pathway through a *rāg*; cf. *pakaḍ*.
Cancal rāg	*Rāg* of light, flowing character; cf. *gambhīr rāg*.
Chāp	Pen name, pseudonym; see also *takhallus*.
Choṭā khayāl	Lit. 'small *khayāl*': medium or fast-tempo section of a *khayāl*; also known as *drut* ('fast') *khayāl*.
Dāyā̃	(Smaller) right-hand drum of the tablā; cf. *bāyā̃*.
Dhrupad	Oldest Hindustani classical genre in the present-day repertory, pre-dating khayāl and typically more serious in style and mood; cf. ṭhumrī.
Drut	Fast (tempo); cf. *madhya lay, vilambit*.
Drut khayāl	Fast-tempo *choṭā khayāl*.
Dugun	At double speed; cf. *ekgun*.
Ekgun	At single speed; cf. *dugun*.
Gamak	Vocal technique involving a heavy shake on each note.
Gamak tān	Melodic run deploying *gamak*.
Gambhīr rāg	*Rāg* of heavy, serious character; cf. *cancal rāg*.
Gat	Instrumental composition; cf. *bandiś*.
Gāyakī	Stylistic characteristics of a vocal genre, *gharānā* or individual artist.
Gharānā	Stylistic school of musicians.
Grah svar	Note that can be used to initiate a phrase; cf. *nyās svar*.
Guru	Teacher, spiritual guide (in Hindu tradition and parlance); see also *ustād*.
Jāti	Class (of *rāg*)—defined by ascending and descending scale types; see also *auḍav, ṣāḍav, sampūrṇ*.
Javārī	(i) Cotton thread applied between the bridge and strings of a tānpurā. (ii) Overtone-filled sound resulting from this physical arrangement.
Jhālā	Final section of an instrumental or dhrupad *ālāp*, in which the performer plays or sings in two registers, with melodic expansion in the higher register over a reiterated tone (usually Sā) in the lower; cf. *joṛ*.

Joṛ	Second section of an instrumental or dhrupad *ālāp*, in which melodic invention is pulsed; cf. *jhālā*.
Kampit	Short ornamental shake or vibrato at the end (or beginning) of a sustained note.
Kaṇ	Grace note; short decorative note preceding a longer note.
Khālī	Unweighted beat or portion of a *tāl* (lit. 'empty'), indicated with a wave; cf. *sam*, *tālī*.
Khāndān	Hereditary line of musicians; cf. *birādarī*.
Kaṭhkā	Rapid melodic embellishment around the beginning of a note, usually involving a degree of force; cf. *murkī*.
<u>Kh</u>ayāl	(i) Genre of Hindustani classical vocal music, partly serious, partly romantic in style. (ii) A performance in this genre. Cf. dhrupad, ṭhumrī.
Komal	Flat (scale degree); cf. *śuddh*, *tivra*.
Lay	Tempo, speed.
Lay bāṇṭ	Delivery of *bandiś* at double-tempo (*dugun*) or faster while *tāl* remains unchanged; cf. *bol bāṇṭ*.
Laykārī	(i) Syncopated (off-beat) rhythmic play. (ii) Any technique used to develop rhythm.
Madhya	Middle, medium—applied to, for example, speed, note register, octave; cf. *mandra*, *tār*.
Madhya lay	Medium-tempo; cf. *drut*, *vilambit*.
Mandra	Lower (for example, note register, octave); cf. *madhya*, *tār*.
Mātrā	Beat, count.
Mehfil	Courtly gathering.
Merukhaṇḍ	Exercise involving strict permutation of a set of notes.
Mīṇḍ	Gliding motion (*glissando*) between notes.
Mukhṛā	Opening phrase (or first line) of a composition (*bandiś*), functioning as a refrain, and, notably in a *baṛā <u>kh</u>ayāl*, anticipating and leading to *sam*.
Murkī	Fast, delicate melodic embellishment at the start of a note; cf. *kaṭhkā*.
Nibaddh	Metred—as in a *tāl* (lit. 'bound', 'tied'); cf. *anibaddh*.
Nyās svar	(i) Note of longer duration (standing note, goal tone); able to be sustained under the conventions of a *rāg*. (ii) Final note. Cf. *grah svar*.
Pakaḍ	Quintessential phrase of a *rāg*, capturing its key features and grammar; cf. *calan*.

Pakhāvaj	Double-headed barrel drum related to tablā—used in dhrupad.
Palṭā	(i) Practise exercise based on a small number of notes and their variation; cf. *alaṅkār*. (ii) More extended melodic phrase for practise, encapsulating key features of a *rāg*. (iii) In tablā playing, variation on a *qāydā* (theme for extemporisation).
Paramparā	Tradition, lineage, succession.
Prahar	Phase of the day or night; lit. 'watch'.
Pūrvaṅg	Lower tetrachord; cf. *uttaraṅg*.
Pūrvaṅg pradhan rāg	*Rāg* with melodic focus in lower tetrachord; cf. *uttaraṅg pradhan rāg*.
Rāg	(i) Principle of melodic organisation based on mode and evoking emotional mood (see *ras*). (ii) A particular exemplar of this principle—for example, Rāg Bhairav.
Ras	Aesthetic flavour (lit. 'juice', 'essence') instilling emotion.
Rasika	*Aficionado*; lover of the arts; informed listener.
Ṣāḍav	Six-note (hexatonic); see also *jāti*; cf. *auḍav, sampūrṇ*.
Śāgird	Student, disciple (in Muslim nomenclature); see also *śiṣyā*.
Sam	Initial beat of a *tāl*, usually the focal point; cf. *khālī*; *tālī*.
Sampūrṇ	Seven-note (heptatonic; lit. 'complete'); see also *jāti*; cf. *auḍav, ṣāḍav*.
Saṃvādī	Second most important or prominent ('con-sonant') note of a *rāg*, complementing *vādī*; cf. *vivādī*.
Sandhi prakāś rāg	*Rāg* performed at twilight.
Sāraṅgī	Bowed string instrument with many sympathetic strings.
Sargam	System of note names based on scale degrees, similar to western *solfège*.
Sargam tān	Melodic run using *sargam* syllables.
Śiṣyā	Student, disciple (in Hindu nomenclature); see also *śāgird*.
Sitār	Plucked, fretted string instrument with additional sympathetic strings.
Śrutī	Microtonal division of octave; lit. 'that which is heard'.
Śruti box	Instrument used to provide drone, either manually with bellowed instrument or electronically.
Sthāī	First part of a composition (*bandiś* or *gat*), usually in lower-to-middle register; cf. *antarā*.
Śuddh	Natural (scale degree); cf. *komal, tivra*.
Svar	Note, tone, pitch.

Tablā	Paired set of hand drums, commonly used as accompanying instrument in Hindustani music.
Takhallus	Pen name, pseudonym; see also *chāp*.
Tāl	(i) Cyclic, metrically structured principle of rhythmic organisation. (ii) A particular exemplar of this principle—for example, *tīntāl*.
Tālī	Relatively prominent beat or portion of a *tāl* cycle, indicated with a clap; cf. *khālī, sam*.
Tālīm	Instruction, tuition (taken from a guru or *ustād*).
Tān	Melodic run or flourish.
Tānpurā	Long necked lute used to provide background drone.
Tār	Upper (note, register, octave); cf. *madhya, mandra*.
Tarānā	(i) Genre or style of singing based on non-semantic syllables, for example, *tā, nā, dhim*. (ii) Final section of a <u>kh</u>ayāl performance in this style.
Ṭhāṭ	Group of *rāgs* defined by a parent scale (under system devised by V. N. Bhatkhande).
Ṭhekā	Sequence of drum strokes (*bols*) defining the flow and shape of a *tāl*.
Ṭhumrī	Light-classical vocal genre, romantic in character; cf. dhrupad, <u>kh</u>ayāl.
Tihāī	Phrase repeated three times.
Tivra	Sharp (scale degree); cf. *komal, suddh*.
Ustād	Teacher, master (in Muslim tradition and parlance); see also *guru*.
Uttaraṅg	Upper tetrachord; cf. *pūrvaṅg*.
Uttaraṅg pradhan rāg	*Rāg* with melodic focus in upper tetrachord; cf. *pūrvaṅg pradhan rāg*.
Vādī	Principal ('sonant') or most prominent note of a *rāg*; cf. *saṃvādī, vivādī*.
Vibhāg	Metrical subgroup within a *tāl*.
Vilambit	Slow (tempo); cf. *drut, madhya lay*.
Vilambit <u>kh</u>ayāl	Slow, initial stage of a <u>kh</u>ayāl performance; also known as *baṛā* ('large') *<u>kh</u>ayāl*.
Vistār	Freely improvised passage over a *tāl*; see also *baṛhat*; cf. *bol ālāp*.
Vivādī	Note foreign to a *rāg*; may be discreetly used in correct context by a knowledgeable performer for expressive purposes; cf. *vādī, saṃvādī*.

References

Ali, Daud (2004). *Courtly Culture and Political Life in Early Medieval India* (Cambridge: Cambridge University Press).

Alter, Andrew Burton (2000). 'Institutional Music Education: Northern Area', in *The Garland Encyclopedia of World Music, Vol. 5—South Asia: The Indian Subcontinent*, ed. by Alison Arnold (New York, NY: Garland), 442–8, https://doi.org/10.4324/9781315086538

Bagchee, Sandeep (1998). *Nād: Understanding Rāga Music* (Mumbai: Eshwar).

Bakhle, Janaki (2005). *Two Men and Music: Nationalism in the Making of an Indian Classical Tradition* (New York, NY: Oxford University Press), https://doi.org/10.1093/acprof:oso/9780195166101.001.0001

Bandopadhyay [Banerjee], Ashok Kumar (2005). *Sanskrit Bānglā Abhidhān* [*Sanskrit–Bengali Dictionary*], rev. 2nd edn (Kolkata: Saudesh).

Bandyopadhyaya, Shripada (1977). *The Origin of Rāga: A Concise History of the Evolution, Growth and the Treatment of Rāga from the Age of Bharatamuni to Bhatkhande*, 2nd edn (New Delhi: Munishram Manoharlal).

Banerjee, Jayasri (1986). 'The Methodology of Teaching Indian Classical Music: A Statement on the Problem', *Journal of the Sangeet Natak Akademi* 79, 11–48, https://archive.org/details/dli.ministry.17126

Beck, Guy L. (1995). *Sonic Theology: Hinduism and Sacred Sound* (Delhi: Motilal Banarsidass), https://doi.org/10.2307/j.ctv2z5510b

Bharata Muni (2006/1989). *The Nātya Śāstra of Bharatamuni*, transl. by a board of scholars, repr. 2nd edn (Delhi: Sri Satguru Publications).

Bhatkhande, Vishnu Narayan (1937). *Hindustani Sangeet Paddhati: Kramik pustak mālikā*, 6 vols. (Hathras: Sangeet Press).

Bhatkhande, Vishnu Narayan (1991/1937). *Hindustani Sangeet Paddhati: Kramik pustak mālikā*, IV (Hathras: Sangeet Press).

Bhatkhande, Vishnu Narayan (1993/1937). *Hindustani Sangeet Paddhati: Kramik pustak mālikā*, VI (Hathras: Sangeet Press).

Bhatkhande, Vishnu Narayan (1994/1937). *Hindustani Sangeet Paddhati: Kramik pustak mālikā*, II (Hathras: Sangeet Press).

Bhatkhande, Vishnu Narayan (1995/1937). *Hindustani Sangeet Paddhati: Kramik pustak mālikā*, III (Hathras: Sangeet Press).

Bhogal, Gurminder Kaur (2017). 'Listening to Female Voices in Sikh *Kirtan*', *Sikh Formations: Religion, Culture, Theory* 13(1–2), 48–77, https://doi.org/10.1080/17448727.2016.1147183

Bhogal, Gurminder Kaur (2022). 'Tracking the Harmonium from Christian Missionary Hymns to Sikh Kirtan', *Yale Journal of Music & Religion* 8(2), Article 1, https://doi.org/10.17132/2377-231X.1240

Bohlman, Philip V. (2002). *World Music: A Very Short Introduction* (Oxford and New York, NY: Oxford University Press).

Böhtlingk, Otto (1855–75). *Sanskrit Wörterbuch, herausgegeben von der kaiserlichen Akademie der Wissenschaften, bearbeitet von Otto Böhtlingk und Rudolph Roth* (St-Petersburg: Eggers), https://www.sanskrit-lexicon.uni-koeln.de/scans/PWGScan/2020/web/index.php

Bor, Joep, and Allyn Miner (2010). 'Hindustani Music: A Historical Overview of the Modern Period', in *Hindustani Music: Thirteenth to Twentieth Centuries*, ed. by Joep Boer, Françoise 'Nalini' Delvoye, Jane Harvey and Emmie te Nijenhuis (New Delhi: Manohar), 197–220.

Bor, Joep, Suvarnalata Rao, Wim van der Meer and Jane Harvey; with Henri Tournier, Lalita du Perron and Robin Broadbank (1999). *The Raga Guide: A Survey of 74 Hindustani Ragas*, text and 4 CDs (Monmouth: Nimbus Records with Rotterdam Conservatory of Music).

Brahaspati, Sulochana (2010). 'Rampur as a Centre of Music', in *Hindustani Music: Thirteenth to Twentieth Centuries*, ed. by Joep Boer, Françoise 'Nalini' Delvoye, Jane Harvey and Emmie te Nijenhuis (New Delhi: Manohar), 267–83.

Brown, Katherine Butler (2003). *Hindustani Music in the Time of Aurangzeb* (PhD diss., King's College London), https://kclpure.kcl.ac.uk/portal/en/studentTheses/hindustani-music-in-the-time-of-aurangzeb

Brown, Katherine Butler (2010). 'The Origins and Early Development of Khayal', in *Hindustani Music: Thirteenth to Twentieth Centuries*, ed. by Joep Boer, Françoise 'Nalini' Delvoye, Jane Harvey and Emmie te Nijenhuis (New Delhi: Manohar), 159–94.

Chakrabarty, Ajoy (2002). *Shrutinandan: Towards Universal Music* (Kolkata: Macmillan India).

Choudhury, Monojit, Anupam Basu and Sudeshna Sarkar (2004). 'A Diachronic Approach for Schwa Deletion in Indo Aryan Languages', in *Proceedings of the ACL Special Interest Group on Computation Phonology*, ed. by John Goldsmith and Richard Wicentowski (Barcelona: Association for Computational Linguistics), 20–6, https://doi.org/10.3115/1622153.1622156

Clarke, David (2013). 'Different Resistances: A Comparative View of Indian and Western Classical Music in the Modern Era', *Contemporary Music Review* 32(2–3), 175–200, https://doi.org/10.1080/07494467.2013.775809

Clarke, David (2017). 'North Indian Classical Music and Lerdahl and Jackendoff's Generative Theory—a Mutual Regard', *Music Theory Online* 23(3), n.p., https://mtosmt.org/issues/mto.17.23.3/mto.17.23.3.clarke.html

Clayton, Martin (2000). *Time in Indian Music: Rhythm, Metre, and Form in North Indian Rāg Performance* (Oxford: Oxford University Press).

Clayton, Martin (2007). 'Observing Entrainment in Music Performance: Video-based Observational Analysis of Indian Musicians' Tanpura Playing and Beat Marking', *Musicae Scientiae*, 11(1), 27–59, https://doi.org/10.1177/102986490701100102

Clayton, Martin, and Veena Sahasrabuddhe (1998). *Khyal: Classical Singing of North India*, video cassette with accompanying booklet (Milton Keynes: Open University Worldwide Ltd).

Daniélou, Alain (2003). *The Rāga-s of Northern Indian Music* (New Delhi: Munshiram Manoharlal).

Das Sharma [Dasasarma], Amal (1993). *Musicians of India: Past and Present: Gharānas of Hindustani Music and Genealogies* (Calcutta: Naya Prokash).

Datta, Asoke Kumar, Ranjan Sengupta, Kaushik Banerjee and Dipak Ghosh (2019). *Acoustical Analysis of the Tanpura: Indian Plucked String Instrument* (Singapore: Springer).

Dennett, Daniel C. (1991). *Consciousness Explained* (London: Penguin).

Deshpande, Vamanrao H. (1987). *Indian Musical Traditions: An Aesthetic Study of the Gharanas of Hindustani Music*, transl. by S. H. Deshpande and V. C. Devadhar, 2nd edn (Bombay: Popular Prakashan).

Deva, B. Chaitanya (1980a). *Indian Music*, 2nd edn (New Delhi: Indian Council for Cultural Relations).

Deva, B. Chaitanya (1980b). *The Music of India: A Scientific Study* (New Delhi: Munishram Manoharlal).

Dhore, Manikrao L., Shantanu K. Dixit and Ruchi M. Dhore (2012). 'Hindi and Marathi to English NE Transliteration Using Phonology and Stress Analysis', *Proceedings of COLING 2012: Demonstration Papers*, ed. by Martin Kay and Christian Boitet (Mumbai: COLING 2012), 111–18.

Doffman, Mark (2019). 'Practical Time Consciousness in Musical Performance', in *Music and Consciousness 2: Worlds, Practices, Modalities*, ed. by Ruth Herbert, David Clarke and Eric Clarke (Oxford and New York, NY: Oxford University Press), 170–86, https://doi.org/10.1093/oso/9780198804352.003.0010

Farrell, Gerry (1986). 'Teaching Indian Music in the West: Problems, Approaches and Possibilities', *British Journal of Music Education* 3(3), 267–78, https://doi.org/10.1017/S0265051700000784

Gonda, Jan (1965). *Change and Continuity in Indian Religious Traditions* (The Hague: Mouton).

Gonda, Jan (1975). 'The Meaning of the Word *Alaṃkāra*', in *Selected Studies, II: Sanskrit Word Studies*, ed. by Jan Gonda (Leiden: E. J. Brill), 258–75.

Hood, Mantle (1960). 'The Challenge of "Bi-Musicality"', *Ethnomusicology* 4, 55–9, https://doi.org/10.2307/924263

Imām, Hakam Karam (1959). 'Effect of Ragas and Mannerism in Singing [Chapter from *Ma'adan ul–mūsiqī* (1865)]', transl. Govind Vidyarthi, *Sangeet Natak Akademi Bulletin* 13–14, 6–14, https://indianculture.gov.in/effect-ragas-and-mannerism-singing

Jairazbhoy, Nazir A. (1971). *The Rāgs of North Indian Music: Their Structure and Evolution* (Middletown, CT: Wesleyan University Press).

Jani, Kalpesh (2019). *Sangeet Aarohee: An Essential Study of Hindustani Classical Music* (Mumbai: BecomeShakespeare.com).

Kashalkar, Sanyukta (2013). 'Comparitive [sic] Study of Ancient Gurukul System and the New Trends of Guru-shishya Parampara', *American International Journal of Research in Humanities, Arts and Social Sciences* 2(1), 81–4.

Katz, Max (2017). *Lineages of Loss: Counternarratives of North Indian Music* (Middletown, CT: Wesleyan University Press).

Kaufmann, Walter (1993/1968). *The Ragas of North India* (Sittingbourne: Asia Publishing House).

Khan, Ali Akbar, and George Ruckert (2021/1998). *The Classical Music of North India: The Music of the Baba Allauddin Gharana as Taught by Ali Akbar Khan at the Ali Akbar College of Music* (New Delhi: Munshiram Manoharlal).

Kiparsky, Paul (1993). 'Pāṇinian Linguistics', in *The Encyclopedia of Languages and Linguistics*, ed. R. E. Asher, 2918–23 (Oxford: Pergamon Press).

Kippen, James (1988). *The Tabla of Lucknow: A Cultural Analysis of a Musical Tradition* (Cambridge: Cambridge University Press).

Kippen, James (2008). 'Working with the Masters', in *Shadows in the Field: New Perspectives for Fieldwork in Ethnomusicology*, ed. by Gregory Barz and Timothy J. Cooley (Oxford and New York, NY: Oxford University Press), 125–40.

Krishna, T. M. (2020). 'Lift the Veil on the Parampara', *The Indian Express* (19 September), https://indianexpress.com/article/opinion/columns/gundecha-brothers-sexual-harassment-hindustani-music-tm-krishna-6601666/

Lallie, Harjinder Singh (2016). 'The Harmonium in Sikh Music', *Sikh Formations: Religion, Culture, Theory* 12(1), 1–14, https://doi.org/10.1080/17448727.2016.1147175

Lath, Mukund (1987). 'An Enquiry into the Rāga-time Association', in *Aspects of Indian Music*, ed. by Sumati Matatkar (New Delhi: Sangeet Natak Akademi), 113–19.

Magriel, Nicolas (1997). 'The Baṛhat Tree', *Asian Music* 28(2), 109–33, https://doi.org/10.2307/834476

Magriel, Nicolas (2001). *Sāraṅgī Style in North Indian Art Music* (PhD diss., School of Oriental and African Studies, University of London).

Magriel, Nicolas, with Lalita du Perron (2013). *The Songs of Khayāl*, 2 vols. (New Delhi: Manohar).

Mittal, Anjali (2000). *Hindustānī Music and the Aesthetic Concept of Form* (New Delhi: D. K. Printworld (P) Ltd).

Mlecko, Joel (1982). 'The Guru in Hindu Tradition', *Numen* 29(1), 33–61, https://doi.org/10.1163/156852782x00132

Monier-Williams, Monier (1899). *Sanskrit-English Dictionary, 1899* (Oxford: Clarendon Press), https://www.sanskrit-lexicon.uni-koeln.de/scans/MWScan/2020/web/index.php

Moutal, Patrick (1997/1991). *A Comparative Study of Selected Hindustānī Rāga-s, Based on Contemporary Practice*, rev. edn (New Delhi: Munishram Manoharlal).

Napier, John James (2006). 'Novelty That Must Be Subtle: Continuity, Innovation and "Improvisation" in North Indian Music', *Critical Studies in Improvisation/Études critiques en improvisation* 1(3), 1–17.

Nārada (1920). *Saṅgīta-makaranda*, ed. by Mangesh Rāmakrishna Telang (Baroda: Central Library), https://sanskritdocuments.org/scannedbooks/musicresearchlibrary.html

Nayar, Sobhana (1989). *Bhatkhande's Contribution to Music* (Bombay: Popular Prakashan).

Neuman, Daniel (1990). *The Life of Music in North India: The Organization of an Artistic Tradition* (Chicago, IL and London: University of Chicago Press), https://archive.org/details/lifeofmusicinnor00neum/page/2/mode/2up

Neuman, Dard (2012). 'Pedagogy, Practice, and Embodied Creativity in Hindustani Music', *Ethnomusicology* 56(3), 426–49, https://doi.org/10.5406/ethnomusicology.56.3.0426

Nijenhuis, Emmie te, and Françoise 'Naline' Delvoye (2010). 'Sanskrit and Indo-Persian Literature on Music', in *Hindustani Music: Thirteenth to Twentieth Centuries*, ed. by Joep Boer, Françoise 'Nalini' Delvoye, Jane Harvey and Emmie te Nijenhuis (New Delhi: Manohar), 35–64.

Nooshin, Laudan, and Richard Widdess (2006). 'Improvisation in Iranian and Indian Music', *Journal of the Indian Musicological Society* 36/37, 104–19.

Phansalkar, Janhavi (2017). 'The Resolute Thinker', *Dhrupad Journal* 1 (Winter), 48–49.

Post, Jennifer C. (2000). 'Women and Music', in *The Garland Encyclopedia of World Music, Vol. 5—South Asia: The Indian Subcontinent*, ed. by Alison Arnold (New York, NY: Garland), 407–17, https://doi.org/10.4324/9781315086538

Powers, Harold S. (1980). 'Language Models and Musical Analysis', *Ethnomusicology* 24(1), 1–60, https://doi.org/10.2307/851308

Powers, Harold S. (1992). 'Reinterpretations of Tradition in Hindustani Music: Omkarnath Thakur contra Vishnu Narayan Bhatkhande', in *The Traditional Indian Theory and Practice of Music and Dance*, ed. by Jonathan Katz (Leiden: E. J. Brill), 9–51.

Powers, Harold S., Frans Wiering, James Porter, James Cowdery, Richard Widdess, Ruth Davis, Marc Perlman, Stephen Jones and Allan Marett (2001). 'Mode', *Grove Music Online*, https://doi.org/10.1093/gmo/9781561592630.article.43718

Qureshi, Regula Burckhardt (2001). 'Other Musicologies: Exploring Issues and Confronting Practice in India', in *Rethinking Music*, ed. by Nicholas Cook and Mark Everest (Oxford and New York, NY: Oxford University Press), 311–35.

Qureshi, Regula Burckhardt (2002). 'Mode of Production and Musical Production: Is Hindustani Music Feudal?', in *Music and Marx: Ideas, Practice, Politics*, ed. by Regula Burkhardt Qureshi (New York, NY and London: Routledge), 81–105.

Qureshi, Regula Burckhardt (2009). '*Sīna ba sīna* or "from father to son": Writing the Culture of Discipleship', in *Theorizing the Local: Music, Practice, and Experience in South Asia and Beyond*, ed. by Richard K. Wolf (Oxford and New York, NY: Oxford University Press), 165–83.

Qureshi, Regula, Harold S. Powers, Jonathan Katz, Richard Widdess, Gordon Geekie, Alastair Dick, Devdan Sen, Nazir A. Jairazbhoy, Peter Manuel, Robert Simon, Joseph J. Palackal, Soniya K. Brar, M. Whitney Kelting, Edward O. Henry, Maria Lord, Alison Arnold, Warren Pinckney, Kapila Vatsyayan, Bonnie C. Wade and Inderjit N. Kaur (2020). 'India, Subcontinent of', *Grove Music Online*, https://doi.org/10.1093/gmo/9781561592630.article.43272

Ranade, Ashok Da. (2006). *Music Contexts: A Concise Dictionary of Hindustani Music* (New Delhi and Chicago, IL: Promilla and Co./Bibliophile South Asia).

Rajput, Vijay (2012). Interview with David Clarke and Indian Music Students (Newcastle University).

Rowell, Lewis (1998). *Music and Musical Thought in Early India* (New Delhi: Munshiram Manoharlal).

Ruckert, George E. (2004). *Music in North India: Experiencing Music, Expressing Culture* (New York, NY and Oxford: Oxford University Press).

Sankaran, Sajan (2020). 'Practices of Music Education in Gurukul and Related Systems', in *Handbook of Education Systems in South Asia*, ed. by P. M Sarangapani and R. Pappu (Singapore: Springer), 1–26, https://doi.org/10.1007/978-981-13-3309-5_6-1

Sanyal, Ritwik, and Richard Widdess (2004). *Dhrupad: Tradition and Performance in Indian Music* (Aldershot and Burlington, VT: Ashgate), https://doi.org/10.4324/9781003347453

Śārṅgadeva (1978). *Saṅgīta-ratnākara, Vol. I*, ed. and transl. by R. K Shringy with Prem Lata Sharma, 2 vols. (Delhi and Varanasi: Motilal Banarsidass).

Śārṅgadeva (2023/1993). *Saṅgīta-ratnākara, Vol. II*, ed. and transl. by R. K Shringy with Prem Lata Sharma, 2 vols. (Delhi: Motilal Banarsidass).

Scarimbolo, Justin (2014). *Brahmans Beyond Nationalism, Muslims Beyond Dominance: A Hidden History of North Indian Classical Music's Hinduization* (PhD diss., University of California, Santa Barbara).

Schippers, Huib (2007). 'The Guru Recontextualized? Perspectives on Learning North Indian Classical Music in Shifting Environments for Professional Training', *Asian Music* 38(1), 123–38, https://doi.org/10.1353/amu.2007.0020

Seeger, Charles (1958). 'Prescriptive and Descriptive Music Writing', *The Musical Quarterly* 44(2), 184–95, https://doi.org/10.1093/mq/xliv.2.184

Singh, Kirit (2023). *Sikh Patronage of Hindustani Music and Śabad Kīrtan in Colonial Punjab, 1857–1947* (PhD diss., SOAS University of London), https://eprints.soas.ac.uk/40269, https://doi.org/10.25501/SOAS.00040269

Slawek, Stephen (1998). 'Keeping it Going: Terms, Practices, and Processes of Improvisation in Hindustānī Instrumental Music', in *In the Course of Performance: Studies in the World of Musical Improvisation*, ed. by Bruno Nettl and Melinda Russell (Chicago, IL and London: University of Chicago Press), 335–68.

Slawek, Stephen (2000). 'The Classical Master–Disciple Tradition', in *The Garland Encyclopedia of World Music, Vol. 5—South Asia: The Indian Subcontinent*, ed. by Alison Arnold (New York, NY: Garland), 457–67.

Snell, Rupert (1991). *The Hindi Classical Tradition: A Braj Bhāṣā Reader* (London: School of Oriental and African Studies).

Snell, Rupert (2003). *Beginner's Hindi* (London: Hodder Education).

Snell, Rupert (2016). *Transliterating Devanagari* (Texas Scholar Works, University of Texas at Austin), http://hdl.handle.net/2152/46080

Sooklal, Anil (1990). 'The Guru-shishya Paramparā: A Paradigm of Religio-cultural Continuity', *Journal for the Study of Religion* 3(2), 15–30.

Sorrell, Neil and Ram Narayan (1980). *Indian Music in Performance: A Practical Introduction* (Manchester: Manchester University Press).

Steiner, Roland (2020). 'Woher hat er das? Zum Charakter des Sanskrit-English Dictionary von Monier-Williams', *Zeitschrift der Deutschen Morgenländischen Gesellschaft* 170(1), 107–17, https://doi.org/10.13173/zeitdeutmorggese.170.1.0107 [English translation available at https://www.academia.edu/42883115/On_the_character_of_Monier_Williams_Sanskrit_English_Dictionary]

Thakur, Omkarnath (2005). *Saṅgītāñjali, Vol. III*, ed. by Premlatā Śarma (Vārāṇasi: Praṇav Smriti Nyās).

Trasoff, David (2010). 'The All-India Music Conferences of 1916–1925: Cultural Transformation and Colonial Ideology', in *Hindustani Music: Thirteenth to Twentieth Centuries*, ed. by Joep Boer, Françoise 'Nalini' Delvoye, Jane Harvey and Emmie te Nijenhuis (New Delhi: Manohar), 331–56.

Trivedi, Madhu (2010). 'Music Patronage in the Indo-Persian Context: A Historical Overview', in *Hindustani Music: Thirteenth to Twentieth Centuries*, ed. by Françoise 'Nalini' Delvoye, Jane Harvey and Emmie te Nijenhuis (New Delhi: Manohar), 65–93.

Tulsidas, Goswami (2015). *Vinay Patrikā*, ed. by Hanuman Prasad Pohar (Gorakhpur: Gita Press).

Van der Meer, Wim (1980). *Hindustani Music in the 20th Century* (The Hague: Martinus Nijhoff), https://doi.org/10.1007/978-94-009-8777-7

Vijay Lakshmi, M. (1996). *A Critical Study of Sangita Makaranda of Narada* (New Delhi: Gyan Publishing House).

Wade, Bonnie C. (1997). *Khyāl: Creativity Within North India's Classical Music Tradition* (New Delhi: Munishram Manoharlal).

Wade, Bonnie C. (1998). *Imaging Sound: An Ethnomusicological Study of Music, Art, and Culture in Mughal India* (Chicago, IL and London: University of Chicago Press).

Wade, Bonnie C. (2004/1999). *Music in India: The Classical Traditions*, rev. edn (New Delhi: Manohar).

Widdess, Richard (1979). 'The Kuḍumiyāmalai Inscription: A Source of Early Indian Music in Notation', *Musica Asiatica* 2, 115–50.

Widdess, Richard (1995). *The Rāgas of Early Indian Music: Modes, Melodies and Musical Notations from the Gupta Period to c. 1250* (Oxford: Clarendon Press).

Widdess, Richard (1996). 'The Oral in Writing: Early Indian Musical Notations', *Early Music* 24(3), 391–406, https://doi.org/10.1093/earlyj/xxiv.3.391

Widdess, Richard (2022). 'Vocable and Syllables in Hindustani Slow-*ālāp* Singing' (unpublished paper, Analytical Approaches to World Music conference, University of Sheffield).

Zadeh, Chloe (2012). 'Formulas and the Building Blocks of *Ṭhumrī* Style—A Study in "Improvised" Music', *Analytical Approaches to World Music* 2(1), n.p., https://iftawm.org/journal/oldsite/articles/2012a/Zadeh_AAWM_Vol_2_1.htm

Online Resources

Ager, Simon (n.d.). *Omniglot*, https://www.omniglot.com/

Cologne Digital Sanskrit Dictionaries (n.d.). *Cologne Digital Sanskrit Dictionaries* (Institute of Indology and Sanskrit Studies, University of Cologne), https://www.sanskrit-lexicon.uni-koeln.de/

Gadre, Sudhir V. (n.d.). *Ocean of Ragas*, http://www.oceanofragas.com/#

ITC Sangeet Research Academy (n.d.). *ITC Sangeet Research Academy*, https://www.itcsra.org/

Moutal, Patrick (n.d.). *Hindustani Rag Sangeet Online*, http://www.moutal.eu/

Nadkarni, Sadashiv (2022). 'Bhimsen Joshi Bhairav 1988', *YouTube*, online video recording, 7 April, https://www.youtube.com/watch?v=gXT3VEKCZRk&ab_channel=SadashivNadkarni

Rao, Suvarnalata, and Wim van der Meer; with Rustom Irai and Salil P. Kawli (n.d.). *Music in Motion*, https://autrimncpa.wordpress.com/

Rasikas (2008). 'Gaiye Ganapati' by Tulsidas – Meaning Request', *Rasikas.org*, https://www.rasikas.org/forums/viewtopic.php?t=5710

Ringe, Prakash Vishwanath and Vishwajeet Vishwanath Ringe (n.d.). *Tanarang*, http://www.tanarang.com/

Sangeetveda1 (2017). 'Bharat Ratna Pandit Bhimsen Joshi sings Ragta: Bhairav', *YouTube*, online video recording, 27 March, https://www.youtube.com/watch?v=p18MARsM92g&ab_channel=Sangeetveda1

Yogapedia (2023). 'Sadhana', *Yogapedia*, https://www.yogapedia.com/definition/4994/sadhana

Discography

Gandharva, Kumar (1993). *Baithak, Raga Malkauns, Vol. 4* (Living Media).

Hangal, Gangubai (1994). *Dr. Smt. Gangubai Hangal: Raga Bhairav and Miyan Ki Malhar*, Classic Raaga Collection (Venus, VCDSP 186).

Joshi, Bhimsen (2016). *Bhimsen Joshi—The Versatile: Khayal, Vol. 3* (Sony, DADC S5500001041/Music Today, CD-A 01041).

Rajput, Vijay (2006). *Twilight Raags from North India* (CD. CETL U4NE-1. UK).

Rajput, Vijay (2024). *Rāg samay cakra* (digital release), https://doi.org/10.11647/OBP.0313#resources

List of Audio Examples

RSC = Rāg samay cakra

TR = Twilight Rāgs from North India

All time codes approximate

1.8.1	*Kaṇ*: Rāg Bhūpālī (*RSC*, Track 9, 00:56–01:17)	p. 19
1.8.2	*Kampit*/'after-*kaṇ*':	p. 20
	(a) Rāg Kedār (*RSC*, Track 10, 00:52–00:58)	
	(b) Rāg Kedār (ibid., 01:01–01:07)	
1.8.3	*Miṇḍ*:	p. 21
	(a) Rāg Mālkauns (*RSC*, Track 12, 00:47–00:53)	
	(b) Rāg Mālkauns (ibid., 01:52–02:04)	
	(c) Rāg Megh (*RSC*, Track 13, 00:40–01:02)	
1.8.4	*Āndolan*:	p. 22
	(a) Rāg Bhairav (*RSC*, Track 1, 00:13–00:26)	
	(b) Rāg Bhairav (ibid., 01:33–01:40)	
	(c) Rāg Mālkauns (*RSC*, Track 12, 02:56–03:02)	
1.8.5	*Gamak*:	p. 23
	(a) Rāg Bhairav (*RSC*, Track 1, 00:26–00:30)	
	(b) Rāg Pūriyā Dhanāśrī (*RSC*, Track 7, 02:46–02:53)	
	(c) Rāg Yaman (*RSC*, Track 9, 05:24–05:32)	
1.8.6	*Kaṭhkā*/*murkī*:	p. 24
	(a) Rāg Kedār (*RSC*, Track 10, 00:17–00:26)	
	(b) Rāg Kedār (ibid., 01:07–01:14)	
	(c) Rāg Bhīmpalāsī (*RSC*, Track 5, 01:29–01:37)	
2.5.1	*Rāg samay cakra*, Track 1	p. 54
2.5.2	*Rāg samay cakra*, Track 2	p. 57
2.5.3	*Rāg samay cakra*, Track 3	p. 60
2.5.4	*Rāg samay cakra*, Track 4	p. 63

2.5.5	*Rāg samay cakra*, Track 5	p. 66
2.5.6	*Rāg samay cakra*, Track 6	p. 69
2.5.7	*Rāg samay cakra*, Track 7	p. 72
2.5.8	*Rāg samay cakra*, Track 8	p. 75
2.5.9	*Rāg samay cakra*, Track 9	p. 78
2.5.10	*Rāg samay cakra*, Track 10	p. 81
2.5.11	*Rāg samay cakra*, Track 11	p. 84
2.5.12	*Rāg samay cakra*, Track 12	p. 87
2.5.13	*Rāg samay cakra*, Track 13	p. 90
2.5.14	*Rāg samay cakra*, Track 14	p. 93
3.2.1	Rāg Bhairav, *ālāp* (*RSC*, Track 1, 00:00–02:01)	p. 99
3.2.2	Rāg Bhairav, *ālāp*: opening (establishing phase) (*RSC*, Track 1, 00:00–00:37)	p. 101
3.2.3	Rāg Bhairav, *ālāp*: intermediate ascending phase (*RSC*, Track 1, 00:38–01:01)	p. 103
3.2.4	Rāg Bhairav, *ālāp*: concluding phase of ascent to *tār* Sā (*RSC*, Track 1, 01:02–01:32)	p. 104
3.2.5	Rāg Bhairav, *ālāp*: descending phase (return to *mahdya* Sā) (*RSC*, Track 1, 01:32–02:01)	p. 104
3.2.6	Rāg Toḍī, *ālāp*: establishing phase (*RSC*, Track 2, 00:00–01:13)	p. 106
3.2.7	Rāg Mālkauns, *ālāp*: establishing phase (*RSC*, Track 12, 00:18–01:37)	p. 106
3.2.8	Ascents beyond *tār* Sā:	p. 107
	(a) in Multānī (*RSC*, Track 6, 00:59–01:14)	
	(b) in Toḍī (*RSC*, Track 2, 01:57–02:18)	
	(c) in Pūriyā Dhanāśrī (*RSC*, Track 7, 01:19–01:59)	
3.2.9	Rāg Śuddh Sāraṅg, *ālāp* (*RSC*, Track 3, 00:00–01:35)	p. 108
3.2.10	Rāg Basant, *ālāp*: first descending phase (*RSC*, Track 14, 00:00–00:29)	p. 109
3.2.11	Rāg Basant, *ālāp*: second descending phase, leading to opening of *bandiś* (*RSC*, Track 14, 00:29–01:06)	p. 109
3.2.12	Rāg Yaman, *ālāp*: turn from ascending to descending phase (*RSC*, Track 9, 02:19–02:56)	p. 110
3.2.13	Rāg Bhīmpalāsī, *ālāp* (*RSC*, Track 5, 00:35–02:26)	p. 110
3.2.14	Rāg Bihāg, *ālāp* (*RSC*, Track 11, 00:00–01:34)	p. 110
3.2.15	Rāg Bhūpālī, *ālāp*: ascending and descending phases (*RSC*, Track 8, 00:34–01:30)	p. 111
3.2.16	Rāg Toḍī, *ālāp* (*RSC*, Track 2, 00:00–02:42)	p. 121

3.3.1	Rāg Bhairav, *choṭā khayāl* (*RSC*, Track 1, 02:00–05:06)	p. 127
3.3.2	Rāg Bhairav, *sthāī* (*RSC*, Track 1, 02:00–02:45)	p. 127
3.3.3	Rāg Bhairav, *antarā* (with lead in) and return to *sthāī* (*RSC*, Track 1, 02:43–03:30)	p. 128
3.3.4	Rāg Bhairav: *gamak* inflections (*RSC*, Track 1):	p. 128
	(a) 02:28–02:36	
	(b) 03:11–03:20	
	(c) 03:02–03:12	
3.3.5	Rāg Bhairav: *sargam tāns* (*RSC*, Track 1, 03:20–03:59)	p. 128
3.3.6	Rāg Bhairav, *choṭā khayāl*: concluding *tihāī* (*RSC*, Track 1, 04:32–05:06)	p. 129
3.3.7	Rāg Brindābanī Sāraṅg, *sthāī* and *antarā* (*RSC*, Track 4, 02:09–03:25)	p. 130
3.3.8	Rāg Bhīmpalāsī, *choṭā khayāl* (*RSC*, Track 5, 02:26–05:20)	p. 130
3.3.9	Rāg Yaman, *sthāī*: first-line accumulation (*RSC*, Track 9, 03:10–04:01)	p. 132
3.3.10	Rāg Toḍī: first-line accumulation:	p. 134
	(a) *sthāī* (*RSC*, Track 2, 02:41–03:50)	
	(b) *antarā* (ibid., 04:14–04:46)	
3.3.11	Rāg Basant: repetition–accumulation:	p. 134
	(a) *sthāī* opening line (*RSC*, Track 14, 00:57–01:25)	
	(b) *antarā* opening line (ibid., 02:03–02:28)	
	(c) *antarā*, third line (ibid., 02:29–02:46)	
3.3.12	Rāg Multānī: *bol ālāp* (*RSC*, Track 6, 01:45–02:22)	p. 135
3.3.13	Rāg Megh: *bol ālāp/vistār* (*RSC*, Track 13, 2:15–03:09)	p. 137
3.3.14	Rāg Yaman: *antarā* and *bol ālāp*, with lead-in (*RSC*, Track 9, 04:32–05:45)	p. 140
3.3.15	Rāg Bihāg: *sargam tāns* (*RSC*, Track 11, 03:47–04:46)	p. 140
3.3.16	Rāg Pūriyā Dhanāśrī: *sargam tāns* in a developmental context (*RSC*, Track 7, 05:03–06:03)	p. 143
3.3.17	*Ākār tāns* in a developmental context:	p. 143
	(a) in Rāg Yaman (*RSC*, Track 7, 05:03–06:03)	
	(b) in Rāg Basant (*RSC*, Track 14, 03:40–04:08)	
3.3.18	Four-note-per-*mātrā ākār tāns*:	p. 143
	(a) in Rāg Śuddh Sāraṅg (*RSC*, Track 3, 04:15–04:37)	
	(b) in Rāg Bhūpālī (*RSC*, Track 8, 04:08–04:26)	

3.3.19	*Bol tāns*:	p. 144
	(a) in Rāg Multānī (*RSC*, Track 6, 03:41–03:50)	
	(b) in Rāg Bhūpālī (*RSC*, Track 8, 02:11–02:19)	
3.3.20	Rāg Mālkauns: *gamak tāns* (*RSC*, Track 12, 04:47–05:15)	p. 144
3.3.21	Rāg Multānī: *behlāvā* (*RSC*, Track 6, 02:34–03:20)	p. 145
3.3.22	Rāg Kedār: *lay bāṇṭ* and *laykārī* (*RSC*, Track 10, 02:30–03:12)	p. 145
3.3.23	*Lay* increase:	p. 147
	(a) Rāg Yaman (*RSC*, Track 9, 06:20–06:49)	
	(b) Rāg Mālkauns (*RSC*, Track 12, 05:48–06:14)	
	(c) Rāg Pūriyā Dhanāśrī (*RSC*, Track 7, 04:41–05:11)	
	(d) Rāg Pūriyā Dhanāśrī (ibid., 05:54–06:32)	
3.3.24	Rāg Pūriyā Dhanāśrī: opening phase (*sthāī* in extended mode) (*RSC*, Track 7, 02:20–03:43)	p. 160
3.3.25	Rāg Pūriyā Dhanāśrī: beginning of elaboration phase (*antarā* in extended mode) (*RSC*, Track 7, 03:43–04:49)	p. 160
4.2.1	Rāg Bhairav: *baṛā khayāl, sthāī* (*TR*, Track 2, 00:00–01:09)	p. 166
4.2.2	Rāg Bhairav: *baṛā khayāl, antarā* (*TR*, Track 2, 11:20–12:20)	p. 166
4.2.3	Rāg Bhairav: *drut khayāl, sthāī* (*TR*, Track 3, 00:41–01:09)	p. 171
4.2.4	Rāg Bhairav: *drut khayāl, antarā* (*TR*, Track 3, 04:26–05:03)	p. 171
4.3.1	Rāg Yaman: *baṛā khayāl, sthāī* (*TR*, Track 5, 00:00–01:24)	p. 191
4.3.2	Rāg Yaman: *baṛā khayāl, antarā* (*TR*, Track 5, 10:04–11:20)	p. 191
4.3.3	*Mukhṛā* of the *sthāī*, with tabla entry (*TR*, Track 5, 00:00–00:08)	p. 195
4.3.4	*Baṛhat*: development of *sthāī* from end of *āvartan* 1 to beginning of *āvartan* 3 (*TR*, Track 5, 00:55–02:31)	p. 197
4.3.5	*Āvartan* 4 (with opening and closing *mukhṛās*): elaboration of Ga and Ḿa (*TR*, Track 5, 03:19–04:33)	p. 198
4.3.6	*Āvartan* 8: prolongation of Ni, leading to *tār* Sā (*TR*, Track 5, 7:52–09:10)	p. 200
4.3.7	*Āvartans* 9 and 10: prolongation of *tār* Sā leading to *antarā* sung complete (*TR*, Track 5, 08:51–11:22)	p. 200
4.3.8	*Āvartan* 11: *laykārī* (*TR*, Track 5, 11:20–12:04)	p. 201
4.3.9	*Āvartan* 12: *sargam tāns* (*TR*, Track 5, 12:26–13:24)	p. 202
4.3.10	*Āvartan* 13: *gamak tāns* (*TR*, Track 5, 13:25–13:47)	p. 202
4.3.11	*Āvartan* 14: *ākār tāns* (*TR*, Track 5, 14:23–15:28)	p. 202
4.3.12	*Āvartan* 15: return to *bol ālāp* singing style (*TR*, Track 5, 15:23–16:35)	p. 202

List of Figures

1.2.1	Scale degrees/note names in *sargam* notation. Created by author (2024), CC BY-NC-SA.	p. 3
1.3.1	Bhatkhande's *ṭhāṭ*s and their scale types (after Powers 1992: 13). Created by author (2024), CC BY-NC-SA.	p. 6
1.4.1	*Tīntāl*: metrical structure and clap pattern. Created by author (2024), CC BY-NC-SA.	p. 8
1.4.2	*Ektāl*: metrical structure and clap pattern. Created by author (2024), CC BY-NC-SA.	p. 10
1.6.1.	*Samay Rāga*—based on twelve time periods (after website of ITC Sangeet Research Academy). Created by author (2024), CC BY-NC-SA.	p. 13
1.6.2	*Rāg samay cakra*—based on eight time periods. Created by author (2024), CC BY-NC-SA.	p. 14
1.8.1	*Kaṇ*: notation of Audio Example 1.8.1. Created by author (2024), CC BY-NC-SA.	p. 19
1.8.2	*Kampit*/'after-*kaṇ*': notation of Audio Example 1.8.2. Created by author (2024), CC BY-NC-SA.	p. 20
1.8.3	*Miṇḍ*: notation of Audio Example 1.8.3. Created by author (2024), CC BY-NC-SA.	p. 21
1.8.4	*Āndolan*: notation of Audio Example 1.8.4. Created by author (2024), CC BY-NC-SA.	p. 22
1.8.5	*Gamak*: notation of Audio Example 1.8.5. Created by author (2024), CC BY-NC-SA.	p. 23
1.8.6	*Kaṭhkā*/*murkī*: notation of Audio Example 1.8.6. Created by author (2024), CC BY-NC-SA.	p. 25
2.3.1	*Bandiś* in Rāg Toḍī: notation of *antarā*. Created by author (2024), CC BY-NC-SA.	p. 50
2.3.2	*Bandiś* in Rāg Mālkauns: notation of *sthāī*. Created by author (2024), CC BY-NC-SA.	p. 51
3.2.1	*Ālāp* in Rāg Bhairav: opening (establishing phase), transcription. Created by author (2024), CC BY-NC-SA.	p. 101
3.2.2	*Ālāp* in Rāg Bhairav: intermediate ascending phase, transcription. Created by author (2024), CC BY-NC-SA.	p. 103

3.2.3	*Ālāp* in Rāg Bhairav: concluding ascending phase, transcription. Created by author (2024), CC BY-NC-SA.	p. 104
3.2.4	*Ālāp* in Rāg Bhairav: descending phase, transcription. Created by author (2024), CC BY-NC-SA.	p. 105
3.2.5	*Ālāp* in Rāg Bhūpālī: ascending and descending phase, transcription. Created by author (2024), CC BY-NC-SA.	p. 112
3.2.6	Relative duration of *ālāp* and composition stages in Hindustani classical genres. Created by author (2024), CC BY-NC-SA.	p. 114
3.2.7	*Rāg samay cakra*: track durations. Created by author (2024), CC BY-NC-SA.	p. 115
3.2.8	*Rāg samay cakra*: *ālāp* and *choṭā khayāl* durations. Created by author (2024), CC BY-NC-SA.	p. 116
3.2.9	*Rāg samay cakra*: *ālāp* durations as percentage of track durations. Created by author (2024), CC BY-NC-SA.	p. 117
3.2.10	*Rāg samay cakra*: durations before and after reaching *tār* Sā within *ālāp*. Created by author (2024), CC BY-NC-SA.	p. 117
3.2.11	Rāg Bhairav, *ālāp*: syllable sequence. Created by author (2024), CC BY-NC-SA.	p. 120
3.2.12	Rāg Toḍī, *ālāp*: syllable sequence. Created by author (2024), CC BY-NC-SA.	p. 121
3.3.1	Rāg Bhairav: *sargam tāns*, notated. Created by author (2024), CC BY-NC-SA.	p. 128
3.3.2	Rāg Bhīmpalāsī, *choṭā khayāl*: repetition structure. Created by author (2024), CC BY-NC-SA.	p. 131
3.3.3	Rāg Yaman, *sthāī*: first-line accumulation. Created by author (2024), CC BY-NC-SA.	p. 133
3.3.4	Rāg Multānī: *bol ālāp*, transcription. Created by author (2024), CC BY-NC-SA.	p. 136
3.3.5	Models for timing of *bol ālāp/vistār* within a *choṭā khayāl* (not drawn to scale). Created by author (2024), CC BY-NC-SA.	p. 138
3.3.6	Rāg Bihāg: *sargam tāns*, notation. Created by author (2024), CC BY-NC-SA.	p. 141
3.3.7	Rāg Kedār: *lay bāṇṭ* and *laykārī*, notation. Created by author (2024), CC BY-NC-SA.	p. 146
3.3.8	Rāg Bhairav, *choṭā khayāl*: (a) event synopsis; (b) event string. Created by author (2024), CC BY-NC-SA.	p. 157
3.3.9	Rāg Pūriyā Dhanāśrī, *choṭā khayāl*: (a) event synopsis; (b) event string. Created by author (2024), CC BY-NC-SA.	p. 159
4.2.1	Notation of *baṛā khayāl*, 'Bālamavā more saīyā̃': (a) *sthāī*; (b) *antarā*. Created by author (2024), CC BY-NC-SA.	p. 167

4.2.2 Opening of 'Bālamavā more saīyā̃', as performed by Gangubai Hangal (1994: Track 1). Created by author (2024), CC BY-NC-SA. p. 168

4.2.3 Notation of *drut khayāl*, 'Suno to sakhī batiyā': (a) *sthāī*; (b) *antarā*. Created by author (2024), CC BY-NC-SA. p. 171

4.2.4 'Suno to': musical and textual rhyme patterns. Created by author (2024), CC BY-NC-SA. p. 173

4.2.5 'Suno to': metrical play. Created by author (2024), CC BY-NC-SA. p. 174

4.2.6 'Suno to': event sequence shown in graphical form. Created by author (2024), CC BY-NC-SA. p. 175

4.2.7 'Suno to': event synopsis. Created by author (2024), CC BY-NC-SA. p. 181

4.2.8 'Suno to': (a) event string; (b) event substrings. Created by author (2024), CC BY-NC-SA. p. 183

4.2.9 'Suno to': event substrings/salient moments. Created by author (2024), CC BY-NC-SA. p. 184

4.3.1 Elements of a typical full-length *khayāl* performance, with durations from VR's Yaman recording (*TR*, Tracks 4–6). Created by author (2024), CC BY-NC-SA. p. 188

4.3.2 Typical event sequence of a *baṛā khayāl*, with time codes of their occurrence in VR's Yaman recording (*TR*, Track 5). Created by author (2024), CC BY-NC-SA. p. 189

4.3.3 Heuristic notation of *bandiś*: (a) *sthāī*; (b) *antarā*. Created by author (2024), CC BY-NC-SA. p. 192

4.3.4 Transcription of *bandiś*: (a) *sthāī*; (b) *antarā*. Created by author (2024), CC BY-NC-SA. p. 194

4.3.5 *Baṛā khayāl* in Rāg Yaman: stages of *baṛhat*. Created by author (2024), CC BY-NC-SA. p. 198

4.3.6 Second part of *baṛā khayāl*: *laykārī* etc. Created by author (2024), CC BY-NC-SA. p. 201

Index

Indexing Policy

Certain terms, conceptually crucial to the content of this book, and hence prevalent within it, potentially yield an unwieldy number of index entries. When these cannot be wholly managed by creating subentries, they have been omitted or selectively treated—other, more fruitful ways to interrogate them are through chapter subheadings, as listed in the Table of Contents; or (when reading the e-book) through an electronic search of the text; or by consulting the Glossary.

However, so that their significance does not go unrecognised, I list such terms in the following 'anti-index', which falls into several groups—viz.:

(i) Wholly omitted terms:

antarā; *āvartan*; *bol ālāp*; expansion [musical] (but *see baṛhat*; development [musical]); Hindustani classical music; khayāl; performance conventions (but *see* performance grammar); phrase; scale (but *see āroh*; *avroh*); *vistār* (but *see baṛhat*); *sthāī*.

(ii) Terms indexed only by their subentries:

ālāp; *baṛā khayāl*; dhrupad; guru; *rāg*; Rajput, Vijay (VR); *svar*; *tān*s.

(iii) Terms indexed only when used outside the *rāg* specifications of Section 2.5:

āroh; *auḍav*; *avroh*; *jāti*; *pakaḍ*; performing time; *prahar*; *ṣāḍav*; *sampūrṇ*; *ṭhāṭ*.

Other important, frequently used terms are indexed selectively. The titles of the book's two accompanying albums, *Rāg samay cakra* and *Twilight Rāgs from North India*, are not indexed. Square brackets are used to indicate a particular usage of a term.

accumulation of intensity 9, 17, 107, 152, 154, 155, 197, 201, 203. *See also* first-line accumulation; *See also* intensification
Adāraṅg. *See* Firoz Khan (Adāraṅg)
ākār 119–120, 197
Akbar, Emperor 28, 36, 122
alaṅkār 19, 42, 101, 113, 193. *See also* ornamentation
ālāp. *See also anibaddh*
ascending phase of 103–105, 107–111, 113, 117, 120
descending phase of 103–105, 108–110, 112–113, 120, 139
duration and proportion of 100, 104–105, 114–117
establishing phase of 102–103, 105–106, 108, 110–111, 113, 120
phase schema of 102, 106–107, 109–110, 112–113, 117, 149
ālāp syllables 119–124, 137
ālapti 99–100, 107, 137
algebra [in musical analysis] 148, 160
Ali, Daud 26
All-India Music Conferences 30
Alter, Andrew 38–39
āndolan/āndolit 5, 21, 24, 54, 90, 101–103
anibaddh xxiii, 44, 99, 115, 126, 136–137, 187–188, 190–191, 193, 195, 197, 201, 204, 206
āroh 5, 63, 75, 105. *See also āroh–avroh*
āroh–avroh 53, 78, 103, 139, 141–142
ati vilambit khayāl 187, 188, 193. *See also baṛā khayāl*
aucār 108, 188
auḍav 5, 53, 78
audience 8, 9, 10, 42, 98, 114, 124, 142, 184, 185, 186, 187, 203, 206. *See also* listeners; *See also rasika*
Aurangzeb, Emperor 28
autoethnography xi, xii, 205. *See also* ethnography; *See also* ethnomusicology, ethnomusicologists
Avadhī [language] 76
avroh 5, 63, 66, 75, 84, 105. *See also āroh–avroh*
Ayers, John xii, 164, 203

Bagchee, Sandeep 145
Bakhle, Janaki 30–33, 37
Bali, Rai Umanath 30
bandiś 18, 44, 52, 126, 127, 130, 189. *See also cīz*
and *ālāp* 99, 105, 108, 114, 119
and *lay* 145–147, 187, 204
and *rāg* 73, 129, 195
and *tāl* 51, 127, 193
hierarchy of components within 151, 155
identity of 134, 168–169, 193, 196
notation of 45, 49, 61, 165, 190–191, 195
performance of 50–51, 126, 149, 174
repetition within 127, 130, 131, 144. *See also* first-line accumulation
text of 17, 46, 88, 137, 165, 172, 190
bandiś. *See also* composition
Bandopadhyay [Banerjee], Ashok Kumar 205
Bandyopadhyaya, Shripada 15, 31
Banerjee, Jayasri 39
Bangha, Imre xii, xiv, xxii, 47
baṛā khayāl. *See also vilambit khayāl*
and *ālāp* 17, 106, 108, 115, 188
and *baṛhat* 17, 106, 138, 196–202
and *laykārī* 18, 201–202
and *tāl* 188, 191, 193–194, 204
bandiś of 17, 165, 167–168, 179, 190–191, 195–196, 200, 204
duration of 188
event sequence of 17, 148, 189
inception of 17, 195
notation of 190–191, 195
speed of 187, 201
temporality of 187, 189–190, 193, 195–196, 203, 206
baṛhat 138, 139, 197. *See also baṛā khayāl*: and *baṛhat*
Barnawi, Shaikh Bahauddin 27
Beck, Guy L. 11
behlāvā 129, 139, 144–145
beloved [in song texts] 61, 67, 73, 165. *See also* loved one, lover [in song texts]
bhajan 8, 76, 126, 164
bhakti tradition 27, 38
Bharata-bhāṣya (Nānyadeva) 15
Bhatkhande, Vishnu Narayan 6, 30–31, 87
and modernisation 4, 30
and *rāg* descriptions 30, 53, 57, 60, 63, 72, 78, 84, 90, 108
and time theory 15, 30, 69, 72
critiques of 30–31
notation system of 3, 30, 49–50, 191
ṭhāṭ system of 6–7, 15, 53
Bhogal, Gurminder Kaur 4
bimusicality xix
bīn 28. *See* also vīṇā
birādarī 36. *See also khāndān, khāndānī*; *See also* hereditary musicians
Bohlman, Philip V. xvii, xviii
Böhtlingk, Otto 205
bol bāṇṭ 18, 145–146, 184, 201
Bor, Joep xxii, 6, 15, 24, 28, 63, 93
Bose, Manali 169
Brahaspati, Sulochana 28, 31
Brahman musicians 32, 36
Braj Bhāṣā [language and poetry] xiv, xv, 46, 48, 73, 88, 172
Bṛhad-deśī (Mataṅga) 15
British [in India] 28, 30
Brown, Katherine Butler 27, 28. *See also* Schofield, Katherine Butler (née Brown)

cakradār 154
calan 60
Chakrabarty, Ajit Kumar 41
Chakrabarty, Ajoy 41–42
chāp. *See* pen name
Chaurasia, Hariprasad xvii, 38
choṭā khayāl 17, 44, 88, 126, 127, 128, 129, 138, 167, 179, 204. *See also drut khayāl*
and *ālāp* 105, 115
closing phase of 150, 182
duration of 44, 52, 116, 130, 147, 188

elaboration phase of 149–150, 154, 156, 160, 182–183
event sequence of 51, 148–149, 156, 159, 174, 179
grammar of 127, 138, 156, 161, 180
musical elements of 151
opening phase of 149, 182
Choudhury, Monojit xvi
chronos 195–196, 199
cīz 126. *See also bandiś*; *See also* composition; *See also gat*
clap pattern [of a *tāl*] 8–10, 50, 173
Clarke, David (DC) xi, xiii, xviii, xix, xxi, xxiii, 16, 46, 104, 113, 164–165, 199
Clayton, Martin xxiv, 8, 10–12, 138, 145, 147, 153, 187–188, 201–202
communalism 31
complexity [musical] 81, 99, 129, 130, 142, 148, 155, 159, 160, 202. *See also* simplicity [musical]
composition 18, 61, 124, 126, 129, 141, 142, 167, 190, 193, 195, 204. *See also bandiś*; *See also cīz*; *See also gat*
notation of 190, 193
consciousness xiii, 11, 16, 20, 108, 118, 124, 137, 148, 161, 185, 188, 203. *See also* unconsciousness, pre-consciousness, non-consciousness
multiple drafts model of xxiii, 185
cross-rhythm 61, 64, 122, 130, 146, 154, 173. *See also laykārī*
cutkulā 27

Ḍāgar *bānī* 12
Dagar [Ḍāgar], Wasifuddin 123
Daniélou, Alain 14
Dartington Hall xviii
Das Sharma [Dasasarma], Amal 34
Datta, Asoke Kumar 11
Debnath, Arun xviii
de le Haye, David xii, 44
Delhi 27, 28, 35. *See also gharānā*: Delhi; *See also* New Delhi
Qavvāls of 27
Sultanate 33, 36
Delvoye, Françoise 'Nalini' 4
Dennett, Daniel xxiii, 185–186
descriptive music writing 49, 167, 194. *See also* prescriptive music writing; *See also* transcription [musical]
Deshpande, M. G. xiii, 72, 76, 84
Deshpande, Vamanrao H. 36, 187–188
deśī [tradition] 28
deśī-rāgā system 7
Deva, B. Chaitanya 12, 15–16
devadāsī 37
Devanāgarī [script] xv, xvi, 3, 45–47, 190
development [musical] 52, 114, 126, 130, 135, 139, 143, 147, 150, 151, 152, 153, 156, 196. *See also* elaboration, musical
dhamār 75
Dholpuri, Mahmood xii, xiii, 101, 131, 143
Dhore, Manikrao L. xvi
dhrupad
ālāp of 99–100, 114, 122–123
and k̲hayāl 17, 22, 28, 115, 122, 124, 154
features of 19, 24, 46, 126, 140, 144–145, 154, 202
syllabary of 122–123
VR's relationship to 123–124
diacritics xv, 47
divine, the 17, 28, 39, 46, 55, 124, 165, 172. *See also* ineffable, the
Doffman, Mark 195
drone 2, 8, 11–12, 101
drut k̲hayāl 70, 144, 164, 169, 174, 183. *See also choṭā k̲hayāl*
du Perron, Lalita xxiii, 46, 58, 88, 172

dugun 145–146, 202
ekgun 145–146
elaboration, musical 99, 111, 137, 138, 145, 152, 198. *See also baṛhat*; *See also choṭā k̲hayāl*: elaboration phase of; *See also* development [musical]; *See also* extemporisation; *See also* improvisation
embodiment xxi, 4, 42
empirical analysis, data, experience, reality 11, 15, 100, 109, 117–118, 126, 179–180, 183–184
ethnography 205. *See also* autoethnography; *See also* ethnomusicology, ethnomusicologists
ethnomusicology, ethnomusicologists xvii, xix, 33, 49. *See also* ethnography
eventfulness [musical] 190, 195. *See also kairos*
event string 157, 160, 182–183
event synopsis 156, 159–160, 180
extemporisation 17, 44, 99, 114, 126, 127, 144, 174, 180, 197, 199. *See also* improvisation

Farrell, Gerry 41–42
female musicians 37
feudalism 37–38
fieldwork 33, 204
film song/filmi 19, 78, 126, 164
Firoz Khan (Adāraṅg) 28
first encounter [as ethnomusicological concept] xvii, xviii
first-line accumulation 132, 134, 139, 144, 150–152, 154, 159–160, 179, 183
flow [musical] 108, 109, 115, 127, 137, 143, 183, 189, 195, 199, 202. *See also rāg*: *cancal*
of a tāl 8–9
folk music 28, 75, 164

Gadre, Sudhir V. xxiii
gamak 19, 22, 23, 24, 91, 101, 128, 144. *See also tāns*: *gamak*
gaṇḍā bandhan ceremony 35
Gandharva, Kumar 108
Gandharva Mahavidyalaya xvii, 30, 37, 67, 76, 169
Gandharva, Sawai xi, xiii, 36, 168
Gaṇeś (Ganesh) 76
gat 115, 126. *See also* composition
gāyakī xviii. *See also* Rajput, Vijay (VR): *gāyakī* of
gharānā 19, 34, 36–37, 99–100, 117, 124, 140
Agra 61
Ajrara xiii

Delhi xiii, xiv, 36
Gwalior 144
Imdad Khan 36
Kirānā xi, 12, 22, 44, 124, 129, 154, 165, 168–169, 187–188, 203
ghazal 126
goal pitch 110, 111, 113. *See also* organising pitch; *See also svar*: *nyās*
Gonda, Jan 26, 38
grah svar. *See svar*: *grah*
grāma-jāti system 7
grāmarāga system 7
grammar [linguistic] 37, 46, 161
grammar [musical] 113. *See also choṭā khayāl*: grammar of; *See also* performance grammar; *See also rāg*: grammar of
Gundecha brothers 12, 38
Gupta era 26
guru. *See also guru-śiṣyā paramparā*; *See also ustād*
attributes of xvii, 32, 35, 39–40
authority of 37, 42
history of 33–34, 37
idealisation of 37–39, 41
payment of. *See guru dakśinā*
problematics of 39
guru dakśinā 35
guru-bahan 35, 204
guru-bhāī 35, 204
gurukul xvii, xviii, 34, 37–38
guru-śiṣyā paramparā xviii, xxi, 32–33, 37, 39
and modernity 32, 38–39
history of 33, 35
problematics of 33, 39
scholarly accounts of 33–34
tropes of 33–35, 41

Hangal, Gangubai 54, 108, 168
Haridas, Swami 36
harmonium xii, xiii, xiv, 2, 101, 131, 139, 143, 174, 185
hereditary musicians 4, 30, 32, 33, 34, 35, 36, 37. *See also birādarī*; *See also khāndān, khāndānī*
female. *See* female musicians
heuristic [approach to notation] 49, 58, 193–194, 200
heuristic [approach to theory] xxiii, 98, 105, 124, 138, 148, 199
Hindavi [language] xv, 47
Hindi [language] xv, 30, 46–47, 52–53, 76, 119, 196. *See* also Hindavi [language]
Hindu culture, religion 5, 27, 30, 32, 34–36, 38, 76, 122
Hindustānī-saṅgīta-paddhati (Bhatkhande) 31
Hood, Mantle xix
Husain Shah Sharqi, Sultan 27
Hussain, Afaq 33–34
Hussain, Fida xii, xiv, 203
Hussain Khan, Sakhawat 31
Hussain, Shahbaz xii, xiv, xxi, 203
Hussain, Zakir xvii
hypotaxis 161, 179, 182, 184. *See also* parataxis

IAST (International Alphabet of Sanskrit Transliteration) xv, 47
ideology xxii, 4
illiteracy 30. *See also* literacy; *See also* orality
Imām, Hakim Karam 122
improvisation 32, 52. *See also* extemporisation
and *ālāp* 17, 99–100, 124, 135
and *bandiś* 126, 129, 131
and *tāl* 9, 188, 206
in a *baṛā khayāl* 17, 189, 196
in a *choṭā khayāl* 18
processes and techniques of 2, 17–18, 42, 126, 129, 142, 174, 197, 204
vs composition 4, 129
ineffable, the xi, 122, 148. *See also* divine, the
intensification 11, 121, 130, 134, 141, 146, 147, 153, 195. *See also* accumulation of intensity
interlude [musical] 131, 139, 143, 149–150, 154, 156
internalisation [of musical material] xix, 41–42, 99, 118, 126, 161, 184, 203
ITC Sangeet Research Academy 13, 38–39

Jahandar Shah, Emperor 29
Jairazbhoy, Nazir A. 7, 15, 31, 69
Jani, Kalpesh 102
jāti 53, 54, 63, 78. *See also grāma-jāti* system
Jaunpur 27
javārī 11
jazz 195
jhālā 99, 114–115
joṛ 99, 114–115
Joshi, Bhimsen xi, xvii, 34, 78–79, 168
and dhrupad 123
and *gharānās* 36, 203
singing style of 22, 36, 129, 140, 164, 168–169

kairos 195, 196, 199. *See also* eventfulness [musical]
kalāvant 122
kampan/kampit 20, 101
kaṇ 19–20, 51, 54, 66, 69, 81, 90, 101, 194
Karnatak tradition xvi, 8, 14, 19, 31, 39, 102
Kashalkar, Sanyukta 38–40
kaṭhkā 24, 25, 103, 200. *See also murkī*
Katz, Jonathan xii, xiv, xxii, 47
Katz, Max 30
Kaufmann, Walter 90
khālī 9–10, 50–51, 127, 137, 141, 146, 156, 173
Khan, Abdul Karim xi, 36
Khan, Abdul Wahid 187
Khan, Ali Akbar xxiv, 24
Khan, Amir 91, 187
Khan, Athar Hussain xii, xiii, 127, 131
Khan, Bade Ghulam Ali (Sabaraṅg) 55
Khan, Fayaz (Prem Pīyā) 61
Khan, Karamutallah 30
Khan, Mahawat (Manaraṅg) 79
Khan, Nasir 35
Khan, Niaz Ahmed 197
Khan, Sabri 33–35

pedagogy xxiii, 33, 36, 37, 38, 100, 187. *See also* oral pedagogy, tradition, transmission
pen name 28, 61, 91
performance grammar xxiii, 156, 160, 161, 179. *See also choṭā khayāl*: grammar of; *See also* grammar [musical]; *See also rāg*: grammar of
performing time. *See samay* principle; *See* time theory [of *rāg*]
Persian [language] 17, 27, 31, 41, 47, 122
Phansalkar, Janhavi 42
phenomenology
  of performance xxiii, 118, 186
  of sound 10–11. *See nād*
play, playfulness 18, 64, 79, 122, 124, 152, 173, 188, 189, 195, 206. *See also laykārī*
Pohar, Hanuman Prasad 76
Post, Jennifer C. 37
Powers, Harold S. 5–7, 15, 31, 161
prahar 13, 72
prakriti 87
pralaya 204, 205, 206. *See also laya* [Sanskr.]
praṇām xix, 35
Prem Pīyā. *See* Khan, Fayaz (Prem Pīyā)
prescriptive music writing 49, 51, 167, 193. *See also* descriptive music writing
prolongation [of svar]. *See svar*: prolongation of
pronunciation xvi, 37, 44–45, 47–48
pūrvaṅg 15. *See also rāg*: *pūrvaṅg pradhan*

qaul 27
qavvāl 122. *See* also Delhi, Qavvāls of
Qureshi, Regula Burkhardt 5–6, 33–37, 122

Rādhā 28, 46, 58, 94, 172
rāg. *See also* modality; *See also rāgs* referred to
  and *ras* 5, 57, 66, 75, 81, 87, 90, 107, 121, 124, 169
  cancal 90, 93
  definition of 5–7
  gambhīr 21, 87, 90, 93, 147
  grammar of 5, 53–54, 69, 93, 102–103, 105–107, 109, 129, 198–199, 203
  monsoon xxi, 14, 21, 44, 90, 137
  parmel-praveśak 69
  pūrvaṅg pradhan 109
  sandhi prakāś 15–16, 107
  specification of 30, 45, 53, 90, 164
  springtime xxi, 14, 44, 93–94, 147
  taxonomy of 6
  uttaraṅg pradhan 93, 117
Rāg Darpan (Faqīrullāh) 28
rāga-rāgini system 6
rāgs referred to
  Aḍānā 109
  Bāgeśrī 66
  Basant xxi, 14, 44, 93, 116–117, 134, 143–144
  Bhairav 5, 21, 44, 54, 99, 101–104, 108, 127, 129, 145, 156, 164–165, 167, 169
  Bhīmpalāsī 25, 66, 69, 110, 130, 142, 149
  Bhūpālī 6, 19, 75, 111–112, 143
  Bihāg 5, 81, 84, 110, 130, 140, 142
  Bilāval 84
  Brindābanī Sāraṅg 60, 63–64, 130
  Darbārī Kānaḍā 109
  Deś 63
  Deśkār 75, 109
  Dhanāśrī 66
  Dhānī 66
  Hamīr 81, 84
  Hansadhvanī 76
  Kalyāṇ 6
  Kamod 81
  Kedār 6, 20, 25, 81, 84, 130, 145, 149
  Lalit 93, 109
  Madhmād Sāraṅg 90
  Malhār 90
  Mālkauns 14, 16, 21, 51, 87, 106, 108, 116, 147, 149, 153
  Māru Bihāg 84
  Mārvā 57, 76
  Megh xxi, 14, 21, 44, 63, 90, 137, 139
  Megh Malhār 90
  Multānī 5, 57, 69, 107, 135, 137–139, 144
  Paraj 93
  Patdīp 66
  Pūriyā Dhanāśrī 22, 69–70, 72, 143, 147, 149, 159
  Pūrvī 72
  Śuddh Sāraṅg 60, 108, 117, 131–132, 143, 149
  Śyām Kalyāṇ 60
  Toḍī 5, 50, 57, 69, 106, 121, 133, 144, 149
  Yaman xviii, xxii, xxiii, 6, 16, 22, 78, 110, 132, 134, 139, 143, 147, 164, 188, 190–191, 195, 198, 200–201
Rajput, Vijay (VR)
  and Kirānā *gharānā* 36, 169
  as guru of DC xi, xviii, xix, xxiii, 100, 123, 190, 199, 204
  biography of xiii, xvii, xviii
  gāyakī of 22, 60–61, 84, 115–116, 119–121, 131, 137, 142, 144–146, 165, 169, 200, 203
  teachers of xi, 22, 34, 36, 55, 61, 67, 72, 76, 79, 82, 84, 91, 164, 169
  thoughts of 24–25, 90, 102, 109, 114, 118, 123–124, 129, 137, 199
Rakha, Alla xiv, xvii
Rampur 28, 31
Ranade, Ashok 24, 52, 99, 102, 126, 196
Rao, Suvarnalata xxii, 108
ras 5, 22, 32, 124. *See also rāg*: and *ras*
  karuṇ 6, 57, 66–67, 107, 121, 169
  śānt 6, 75, 87
  śṛṅgār 5, 81, 169
  vīr 6, 87, 90
rasika xi, 98
recordings, historic 36, 49, 100, 168–169
register [musical] 3, 17, 99, 142, 151, 152, 155, 184, 195, 197, 202. *See also pūrvaṅg*; *See also uttaraṅg*
  and syllable choice 123
repetition
  in *riyāz* 41–42, 126, 129

musical 91, 128, 129, 130, 131, 134, 151, 159, 179. *See also* *bandiś*: repetition within; *See also* first-line accumulation
rhythmic density 147, 153. *See also* *lay* density
Ringe, Prakash Vishwanath and Vishwajeet Vishwanath xxiii, 72, 84, 90
riyāz 34, 41, 42, 54. *See also* repetition: in *riyāz*
Roth, Rudolph 205
Rowell, Lewis 11–12
Roy, Sudipta xii, xxiii, 190, 204–205
Ruckert, George E. xxiv, 24, 129, 138, 196

Sabaraṅg. *See* Khan, Bade Ghulam Ali (Sabaraṅg)
Sadāraṅg. *See* Ni'mat Khan (Sadāraṅg)
ṣāḍav 5, 53, 78
śāgird 32, 35, 37. *See* also *śiṣyā*
Sahasrabuddhe, Veena xiii, xxiv, 42, 187
sam 8–10, 17, 50, 129, 134, 141, 146, 154, 156, 167–168, 196–197
samay principle 15, 44, 54, 69, 187. *See also* time theory [of *rāg*]
history of 14
sampūrṇ 5, 53–54, 78
saṃvādī. *See* *svar*: *vādī* and *saṃvādī*
Saṅgīta-makaranda (Nārada) 14–15
Saṅgīta-ratnākara (Śārṅgadeva) 15, 31, 99–100, 107
Sankaran, Sajan 38
Sanskrit [language] xv, 3, 5, 13, 26, 32, 41, 47–48, 99, 161, 204–206
Sanyal, Ritwik xxiv, 2, 20, 24, 48, 100, 102, 107, 113, 122–123, 144
Sāraṅg *aṅg* 60, 63, 90
sāraṅgī xiii, xxiv, 2, 33, 35, 41
sargam notation 2–4, 45, 49–50, 191, 193
sargam syllables 18, 119, 128, 140, 142, 197, 202
sarod xxiv, 24, 30–31, 41
śāstras 4, 100, 102, 106, 124
Scarimbolo, Justin 32
Schippers, Huib 38
Schofield, Katherine Butler (née Brown) 4, 27. *See also* Brown, Katherine Butler
schwa xv, 48
secularisation [of music] 28, 30, 203
Seeger, Charles 49, 167, 193–194
Shah Jahan, Emperor 28
Shankar, Ravi xvii
Sher Muhammed, Shaikh 27
Shukla, Richa 169
Sikh scholars, musicians 4
silsilā 32. *See also* *guru-śiṣyā paramparā*
simplicity [musical] 19, 75, 99, 127, 128, 130, 140, 142, 148, 150, 151, 152, 154, 156, 157. *See also* complexity [musical]
Singh, Kirit 4
śiṣyā xi, xviii, xix, xxiii, 32, 34, 35, 38, 39, 40, 41, 190, 204, 206. *See also* *guru-śiṣyā paramparā*; *See also* *śāgird*
Śiva 54, 76, 122
Slawek, Stephen 2, 39
smartphone 11, 38, 190
Snell, Rupert 46–48
sonata 189
song. *See* *bandiś*
Sooklal, Anil 38
Sorrell, Neil xxiv, 9–10, 42
śruti 4–5, 11, 32, 54
śruti box 11
staff notation 49, 50. *See also* *sargam* notation
status [of musicians] 11, 35, 38, 40
Steiner, Roland 205
Sufi culture, musicians 27, 36, 122
svar. *See also* *svar* space
anugāmī 87
grah 106, 111
nyās 87, 105, 111, 113, 197, 198, 199. *See also* goal pitch; *See also* organising pitch
prolongation of 103, 137, 152, 168, 199
samvad 87
vādī and *saṃvādī* 5, 21, 53–54, 72, 75, 90, 102, 105–106, 113
vivādī 81, 84
svar space 102, 106, 108, 110–113, 199
syllables. *See* *ālāp* syllables; *See* dhrupad: syllabary of; *See* register [musical]: and syllable choice; *See* *sargam* syllables; *See* *tarānā*; *See* vocables
syntax 41, 53, 122, 123, 137, 159, 179, 185, 186. *See also* *choṭā khayāl*: grammar of; *See also* grammar [musical]; *See also* performance grammar; *See also* *rāg*: grammar of

tabla xiii, 2, 8–9, 17, 33, 44, 99, 127, 129, 131, 134, 147, 150, 188, 193, 195
bols 3, 10
takhallus. *See* pen name
tāl 2, 8, 9, 17, 32, 50, 99, 123, 126, 134, 137, 142, 145, 156, 167, 205, 206. *See also* *bandiś*: and *tāl*; *See also* *baṛā khayāl*: and *tāl*; *See also* clap pattern [of a *tāl*]; *See also* improvisation: and *tāl*; *See also* *tāls* referred to
tālī 9–10, 50, 169
tālīm xi, xviii, 35
tāls referred to
dādrā 8
drut ektāl 10, 109, 143, 169
ektāl 8–10, 94, 173
jhaptāl 8
keharvā 8
madhya lay tīntāl 64, 127
rūpak 8–9
tīntāl 8–10, 50, 128, 136, 141–142, 145–146, 156
vilambit ektāl 165, 167–168, 188, 193, 200
vilambit tīntāl 168
Talwalkar, Padma 108
tānpurā 2, 11, 35, 101, 203
tāns
ākār 18, 91, 140, 142–144, 147, 153, 156, 179, 182, 202
bol 18, 134, 140, 142, 144, 153
gamak 18, 22–23, 140, 144, 153, 202
sargam 18, 128, 140, 142–143, 146–147, 153, 201

Tānsen, Miyā̃ 28, 36, 57
tantrism 38
tarānā 18, 27, 66, 122–124
tawāīf 37
Telang, Mangesh Rāmakrishana 15
temporality 190, 195. *See also baṛā khayāl*: temporality of
Thakur, Omkarnath 7, 15, 87
ṭhāṭ 6, 69, 84. *See also* Bhatkhande, Vishnu Narayan: *ṭhāṭ* system of
ṭhekā 9–10, 193
theory 4, 6, 31, 100, 148, 205. *See also* heuristic [approach to theory]; *See also* time theory [of *rāg*]; *See also* western music: theory of
  and practice xii, xxi, 4, 25, 98, 124, 142, 206
  formal xxiii, 112, 127, 161
  limits of xi, xii, 186
  of *ālāp* 124
  of emotion 5
  withholding of 42
ṭhumrī 8, 17, 19, 46, 75, 126, 140, 164
tihāī 129, 131, 150, 154, 157
time theory [of *rāg*] 15. *See also* Bhatkhande, Vishnu Narayan: and time theory; *See also samay* principle
transcription [musical] xxiii, 30, 50, 101, 103, 104, 105, 112, 119, 132, 134, 135, 146, 166, 193, 194, 199, 200. *See also* descriptive music writing; *See also* heuristic [approach to notation]
transliteration xv, 46, 47, 48, 119, 190
Trasoff, David 30
Trivedi, Madhu 28
trope xxii, 46, 67, 172, 190. *See also guru-śiṣyā paramparā*: tropes of
Tulsidas, Goswami 76
Tyagi, Manjusree 61, 91

unconsciousness, pre-consciousness, non-consciousness xxiii, 16, 100, 123, 134, 148, 161, 179, 185. *See also* consciousness
Urdu [language] xiv, xv, 31, 32, 34, 41, 44, 47, 119. *See also* Hindavi [language]
ustād 32, 33, 34, 36, 37, 39, 40, 41, 42, 49. *See also* guru
uttaraṅg 15. *See also rāg*: *uttaraṅg pradhan*

vādī. *See svar*: *vādī* and *saṃvādī*
vakra motion 81, 104
Van der Meer, Wim xxii, 32, 34, 108, 187
variants. *See also* variation [musical]
  of a *bandiś* 46, 49, 58, 169
  of a *rāg* 54, 90
  of a song text 55
  of genres 27
  of musical figures 2, 110, 120, 131
  of performance principles 105, 114
variation [musical] 51, 115, 129, 134, 145, 146, 151, 154, 159, 168, 197, 201. *See also* variants
varṇam 126
Vedas, Vedic era 11, 30, 32, 33, 34, 37
Vedi, Dilip Chandra 34
vibhāg 8, 9, 10, 50, 134, 137, 146, 169
Vijay Lakshmi, M. 15
vilambit khayāl 164, 187. *See also ati vilambit khayāl*; *See also baṛā khayāl*
vīṇā 31. *See also* bīn
Vinay-Patrikā (Tulsidas) 76
vivādī. *See svar*: *vivādī*
vocables 119, 120. *See also ālāp* syllables; *See also* dhrupad: syllabary of

Wade, Bonnie C. 12, 13, 15, 28, 34, 36, 79
western music 8, 19, 20, 33, 44, 189. *See also* staff notation
  theory of 100, 102, 113, 185
western musicians, musicologists xxiv, 34
Widdess, Richard xii, xxiv, 2, 4, 6, 7, 12, 15, 20, 23, 100, 102, 107, 113, 122, 123, 126, 144

YouTube 169

Zadeh, Chloe 2, 126
zamīndār 38

About the Team

Alessandra Tosi was the managing editor for this book.

Adèle Kreager proof-read this manuscript. The author indexed it.

Katy Saunders designed the cover. The cover was produced in InDesign using the Fontin font.

Cameron Craig typeset the book in InDesign and produced the paperback and hardback editions. The main text font and heading font is Noto Serif.

Cameron also produced the PDF and HTML editions. The conversion was performed with open-source software and other tools freely available on our GitHub page at https://github.com/OpenBookPublishers.

Jeremy Bowman created the EPUB.

This book was peer-reviewed by two referees. Experts in their field, these readers give their time freely to help ensure the academic rigour of our books. We are grateful for their generous and invaluable contributions.

This book need not end here...

Share

All our books — including the one you have just read — are free to access online so that students, researchers and members of the public who can't afford a printed edition will have access to the same ideas. This title will be accessed online by hundreds of readers each month across the globe: why not share the link so that someone you know is one of them?

This book and additional content is available at:
https://doi.org/10.11647/OBP.0313

Donate

Open Book Publishers is an award-winning, scholar-led, not-for-profit press making knowledge freely available one book at a time. We don't charge authors to publish with us: instead, our work is supported by our library members and by donations from people who believe that research shouldn't be locked behind paywalls.

Why not join them in freeing knowledge by supporting us:
https://www.openbookpublishers.com/support-us

You may also be interested in:

Tellings and Texts
Music, Literature and Performance in North India
Francesca Orsini and Katherine Butler Schofield (Eds)

https://doi.org/10.11647/obp.0062

Feeding the City
Work and Food Culture of the Mumbai Dabbawalas
Sara Roncaglia and Angela Arnone

https://doi.org/10.11647/obp.0031

Tales of Darkness and Light
Soso Tham's The Old Days of the Khasis
Soso Tham

https://doi.org/10.11647/obp.0137

www.ingramcontent.com/pod-product-compliance
Lightning Source LLC
Chambersburg PA
CBHW082013220426
43670CB00015B/2621
* 9 7 8 1 8 0 0 6 4 8 0 7 4 *